PRIVATE PASSIONS

Private Passions   MICHAEL BERKELEY

Private Passions is a Classic Arts Production for BBC Radio 3

Executive Producer WENDY THOMPSON

faber and faber

First published in 2005
by Faber and Faber Limited
3 Queen Square London WC1N 3AU

Typeset by RefineCatch Limited, Bungay, Suffolk
Printed in England by Mackays of Chatham

A CIP record for this book
is available from the British Library

ISBN 0–571–22884–4

10 9 8 7 6 5 4 3 2 1

Contents

Introduction

A genuine passion for music is the one thing we really look for in guests for *Private Passions*. The criteria is not fame and celebrity (or a new book) for their own sake, but in the ability of someone to convey the role and importance of music in their lives as illustrated by particular pieces. Psychologists say that we reveal far more of our personalities when apparently talking about subjects other than ourselves, which is why psychoanalysts will often encourage clients to tell stories rather than tackle their own problems head-on (see Adam Phillips, p. 67). In its abstraction, its refusal to be specific, music offers an even safer haven for the expression and discussion of emotion. Describing this most elliptical of art forms in words is a very particular challenge, but in harnessing the language of another discipline, we sometimes find a fresh insight into music, one that may not come so naturally to the musicologist: the analogy, say, between cell structure and thematic development, expressionist painting and the work of Berg; or the cathedral-like architecture of Bruckner. Music engages us directly: in the ten years that I have sat opposite guests recording *Private Passions*, the most unlikely people have been reduced to tears by a significant piece. Several guests know that they may weep and apologise in advance for their tears. The friends of Tom Courtenay, for instance, warned that he was a copious and frequent crier. Tears may arise because the music is linked to some memorable event – a marriage or a death – or simply because of the pure power of music and its ability to move the listener. Sometimes it is the two combined.

Time and again, sculptors, painters, architects, novelists, poets, actors and film-makers describe their work as aspiring to the condition of music. So what is it about music that gives it this secret, almost sacred power? I think it must be precisely its non-specific nature, the fact that we can read into it as we choose, can invest it with our own private emotions and bend it to our psychological and emotional needs. Paradoxically, composers may bare their souls and reveal nothing, yet their music shines a light on and into us, the listeners.

There is, too, a synchronicity that is the sole preserve of music, especially in the world of opera. For example, quintets and quartets from Beethoven (*Fidelio*), Mozart (*The Marriage of Figaro*), and Verdi (*Falstaff*) often get requested simply to illustrate their unique ability to voice several contrasting emotional points of view simultaneously. Thus, for many, music is capable of the ultimate catharsis. Musicians themselves often take this quality for granted and that is why, as the programme has progressed, I have become fascinated by how non-musicians describe what they hear when listening to music and the way in which they relate it to their lives.

And of course it is not just artists; some of the most illuminating conversations have been with theologians (music as religion), philosophers, scientists and doctors, where we have been able to take a journey into the physiology and psychology of music – how we process it and respond to it in the body; why our minds are so attracted to the sad and tragic music that dominates these lists. Indeed, in the best editions I feel that I am always learning something new, either musical or intellectual. Broadcasting is at its finest when the listener feels that he or she is eavesdropping on a private conversation.

So when in 1995 Radio 3 said that they were looking for an independent company to make an hour-long programme similar to the old *Man of Action* but in the form of an interview rather than a monologue I pricked up my ears. I had in fact been easing myself out of broadcasting and, having just taken on the artistic direction of the Cheltenham International Festival of Music, was keen to preserve time for my primary occupation as a composer. But ever since John Freeman's *Face to Face*, I had toyed with the possibility of a forum with music as the common denominator, where I could marry my somewhat messianic desire to share music more widely with my experience of communication through broadcasting.

Initially Radio 3 and its then controller, Nicholas Kenyon, shared out this important commission, and so we began with two companies making the programme: Ladbroke Radio, who used a West End studio, and Classic Arts, who were based in the Midlands and used a room in my house. We searched around for the right format and title, and eventually I came up with *Private Passions*, since it seemed important to emphasise that the programme was going to concentrate largely on people for whom music was indeed a private rather than a public or professional passion. I wanted to show how the non-musicological articulation of a love of music could be strangely affecting. Meeting people from all walks of life, I have been struck by how their passion for music creates an immediate bond and a shared sense of the fragility of the human condition. It is as though in the face of these great yet abstract creations we are somehow humbled, belittled, and that, in the communion of listening together, we begin to redress in a minute way the balance between man's desire to destroy and the ability to create. The best (and easiest) programmes have featured speakers who barely mention their own achievements and lives, since they have so much to say about the music they have chosen. These have ranged from the architect, Daniel Libeskind, to the actor and comedian Stephen Fry (who was one of the few speakers to choose entirely happy and funny music).

It soon became clear that, much as I liked both teams, dealing with two executive producers (who were frequently chasing the same guests and wanting to record on the same day) was unproductive. It was the combination of experience and venue that determined the way forward. Classic Arts had already assembled a first-rate ex-Radio 3 team including engineers from Ninth Wave Audio. They had built an entire sound desk in a little room at the top of our Notting Hill house and wired it through to the spare bedroom/studio, which meant that friends coming to stay would be greeted by a loudspeaker embossed with *Private Passions* at one end of the bed and a closed-circuit television camera at the other! I always enjoy offering the likes of Juliet Stevenson and Joanna Lumley a cup of tea in the kitchen, complete with inquisitive but friendly Labrador, and then inviting them up through the usual domestic detritus to this well-equipped 'bedroom'. Since Otter, the Labrador, has his basket in the downstairs loo, the caninely challenged have to be reassured about the safety of their 'comfort stop', which is obviously benignly observed from rather close quarters. Actually, I am convinced that all this informality leads to a more open, relaxed and intimate conversation than might be obtained deep in the anonymous bowels of Broadcasting House.

It is curious how certain imperatives emerge from the programme. The simple fact of listening to all the music as we make the programme often turns out to be an oasis in a hectic day. Invariably people say that they enjoyed the exercise far more than they had anticipated. High-powered doctors and politicians like Robert Winston and William Hague and journalists like Jon Snow are so unused to the luxury of sitting back, hearing and dissecting their favourite pieces that they enter into a sort of lacuna, almost a form of therapy, with music the catalyst.

I have learnt not to discuss the music with my guest prior to the programme since the second time you are told something it is never quite as spontaneous. The producer of the day will have been through the selection with the guests and made notes enabling me to lead the conversation towards the next composer or artist without having to use the familiar phrase '. . . and your next disc?' I will have read press cuttings and articles on our subject and anything they themselves have written. While we try not to be just another PR opportunity for someone with something to sell, inevitably, really interesting people from around the world (the late Edward Said or Mario Vargas Llosa, for example) are often only in the country for a short while and you have to grab them when you can.

There are certain guests whose musical choices seem to mirror their personalities, their work and even their appearance. I am thinking in particular of that wonderful bear-like sculptor Eduardo Paolozzi, whose music, you will see, had the same kind of massiveness as his sculpture. Is it too fanciful to make the connection between an eminent England fast bowler's long run-up and the almost two hundred bars of pedal E flat that begin Wagner's *Das Rheingold* and the *Ring* cycle (p. 213)? Quentin Blake, the artist and children's book illustrator, chose music that seemed to realise in sound the wit and quirkiness of his art. I have tried to point up particularly striking instances of this kind in the pages that follow.

Another rewarding area has been music from foreign climes introduced by natives or enthusiasts. Indian music, for example, explained by Gita Mehta and Mark Tully, and from nearer to home, Barrie Gavin's remarkable recording of Gaelic singing, an unforgettably haunting sound. We have also had a series of eminent jazz musicians like Dave Holland (who played bass for Miles Davis), because I find their take on classical music refreshing and idiosyncratic. Occasionally, then, we break our 'non-musician' rule for particularly eminent artists or composers whose musical passions may surprise us. The great Hungarian composer, György Ligeti (African drumming and Indonesian gamelan) was one such – and who would have guessed that Harrison Birtwistle was so intrigued by the vocal dexterity of Roy Orbison? Actually, we made the point about boundary-crossing and catholicity of taste when, in our first programmes, Elvis Costello revealed his passion for Purcell, and Germaine Greer became the first of many to play that devastating contemporary hymn of despair, 'Is That All There Is?' sung with a disarming sense of tragedy by Peggy Lee. Strangely, it seemed to sit naturally between Mahler and Brahms. Neil Tennant of The Pet Shop Boys spoke passionately about music he loathed and loved at the Proms. His taste was later to be contradicted (forcibly) by his best mate, Janet Street-Porter. David Hare set one running when he described his utter loathing of opera because of its 'lack of realism' – an argument that has recurred with many from the theatre, most taking issue with equal strength, including a distinguished Hare exponent, Richard Eyre. Straight talking and controversy came early in the series when Chad Varah, founder of the Samaritans, startled the Radio 3 audience with his enthusiastic espousal of masturbation. He explained how children who were made to feel guilty about this activity often suffered psychological damage. We have even sent ourselves up with, thanks to John Sessions, the great 112-year-old percussionist, Manfred Stürmer – how sad that Brahms declined his invitation to create the first Concerto for Spoons and Washboard!

I am hopeless at remembering dates and details and am often floored when asked 'What did (for example) Dudley Moore choose?' So I have myself longed for a book to which I can refer, not only to give that answer but also in order to furnish details of the recording and points of particular interest. So here it is and I hope it settles many squabbles, aids the memory and provokes new acquisitions – it is, after all, a compendium that provides a pretty good way to start and augment a library. There is also a lot of fun to be had. Who chose a Beethoven piano concerto performed by the Glenn Miller Orchestra? Did you know that John Peel loved classical music? And why did Denis Healey leave the recording with scratched Private Parts?

Michael Berkeley

Acknowledgements

I should like to thank Nicholas Kenyon who, as Controller of Radio 3, initially commissioned the series, and Roger Wright, the present Controller, who has continued to give it his total support. Also at Radio 3, Brian Barfield, Abigail Appleton and Dr John Evans have done their very best to keep us on the rails and curb our worst excesses. I am very grateful to Wendy Thompson and Jim Hiley, the respective Executive Producers for Classic Arts and Ladbroke Radio, who launched the series and to Wendy for her ten years at the tiller ever since. Our principal producers over the years have been Sarah Devonald, who did much to help shape the format of the programme, Martin Cotton, Chris Marshall and Sarah Cropper. The programme gets on the air thanks to our technical experts at Ninth Wave Audio, Tony Wass, Tim Allcock and Alex Anderson. Finally, we have been extremely fortunate in having two wonderful researchers in Katherine Warren and Helen Anderson and at Faber, an editorial maestro in Belinda Matthews tirelessly supported by chorus master Kate Ward.

Explanatory notes

Wherever possible we have included all guests, recording details and numbers. However, some LPs no longer exist or music was taken from a film soundtrack or private recording. Furthermore information from some of the very early programmes was not always precisely listed or archived and despite our best efforts to retrieve it, there are still a few omissions.

Where a reading was requested by me from a poet or writer as opposed to being one of the guests' own selections (e.g. Gielgud reading Shakespeare), we have listed it in square [] brackets.

The occupation of each guest is stated as it was at the time of the recording.

Private Passions – *the lists*

The introductory fanfare that opens the programme comes from a suite of incidental music written originally for a BBC Radio 3 series on Chaucer called *Ladies Lost and Found* produced by Piers Plowright (see p. 175).

¶ Michael Berkeley, 'The Wakeful Poet' from *Music from Chaucer* BBQ 003, Chandos ABTD 1190 or Onyx Meridian CDE 44462

Elvis Costello, singer/songwriter

¶ Schubert, Sonata D571 (a single movement work), András Schiff (piano)
Decca 440 305 2
¶ Mozart, 'Parto, parto, ma tu ben mio' (from *La clemenza di Tito*), Anne Sofie von Otter (Sesto)/English Baroque Soloists/John Eliot Gardiner
Archiv 431 807 2
¶ Weill, 'My Ship' (from *Miles Ahead*), Miles Davis (trumpet)/Gil Evans (arranger and conductor)
CBS 4460606 2
¶ Von Koch, 'Wild Swans', Anne Sofie von Otter (mezzo-soprano)/Bengt Forsberg (piano)
BBC tape
¶ Britten, Corpus Christi carol (from *Grace*), Jeff Buckley
Columbia 475 928 2
¶ Stravinsky, 'Marche royale' (from *L'histoire du soldat*), chamber group directed by Igor Stravinsky, rec. 1932
Vogue 665002 B
¶ Purcell, Fantasia No. 5 à 4 in B flat Z736, Fretwork
Virgin veritas 7243 545062 2
¶ Byrd, 'Ye Sacred Muses', Alfred Deller/Wenzinger Consort of Viols (of the Schola Cantorum Basiliensis)
Vanguard 08 5068 71

Our first victim, and in many ways an ideal one in that he was not confined by the boundaries of pop music but took a truly practical interest in, for example, Purcell. In the Britten, Jeff Buckley's extraordinarily pure falsetto voice created quite a stir.

Germaine Greer, writer and academic

¶ Handel, 'Heart, the Seat of Soft Delight' (from *Acis and Galatea*), Joan Sutherland (Galatea)/Philomusica of London/Adrian Boult
Decca 436 229 2

¶ Johann Ritter von Herbeck, 'Pueri concinite', Placido Domingo/
Vienna Boys' Choir/Helmuth Froschauer
RCA 07863 533835 2
¶ François Couperin, 'L'evaporée' (*Pièces de clavecin*, Book 3,
5th ordre), Gustav Leonhardt
Philips 420 939 2
¶ Victoria, Tenebrae responsories, The Sixteen/Harry Christophers
Virgin Classics VC 791440 2
¶ John Cage, *Organ Music*
¶ Mahler, 'Der Tambourg'sell' (from *Des Knaben Wunderhorn*),
Andreas Schmidt (baritone)/Concertgebouw Orchestra/Leonard
Bernstein
DG 427 302 2
¶ Leiber/Stoller, 'Is That All There Is?', Peggy Lee
Capitol CDP 790552 2
¶ Brahms, 'Gesang aus Fingal' (Four Songs, Op. 17, No. 4), Ensemble
Vocal Michel Piquemal
Arion ARN 68132
¶ Schubert, 'Der blinde Knabe' D833, Barbara Hendricks/Radu Lupu
EMI CDC 747 549 2

*Visited the good Doctor in her Cambridge rooms and discovered her
passion for singing in a choir, both because of a love of the human voice
and the sense of community. The first person to choose a regular
favourite, the haunting 'Is That All There Is?' with Peggy Lee. A lovely
Brahms part-song perhaps gave to some of us an answer of sorts.*

29 APRIL 1995
Simon Russell Beale, actor

¶ Rachmaninov, Cello Sonata (third movement), Mstislav
Rostropovich/Vladimir Horowitz (rec. at Carnegie Hall 85th
anniversary concert)
Sony Classical CD 46743/A
¶ Monteverdi, 'Quia fecit mihi magna' (from Magnificat, Vespers,
1610), John Shirley-Quirk (baritone)/Michael Rippon (bass)/
Monteverdi Choir and Orchestra/John Eliot Gardiner
Decca 414 574 2

◄ Richard Strauss, finale from *Elektra*, Birgit Nilsson (Elektra), Marie Collier (Chrysothemis)/Vienna Philharmonic Orchestra/Georg Solti
Decca 417 347 2
◄ Finzi, 'The Salutation' (from *Dies natalis*), Martyn Hill (tenor)/City of London Sinfonia/Richard Hickox
Virgin Classics vc 790118 2
◄ Duparc, 'Chanson triste', Elly Ameling (soprano)/San Francisco Symphony Orchestra/Edo de Waart
Philips 410 043 2
◄ Ravel, 'Le jardin féerique' (from *Ma mère l'oye*), Ulster Orchestra/Yan Pascal Tortelier
Chandos CHAN 9203
◄ Bach, Kyrie (from Mass in B minor), Netherlands Chamber Choir/Orchestra of the 18th Century/Frans Brüggen
Philips 426 402 2

Brought the same kind of savage focus to his choice of music as he does to his roles. We agreed on the white-hot nature of Richard Strauss's early operas and, in particular, Elektra *with the muscular Solti in charge. Duparc has emerged as one of the programme's great unsung heroes.*

6 MAY 1995
Denis Healey, politician

◄ Beethoven, String Quartet Op. 130 (fifth movement, Cavatina), Amadeus Quartet
DG 423 480–2
◄ Rossini, 'Nacqui all'affanno . . . Non più mesta' (from *La cenerentola*), Maria Callas (Angelina)/Philharmonia/Antonio Tonini
EMI 749 428–2
◄ Puccini, 'In questa reggia' (from *Turandot*), Eva Turner (Turandot)/Orchestra conducted by Stanford Robinson, rec. 1933
EMI 760 791–2
◄ Mozart, Lacrimosa (from Requiem, K626), Leipzig Radio Chorus/Dresden Staatskapelle/Peter Schreier
Philips 411 420–2
◄ Schubert, 'The Shepherd on the Rock', D965, Elisabeth Schumann (soprano)/Reginald Kell (clarinet)/George Reeves (piano)
EMI CHS 763 040–2

¶ Bach, Gigue from Partita No. 1 in B flat BWV 825, Dinu Lipatti (piano)
EMI CDH 769 800–2
¶ Beethoven, Piano Concerto No. 5, 'Emperor' (finale)
¶ Richard Strauss, Trio from Act III of *Der Rosenkavalier*, Kiri te Kanawa/Anne Sofie von Otter/Barbara Hendricks/Dresden Staatskapelle/Bernard Haitink
EMI CDC 754 262–2

Seated comfortably in an armchair the irresistible Denis was soon joined by Charlie, our ginger tom. He settled down in the ex-Chancellor's lap as he expounded on his love of . . . Then I noticed Charlie beginning to make bread. Ever the consummate professional, Denis did not blink, and even managed to continue with the merest of grimaces when a set of claws were suddenly dug enthusiastically into his groin!

13 MAY 1995
Harriet Walter, actress

¶ Prokofiev, 'Death of Tybalt' (from *Romeo and Juliet*), Orchestra of the Royal Opera House/Mark Ermler
ROG 30
¶ Bach, Trio Sonata (second movement from *The Musical Offering*), Musica Antiqua Köln/Reinhard Goebel
Archiv 413 643
¶ Poulenc, Domine Deus (from *Gloria*), Donna Deam (soprano)/Cambridge Singers/City of London Sinfonia/John Rutter
Collegium COL CD 108
¶ Beethoven, Symphony No. 5 (first movement), Berlin Philharmonic Orchestra/Herbert von Karajan
DG 419 051 2
¶ Monteverdi, *Beatus vir*, Les Arts Florissants/William Christie
Harmonia Mundi HM 901250
¶ Elgar, Cello Concerto (second movement), Jacqueline du Pré/London Symphony Orchestra/John Barbirolli
EMI CDM 763 286 2
¶ Chopin, Nocturne in C sharp minor, Op. 27, No. 1, Daniel Barenboim
DG 415 117 2

Terry Waite, former envoy to Archbishop of Canterbury

❡ Jobim/Lees, 'Quiet Night of Quiet Stars', Oscar Peterson Trio
Verve 810 047 2
❡ Chopin, Ballade No. 1 in G minor, Vladimir Horowitz (rec. 1968 at
Carnegie Hall)
Sony Classical sk 53465
❡ Penderecki, *Utrenya* (from Part II: 'The Resurrection of Christ'),
Warsaw National Philharmonic Orchestra and Choir/Andrzej
Markowski
Muza PNCD 018
❡ J. M. Nicholas arr. B. Davies, 'Great is he, the Lord eternal',
Warrington Male Voice Choir
Priory PRC 513
❡ Elgar, *The Dream of Gerontius* (Part II, Prelude and 'I Went to
Sleep'), Richard Lewis (tenor)/Janet Baker (mezzo-soprano)/Hallé
Orchestra/John Barbirolli
EMI CDM 763 187 2
❡ Peter Melville Smith, Fanfare, Brass Ensemble and Choirs of Eton
College/Paul Plummer
Capriole CAPCD 1005
❡ Malcolm Boyle, 'Thou, O God, are praised in Sion', Brass Ensemble
and Choirs of Eton College/Paul Plummer
Capriole CAPCD 1005
❡ Gurney, 'Sleep', Benjamin Luxon (baritone)/David Willison (piano)
Chandos CHAN 8831
❡ Elgar, arr. Paul Cassidy, 'Chanson de matin', Op. 15, No. 2, Brodsky
Quartet
Teldec 2292 46015 2

*The enduring and sustaining power of music as memory, as recalled by
someone imprisoned and in very real fear for his life.*

27 MAY 1995
P. D. James, writer

❡ Bach, Gloria, In terra Pax (from Mass in B minor), Monteverdi
Choir/English Baroque Soloists/John Eliot Gardiner
Archiv 415 515–2

¶ Handel, 'Dopo notte' (from *Ariodante*), Janet Baker (Ariodante)/
English Chamber Orchestra/Raymond Leppard
Philips 426 450–2
¶ Finzi, 'His Golden Locks' (from *Farewell to Arms*), Martyn Hill/
City of London Sinfonia/Richard Hickox
Virgin VC 79–718–2
¶ Gibbons, Psalm 145, Choir of King's College, Cambridge/David
Willcocks
Decca 433 677–2
¶ Fauré, Agnus dei and Libera me (from Requiem, Op. 48), Stephen
Varcoe (baritone)/Cambridge Singers/City of London Sinfonia/
John Rutter
Conifer CDCFRA 122
¶ Mozart, 'Soave sia il vento' (from *Così fan tutte*, Act I), Elisabeth
Schwarzkopf (Fiordiligi)/Nan Merriman (Dorabella)/Sesto
Bruscantini (Don Alfonso)/Philharmonia/Herbert von Karajan
EMI CDH 769636 2
¶ Schubert, 'An die Musik', Kathleen Ferrier (contralto)/Phyllis Spurr
(piano)
Decca 430 096–2
¶ Gimbel/Fox, 'Killing Me Softly with His Song', Cleo Laine/
John Williams
RCA RS 1094

3 JUNE 1995
Adam Mars-Jones, writer and journalist

¶ Reger, Chorale Prelude: 'Wachet auf', Op. 67, No. 41, Roger Fisher
(organ)
Vista
¶ Gesualdo, *Dolcissima mia vita*, Monteverdi Choir/John Eliot
Gardiner
Decca 440 032–2
¶ Don van de Vliet, 'Hair Pie: Bake 2' (from *Trout Mask Replica*),
Captain Beefheart and his Magic Band
Reprise 927 196–2
¶ Pärt, 'Mein Weg hat Gipfel und Wellentaler', Christopher Bowers-
Broadbent (organ)
ECM 849 655–2

♪ Poulenc, 'Sicilienne' and 'Carillon' (from *Suite française*), Francis
Poulenc
Sony Classical CD 47684
♪ Schubert, *Lebensstürme*, D947, Imre Rohmann/András Schiff (piano
duet)
Hungaroton HCD 11941–2
♪ Bach, Chorale Prelude: 'O Mensch, bewein dein Sünde gross', Lionel
Rogg (organ)
Harmonia Mundi HMX 290775
♪ Godowsky, Study No. 27 (on Chopin's Op. 25, No. 2), Ian Hobson
(piano)
Arabesque z6537

The kind of guest who makes my task easy and delightful, and I loved the
idea of pairing Arvo Pärt and Captain Beefheart. Agreed that Gesualdo's
chromatic and visionary harmony was just as surprising as his
murderous life!

10 JUNE 1995
John Nettles, actor

♪ Canteloube, 'Baïlèro' (from *Songs of the Auvergne*), Kiri te Kanawa/
English Chamber Orchestra/Jeffrey Tate
Decca 410 004–2
♪ Walton, Charge and Battle Music (from *Henry V* film score),
Christopher Plummer (narrator), Academy of St Martin-in-the-
Fields/Neville Marriner
Chandos CHAN 8892
♪ John Ireland, *The Island Spell*, Christopher Headington (piano)
Kingdom KCL CD 2017
♪ Joan Baez, 'All in Green' (from *Love Song*), Joan Baez
Vanguard VSD 80
♪ Mozart, Clarinet Concerto (second movement), Gervase de Peyer
(clarinet)/London Symphony Orchestra/Peter Maag
Decca 433 727–2
♪ Shakespeare/Best, 'Under the Greenwood Tree', Martin Best (voice
and guitar)
Grosvenor GRS 1013

¶ March, 'The Cornish Troubadour' (arr. K. Polmear), Camborne Town Band/Derek Greenwood
Sound News SM 152
¶ Beethoven, Symphony No. 6, 'Pastoral' (finale), Leipzig Gewandhaus Orchestra/Kurt Masur
Philips 416 278–2

17 JUNE 1995
Toyah Willcox, actress

¶ Kate Bush (details not known)
¶ Beethoven, Symphony No. 7 (second movement), Royal Liverpool Philharmonic Orchestra/Charles Mackerras
CD EMX 2212
¶ Stravinsky, two dances from *The Firebird* (1910), Columbia Symphony Orchestra/Igor Stravinsky
Sony Classical CD 46291 A
¶ Mozart, Serenade for 13 wind instruments in B flat, K361 (second movement) (from soundtrack of film *Amadeus*), Academy of St Martin-in-the-Fields/Neville Marriner
Metronome 825 127 2
¶ Elgar, *Enigma Variations* (No. 9, 'Nimrod'), City of Birmingham Symphony Orchestra/Simon Rattle
EMI CDC 555001 2
¶ Holst, 'Mars' (from *The Planets*), BBC Symphony Orchestra/Andrew Davis
Teldec 4509 94541 2
¶ Tippett/Sheppard, No. 32 from '66 Shades of Lipstick', Toyah Willcox
UK Editions EEGCD 64

24 JUNE 1995
John Mortimer, writer and lawyer

¶ Puccini, 'E lucevan le stelle' (from *Tosca*, Act III), Placido Domingo (Cavaradossi)/Orchestra of the Royal Opera House/Giuseppe Sinopoli
DG 4317752
¶ Mozart, Sinfonia concertante, K364 (finale), Jascha Heifetz (violin)/William Primrose (viola)/RCA Victor Orchestra/Izler Solomon
RCA 09026 61779–2

❡ Brahms, Symphony No. 4 (third movement), Cleveland
Sony SBK 46330
❡ Johann Strauss II, 'How Sad It Is' (from *Die Fledermaus*)
❡ Verdi, Dies irae (from Requiem), Vienna State Opera Chorus/Vienna
Philharmonic Orchestra/Claudio Abbado
DG 4358842
❡ Richard Strauss, 'Beim Schlafengehen' (No. 3 from *Four Last Songs*),
Jessye Norman (soprano)/Leipzig Gewandhaus Orchestra/Kurt Masur
Philips 464 742–2
❡ Cole Porter, 'Let's Face the Music and Dance', Fred Astaire
❡ Rossini, 'Una voce poco fa' (from *The Barber of Seville*, Act I), Maria
Callas (Rosina)/Philharmonia/Alceo Galliera
Angel 66671

*One of our few 'location' recordings. We went to the playwright's house
forty minutes west of London and in the middle of woodlands. It is still
suffused with the spirit of Mortimer's* A Voyage Round My Father. *John
looking wonderfully Rumpole-like. Fortunately, his actress daughter,
Emily, does not remind me of Rumpole.*

1 JULY 1995
Chad Varah, founder, The Samaritans

❡ Scarlatti, Sonata in A minor, Kk54, Vladimir Horowitz (piano)
Sony SK53460
❡ Satie, *Gymnopédie* No. 1 (orch. Debussy), Academy of St Martin-in-
the-Fields/Neville Marriner
Philips 4622 772
❡ Handel, 'Date serta' (from motet *Silete Venti* for soprano and
orchestra), Ann Mackay (soprano)/European Community Chamber
Orchestra
ASV 766
❡ Byrd, Agnus Dei (from Mass for 4 voices), Tallis Scholars/Peter
Phillips
Gimell 345
❡ Grainger, 'Brigg Fair' (arr. for tenor and chorus), James Gilchrist
(tenor)/Polyphony/Stephen Layton
Hyperion 66793

¶ Handel, Dixit Dominus (Psalm 110) HWV 232, Ann Mackay, Isobel
Buchanan (sopranos), Choir of King's College Cambridge/English
Chamber Orchestra/Stephen Cleobury
Decca 448242
¶ Tchaikovsky, Piano Concerto No. 2 (second movement), Peter
Donohoe (piano)/Bournemouth Symphony Orchestra/Rudolf Barshai
EMI 585540–2
¶ Sibelius, 'Flickan kom ifran sin' (The maiden's tryst) from Five
Songs, Op. 37, Anne Sofie von Otter (mezzo-soprano)/Bengt Forsberg
(piano)
B15 457
¶ Bach, Concerto for oboe, violin and strings in C minor, BWV 1060
(second movement, Adagio), Anthony Robson (oboe)/Elizabeth
Wallfisch (violin/director)/Orchestra of the Age of Enlightenment
Virgin 61558

8 JULY 1995

Simon Jenkins, journalist

¶ Mozart, Piano Concerto No. 27, K595 (second movement), Clifford
Curzon (piano)/English Chamber Orchestra/Benjamin Britten
Decca 4684912
¶ Schubert, 'The Shepherd on the Rock', D965, Kathleen Battle
(soprano)/Karl Leister (clarinet)/James Levine (piano)
¶ Beethoven, Symphony No. 7 (fourth movement), Orchestre
Révolutionnaire et Romantique/John Eliot Gardiner
Archiv 4399002
¶ Satie, La belle excentrique, Aldo Ciccolini, Gabriel Tacchino (pianos)
EMI 567 239–2
¶ Dolly Parton, 'I Will Always Love You', Whitney Houston
Sony 67582
¶ Joplin, Elite Syncopations, arr. J. C. Starkey, Jonathan Starkey (piano)
¶ Rossini, Cujus animam gementem, from Stabat mater, Arthur Davies
(tenor)/LSO Chorus/City of London Sinfonia/Richard Hickox
CHAN 8780
¶ Verdi, excerpt from Rigoletto, Luciano Pavarotti (Duke)/Bologna
Municipal Theatre Chorus and Orchestra/Riccardo Chailly
Decca 4258642

Bernice Rubens, writer

♪ Dvořák, Cello Concerto (third movement), Mstislav Rostropovich (cello)/Boston Symphony Orchestra/Seiji Ozawa
Elatus 0927467272
♪ Richard Strauss, 'Beim Schlafengehen' (No. 3 from *Four Last Songs*), Jessye Norman (soprano)/Leipzig Gewandhaus Orchestra/Kurt Masur
Philips 4647422
♪ Charles Ives, *General William Booth Enters into Heaven* (excerpt), Gregg Smith Singers, Ithaca College Concert Choir, Texas Boys' Choir/Columbia Chamber Orchestra/Gregg Smith
Columbia MS 6921
♪ Schubert, String Quintet in C major, D956 (second movement), Cleveland String Quartet/Yo-Yo Ma (cello)
CBS 074643913423
♪ Mozart, String Quartet in C major, 'Dissonance', K365 (second movement), Amadeus String Quartet
DG 474 002
♪ Mozart, 'Mi tradi quell'alma ingrata', (from *Don Giovanni*, Act II), Munich Radio Orchestra/Leonard Slatkin
People's Guide Opera 70651

Sir Alistair Morton, Chairman of Eurotunnel

♪ Spencer Williams, *Basin Street Blues*, Duke Ellington (piano, conductor)/Johnny Hodges (saxophone)
Vene 823 637–2
♪ Stravinsky, 'Disappearance of the Palace' and 'Kastchei's Enchantments' (from *The Firebird*, scene 2), National Youth Orchestra of Great Britain/Christopher Seaman
IMP Classics CIMPC921
♪ Elgar, Cello Concerto (first movement), Jacqueline du Pré (cello)/London Symphony Orchestra/John Barbirolli
EMI 555 527–2
♪ Matshikizia, excerpt from *King Kong*, original cast recording/Stanley Glasser
Decca SKL–4132 (LP)

13

§ Rutter, 'For the Beauty of the Earth', St John's College Johannesburg Choir

§ Verdi, 'Vedi come il buon vegliardo' (from *Ernani*, Act I), Leontyne Price (soprano), Fernando Iacopucci and Carlo Bergonzi (tenors), Ezio Flagello (bass)/RCA Italiana Chorus and Orchestra
RCA 6503

§ Verdi, 'Ah! Veglia, o donna' (from *Rigoletto*, Act I), June Anderson (soprano), Leo Nucci (baritone)/Bologna Municipal Theatre Orchestra/Riccardo Chailly
London 425 864–2

29 JULY 1995
Patricia Hodge, actress

§ Fauré, Libera me (from Requiem, Op. 48), Olaf Bär (baritone)/Choir of King's College, Cambridge/English Chamber Orchestra/Stephen Cleobury
EMI CDC 7498 80–2

§ Chopin, Polonaise for piano in A flat major, 'Eroica', Op. 53, Maurizio Pollini (piano)
EMI 7 64354

§ Mahler, Symphony No. 5 (fourth movement, Adagietto), Concertgebouw Orchestra/Bernard Haitink
Philips 446 500–2

§ Morricone, 'Gabriel's Oboe' (No. 2 from film score *The Mission*), orchestra conducted by Ennio Morricone
Virgin 86001

§ Bernstein, excerpt from Symphony No. 3, 'Kaddish', Michael Wager (speaker)/Vienna Youth Choir, Vienna Boys' Choir/Israel Philharmonic Orchestra/Leonard Bernstein
DG 459552

§ Widor, Toccata (from Symphony for Organ No. 5 in F minor), Charles-Marie Widor (organ)
Composers in Person 5550372

§ Weill, 'Girl of the Moment' (from *Lady in the Dark*), Adolph Green, Risë Stevens, John Reardon/Orchestra/Lehman Engel
Sony 62869

5 AUGUST 1995
Sir Jeremy Isaacs, General Director of the Royal Opera House

¶ Schubert, Sonata in B flat major, D960 (first movement), Alfred Brendel (piano)
Philips 4387032
¶ Janáček, *The Cunning Little Vixen* (Act I, Prelude), Vienna Philharmonic Orchestra/Charles Mackerras
Decca 4171292
¶ Rossini, 'Pourquoi ta presence' (from *William Tell*, Act IV), Nicolai Gedda (tenor), Gabriel Bacquier (baritone)/Ambrosian Opera Chorus/Royal Philharmonic Orchestra/Lamberto Gardelli
EMI CDMD 69951
¶ Haydn, Kyrie (from Mass in D minor, *Missa in angustiis*), Choir of King's College, Cambridge/London Symphony Orchestra/David Willcocks
Decca 4550202–1
¶ Mozart, Symphony No. 38, 'Prague', K504 (first movement), New York Symphony Orchestra/Bruno Walter
Sony SM2K 64474
¶ Beethoven, 'O namenlose Freude' (from *Fidelio*, 1814 version, Act II), Christa Ludwig (Leonore), Jon Vickers (Florestan)/Philharmonia/Otto Klemperer
EMI 67361

12 AUGUST 1995
Irene Thomas, radio personality

¶ Julia Ward Howe, 'Battle Hymn of the Republic', Val Doonican/George Mitchell Choir
¶ Wagner, 'Liebestod' (from *Tristan und Isolde*, Act III), Kirsten Flagstad (Isolde)/Philharmonia/Wilhelm Furtwängler
EMI 556 254–2
¶ Orazio Vecchi, 'Fa una canzona' (madrigal), Robert Shaw Chorale
¶ J. H. Hewitt, 'All Quiet along the Potomac Tonight', Lansdowne Orchestra/G. Mitchell
¶ A. C. Green, arr. Neil Richardson, *Sunset*, Band of the Royal Marines/M. R. Goss

¶ Traditional Welsh, 'Bugeilio'r gwenith gwyn' (Watching the white wheat), Thomas L. Thomas (voice)/Enid Simon (harp)
¶ Britten, 'Moonlight' (No. 3 of *Four Sea Interludes from Peter Grimes*), Orchestra of the Royal Opera House/Benjamin Britten
Decca 4676 82–2
¶ Schumann, 'Berg und Burgen schaun herunter' (No. 7 of *Liederkreis*, Op. 24), Thomas Allen (baritone)/Roger Vignoles (piano)
¶ Gounod, 'Avant de quitter' (from *Faust*, Act II), Thomas Allen (baritone)/Paris Opéra Orchestra/Georges Prêtre
EMI CDS 7474938
¶ Verdi, 'Tacea la notte placida' (from *Il Trovatore*, Act I), Renata Tebaldi (soprano)/Geneva Theatre Orchestra/Alberto Erede
Double Decca 4487432
¶ Verdi, Tuba mirum (from Requiem), Brighton Festival Chorus, Royal Choral Society/Royal Philharmonic Orchestra/Owain Arwel Hughes
EMI (Classics for Pleasur) 2503

26 AUGUST 1995
Albert Roux, chef

¶ Wesley Wilson, 'Gimme a Pigfoot', Billie Holiday/Sy Oliver orchestra
Naxos 8.120750
¶ Bach, Gigue from Suite for Cello No. 3 in C, BWV1009, Paul Tortelier (cello)
EMI 562 8788–2
¶ Saint-Saëns, *Danse macabre*, City of Birmingham Symphony Orchestra/Louis Frémaux
Eminence CDEMX2266
¶ Puccini, 'Nessun dorma' (from *Turandot*, Act III), Placido Domingo (Calaf)/Vienna Philharmonic Orchestra/Herbert von Karajan
DG 23855
¶ Bruch, Violin Concerto No. 1 in G minor, Op. 26 (second movement), Pinchas Zukerman (violin)/Los Angeles Philharmonic Orchestra/Zubin Mehta
Essential Classics SBK 48274

¶ Mozart, Requiem aeternam (from Requiem, K626), Anna Tomowa-Sintow (soprano)/Vienna Philharmonic Chorus and Berlin Philharmonic Orchestra/Herbert von Karajan
Galleria 459409–2
¶ Louiguy, 'La vie en rose', Edith Piaf
Naxos 8.120553
¶ Reynaldo Hahn, 'Offrande', Maggie Teyte (voice)
Naxos 8.110757–58
¶ Massenet, 'Si tu veux, Mignonne', Reynaldo Hahn (baritone)/Joseph Benvenuti (piano)
Pearl GEMM 0003

2 SEPTEMBER 1995
Leopold de Rothschild, Chair, RCM (1987–99)

¶ Mozart, Menuetto and Trio from Serenade in D major, K203, Iona Brown (violin)/Academy of St Martin-in-the-Fields/Neville Marriner
¶ Bach, Prelude and Fugue in A major (from *The Well-tempered Clavier*, Book 2), Sviatoslav Richter (piano)
RCA Gold Seal GD 60949
¶ Handel, Concerto Grosso in B minor, Op. 6, No. 12 (third movement), English Chamber Orchestra/Raymond Leppard
Philips 454363–2
¶ Cavalli, extract from *La Calisto*, Janet Baker (mezzo-soprano), James Bowman (countertenor)/London Philharmonic Orchestra/Raymond Leppard
Rosette 4762176
¶ Parry, *An Ode on the Nativity*, Teresa Cahill (soprano)/Royal College of Music Choir/London Philharmonic Orchestra/David Willcocks
¶ Mozart, Piano Concerto No. 18 in B flat major, K456 (second movement), Mitsuko Uchida (piano)/English Chamber Orchestra/ Jeffrey Tate
Philips Duo 468540–2
¶ Gilbert/Sullivan, 'The Sun, Whose Rays are All Ablaze' (from *The Mikado*, Act II), Lesley Garrett (Yum-Yum)/Orchestra of English National Opera/Peter Robinson
TER 1121
¶ Meyerbeer, 'Rare Flower', Charlotte de Rothschild (soprano)/ Malcolm Martineau (piano)

Ian Hislop, journalist and broadcaster

¶ Mozart, Overture to *The Marriage of Figaro*, Concertgebouw Orchestra/Nikolaus Harnoncourt
Teldec 4509 908 612
¶ Mickey Newbury, *An American Trilogy* (Dixie/John Brown/All My Trials), Elvis Presley/Orchestra
¶ Bruckner, Symphony No. 4, 'Romantic' (fourth movement), Philadelphia Orchestra/Wolfgang Sawallisch
EMI 555119–2
¶ Emilio de'Cavailieri, 'O che nuovo miracolo' (*ballo* from 6th Florentine Intermedio, 1589), Taverner Consort/Taverner Choir/Taverner Players/Andrew Parrott
Reflexe 7479982
¶ Purcell, 'Crown the Altar, Deck the Shrine', from 'Celebrate this festival' (*Birthday Ode for Queen Mary*, 1693), James Bowman (countertenor)/King's Consort/Robert King
Hyperion 66412
¶ Anon, 'Ayo visto lo mappamundi' (fifteenth-century Neapolitan *barzeletta*), Waverley Consort/Michael Jaffee
Virgin 61815
¶ Walton, arr. Colin Matthews, 'Spitfire Music' and 'Battle in the Air' (from *The Battle of Britain* suite), London Philharmonic Orchestra/Carl Davis
EMI 565585–2
¶ Tchaikovsky, Serenade for Strings, Op. 48 (second movement, Waltz), Moscow Soloists/Yuri Bashmet
RCA ARI60368RD
¶ Palestrina, 'Hodie Christus natus est', motet for four voices, Vienna Boys' Choir/Hans Gillesberger

16 SEPTEMBER 1995
Dennis Marks, TV and radio producer

¶ Schubert, Piano Trio in E flat major, D897 (Notturno), Beaux Arts Trio of New York
Philips 438700

❡ Mahler, 'Ich bin der Welt abhanden gekommen' (No. 4 from *Rückert-Lieder*), Janet Baker (mezzo-soprano)/London Symphony Orchestra/Michael Tilson Thomas
Masterworks 44553
❡ Monteverdi, 'Laetatus sum' (from Vespers, 1610), Monteverdi Choir/English Baroque Soloists/His Majesty's Sagbutts and Cornetts/John Eliot Gardiner
DG 4295652
❡ Janáček, *The Cunning Little Vixen* (Act III, final scene), Dalibor Jedlička (Forester), Peter Saray (Frog)/Vienna Philharmonic Orchestra/Charles Mackerras
Decca 4171292
❡ Debussy, *Arabesque* No. 1 in E major, Walter Gieseking (piano)
VAI A 1117
❡ Tippett, Interlude and second movement from Concerto for violin, viola, cello and orchestra, György Pauk (violin), Nobuko Imai (viola), Ralph Kirshbaum (cello)/London Symphony Orchestra/Colin Miles

23 SEPTEMBER 1995
Sir Edwin Nixon, former Deputy Chairman of NatWest

❡ Mozart, Credo (from Mass in C minor, K427), Sylvia McNair (soprano)/Monteverdi Choir/English Baroque Soloists/John Eliot Gardiner
Philips 4202102
❡ Bernstein, 'America' (from *West Side Story*)
❡ Monteverdi, 'Deus in adjutorium meum intende' (Intonation), and 'Domine ad adjuvandum' (from Vespers, 1610), Monteverdi Choir/English Baroque Soloists/John Eliot Gardiner
Decca 414 572
❡ Verdi, 'Orfanella il tetto umile . . . Figlia! A ta nome' (from *Simon Boccanegra*, Act I), Kiri te Kanawa (soprano), Leo Nucci (baritone)/Orchestra of La Scala, Milan/Georg Solti
Decca 425628–2
❡ Richard Strauss, 'Wiegenlied', Op. 41, No. 1, Jessye Norman (soprano)/Leipzig Gewandhaus Orchestra/Kurt Masur
Philips 0289 4756 3631
❡ Chopin, Polonaise in A, 'Military', Op. 40, No. 1, Vladimir Ashkenazy (piano)

¶ Brahms, *Academic Festival Overture*, Op. 80, BBC Symphony Orchestra/John Pritchard

30 SEPTEMBER 1995
David Hockney, painter

¶ Richard Strauss, 'Falcon Aria' (from *Die Frau ohne Schatten*, Act II), René Kollo (Emperor)/Bavarian Radio Symphony Orchestra/Wolfgang Sawallisch
EMI CDC 749077–2
¶ Mozart, 'Bald prangt, den Morgen zu verkunden' (from *The Magic Flute*), Lucia Popp (Pamina)/Tolz Boys' Choir/Bavarian Radio Symphony Orchestra/Bernard Haitink
EMI CDC 747953–2
¶ Ravel, 'Five o'clock Foxtrot' (from *L'enfant et les sortilèges*), Jocelyne Taillon (Chinese cup), Philip Langridge (Teapot)/London Symphony Orchestra/André Previn
EMI CDC 747169–2
¶ Stravinsky, 'Song of the Nightingale' (from *Le rossignol*), Phyllis Bryn-Julson (Nightingale), Neil Howlett (Emperor)/BBC Symphony Orchestra/Pierre Boulez
Erato 2292–45627–2
¶ Wagner, Prelude to *Tristan und Isolde*, Philharmonia/Wilhelm Furtwängler
EMI CDC 747322–2
¶ Bartók, String Quartet No. 2 (second movement, Allegro molto capriccioso), Takács Quartet
Hungaroton HCD 12502–2

Having spent many happy hours in his studio discussing music and the visual arts, I knew that David would be fascinating on what he sees when he hears music and what he hears when he looks at art. Pity we could not include Leo the singing dog, a regular at David's house and, seriously, a stunning improviser when accompanied on the accordion by his owner, Jean-Pierre.

Bamber Gascoigne, writer and broadcaster

¶ Verdi, 'È grave il sacrifizio' (from *La traviata*, Act II), Leo Nucci (Germont), Angela Gheorghiu (Violetta)/Orchestra of the Royal Opera House/Georg Solti
Decca 448 120–2
¶ Berlioz, 'Absence' (from *Les nuits d'été*), Maggie Teyte (mezzo-soprano)/London Philharmonic Orchestra/Leslie Heward
EMI 556 5198–2
¶ Mercadante, Overture to *La testa di bronzo*, Philharmonia/David Parry
Opera Rara ORCH 104
¶ Mozart, Finale of Act III, *The Marriage of Figaro*, Samuel Ramey (Figaro), Lucia Popp (Susanna), Thomas Allen (Almaviva), Kiri te Kanawa (Countess Almaviva), Philip Langridge (Don Curzio), Robert Tear (Don Basilio), Giorgio Tadeo (Antonio), Kurt Moll (Doctor Bartolo)/London Philharmonic Orchestra/Georg Solti
Decca 410 153–2
¶ 'Babuji dheere chalna', Gheeta Dutt
Ace CDORBD 056
¶ Stravinsky, 'Petrushka's Room' (from *Petrushka*), Philadelphia Orchestra/Leopold Stokowski
¶ Britten, 'The Splendour Falls' (from *Serenade*, Op. 31), Peter Pears (tenor)/Barry Tuckwell (horn)/English Chamber Orchestra/Benjamin Britten
Decca 417 153–2

David Pountney, opera producer

¶ Janáček, String Quartet No. 1, 'Kreutzer Sonata' (first movement), Britten Quartet
EMI CDC 7547876–2
¶ Gershwin, 'Just Another Rumba', Joan Morris (mezzo-soprano)/William Bolcom (piano)
Nonesuch 7559–79151–2
¶ Maxwell Davies, 'Resurrection' (from *Revivalist Rally*), Neil Jenkins (Hot Gospeller)/soloists/BBC Philharmonic Orchestra/Peter Maxwell Davies
Collins 70342

¶ Shostakovich, 'Can-can', 'Ophelia's Ditty', 'Lullaby' (from *Hamlet*), Louise Winter (mezzo-soprano)/City of Birmingham Symphony Orchestra/Mark Elder
Cala CACDD 1021
¶ Schubert, Sonata in A minor D784 (second movement, Andante), Imogen Cooper (piano)
Ottavo OTRC 68608
¶ Dvořák, *Kate and the Devil* (Finale of Act I), Richard Novák (Devil Marbuel), Anna Barová (Kate), Daniela Suryová(Mother), Miloš Ježil (Shepherd Jirka)/Brno Janáček Opera Chorus and Orchestra/Jiří Pinkas
Supraphon 11 1800–2 612
¶ Purcell, 'Dance of Fairies', 'Sing while we Trip It', 'See, Even Night Herself is Here' (from *The Fairy Queen*, Act II), Judith Nelson, Jennifer Smith (sopranos)/Monteverdi Choir/English Baroque Soloists/John Eliot Gardiner
Archiv 419 221–2

21 OCTOBER 1995
Dudley Moore, actor

¶ Mahler, 'In diesem Wetter' (from *Kindertotenlieder*), Kathleen Ferrier (contralto)/Vienna Philharmonic Orchestra/Bruno Walter
EMI CDH 761003 2
¶ Chopin, Ballade No. 1, Op. 23, Vladimir Horowitz (piano)
CBS M3K 44681
¶ Mozart, Domine Jesu (from Requiem, K626), Barbara Bonney (soprano), Anne Sofie von Otter (mezzo-soprano), Hans-Peter Blochwitz (tenor), Willard White (bass)/Monteverdi Choir/English Baroque Soloists/John Eliot Gardiner
Philips 420 197–2
¶ Massenet, 'Meditation' (from *Thaïs*), Michael Davis (violin)/BBC Symphony Orchestra and Chorus/Andrew Davis
Teldec 4509–97868–2
¶ Bach, Fugue in B minor, BWV 544, Lionel Rogg (organ)
Harmonia Mundi HMX 290783
¶ Rachmaninov, Piano Concerto No. 2 (second movement), Sviatoslav Richter (piano), Warsaw National Philharmonic Orchestra/Stanislaw Wislocki
DG 429 918–2

¶ Beethoven, Symphony No. 3, 'Eroica' (second movement), Cleveland Orchestra/George Szell
Sony SBK 46328
¶ Weelkes, 'When David Heard', Winchester Cathedral Choir/ David Hill
Hyperion CDA 66477

I felt very badly about assuming that cuddly Dudley was high as a kite only to find out subsequently that he was in fact dying from a brain disorder. Still, that did not prevent him from being his usual charming and entertaining self, and I guess that he and Peter Cook might even have found something black and amusing in my misdiagnosis.

28 OCTOBER 1995
Elizabeth Esteve-Coll, Director of the Victoria and Albert Museum

¶ Scarlatti, Sonata in D major, Kk490, Wanda Landowska (harpsichord), rec. 1940
EMI Classics CDH 7 64934 2
¶ Trad. Spanish, arr. G. Tarrago, 'El Rossinyol', Victoria de los Angeles (soprano), Renata Tarraga (guitar)
HMV ASD 3085
¶ Britten, Sanctus (from *War Requiem*, Op. 66), Galina Vishnevskaya (soprano)/Bach Choir, London Symphony Orchestra Chorus/London Symphony Orchestra/Benjamin Britten
Decca 414 385–2
¶ *Bella Ciao* (traditional Sicilian peasant songs)
Harmonia Mundi HMV 734
¶ Saint-Saëns, 'Mon coeur s'ouvre à ta voix' (from *Samson and Delilah*, Act II), Marian Anderson (Delilah)/Orchestra/Lawrence Collingwood, rec. 1930
Nimbus N17801
¶ Shostakovich, Violin Concerto (first movement, 'Nocturne'), Maxim Vengerov (violin)/London Symphony Orchestra/Mstislav Rostropovich
Teldec 4509–98143–2
¶ Mozart, Quintet for piano and wind, K452 (Larghetto), Mitsuko Uchida (piano)/Neil Black (oboe)/Thea King (clarinet)/Frank Lloyd (horn)/Robin O'Neill (bassoon)
Philips 422 592–2

Fiona Shaw, actress

❡ Mozart, Requiem aeternam (from Requiem, K626), Monteverdi Choir/English Baroque Soloists/John Eliot Gardiner
Phs 420 197–2
❡ Rachmaninov, Piano Concerto No. 2 (first movement), Sviatoslav Richter/Warsaw Philharmonic/Stanislaw Wislocki
DG 429 920–2
❡ Honegger, *Joan of Arc at the Stake* (scene 7 and part of scene 8), Marthe Keller (Joan)/Choir of Radio France/French National Orchestra/Seiji Ozawa
DG 429 412–2
❡ Britten, 'Adam lay i-bounden' (from *A Ceremony of Carols*), Choir of Christ Church, Oxford/Francis Grier
ASV CD QS 6030
❡ John Field, Nocturne No. 7 in C major, Miceál O'Rourke (piano)
Chandos CHAN 8720
❡ John Tavener, *The Protecting Veil* (opening movement), Steven Isserlis (cello)/London Symphony Orchestra/Gennadi Rozhdestvensky
EMI 561 849–2
❡ Mozart, 'Mi tradi quell'alma ingrate' (from *Don Giovanni*, Act II), Martina Arroyo (Elvira)/Orchestra of the National Theatre of Prague/Karl Böhm
DG 429 873–2

Noel Annan, diplomat and writer

❡ Mozart, Concerto for flute and harp K299 (second movement), James Galway (flute), Fritz Helmis (harp)/Berlin Philharmonic Orchestra/Herbert von Karajan
EMI CDC 763604 2
❡ Tchaikovsky, *Eugene Onegin* (final scene), Bernd Weikl (Onegin), Teresa Kubiak (Tatiana)/Orchestra of the Royal Opera House/Georg Solti
Decca 417 413–2
❡ Purcell, Chaconne (from *The Fairy Queen*), Heidelberg Chamber Orchestra/Justus von Websky
Oryx EXP 54

¶ Bach, Sanctus (from Mass in B minor), BBC Chorus/Philharmonia/
Otto Klemperer
EMI CMS 763364
¶ Schubert, 'Im Frühling', Elisabeth Schwarzkopf (soprano)/Edwin
Fischer (piano)
EMI CDC 747326 2
¶ Weill, 'Surabaya Jonny' (from *Happy End*), Lotte Lenya/Orchestra/
Roger Bean
CBS 66269
¶ Purcell, 'Halcyon Days' (from *The Tempest*), Jennifer Vyvyan
(soprano)/Philomusica of London/Anthony Lewis
Oiseau Lyre SOL 60002

18 NOVEMBER 1995
Jonathan Miller, doctor, writer and director

¶ Spencer Williams, *Tishomingo Blues*, Will Bill's Stompers, rec. 1947
Artist's private recording
¶ Monteverdi, final duet from *The Coronation of Poppea*, Danielle Borst
(Poppea), Guillemette Laurens (Nero)/Concerto vocale/René Jacobs
Harmonia Mundi HMC 901330–32
¶ Schubert, Adagio in E flat, D897 (Notturno), Beaux Arts Trio
Philips 422836–2
¶ Bach, 'Erbarme dich' (from *St Matthew Passion*), Michael Chance
(countertenor)/English Baroque Soloists/John Eliot Gardiner
Archiv 4272226250–2
¶ Janáček, Introduction to *The Cunning Little Vixen*, Vienna
Philharmonic Orchestra/Charles Mackerras
Decca 417130–2
¶ Beethoven, Piano Concerto No. 4 (first movement), Wilhelm
Backhaus/Vienna Philharmonic Orchestra/Clemens Krauss
Decca 425962–2
¶ Trad., Rag bilaskhani todi, Imrat Khan (sitar)/Shafaatullah Khan
(tabla)/Vajahat Khan (tamburas)
Nimbus NI 5153
¶ Mozart, 'Sull'aria' and 'Che soave zeffiretto' (from *The Marriage of
Figaro*), Margaret Price (Countess), Kathleen Battle (Susanna)/Vienna
Philharmonic Orchestra/Riccardo Muti
EMI CDC 747978–80

Brilliant on music and the mind and wide-ranging enthusiasms with, of course, a particular insight into opera.

25 NOVEMBER 1995
Charles Rosen, pianist and musicologist

¶ Wagner, 'Immolation Scene' (from *Götterdämmerung*), Birgit Nilsson (Brünnhilde), Gottlob Frick (Hagen)/Vienna Philharmonic Orchestra/ Georg Solti
Decca 414 119–2

¶ Carter, Double Concerto, Charles Rosen (piano)/Paul Jacobs (harpsichord)/English Chamber Orchestra/Frederick Prausnitz
CBS 72717

¶ Mozart, 'Di scrivermi ogni giorno' (from *Così fan tutte*, Act I), Carol Vaness (Fiordiligi), Delores Ziegler (Dorabella), Dale Duesing (Guglielmo), John Aler (Ferrando), Claudio Desderi (Don Alfonso)/ London Philharmonic Orchestra/Bernard Haitink
EMI CDC 7 47727

¶ Chopin, Waltz in C sharp minor, Op. 64, No. 2, Josef Hofmann (piano)
IPL 103

¶ Bellini, 'O rendetemi la speme' (from *I Puritani*), Joan Sutherland (Elvira), Nicolai Ghiaurov (Sir Giorgio), Piero Cappuccilli (Sir Riccardo Forth)/London Symphony Orchestra/Richard Bonynge
Decca 417 590–2

¶ Webern, 'Eingang' (from *Five Songs on Poems by Stefan George*, Op. 4), Heather Harper (soprano)/Charles Rosen (piano)
Sony CD 45845

¶ John Browne, Stabat mater, Taverner Choir/Andrew Parrott
EMI CDC 749661 2

¶ Bach, Prelude and Fugue in C minor, BWV 871 (from *The Well-tempered Clavier*, Book 2), András Schiff (piano)
Decca 417 237–2

2 DECEMBER 1995
Julian Barnes, writer

¶ Mozart, Sonata in E flat, K282 (first movement), András Schiff
Decca 421 110–2

¶ Berlioz, 'Villanelle' (from *Les nuits d'été*), Régine Crespin (soprano)/
Orchestre de la Suisse Romande/Ernest Ansermet
Decca 417 813–2
¶ Satie, *Gnossienne* No. 4, Pascal Rogé (piano)
Decca 410 220–2
¶ Brassens, 'Le 22 septembre', Georges Brassens
Philips 836 293–2
¶ Sibelius, Symphony No. 4 (first movement), City of Birmingham
Symphony Orchestra/Simon Rattle
EMI CDC 747711 2
¶ Coward, 'Don't Let's Be Beastly to the Germans', Noël Coward
EMI Coward 13
¶ Gounod, Credo (from *St Cecilia Mass*), Choeurs de Radio France/
Nouvel Orchestre Philharmonique de Radio France/Georges Prêtre
EMI CDC 747094 2
¶ Ravel, 'Blues' (from Violin Sonata), Jean-Jacques Kantorow (violin)/
Philipp Muller (piano)
Erato ECD 71569

*Fascinating how the feeling for France that so informs his writing is
followed through in his love of music.*

9 DECEMBER 1995
John Bird, actor

¶ Haydn, String Quartet in B flat, Op. 76, No. 4 (first movement),
Takács Quartet
Decca 425 467–2
¶ Schoenberg, Three Pieces for chamber orchestra, Schoenberg
Ensemble/Reinbert de Leeuw
Musica Mundi CD 311 009
¶ Schoenberg, *Herzgewächse*, Lucy Shelton (soprano)/Da Capo
Players/Oliver Knussen
Bridge BCD 9032
¶ Beethoven, Sonata in A, Op. 101 (second movement), Alfred Brendel
(piano)
Philips 438 472–2
¶ Debussy, 'Étude pour les octaves', Martino Tirimo (piano)
IMP MCD 14

❡ Boulez, *Éclat*, Ensemble Intercontemporain/Pierre Boulez
Sony sk 45839
❡ Bach, Prelude in C sharp major (from *The Well-tempered Clavier*,
Book 1), Libby Crandon (piano)
Private recording
❡ Stravinsky, *Variations – Aldous Huxley in memoriam*, Columbia
Symphony Orchestra/Robert Craft
Sony smk 46302
❡ Schumann, 'Sphinxes', 'Papillons' (from *Carnaval*), Cristina Ortiz
(piano)
imp pcd 899

There was something so natural about his love of contemporary music
that it could not fail to be infectious. Boulez and Webern are John's
musical bread and butter and his analogy with a walk in a strange but
magical wood made one hear innovative sounds and colours with a new
and fresh ear. For me, an ideal guest.

16 DECEMBER 1995
Marjorie Wallace, chief exective, SANE

❡ Annie F. Harrison, 'In the Gloaming', Stuart Burrows (tenor)/John
Constable (piano)
Oiseau Lyre dslo 43
❡ Gounod, 'Repentir', Cheryl Studer (soprano)/London Symphony
Orchestra/Ion Martin
dg 435 387–2
❡ Puccini, 'Recondite armonia' (from *Tosca*, Act I), José Carreras
(Cavaradossi), Fernando Corena (Sacristan)/Berlin Philharmonic
Orchestra/Herbert von Karajan
dg 413 815–2
❡ Meredith Wilson, 'Till There Was You' (from *The Music Man*),
Barbara Cook/Robert Preston
Angel zdm 764663 2
❡ Verdi, 'Dinale' (from *La traviata*, Act III), Matteo Manuguerra
(Germont), Joan Sutherland (Violetta), Luciano Pavarotti (Alfredo),
Marjon Lambriks (Annina), Giorgio Taddeo (Dottore)/National
Philharmonic Orchestra/Richard Bonynge
Decca 410 154–2

❡ Elgar, 'As Torrents in Spring', Louis Halsey Singers/Louis Halsey
Decca KCSP 598
❡ Chopin, Waltz in A flat, Op. 69, No. 1, Artur Rubinstein (piano)
RCA RD 89564
❡ Fauré, In paradisum (from Requiem, Op. 48), Choir of King's
College, Cambridge/New Philharmonia Orchestra/David Willcocks
EMI CDM 764715 2
❡ Mahler, Symphony No. 5 (fourth movement, Adagietto), New
Philharmonia Orchestra/John Barbirolli
EMI CDM 769186 2

23 DECEMBER 1995
Barry Humphries, actor

❡ Villa-Lobos, 'Samba Classico', Teresa Berganza (mezzo-soprano)/
Juan Antonio Alvarez Parejo (piano)
Claves CD 50–8401
❡ Grainger, 'On Arrival Platform Humlet', Paul Coletti (viola)
Hyperion CDA 66687
❡ Chabrier, 'L'île heureuse', Jacques Jansen (baritone)/Jacqueline
Bonneau (piano)
Decca LXT 2774
❡ Křenek, 'The Farewell Song' (from *Jonny spielt auf*), Ludwig
Hoffman/Orchestra of the State Opera House, Berlin
Parlophone E 10698
❡ Damase, 'Variations on the Wedding March', Claude Delangle
(saxophone)/Jean-Michel Damase (piano)
Private recording
❡ Mompou, 'Damunt de tu nomes les flors', Montserrat Caballé
(soprano)/Frederic Mompou (piano)
Vergara 701 TL
❡ Delius, 'They Are Not Long, the Weeping and the Laughter' (from
Songs of Sunset), John Cameron (baritone)/Beecham Choral Society/
Royal Philharmonic Orchestra/Thomas Beecham
EMI CDS 747509 2
❡ Varèse, *Octandre*, Ensemble Intercontemporain/Pierre Boulez
Sony CD 45844

13 JANUARY 1996
Ken Russell, film and television director

¶ Brahms, Symphony No. 3 (second movement), Berlin Philharmonic Orchestra/Wilhelm Furtwängler
Music and Art CD 804 (4) A-D
¶ Milhaud, *Saudades do Brasil* (No. 4, 'Copacabana', No. 5, 'Ipanema', No. 6, 'Gavea'), Orchestre du Théâtre des Champs-Élysées/Darius Milhaud
EMI CDC 7 546 042
¶ Stan Kenton, 'Lover' (from *Kenton in Hi-Fi*), Stan Kenton/Vido Musso/Milt Bernhardt
Capitol Jazz CPP 7 98451 2
¶ Prokofiev, 'Waltz' (from *War and Peace* symphonic suite), Philharmonia/Neeme Järvi
Chandos CHAN 9096
¶ Elgar, Symphony No. 2 (third movement, 'Presto'), London Symphony Orchestra/Jeffrey Tate
EMI CDC 7 54192 2
¶ Carmichael/Mercer, 'Skylark', Linda Ronstadt/Nelson Riddle/Orchestra
Asylum 960387 2
¶ John Adams, *Grand Pianola Music* (Part II, 'On the Dominant Divide'), Ellen Corver, Sepp Grotenhuis, Lindsay Wagstaff, Kym Amps, Ruth Holton/Netherlands Wind Ensemble/Mosko
Chandos CHAN 9363

20 JANUARY 1996
David Hare, playwright

¶ Stanley Myers, theme from *Heading Home*, Stanley Myers
Private recording
¶ Berlioz, *La mort de Cleopatre*, Jessye Norman (soprano)/Orchestre de Paris/Daniel Barenboim
DG 439 404–2
¶ Beethoven, Symphony No. 7 (second movement), New York Philharmonic Orchestra/Arturo Toscanini
BMG Classics GD 60316
¶ Ravel, *Tzigane*, Christian Ferras (violin)/Pierre Barbizet (piano)
EMI 7 672182

❡ Bach, *Goldberg Variations*, BWV 988 (Variations 4–8), Glenn Gould (piano)
Sony Classical SMK 52685
❡ Miles Davis, 'Diner au Motel' (from *Ascenseur pour l'echafaud*),
Miles Davis
Fantasia 836 305–2
❡ Figgis, 'Ben and Sara' (theme) (from soundtrack for *Leaving Las Vegas*), Mike Figgis and Dave Hartley
Pangaea 72438 36071 29

Simply cannot stand opera. Finds its lack of realism impossible to surmount. These trenchant views have led to some furious arguments in subsequent programmes so I have been extremely grateful to David ever since!

27 JANUARY 1996
Sian Phillips, actress

❡ Schubert, Impromptu No. 3 in G flat, Op. 90, D899, Alfred Brendel (piano)
Philips 422 237–2
❡ Pergolesi, Fac ut ardeat cor meum (from Stabat mater), June Anderson, Cecilia Bartoli (voices)/Sinfonietta de Montreal/Charles Dutoit
Decca 436 209–2
❡ Mozart, Piano Concerto No. 19, K459 (first movement), Maurizio Pollini (piano)/Vienna Philharmonic Orchestra/Karl Böhm
DG 413 793–2
❡ Gershwin, 'Bess, You Is My Woman Now' (from *Porgy and Bess*), Willard White (Porgy), Leona Mitchell (Bess)/Cleveland Orchestra/Lorin Maazel
Decca 414 559–2
❡ Mozart, 'Porgi amor' (from *The Marriage of Figaro*), Jessye Norman (Countess)/BBC Symphony Orchestra/Colin Davis
Philips 426 196–2
❡ Bernstein, 'Glitter and Be Gay' (from *Candide*), Barbara Cook (voice)
CBS Masterworks MK 38732

Sir Isaiah Berlin, philosopher

❡ Bellini, 'Casta diva' (from *Norma*, Act I), Rosa Ponselle (Norma)/
Orchestra and Chorus of the Metropolitan Opera House, New York/
Giulio Setti
RCA GB 87810
❡ Schubert, Sonata in A, D959, Alfred Brendel (piano)
Philips 422 229–2
❡ Beethoven, String Quartet No. 13 in B flat, Op. 130 (fifth movement,
Adagio molto espressivo), Busch Quartet
Masterworks Portrait MPK 47687
❡ Bach, Brandenburg Concerto No. 5 (first movement, Allegro), Alfred
Cortot (piano)/Jacques Thibaud (violin)/Roger Cortot (keyboard)
Biddulph LAB 028
❡ Mozart, Act II finale from *The Marriage of Figaro*, Samuel Ramey,
Thomas Allen, Kiri te Kanawa, Lucia Popp, Giorgio Taddeo, Jane Berbié,
Robert Tear, Kurt Moll/London Philharmonic Orchestra/Georg Solti
Decca 410 151–2

*Wickedly naughty on the subject of Stravinsky and his rivalry with
Britten, of whom Igor said, 'He is the greatrest accompanist I have ever
heard; that is my opinion of Benjamin Britten.' Strange how even the
most celebrated remain childishly insecure. Very moving to hear an
account of Berlin as a child watching the White Army riding below his
first-floor window as Russia dissolved into turmoil.*

Professor Steve Jones, geneticist

❡ Richard Strauss, 'Da geht er hin, der aufgeblasener schlechter Kerl'
(from *Der Rosenkavalier*, Act I), Elisabeth Schwarzkopf (Marschallin)/
Philharmonia/Herbert von Karajan
EMI CDC 749 355/57 2
❡ Bach, Chaconne (from Partita for violin No. 2), Andrés Segovia
(guitar)
MCA 42068
❡ Steve Reich, *Tehillim* for voice and ensemble (Part II: fast),
Schoenberg Ensemble Percussion Group, The Hague/Reinbert de Leeuw
Elektra Nonesuch 7559 79295–2

¶ The Ramblers Dance Band, 'Agyanka Dabre', The Ramblers Dance
Band
Flame Tree FLTRCD 526
¶ Beethoven, String Quartet No. 16 in F, Op. 135 (second movement),
Lindsay String Quartet
ASV CD DCA 604
¶ Monteverdi, Sonata sopra Sancta Maria (from Vespers, 1610),
Monteverdi Choir/English Baroque Soloists/His Majesty's Sagbutts
and Cornetts/John Eliot Gardiner
Archiv 429 565–2
¶ Purcell, 'In the Midst of Life' (from *Music for the Funeral of Queen
Mary*), Choir of Winchester Cathedral/David Hill
Argo 436 833–2
¶ Bach, arr. Elgar, Fantasia and Fugue in C minor, BWV 537, Op. 86,
London Philharmonic Orchestra/Adrian Boult
EMI CDM 7 631 332

*I always enjoy finding musical analogies for science and vice versa. We
discovered some fascinating common ground in the approach to music
and genetics.*

17 FEBRUARY 1996
Patricia Routledge, actress

¶ Lennox Berkeley, 'The Lord is my shepherd', Op. 91, No. 1, Choir of
St Paul's Cathedral/Andrew Lucas (organ)/John Scott
Hyperion CDA 66758
¶ Shostakovich, Suite: *The Adventures of Korzinkina*, Op. 59, Chorus
and Symphony Orchestra of the USSR Ministry of Culture/Gennadi
Rozhdestvensky
Olympia OCD 194
¶ Dvořák, String Quartet No. 12 in F, 'American' Op. 96 (second
movement, Lento), Amadeus Quartet
DG Galleria 437 251–2
¶ Tchaikovsky, *Variations on a Rococo Theme* for cello and orchestra,
Op. 33 (Variations 4–7), Mstislav Rostropovich/Berlin Philharmonic
Orchestra/Herbert von Karajan
Polydor DP 413 819–2

¶ Gluck, 'Che farò senza Euridice' and 'Dance of the Blessed Spirits' (from *Orfeo ed Euridice*), Janet Baker (mezzo-soprano)/English Chamber Orchestra/Raymond Leppard
Philips 422 950–2

24 FEBRUARY 1996
Sir Magdi Yacoub, heart surgeon

¶ Mozart, Fantasia in C, K395, Jorge Demus (piano)
Harmonia Mundi HM 484
¶ Franck, *Panis angelicus*, Jessye Norman (soprano)/Royal Philharmonic Orchestra/Alexander Gibson
Philips 432 546–2
¶ Bob Marley, 'Three Little Birds', Bob Marley and the Wailers
Island CID 103
¶ Handel, 'Let the Bright Seraphim' (from *Samson*), Kiri te Kanawa (soprano)/Choir of St Paul's Cathedral/London Symphony Orchestra/Colin Davis
¶ Mozart, Lacrimosa (from Requiem, K626), John Alldis Choir/English Chamber Orchestra/Daniel Barenboim
EMI CZS 762893/94 2
¶ Bach, Prelude No. 1 in C (from *The Well-tempered Clavier*, Book 1), Glenn Gould (piano)
Sony Classical SM2K 55 600
¶ Bach, 'Ich habe genug' (from Cantata No. 82), Janet Baker (mezzo-soprano)/Bath Festival Orchestra/Yehudi Menuhin
HMV ASD 2302
¶ Charpentier, Te Deum, Les Arts Florissants/William Christie
¶ Bach, Concerto for Two Violins, BWV 1043 (second movement, Largo ma non tanto), David and Igor Oistrakh (violins)/Leipzig Gewandhaus Orchestra/Franz Konwitschny
Berlin Classics BC 2130–2

Surgeons often operate with music playing, though as a patient I might baulk at the Lacrimosa from the Mozart Requiem!

James MacMillan, composer

¶ Byrd, Kyrie (from Mass for Four Voices), Choir of Winchester Cathedral/David Hill
Argo 430 164–2
¶ Galina Ustvolskaya, *Composition* No. 3 (Benedictus qui venit), London Musici/Mark Stephenson
Conifer 75605 51194 2
¶ John Casken, *Vaganza* (third movement), Northern Sinfonia/John Casken
Collins Classics 14242–2
¶ Beethoven, 'O namenlose Freude' (from *Fidelio*, Act II), Jon Vickers (Florestan), Christa Ludwig (Leonora)/Philharmonia Chorus and Orchestra/Otto Klemperer
EMI CMS 7 69324 2
¶ Bach, Fugue No. 21 in B flat (from *The Well-tempered Clavier*, Book 1), András Schiff (piano)
Decca 414 388–2
¶ Mozart, Clarinet Quintet in A, K581 (first movement), Benny Goodman/Budapest String Quartet
RCA RD 85275
¶ Trad., 'MacCrimmon's Lament', Heather Heywood
CDTRAX 054
¶ Messiaen, *Et exspecto resurrectionem mortuorum*, Cleveland Orchestra/Pierre Boulez
DG 445 827–2
¶ Wagner, Prelude and opening scene of *Götterdämmerung*, Helen Watts, Grace Hoffman, Anita Valkki (Norns)/Vienna Philharmonic Orchestra/Georg Solti
Decca 414 1162

Michael Ignatieff, writer and journalist

¶ Schoenberg, *Verklärte Nacht*, Orpheus Chamber Orchestra
DG 429 233–2
¶ Bach, Concerto in F, 'Italian' BWV 971 (third movement, Presto), Glenn Gould (piano)
CBS Masterworks CBS MYK 42527

♪ Hoagy Carmichael, 'Stardust', Ben Webster (saxophone), Teddy
Wilson (piano), Orsted Pederson (bass), Makaya Ntsoko (drums)
Storyville STCD 41181
♪ Beethoven, Piano Concerto No. 4 (second movement, Andante con
moto), Alfred Brendel (piano)/London Symphony Orchestra/Bernard
Haitink
Philips 4208552
♪ Mahler, Symphony No. 2, 'Resurrection' (fourth movement,
'Urlicht'), Janet Baker (mezzo-soprano)/City of Birmingham
Symphony Orchestra/Simon Rattle
EMI CDS 7 47962 8
♪ Schubert, Quintet in A major, 'Trout' (third movement, Scherzo),
Emil Gilels (piano)/members of Amadeus Quartet with Rainer
Zepperitz (double bass)
DG 413 452–3
♪ Gershwin, 'Summertime' (from *Porgy and Bess*)/Ella Fitzgerald,
Louis Armstrong/Orchestra/Russell Garcia
Verve 827 475–2

16 MARCH 1996
John Peel, broadcaster and writer

♪ Saint-Saëns, Piano Concerto No. 2 in G minor, Op. 22 (third
movement, Presto), Cécile Licard (piano)/London Philharmonic
Orchestra/André Previn
CBS MK 39153
♪ Allegri, Miserere, Choir of King's College, Cambridge/Roy Goodman
(treble)/David Willcocks
Decca 421147–2
♪ Gottschalk, *Ojos Criollos, Danse cubaine*, Vienna State Opera
Orchestra, Berlin Symphony Orchestra/Cary Lewis, Eugene List
(pianos)/Igor Buketoff and Samuel Adler (conds)
Vox Box 1154842
♪ Neil Young, 'Rockin' in the Free World', Neil Young
Reprise 9352–41406–2
♪ Conlon Nancarrow, Study for Player-Piano No. 21, Conlon
Nancarrow
1750 Arch Records S1786B

♪ Bruch, Violin Concerto, Op. 26 (second movement), Kyung-Wha Chung (violin)/Royal Philharmonic Orchestra/Rudolph Kempe
Decca 417 707–2
♪ Gershwin, *Rhapsody in Blue*, Michael Tilson Thomas (piano and conductor)/Los Angeles Philharmonic Orchestra
CBS MK 39699

In all the acres of newsprint devoted to John's tastes, following his untimely death, not one article mentioned his love of classical music. I loved the way that his curiosity was expressed uniquely by asking me to choose something that I thought he might like and that might surprise him. I suggested the Nancarrow which he subsequently broadcast on Radio 1, where I am sure it genuinely intrigued.

23 MARCH 1996
Sir Colin Davis, conductor

♪ Bruckner, Symphony No. 6 (second movement), New Philharmonia Orchestra/Otto Klemperer
EMI 562 621–2
♪ Berlioz, Act III finale from *Les Troyens*, Jon Vickers (Aeneas), Josephine Veasey (Dido), Roger Soyer (Narbal), Anthony Raffell (Panthus), Anne Howells (Ascanius), Ian Partridge (Iopas)/Orchestra and Chorus of the Royal Opera House/Colin Davis
Philips 416 432–2
♪ Beethoven, fugue section of Credo (from *Missa solemnis*, Op. 123), Luba Organosova (soprano), Jadwiga Rappé (alto), Uwe Heilmann (tenor), Jan-Hendrik Rootering (bass)/Bavarian Radio Symphony Orchestra/Colin Davis
BMG/RCA 09026 60967 2
♪ Britten, Act I, scene 2 from *Peter Grimes*, Peter Pears (Grimes), Marion Studholme, Iris Kelly (Nieces), Raymond Nilsson (Bob Boles), James Pease (Captain Bulstrode), Geraint Evans (Ned Keene), Jean Watson (Auntie), David Kelly (Hobson), Claire Watson (Ellen Orford)/Orchestra and Chorus of the Royal Opera House/Benjamin Britten
Decca 414 577–2
♪ Mozart, Divertimento for string trio in E flat, K563 (second movement, Adagio), Grumiaux Trio
Philips 422 696–2

♪ Tippett, Act II, scene 3 from *The Midsummer Marriage*, Elizabeth Harwood (Bella)/Orchestra of the Royal Opera House/Colin Davis
Lyrita SRCD 2217

Despite a necessary degree of single-minded determination, Colin always gives me the feeling of being humbled by the great scores that he conducts, and this was a quality much in evidence here too.

30 MARCH 1996
Carl Davis, composer and conductor

♪ Bernstein, 'Danzon' (3rd Dance Variation from *Fancy Free*),
New York Philharmonic Orchestra/Leonard Bernstein
Sony SM3K 47154
♪ Puccini, 'Chi il bel sogno di Doretta' (from *La rondine*), Kiri te Kanawa (Magda)/London Philharmonic Orchestra/John Pritchard
CBS CD 37298
♪ Schubert, *Moment Musical* in F minor D780/3, Radu Lupu (piano)
Decca 417 785–2
♪ Monteverdi, 'Messenger's Aria' (from *Orfeo*), Anne Sofie von Otter (Messenger)/Mark Tucker (1st Shepherd)/Nigel Robson (2nd Shepherd)/English Baroque Soloists/John Eliot Gardiner
Archiv 419 251–2
♪ Richard Strauss, 'Wiegenlied' Op. 41, No. 1, Elisabeth Schwarzkopf (soprano)/London Symphony Orchestra/George Szell
EMI CDC 747276 2
♪ Walton, 'Spitfire Music' (from *Battle of Britain* suite), London Philharmonic Orchestra/Carl Davis
EMI CDC 747944 2
♪ McCartney/Davis, 'The World You're Coming Into' (from *Liverpool Oratorio*), Kiri te Kanawa (soprano)/Jeremy Budd (treble)/Royal Liverpool Philharmonic Orchestra/Carl Davis
EMI CDC 754373 2
♪ Mozart, Quintet in G minor, K516 (third movement, Adagio ma non troppo), Melos Quartet/Franz Beyer (viola)
DG 419 773–2
♪ Davis, *Pride and Prejudice*, opening titles, Melvyn Tan (fortepiano)/Orchestra/Carl Davis
EMI 7243 836090 2

¶ Bach, Overture (from Suite No. 3 in D), Bath Festival
Orchestra/Yehudi Menuhin
EMI CZS 767350 2

6 APRIL 1996
Sir David Attenborough, naturalist and broadcaster

¶ Ellington, 'Stompy Jones', Duke Ellington (piano)/Johnny Hodges
(alto saxophone)/ Harry 'Sweets' Edison (trumpet)/Al Hall (bass)/Les
Spann (guitar)/Jo Jones (drums)
Verve 821 578 2
¶ Tomkins, 'When David Heard', Tallis Scholars/Peter Phillips
Gimell CDGIM 024
¶ Handel, 'And the Glory of the Lord' (from *Messiah*), English
Concert/English Concert Choir/Trevor Pinnock
Archiv 423 630 2
¶ Scarlatti, Sonata in G major, Longo 209, Vladimir Horowitz (piano)
CBS CD 42534
¶ Mahler, 'Ich bin der Welt abhanden gekommen' (No. 4 from
Rückert-Lieder), Janet Baker (mezzo-soprano)/New Philharmonia
Orchestra/John Barbirolli
EMI CDC 747 793 2
¶ Mozart, 'Soave sia il vento' (from *Così fan tutte*, Act I), Montserrat
Caballe (Fiordiligi)/Janet Baker (Dorabella)/Richard van Allan (Don
Alfonso)/Orchestra of the Royal Opera House/Colin Davis
Philips 422 818 2
¶ Britten, 'The Pagodas' (from *The Prince of the Pagodas*, Act 2),
London Sinfonietta (including James Holland, percussion, John
Constable, keyboard)/Oliver Knussen
Virgin Classics VCD 791103/A 2
¶ Monteverdi, 1st Versicle and Response (from Vespers, 1610), David
Thomas/Taverner Choir and Players/Andrew Parrott
EMI CDC 747078 2

*Passionate not just about music but also the medium of communicating
it. Castigated the BBC for allowing its public-service ethos to slip and for
pandering to ratings at the expense of quality. That said, it is good to see
that David's wild-life programmes still enchant us almost every week.*

Jilly Cooper, writer

¶ Beethoven, Quintet in E flat (first movement, Allegro), Wind Soloists of the Chamber Orchestra of Europe
ASV CD COE 807

¶ Gilbert/Sullivan, 'Now, Marco Dear' (from *The Gondoliers*), Mary Sansom (Gianetta)/Joyce Wright (Tessa)/Thomas Round (Marco)/ Alan Styler (Giuseppe)/New Symphony Orchestra of London/Isidore Godfrey
London 417 254–2

¶ Richard Strauss, *Ein Heldenleben* (closing section), Chicago Symphony Orchestra/Daniel Barenboim
Warner 0630 14342–2

¶ Britten, 'Sentimental Sarabande' (from *Simple Symphony*, Op. 4), English String Orchestra/William Boughton
Nimbus NI 5025

¶ Chopin, 'Andantino' (from *Fantasia on Polish Airs*, Op. 13), Idil Biret (piano)/Czecho-Slovak State Philharmonic Orchestra/Robert Satanovsky
Naxos 8.550368

¶ Richard Strauss, 'Night and Sunrise' (from *An Alpine Symphony*), Berlin Philharmonic Orchestra/Herbert von Karajan
DG 439 017–2

¶ Brahms arr. Joachim, Hungarian Dance No. 3 in F, Marat Bisengaliev (violin)/John Lenehan (piano)
Naxos 8.553026

¶ Mozart, 'Ah! taci, ingiusto core' (from *Don Giovanni*, Act II), Kiri te Kanawa (Donna Elvira)/Ruggero Raimondi (Don Giovanni)/José van Dam (Leporello)/Paris Opéra Orchestra/Lorin Maazel
CBS M3K 35192

Naughty in that she began to turn the tables on me by reverting to her journalistic instincts and the role of inquisitor – an honourable draw, I think!

20 APRIL 1996
Juliet Stevenson, actress

¶ Bach, 'Und von der sechsten Stunde' and 'Wenn ich einmal soll scheiden' (from *St Matthew Passion*), Peter Schreier (Evangelist)/ Dietrich Fischer-Dieskau (Jesus)/Vienna Singverein/Berlin Philharmonic Orchestra/Herbert von Karajan
DG 419 789–2
¶ Britten, *The Turn of the Screw* (scene 8), Peter Pears (Peter Quint)/ David Hemmings (Miles)/Arda Mandikian (Miss Jessel)/Olive Dyer (Flora)/Jennifer Vyvyan (Governess)/Joan Cross (Mrs Grose)/English Opera Group Orchestra/Benjamin Britten
London 425 672–2
¶ Reid/Shamblin, 'I Can't Make You Love Me', Bonnie Raitt
Capitol CDP 796111 2
¶ Schubert, Arpeggione Sonata, D821 (first movement, Allegro Moderato), Yuri Bashmet (viola)/Mikhail Muntian (piano)
RCA RD 60112
¶ Richard Strauss, 'Beim Schlafengehen' (from *Four Last Songs*), Jessye Norman (soprano)/Leipzig Gewandhaus Orchestra/Kurt Masur
Philips 411 052–2
¶ James MacMillan, Sanctus (from *Busqueda*), Juliet Stevenson (speaker)/Charlotte Spink, Ruth Anderson, Anna Bentley (sopranos)/ Scottish Chamber Orchestra/James MacMillan
RCA 09026–62669–2
¶ Leonard Cohen, 'Famous Blue Raincoat', Jennifer Warnes
RCA PD 90048

I am always fascinated by how exposure to contemporary music inevitably brings an understanding and love of it. It was through taking part as a narrator in Busqueda *that Juliet came to get under the skin of the score. As a reward, she was one of the few guests who has been allowed to sneak in one of Richard Strauss's lovely* Four Last Songs. *We try and discourage its over-use and as a result (see Josceline Dimbleby, p. 368) have shed light on some of the other equally beautiful Strauss songs.*

Simon Callow, actor and director

♪ Kevin Malpass, Music from 'Shades', Catherine Musker (viola)/Ron Asprey (saxophone)/Phil Steriopulos (bass)/Kevin Malpass (keyboard)
Private recording
♪ Cole Porter, 'In the Still of the Night', Leslie A. Hutchinson
Happy Days CDHD 213
♪ Mahler, Symphony No. 8 (final section of Part II), John Mitchinson (Dr Marianus)/Various choruses and London Symphony Orchestra/ Leonard Bernstein
CBS 42199/C
♪ Bizet/Oscar Hammerstein II, 'De Cards Don' Lie' and 'Dat ol' Boy' (from *Carmen Jones*), Sharon Benson and original London cast/dir. Henry Lewis
EMI CDC 754351 2
♪ Mozart, Serenade in B flat, K361 (Adagio), London Mozart Players Wind Ensemble/Jane Glover
Novello NVLCD 103
♪ Prokofiev, Violin Concerto No. 2 (second movement), Shlomo Mintz/Chicago Symphony Orchestra/Claudio Abbado
DG 410 524 2
♪ John White, 'Waltz' from incidental music to *Les Enfants du Paradis*, John White (synthesiser)
Private recording
♪ Saint-Saëns, 'Mon coeur s'ouvre à ta voix' (from *Samson and Delilah*, Act II), Marian Anderson (Delilah)/Orchestra/Lawrence Collingwood, rec. 1930
Nimbus NI7801

Dynamic, intelligent and passionate – not hard to see why he is such a gifted actor.

4 MAY 1996
Ernst Gombrich, art historian

♪ Bach, Concerto in E major, BWV 1042 (second movement, Adagio), Adolf Busch (violin)/Busch Chamber Players
Odyssey Y 34895

¶ Beethoven, String Quartet No. 13 in B flat major, Op. 130 (third movement, Andante con moto, ma non troppo), Busch Quartet
Sony MPK 47687
¶ Haydn, Qui tollis peccata mundi (from the 'Nelson' Mass), Lisa della Casa (soprano)/George London (bass)/Vienna Akademie Chorus/Vienna Symphony Orchestra/Jonathan Sternberg
Nixa HLP 2004
¶ Mozart, Laudate Dominum (from Vesperae solennes de confessore, K339), Teresa Stich-Randall (soprano)/Chorus of Sarrebrück Conservatory/Chamber Orchestra of the Sarre/Karl Ristenpart
Philips 426275–2
¶ Mozart, String Quartet in B flat major, K458 (third movement, Adagio), Amadeus Quartet
DG 423 303–2
¶ Schubert, Sonata in G major, D894 (third movement, Menuetto), Alfred Brendel (piano)
Philips 422 340–2
¶ Beethoven, Sonata No. 8 in G major, Op. 30, No. 3 (last movement, Allegro vivace), Adolf Busch (violin)/Rudolf Serkin (piano)
Odyssey Y 34893

A great art historian but musically rooted and marooned in the first great Viennese School. Fortunate that he had a somewhat broader view of art.

11 MAY 1996
Joanna Trollope, writer

¶ Gershwin, 'Summertime' (from *Porgy and Bess*), Harolyn Blackwell (Clara)/Glyndebourne Chorus/London Philharmonic Orchestra/Simon Rattle
EMI CDC 749569 2
¶ Britten, 'Dawn' (from *Four Sea Interludes from Peter Grimes*), BBC Symphony Orchestra/Andrew Davis
Teldec 9031–73126–2
¶ Mozart, Laudamus te (from Mass in C minor, K427), Diana Montague (soprano)/English Baroque Soloists/John Eliot Gardiner
Philips 420 210–2

¶ Telemann, Concerto in D for three trumpets (first and second movements), Friedemann Immer, Michael Laird, Iain Wilson (trumpets)/Academy of Ancient Music/Christopher Hogwood
Oiseau Lyre 411 949–2
¶ Vaughan Williams, *Fantasia on a Theme by Thomas Tallis*, New York Philharmonic Orchestra/Dimitri Mitropoulos
Sony SRCR 8463
¶ Rodgers/Hart, 'Manhattan', Ella Fitzgerald
Polydor 515 575–2
¶ Fauré, In paradisum (from Requiem, Op. 48), Monteverdi Choir/ Salisbury Cathedral Boy Choristers/Orchestre Révolutionnaire et Romantique/John Eliot Gardiner
Philips 438 149–2
¶ Górecki, Symphony No. 3 (opening of third movement), Dawn Upshaw (soprano)/London Sinfonietta/David Zinman
Elektra Nonesuch 7559–79282–2

18 MAY 1996
Oz Clarke, wine critic

¶ Puccini, 'Che gelida manina' (from *La bohème*, Act I), Jussi Björling (Rodolfo), Victoria de los Angeles (Mimì)/RCA Victor Symphony Orchestra/Thomas Beecham
EMI CDS 747235 8
¶ Purcell, 'When I Am Laid in Earth' (from *Dido and Aeneas*), Ann Murray (Dido)/Concentus Musicus Wien/Nikolaus Harnoncourt
Teldec 8.42919
¶ Sondheim, 'There was a Barber and his Wife' (from *Sweeney Todd*), Len Cariou (Sweeney Todd), Angela Lansbury (Mrs Lovett)
RCA CBL2 3379/A
¶ Stephen Oliver, 'The Battle of Pelennor Fields' (from *The Lord of the Rings*), Oz Clarke/Ensemble/Stephen Oliver
BBC REH 415
¶ Tom Waits, 'The Piano Has Been Drinking (Not Me)', Tom Waits
Asylum 960612–2
¶ Trad., 'She Moved Through the Fair', Oz Clarke
specially recorded
¶ Leiber/Stoller, 'King Creole', Elvis Presley
RCA PD 90100

❡ Bach, 'O Mensch, bewein dein Sünde gross' (from *St Matthew Passion*),
Monteverdi Choir/English Baroque Soloists/John Eliot Gardiner
Archiv 427 648–2
❡ Robin/Rainger, 'Thanks for the Memory' (from *The Mitford Girls*),
Patricia Hodge (Nancy), Lucy Fenwick (Jessica), Julia Sutton (Pamela),
Patricia Michael (Diana), Colette Gleeson (Unity), Gay Soper
(Deborah)/John Owen Edwards (piano)
Philips 6359 088

25 MAY 1996
Anthony Storr, psychiatrist and writer

❡ Liszt, *Unstern-Sinistre*, Alfred Brendel (piano)
Philips 446 943 2
❡ Bach, Menuets I and II from Partita No. 1 in B flat, Dinu Lipatti
(piano)
EMI CDC 747517 2
❡ Chopin, Nouvelles Etudes Nos 1 and 2, Artur Rubinstein (piano)
RCA RD 89911
❡ Duparc, *L'invitation au voyage*, Elly Ameling (soprano)/San
Francisco Symphony Orchestra/Edo de Waart
Philips 410 043 2
❡ Haydn, String Quartet in F minor (Adagio), Quatuor Mosaïques
Astrée E 8785
❡ Mozart, String Quintet in C, K515 (fourth movement, Allegro),
Arthur Grumiaux, Arpad Gerécz (violins)/Georges Janzer, Max
Lesueur (violas)/Eva Czako (cello)
Philips PHCP 4968
❡ Schubert, 'Abschied' (from *Schwanengesang*, D957), Wolfgang
Holzmair (baritone)/Imogen Cooper (piano)
Philips 442 460 2
❡ Handel, Organ Concerto in B flat major, Op. 4, No. 2 (second
movement, Allegro), Ton Koopman/Amsterdam Baroque Orchestra
Erato ECD 88138

*Discussed the nature of sad and tragic music and why we are so drawn to
it, especially when we are feeling unhappy. However, he pointed out that
clinically depressed people cannot listen to anything; that is what
blackness is really about. Emotionally, I guess that we are essentially
voyeurs, in the best sense of the word.*

45

Joe Melia, actor

❡ Williams/Vodex/Havez, 'The Darktown Poker Club', Phil Harris and his Orchestra
RCA NL 89526

❡ Britten, 'Elegy' (from *Serenade*), Peter Pears (tenor)/Dennis Brain (horn)/Boyd Neel String Orchestra/Benjamin Britten
Decca 425 996–2

❡ Loesser, Overture and Racetrack Trio (from *Guys and Dolls*), Stubby Kaye/Johnny Silver/Douglas Deane (original Broadway cast recording)
MCA MCL 1659

❡ Verdi, *Falstaff* (opening of Act II), Tito Gobbi (Falstaff), Renato Ercolani (Bardolph), Nicola Zaccaria (Pistol), Fedora Barbieri (Mistress Quickly)/Philharmonia/Herbert von Karajan
EMI CDS 749669 2

❡ Wagner, 'Hagen Summons the Vassals' (from *Götterdämmerung*, Act II), Gottlob Frick (Hagen)/Vienna State Opera Chorus/Vienna Philharmonic Orchestra/Georg Solti
Decca 414 115–2

❡ Richard Strauss, 'Moonlight Music' (from the last scene of *Capriccio*), Bavarian Radio Symphony Orchestra/Karl Böhm
DG 419 023–2

❡ Beethoven, String Quartet in E flat major, Op. 127 (third movement, Scherzando vivace), Hungarian Quartet
EMI CDZ 767241 2

❡ Liszt, *Les préludes*, New Symphony Orchestra of London/Adrian Boult
Chesky CD 53

Carmen Callil, publisher and writer

❡ D. Harrison/R. Elton, 'Give me a Ticket to Heaven', Benjamin Luxon (baritone)/David Willison (piano)
Argo ZFB 95

❡ Bellini, 'Prendi: l'anel ti dono' (from *La sonnambula*), Joan Sutherland (Amina), Luciano Pavarotti (Elvino)/National Philharmonic Orchestra/Richard Bonynge
Decca 417 424–2

¶ Stephen Foster, 'Ah! May the Red Rose Live Alway', Thomas Hampson (baritone)/Jay Ungar (violin)/Molly Mason (guitar)/David Alpher (piano)
Angel CDC 754621 2
¶ Schubert, String Quintet in C, D956 (second movement, Adagio), Australia Ensemble
Tall Poppies TP 011
¶ Jerome Kern, 'Can't Help Loving That Man', Helen Morgan/Irene Dunne/Paul Robeson/Hattie McDaniel
Vertinge 2004
¶ Verdi, 'Dio, che nell'alma infondere amor' (from *Don Carlo*), Placido Domingo (Don Carlo), Sherrill Milnes (Rodrigo)/Ambrosian Opera Chorus/Orchestra of the Royal Opera House/Carlo Maria Giulini
EMI CDC 747701 2
¶ Richard Strauss, 'Beim Schlafengehen' (from *Four Last Songs*), Elisabeth Schwarzkopf (soprano)/Berlin Radio Symphony Orchestra/George Szell
EMI CDC 747276 2
¶ Trad., Tantum Ergo, Monks of Kergonan Abbey
Studio SM 1216.55

15 JUNE 1996
Oliver Knussen, composer and conductor

¶ Carter, *A Celebration of Some 100 x 150 Notes*, London Sinfonietta/Oliver Knussen
Virgin VC 791503 2
¶ Berlioz, 'Ride to the Abyss' (from *The Damnation of Faust*), David Poleri (Faust), Martial Singher (Mephistopheles)/Harvard Glee Club/Radcliffe Choral Society/Boston Symphony Orchestra/Charles Munch
RCA 87940
¶ Britten, 'Apparition of the Spirit' (from *Curlew River*), Peter Pears (Madwoman), Harold Blackburn (Abbott), John Shirley-Quirk (Ferryman), Brian Drake (Traveller), Bruce Webb (Voice of the Spirit)/English Opera Group/Benjamin Britten
Decca 421 858–2
¶ Mussorgsky, opening of Act II of *Boris Godunov*, Halina Lukomska (Xenia), Bozena Brun-Baranska (Nurse), Wiera Baniewicz (Fyodor)/Polish National Radio Symphony Orchestra/Jerzy Semkow
EMI CDS 754377 2

❡ Schoenberg, orchestral interlude from *Gurrelieder*, Philadelphia
Orchestra/Leopold Stokowski
Pearl GEMM CDS 9066
❡ Stravinsky, *Four Russian Peasant Songs*, Gregg Smith Singers/anon.
horn players/Igor Stravinsky
Sony SM2K 46298
❡ Stravinsky, *Movements* for piano and orchestra No. 4, Charles Rosen
(piano)/Columbia Symphony Orchestra/Igor Stravinsky
Sony SMK 46395
❡ Busoni, *Berceuse élégiaque* (opening), New Philharmonia Orchestra/
Frederick Prausnitz
Argo ZRG 757
❡ Ravel, *Valses nobles et sentimentales* (conclusion), Boston Symphony
Orchestra/Seiji Ozawa
DG 439 432–2
❡ Tchaikovsky, 'Pas d'action' (from *The Sleeping Beauty*), Leopold
Stokowski and his Symphony Orchestra
HMV ALP 1002
❡ Pérotin, 'Viderunt omnes' (opening), Early Music Consort of
London/David Munrow
Archiv 415 292–2

*Curious how really gifted interpreters and creators of new music are not
in the least forbidding, but infectious in their enthusiasm and knowledge
(see also Ligeti, Birtwistle and Benjamin).*

22 JUNE 1996
Ian McEwan, writer

❡ Jonnie Johnson/Keith Richards, 'Tanqueray', Jonnie Johnson
(and band)
Elektra Nonesuch 7559 61149 2
❡ Purcell, Funeral Sentence, 'Man that is Born of a Woman', Taverner
Consort, Choir and Players/Andrew Parrott
EMI CDC 749635 2
❡ Wynton Marsalis, 'Hesitation', Wynton Marsalis (trumpet)/Branford
Marsalis (saxophone)/Tony Williams (piano)/Ron Carter (bass)
CBS CD 85404

¶ Bach, *Goldberg Variations*, BWV 988 (Variation 11), Gustav Leonhardt (harpsichord)
Vanguard VBD 175
¶ Bach, Three-part Invention in C minor, Glenn Gould (piano)
CBS CD 42269/B
¶ Britten, 'Near the Black Mountains there I Dwelt' (from *Curlew River*), Peter Pears (Madwoman)/English Opera Group/ Benjamin Britten
London 421 858 2
¶ L. Cohen, 'Hallelujah', Jeff Buckley
Columbia 475928 2
¶ Lennox Berkeley, Sonatina (second movement), Kenneth Smith (flute)/Paul Rhodes (piano)
ASV CDDCA 768
¶ Mozart, String Quintet in G minor, K516 (third movement, Adagio ma non troppo), Amadeus Quartet/Cecil Aronowitz (viola)
DG 431 151 2

I knew that he played the flute and having read his novels, so full of science, was hardly surprised to find the figure of J. S. Bach looming large.

29 JUNE 1996
Sir Robin Knox-Johnston, yachtsman

¶ Benny Goodman Orchestra, 'Sing, Sing, Sing', Benny Goodman Orchestra, live at Carnegie Hall, January 1938
CBS 450983 1/A
¶ Acker Bilk, 'Stranger on the Shore', Acker Bilk with the Leon Young String Chorale
Philips 830 779–2
¶ Tchaikovsky, Fantasy overture, *Romeo and Juliet*, Chicago Symphony Orchestra/Daniel Barenboim
DG 427815–2
¶ Rogers/Hammerstein, 'Everything's Up to Date in Kansas City' (from *Oklahoma*), Wilton Clary as Will Parker, with an unspecified male voice chorus and orchestra under the direction of Lehman Engel
Sony Broadway SK 53326
¶ Grieg, Piano Concerto (first movement), Jean-Marc Luisada (piano)/London Symphony Orchestra/Michael Tilson Thomas
DG 439 913–2

¶ Gilbert/Sullivan, 'Where is the Plaintiff?' and 'Comes a Broken Lover' (from *Trial by Jury*), Ann Hood (Angelina), Donald Adams (Usher), Kenneth Sandford (Counsel for the Plaintiff)/D'Oyly Carte Opera Company/Orchestra of the Royal Opera House/Isidore Godfrey
Decca London 417 358–2
¶ Handel, 'Allegro' and 'Hornpipe' from *Water Music* suite in D major, English Baroque Soloists/John Eliot Gardiner
Erato ECD 88005
¶ Sibelius, *Finlandia*, Scottish National Orchestra/Alexander Gibson
Chandos CHAN 6508
¶ Julian Slade, 'We Said We Wouldn't Look Back' (from *Salad Days*), John Warner (Timothy), Eleanor Drew (Jane), with Edward Rubach and Robert Docker (pianos). Original cast recording

6 JULY 1996
David Sylvester, art critic

¶ Purcell, 'Hark, each Tree' (*Ode on St Cecilia's Day*, 1692), Simon Woolf (soprano), John Shirley-Quirk (bass)/English Chamber Orchestra/Charles Mackerras
Archiv 2533 042
¶ Bach, Recitative, 'Die Welt, das Sündenhaus', and Aria, 'Wie jammern mich doch die verkehrten Herzen' (from Cantata No. 170, *Vergnügte Ruh, Beliebte Seelenlust*), Janet Baker (mezzo-soprano)/Philip Ledger (organ)/Academy of St Martin-in-the-Fields/Neville Marriner
Decca 430 260 2
¶ Chopin, Prelude in E minor, Alfred Cortot
Music and Arts Programs of America CD317
¶ Guillaume de Machaut, Gloria (from Messe de Notre Dame), Hilliard Ensemble/Paul Hillier
Hyperion CDA 66358
¶ Bach, Fugue from *The Musical Offering*, London Symphony Orchestra/Pierre Boulez
Sony Classical SM3K 45845
¶ Birtwistle, 'Tenebrae' (from *Three Settings of Celan* for soprano and five instruments), Christine Whittlesey (soprano)/Ensemble Intercontemporain/Pierre Boulez
DG 439 910 2

¶ Beethoven, 'Mir ist so wunderbar' (from *Fidelio*, Act I), Sena Jurinac (Marzelline), Martha Mödl (Leonore), Gottlob Frick (Rocco), Rudolf Schock (Jaquino)/Vienna Philharmonic Orchestra/Wilhelm Furtwängler
Rodolphe Productions RPC 32494

14 SEPTEMBER 1996
Marina Warner, writer and academic

¶ John Adams, 'Night Chorus' (from *The Death of Klinghoffer*), London Opera Chorus/Orchestra of the Opéra de Lyon/Kent Nagano
Elektra Nonesuch 7559–79281–2
¶ Monteverdi, *Il combattimento di Tancredi e Clorinda* (conclusion), Laerte Malaguti (Testo), Elisabeth Speiser (Clorinda)/Mainz Chamber Orchestra/Gunter Kehr
Turnabout TV 34018S
¶ John Woolrich, *The Turkish Mouse*, Mary Wiegold (soprano)/The Composers Ensemble/Dominic Muldowney
NMC NMC D003
¶ Stravinsky, 'Petits airs au bord du ruisseau' (from *L'histoire du soldat*), Martial Singher (The Devil)/Ensemble/Leopold Stokowski
Vanguard 08 8004 71
¶ Schubert, 'Gretchen am Spinnrade', Elisabeth Schwarzkopf (soprano)/Edwin Fischer (piano)
EMI CDH 764026 2
¶ Allan, Strange Fruit, Billie Holiday/Frank Newton and his Orchestra
Affinity CDAFS 1019/G
¶ Ravel, 'Le jardin féerique' (from *Ma mère l'oye*), New York Philharmonic/Leonard Bernstein
Sony SMK 47545
¶ Dvořák, Cello Concerto (first movement), Mstislav Rostropovich (cello)/Royal Philharmonic Orchestra/Adrian Boult
Laserlight 16223

Marina explored John Woolrich's music when writing the libretto for his opera, The House of Crossed Desires.

Nigel Rees, radio personality

¶ Haydn, Kyrie (from the 'Nelson' Mass), Sylvia Stahlman (soprano), Helen Watts (contralto), Wilfred Brown (tenor), Tom Krause (bass)/ Choir of King's College, Cambridge/London Symphony Orchestra/ David Willcocks
Decca 421 146–2

¶ Skryabin, Etude in C sharp minor, Op. 2, No. 1, Vladimir Horowitz (piano)
Sony S3K 53461

¶ Gay, 'Virgins are like the Fair Flower' (from *The Beggar's Opera*), Kiri te Kanawa (Polly Peachum)/National Philharmonic Orchestra/ Richard Bonynge
Decca 430 066–2

¶ Tchaikovsky, Gremin's aria (from *Eugene Onegin*, Act III), Nicolai Ghiaurov (Prince Gremin)/Orchestra of the Royal Opera House/ Georg Solti
Decca 417 413–2

¶ Rachmaninov arr. Wood, Prelude in C sharp minor, Symphony Orchestra/Sir Henry Wood, rec. 1930
Dutton Lab 2cd ax 2022

¶ Mendelssohn, Overture, *Ruy Blas*, London Symphony Orchestra/ Claudio Abbado
DG 423 104–2

¶ Mozart, Piano Concerto in D minor K466 (second movement, Romance), Vladimir Ashkenazy (piano)/London Symphony Orchestra/Hans Schmidt-Isserstedt
Decca 417 726–2

Tessa Blackstone, academic and politician

¶ Tchaikovsky, 'Waltz' (from *The Sleeping Beauty*, Act I), Kirov Orchestra, St Petersburg/Valery Gergiev
Philips 434 922–2

¶ Mahler, 'Der Abschied' (sixth movement of *Das Lied von der Erde*), Janet Baker (mezzo-soprano)/Royal Concertgebouw Orchestra/ Bernard Haitink
Philips 432 279–2

¶ Stravinsky, 'The Tresses' (Tableau 1 from *Les noces*), New London Chamber Choir and Instrumental Ensemble/James Wood
Hyperion CDA 66410
¶ Beethoven, Symphony No. 8 (fourth movement, Allegro vivace), Philharmonic Symphony Orchestra of London/Hermann Scherchen
MCA MCAD2–9802-B
¶ Kern, 'Pick Yourself Up', Fred Astaire/Johnny Green and his Orchestra
Columbia C2K 44233
¶ Mozart, 'Voi che sapete' (from *The Marriage of Figaro*, Act II), Frederica von Stade (Cherubino)/London Philharmonic Orchestra/ Georg Solti
Decca 417 395–2
¶ Wagner, Prelude to *Die Meistersinger von Nürnberg*, Orchestra of the German Opera, Berlin/Eugen Jochum
DG 415 278–2
¶ Mozart, Violin Concerto No. 3, K216 (third movement, Rondo, allegro), Anne-Sophie Mutter (violin)/Berlin Philharmonic Orchestra/ Herbert von Karajan
DG 415 327–2

5 OCTOBER 1996
Craig Raine, poet

¶ Haydn, Kyrie (from *Missa in tempore belli*), Sylvia McNair (soprano), Delores Ziegler (mezzo-soprano), Hans-Peter Blochwitz (tenor), Andreas Schmidt (baritone)/RIAS Chamber Choir/Berlin Philharmonic Orchestra/James Levine
DG 435 853–2
¶ Puccini, *Tosca* (conclusion of Act II), Maria Callas (Tosca), Tito Gobbi (Scarpia)/Paris Conservatoire Orchestra/Georges Prêtre
EMI CMS 769974–2
¶ Bizet/Oscar Hammerstein II, 'Beat Out Dat Rhythm on a Drum' (from *Carmen Jones*), Pearl Bailey/Orchestra and Chorus/Herschel Burke Gilbert
RCA 1881–2-R
¶ Charles Ives, *Memories (Very Pleasant: Rather Sad)*, Jan DeGaetani (mezzo-soprano)/Gilbert Kalish (piano)
Nonesuch H 71325

❡ Tchaikovsky, 'Chinese Dance' (from *The Nutcracker*), Berlin Philharmonic Orchestra/Herbert von Karajan
DG 419 175–2
❡ Stravinsky, 'Marche royale' (from *L'histoire du soldat*), Columbia Chamber Ensemble/Igor Stravinsky
Sony SM3K 46291
❡ Handel, 'Ev'ry Valley Shall Be Exalted' (from *The Messiah*), Paul Elliott (tenor)/Academy of Ancient Music/Christopher Hogwood
Oiseau Lyre 400 086–2
❡ Mahler, 'Wenn dein Mütterlein tritt zur Tür herein' (from *Kindertotenlieder*), Christa Ludwig (contralto)/Berlin Philharmonic Orchestra/Herbert von Karajan
DG 415 098–2
❡ S. Silverstein, 'Sylvia's Mother', Dr Hook and the Medicine Show
Capitol CDP 746620 2
❡ Mussorgsky arr. Yamashita, 'Ballet of the Chicks in their Shells' (from *Pictures at an Exhibition*), Kazuhito Yamashita (guitar)
RCA RCD 14205

12 OCTOBER 1996
George Melly, jazz musician

❡ Porter, 'Let's Do It', Noël Coward/Carl Hayes and his Orchestra
Sony CD 47253
❡ Heyman/Sour/Eyton/Green, 'Body and Soul', Coleman Hawkins, rec. 1939
RCA ND 85717
❡ Max Miller, 'Here's a Funny Thing' (from *Max at the Met*), Max Miller
Flashbacks FBLP 8089
❡ Gilbert/Sullivan, 'Take a Pair of Sparkling Eyes' (from *The Gondoliers*), Richard Lewis (tenor)/Pro Arte Orchestra/Malcolm Sargent
EMI CMS7 64394–2
❡ Respighi, Prologue from *The Birds*, San Francisco Symphony Orchestra/Edo de Waart
Philips 411 419–2
❡ Stravinsky, 'Danse sacrale' (from *The Rite of Spring*), Columbia Symphony Orchestra/Igor Stravinsky
Sony SM3K 46291

¶ Walton, 'Popular Song' (from *Façade* suite), Philharmonia/William Walton
EMI CDH 565006 2
¶ Sidney Bechet, 'Egyptian Fantasy', Sidney Bechet and his New Orleans Feetwarmers
RCA ND 90317
¶ Satie, 'Airs à faire fuir', Aldo Ciccolini (piano)
EMI CDC 749760 2

19 OCTOBER 1996
Paul Bailey, writer

¶ Mozart, 'Porgi amor' (from *The Marriage of Figaro*), Sena Jurinac (Countess)/Glyndebourne Festival Orchestra/Vittorio Gui
CFP CD-CFP 4724
¶ Brahms, Sonata No. 1 in G, Op. 78 (first movement, Vivace ma non troppo), Gioconda de Vito (violin)/Edwin Fischer (piano)
Testament SBT 1024
¶ Verdi, 'Dio, che nell' alma infondere amor' (from *Don Carlo*), Placido Domindo (Don Carlos), Sherrill Milnes (Rodrigo)/Ambrosian Opera Chorus/Orchestra of the Royal Opera House/Carlo Maria Giulini
EMI CDC 747701 2
¶ Trad. arr. Jacobson, 'Ca' the Yowes', Kathleen Ferrier (contralto)/John Newmark (piano)
Decca 417 192–2
¶ Bach arr. Busoni, 'Nun komm', der Heiden Heiland', BWV 659, Dinu Lipatti (piano)
EMI CZS 767163 2
¶ Schubert, 'Der Leiermann' (from *Winterreise*), Peter Schreier (tenor)/András Schiff (piano)
Decca 436 122–2
¶ Janáček, 'S Bohem, rodný kraju' (from *The Diary of One who Disappeared*), Peter Keller (tenor)/Mario Venzago (piano)
Accord 220312
¶ Berg, 'Interlude: Invention on a key (D minor)' (from *Wozzeck*), Vienna Philharmonic Orchestra/Christoph von Dohnányi
Decca 417 348–2

A regular and discerning listener; an ex-actor, so a hilarious mimic, and a reliable purveyor of outrageous gossip.

Hermione Lee, writer and academic

♪ Britten, 'Parade' and 'Départ' (from *Les illuminations*), Peter Pears (tenor)/English Chamber Orchestra/Benjamin Britten
Decca 417 153–2

♪ Verdi, *Falstaff* (beginning of Act I, scene 2), Rosalind Elias (Meg), Ilva Ligabue (Alice), Giulietta Simionato(Quickly), Mirella Freni (Nannetta), John Lanigan (Dr Caius), Piero de Palma (Bardolph), Alfredo Kraus (Fenton), Giovanni Foiani (Pistol), Robert Merrill (Ford)/RCA Italiana Orchestra/Georg Solti
Decca 417 170–2

♪ Beethoven, String Quartet in B flat, Op. 130 (fifth movement, Cavatina), Quartetto Italiano
Philips 426 050–2

♪ Haydn, Et Resurrexit (from *Theresienmesse*), Janice Watson (soprano), Pamela Helen Stephen (mezzo-soprano), Mark Padmore (tenor), Stephen Varcoe (baritone)/Collegium Musicum 90/ Richard Hickox
Chandos CHAN 0592

♪ Bach arr. Rowland Jones, Courante (from Cello Suite No. 3, BWV 1009), Simon Rowland Jones (viola)
Meridian CDE 84270

♪ Janáček, String Quartet No. 2, 'Intimate Letters' (second movement, Adagio), Alban Berg Quartet
EMI CDC 555457–2

♪ Schubert, Sonata in A, D959 (second movement, Andantino), András Schiff (piano)
Decca 440 309–2

♪ Mozart, 'Cosa mi narri' and 'Sull'aria' (from *The Marriage of Figaro*), Charlotte Margiono (Countess), Barbara Bonney (Susanna)/Royal Concertgebouw Orchestra/Nikolaus Harnoncourt
Teldec 4509 90861–2

Genista Mcintosh, Executive Director of the National Theatre

¶ Rossini, Kyrie (*Petite messe solennelle*), City of Birmingham Symphony Orchestra Chorus/Nettle-Markham Piano Duo/ Peter King (harmonium)/Simon Halsey (conductor)
Conifer CDCF 184
¶ Prokofiev, Piano Concerto No. 1, Op. 10, Andrei Gavrilov (piano)/London Symphony Orchestra/Simon Rattle
EMI CDM 764 329 2
¶ Mozart, Laudamus te (from Mass in C minor), Arleen Augér/ Academy of Ancient Music/Christopher Hogwood
Decca 430 122 2
¶ Woolfenden, 'Come unto these Yellow Sands' (*The Tempest*), Ian Charleson/Royal Shakespeare Company Wind Ensemble/Guy Woolfenden
Ariel Records DLC 6791
¶ Biber, Sonata and 'Die liederliche Gesellschaft von allerlei Humor' (drunken part-writing), (first and second movements from *Battalia à 10*), New London Consort/Philip Pickett (director)
Oiseau Lyre 436460–2
¶ Stravinsky, 'O God, Protect Dear Tom', (from *The Rake's Progress*, Act I), Cathryn Pope (Anne)/London Sinfonietta/Riccardo Chailly
Decca 411 645 2
¶ Rodgers/Hart, 'Ten Cents a Dance', Ruth Etting, rec. 1930
ASV CD AJA 507
¶ Puccini, 'Signore, ascolta' (from *Turandot*, Act I), Barbara Hendricks (Liù), Placido Domingo (Calaf)/Vienna Philharmonic Orchestra/ Herbert von Karajan
DG 423 856 2

9 NOVEMBER 1996
Cleo Laine, jazz singer

¶ Fauré, 'En sourdine', Janet Baker (mezzo-soprano)/Raymond Leppard (piano)
BBC Music Magazine CD Vol. IV

♪ Rutter, 'What Sweeter Music', Cambridge Singers/City of London Sinfonia/John Rutter
Collegium Colcd 111
♪ Horace Silver, 'Ecaroh', Turtle Island String Quartet
WD 0114
♪ Santer, 'Pan', Stan Getz (saxophone)/strings and woodwind/ Hershey Kay (director)
Verve SVSP29/30
♪ John Dankworth, 'Sinners Rue', Jacquie Dankworth/New Perspectives
Spotlite SP3 CD 559
♪ Sondheim, 'Not a Day Goes By' (from *Symphonic Sondheim*), London Symphony Orchestra/Don Sebesky
Wea 9031 72119 2
♪ Vivaldi, *Spring* (from *The Four Seasons*; first movement), Peter Fisher (violin)/London Concertante
CMG 001
♪ Carroll Coates, 'Love Comes and Goes', Cleo Laine/George Shearing/ Orchestra
RCA Victor 09026 61419 2
♪ Herrick/Purcell, 'Passing By', Paul Robeson/Lawrence Brown
CD MOIR 415
♪ Gershwin, 'Soon', Eddie Daniels/David Grusin
GRPGRD 2005

16 NOVEMBER 1996
Dr Oliver Sacks, psychoanalyst and writer

♪ Bach, Final chorus from *St John Passion*, Monteverdi Choir/English Baroque Soloists/John Eliot Gardiner
Archiv 419 325/6 2
♪ Chopin, Mazurka in B flat, Op. 7, No. 1, Artur Rubinstein (piano)
EMI CDH 764 698/9 2
♪ Mozart, *Don Giovanni* (part of final scene), Franz Crass, Nicolai Ghiaurov/New Philharmonia Orchestra/Otto Klemperer
EMI CMS 763 841 2
♪ Stravinsky, 'Infernal Dance' and 'Berceuse' (from *The Firebird*), New York Philharmonic Orchestra/Pierre Boulez
CBS CD 42396

¶ Mozart, Sinfonia concertante, K 364 (second movement, Andante), Arthur Grumiaux (violin)/Arrigo Pelleccia (viola)/London Symphony Orchestra/Colin Davis
Philips PHCP 4919
¶ Schubert, 'Der Müller und der Bach' (from *Die schöne Müllerin*), Dietrich Fischer-Dieskau (baritone)/Gerald Moore (piano)
EMI CDC 747 173 2

23 NOVEMBER 1996
Sir John Drummond, writer, broadcaster and festival director

¶ Stravinsky, *Les noces* (second tableau), Anny Mory (soprano), Patricia Parker (mezzo-soprano), John Mitchinson (tenor), Paul Hudson (bass)/Martha Argerich, Krystian Zimerman, Cyprien Katsaris, Homero Francesch (pianos)/English Bach Festival Chorus and Percussion Ensemble/Leonard Bernstein
DG 423 251–2
¶ Poulenc, 'La reine des mouettes' and 'C'est ainsi que tu es' (from *Métamorphoses*), Felicity Lott (soprano)/Graham Johnson (piano)
Hyperion CDA 66147
¶ Bortnyansky, *Songs of the Cherubim* No. 7 (conclusion), Russian Republican Academic Choir/Alexander Yurlov
Melodiya C 01648
¶ Chopin, Sonata No. 3 in B minor, Op. 58, Evgeny Kissin (piano)
RCA 09026 62542 2
¶ Berg, 'Die Nachtigall' (from *Seven Early Songs*), Kari Lövaas (soprano)/North German Radio Symphony Orchestra/Herbert Blomstedt
DG 437 719–2
¶ Verdi, Macbeth/Banquo duet (from *Macbeth*, Act I, scene I), Sherrill Milnes (Macbeth), Ruggero Raimondi (Banquo)/Ambrosian Opera Chorus/New Phiharmonia Orchestra/Riccardo Muti
EMI CMS 764339 2
¶ Shelley, 'Ode to the West Wind', Sir John Gielgud
BBC REGL 351
¶ Haydn, Symphony No. 49 in F minor, 'La Passione', Philharmonia Hungarica/Antál Dorati
Decca 425 915–2

❡ Kern, 'The Way you Look Tonight', Fred Astaire/Johnny Green and his Orchestra
Columbia C2K 44233

Tireless champion for innovation and excellence, and for many years an unapologetic and outspoken critic of the mediocre. Able, I think, to smile at himself too!

30 NOVEMBER 1996
Eleanor Bron, actress

❡ Poulenc, 'Villageoises' (*Petites pièces enfantines*), Pascal Rogé (piano)
Decca 425 862 2
❡ Respighi, *Pines of Rome* (first movement, 'I pini di Villa Borghese'),
Philadelphia Orchestra/Riccardo Muti (conductor)
EMI CDC 747316 2
❡ Schubert, 'Im Frühling', Dietrich Fischer-Dieskau (baritone)/Gerald Moore (piano)
EMI CDM 565672
❡ Bartók, *Duke Bluebeard's Castle* (Doors 4 and 5), Christa Ludwig (Judith), Walter Berry (Bluebeard)/London Symphony Orchestra/ István Kertész (conductor)
Decca 414 167 2
❡ Mulligan, 'Utter Chaos', Gerry Mulligan (baritone saxophone)/Art Farmer (trumpet)/Bill Crow (bass)/Dave Bailey (drums)
Jazz Hour with JHR 73577
❡ Franck, Piano Quintet (third movement), Sviatoslav Richter (piano)/Borodin Quartet
Philips 432 142 2
❡ Chopin, Etude in A flat, Op. 25, No. 1, Maurizio Pollini (piano)
DG 413 794 2

7 DECEMBER 1996
Malcolm Bradbury, novelist and academic

❡ Canteloube, 'Baïlèro' (from *Songs of the Auvergne*), Victoria de los Angeles (soprano)/Lamoureux Orchestra/Jean-Pierre Jacquillat
EMI CDC 555095−2

❡ Bernstein, 'The Best of All Possible Worlds' (from *Candide*), Max Adrian, Barbara Cook, Robert Rounseville/Chorus Orchestra/Samuel Krachmalnick (from the original Broadway production)
Sony SK 48017
❡ Mozart, Oboe Concerto in C, K314 (first movement, Allegro aperto), Lothar Koch (oboe)/Berlin Philharmonic Orchestra/Herbert von Karajan
EMI CDM 764355 2
❡ Copland, 'Simple Gifts', Thomas Hampson (baritone)/Saint Paul Chamber Orchestra/Hugh Wolff
Teldec 4509 98825–2
❡ Bach, Brandenburg Concerto No. 4 (first movement, Allegro), English Chamber Orchestra/Raymond Leppard
Philips 420 346–2
❡ Dvořák, Serenade for Strings (first movement, Moderato), English Chamber Orchestra/Charles Mackerras
CFP CD-CFP 4597
❡ Reicha, Clarinet Quintet, Op. 107 (second movement, Andante siciliano), Vlastimil Mares (clarinet)/Stamic Quartet
Supraphon SU 0051–2131
❡ Michael Nyman, 'The Disposition of the Linen' (from *The Draughtsman's Contract*), Michael Nyman Band
Charisma CASCD 1158

14 DECEMBER 1996
Alan Hollinghurst, writer

❡ Mozart, 'E Susanna non vien' and 'Dove sono i bei momenti' (from *The Marriage of Figaro*, Act III), Lisa della Casa (Countess)/Vienna Philharmonic Orchestra/Erich Kleiber
Decca 417317 2
❡ Janáček, String Quartet No. 2, 'Intimate Letters' (third movement), Janáček Quartet
Supraphon SUAST 50556
❡ Wagner, 'O sink hernieder' (from *Tristan und Isolde*, Act II), Ludwig Suthaus (Tristan), Kirsten Flagstad (Isolde)/Philharmonia/Wilhelm Furtwängler
EMI CEDC 747 323 2

¶ Schumann, 'Papillons', 'Lettres dansantes', 'Chiarina, 'Chopin' and 'Estrella' (from *Carnaval*), Arturo Benedetti Michelangeli

EMI CDC 749 325 2

¶ Vaughan Williams, 'Minuet of the Sons of Job and Their Wives', scene 3 from *Job (A Masque for Dancing)*, London Symphony Orchestra/Adrian Boult

EMI CDM 769 710 2

¶ Adès, 'Maid's Champagne Aria' (from *Powder Her Face*), Valdine Anderson/Almeida Ensemble/Thomas Adès (conductor)
Classic Arts recording

¶ Mahler, Symphony No. 3 (opening of first movement), London Symphony Orchestra/Jascha Horenstein
Unicorn UKCD 2006

Having often sat next or near to Alan at various new music concerts I felt fairly confident that this would be a wide-ranging list discussed with real insight. Not disappointed.

21 DECEMBER 1996
Sir Claus Moser, former Chairman of the Royal Opera House (1965–87)

¶ Schubert, *Moment Musical* No. 3 in F minor, D780, Imogen Cooper (piano)
Ottavo OTR C128715

¶ Monteverdi, 'Deus in adjutorium' (from Vespers, 1610), Robert Tear (tenor)/Monteverdi Choir and Orchestra/Philip Jones Brass Ensemble/ John Eliot Gardiner
Decca 414 572–2

¶ Mozart, 'Riconosci in quest'amplesso' (from *The Marriage of Figaro*, Act III), Claudio Desderi (Figaro), Gianna Rolandi (Susanna), Richard Stilwell (Count), Felicity Lott (Countess), Arthur Korn (Bartolo), Alexander Oliver (Don Curzio)/London Philharmonic Orchestra/Bernard Haitink
EMI CDS 749753 2

¶ Schubert, 'Gute Nacht' (from *Winterreise*), Dietrich Fischer-Dieskau (baritone)/Alfred Brendel (piano)
Philips 411 463–2

❦ Beethoven, Sonata in A flat, Op. 110 (Fuga: Allegro ma non troppo), Alfred Brendel (piano)
Philips 412 789–2
❦ Wagner, 'Wotan's Farewell' (from *Die Walküre*), Hans Hotter (Wotan)/Vienna Philharmonic Orchestra/Georg Solti
Decca 414 105–2
❦ Beethoven, String Quartet in C, Op. 59, No. 3 (fourth movement, Allegro molto), Amadeus Quartet
DG 423 473–2
❦ Mozart, Piano Concerto No. 23 in A, K488 (second movement, Adagio), Murray Perahia (piano)/English Chamber Orchestra
CBS CD 39064

28 DECEMBER 1996
Dame Edna Everage (a.k.a. Barry Humphries)

❦ Khatchaturian, 'Sabre Dance', The Andrew Sisters
Magic AWE 4
❦ William Garret James, 'Bush Night Song', Peter Dawson (baritone)/Gerald Moore (piano)
Pearl GEMM CD 9384
❦ Grainger, 'The Gum-suckers' March' (from *In a Nutshell*), English Sinfonia/Neville Dilkes
EMI CDM 7 63520 2
❦ Bishop, 'Home Sweet Home', Joan Sutherland (Soprano)/Australian Pops Orchestra/Douglas Gamley
WEA 9031–72815–2
❦ Lehár, 'Girls were Made to Love and Kiss' (from *Paganini*), Richard Tauber (tenor)/Lyceum Theatre Orchestra/Frank Collinson
Testament SBT 1006
❦ Charles Williams, 'The Dream of Olwen', Arthur Dulay (piano)/Charles Williams and his Concert Orchestra
HMV CDHMV 6
❦ Rutland Boughton, 'Faery Song' (from *The Immortal Hour*), Webster Booth (tenor)/John Cockerill (harp)
EMI GX 2547
❦ May Brahe, 'Bless this House', John McCormack (tenor)/Edwin Schneider (piano)
BBC REB 689

❡ John Antill, 'A Rain Dance' (from *Corroboree*), London Symphony Orchestra/Eugene Goossens
Everest EVC 9007
❡ Purcell, 'Nymphs and Shepherds', Manchester Children's Choir
EMI CDEM 1465
❡ Carl Davis, 'Why Do We Love Australia?' (from *The Last Night of the Poms*), Dame Edna Everage/New Antipodean Singers/London Symphony Orchestra/Carl Davis
EMI EMC 2743

We were agog to see how the Dame would be attired for her passions – most of which are hardly private. It was a tribute to the power of the imagination as the immaculately attired Barry Humphries told me to don earphones, close my eyes and sally forth. 'I do like your dress, Dame Edna,' I said. 'I can tell that, Michael, from the way your hand is slowly travelling up my thigh,' came the svelte reply. What made both this and the straight Barry Humphries programme (see p. 29) a true delight was the genuine and informed love of music on display. There were many pearls of wisdom, including a description of both Percy Grainger's music and his Pubic Hair Museum.

4 JANUARY 1997
David Malouf, Australian novelist, poet and librettist

❡ Richard Strauss, *Metamorphosen* (end), Berlin Philharmonic Orchestra/Herbert von Karajan
DG 410 892–2
❡ Schubert, 'Wandrers Nachtlied' II, Dietrich Fischer-Dieskau (baritone)/Gerald Moore (piano)
DG 431 085–2
❡ Chopin, Waltz No. 10 in B minor, Op. 69, No. 2, Dinu Lipatti (piano)
EMI CDC 747390 2
❡ Haydn, String Quartet in F minor, Op. 77 No. 2 (Andante), Amadeus Quartet
DG 429 190–2
❡ Bach, Fugue No. 24 in B minor, BWV 869 (from *The Well-tempered Clavier*, Book II), Sviatoslav Richter (piano)
RCA GD 60949/A–D

♪ Mozart, 'Tutto e tranquillo e placido' and 'Gente, gente, all'armi' (from *The Marriage of Figaro*), Mirelli Freni (Susanna), Jessye Norman (Countess)/BBC Symphony Orchestra/Colin Davis

5 APRIL 1997
Roger Scruton, writer and philosopher

♪ Victoria, 'Caligaverunt oculi mei', 'Si est dolor', 'O vos omnes' (from Tenebrae Responsories), Westminster Cathedral Choir/George Malcolm
Decca 425 078–2
♪ Janáček, Sinfonietta (conclusion), Brno State Philharmonic Orchestra/František Jílek
Supraphon 11 0282–2
♪ Bach, Concerto for Two Violins in D minor, BWV 1043 (first movement, Vivace), Adolf Busch, Frances Magnes (violins)/Busch Chamber Players
Odyssey Y 34895
♪ Berg, Violin Concerto (conclusion), Yehudi Menuhin (violin)/BBC Symphony Orchestra/Pierre Boulez
EMI CDM 763989 2
♪ Brahms, 'Geistliches Wiegenlied', Op. 91, No. 2, Jessye Norman (soprano)/Wolfram Christ (viola)/Daniel Barenboim (piano)
DG 413 311–2
♪ Barber, *Knoxville: Summer of 1915*, Dawn Upshaw (soprano)/ Orchestra of St Luke's/David Zinman
Nonesuch 7559 79187–2
♪ Wagner, 'Brünnhilde Pleads with Wotan' (from *Die Walküre*), Régine Crespin (Brünnhilde)/Berlin Philharmonic Orchestra/Herbert von Karajan
DG 425 145–2
♪ Schubert, Symphony No. 9 in C (trio from the Scherzo), Berlin Philharmonic Orchestra/Wilhelm Furtwängler
DG 415 660–2

Sir John Tusa, broadcaster and Managing Director of the Barbican Centre

❡ Beethoven, String Quartet Op. 59, No. 3, 'Razumovsky' (finale), Hungarian Quartet
CDZ 767 239

❡ Verdi, 'Di quella pira' (from *Il trovatore*, Act III), Giovanni Martinelli/orchestra conducted by Walter Rogers
Nimbus NI 7826

❡ Schubert, Sonata in B flat, op. posth. D960 (third movement, Scherzo: Allegro vivace con delicatezza), Artur Schnabel (piano)
Arabesque Z 6575

❡ Schubert, 'Liebesbotschaft' (from *Schwanengesang*), Olaf Bär (baritone)/Geoffrey Parsons (piano)
EMI CDC 749997 2

❡ Dvořák, Piano Quintet in A, Op. 81, Sviatoslav Richter (piano)/Borodin Quartet
Philips 412 429 2

❡ Alexandrov, USSR National Anthem (part), Bolshoi Theatre Orchestra/Yuri Simonov
Boheme Music CDBM R009166

❡ Verdi, Rodrigo's death scene from *Don Carlos* (Act IV, scene 2), Tito Gobbi (Rodrigo)/Orchestra of the Opera Theatre of Rome/Gabriele Santini
EMI CDM 764645 2

❡ Schumann, Toccata, Op. 7, Sviatoslav Richter (piano)
DG 435 751 2

What with running or helping to run the Barbican, ENO and Wigmore Hall, one might think his time was spoken for, but I would regularly see him at Cheltenham and other venues where something of interest was happening.

19 APRIL 1997
Lord (Robert) Armstrong, former civil servant

❡ Vaughan Williams, *A Sea Symphony* (Scherzo: 'The Waves'), London Philharmonic Choir/London Philharmonic Orchestra/Bernard Haitink
EMI CDC 749911 2

❡ Byrd, 'Justorum animae', Christ Church Cathedral Choir/Stephen Darlington (director)
Nimbus NI 5237
❡ Handel, Fugue in C minor, Op. 3, No. 6, Paul Nicholson (harpsichord)
Hyperion CDA 66932
❡ Richard Strauss, 'Moonlight Music' (from last scene of *Capriccio*), Philharmonia/Wolfgang Sawallisch
EMI CDC 749015 2
❡ Mozart, Quintet for piano and wind K452 (second movement), Alfred Brendel (piano)/Heinz Holliger (oboe)/Roger Brenner (clarinet)/Hermann Baumann (horn)/Klaus Thunemann (bassoon)
Philips 490 182 2
❡ Bach, 'Jesu, meine Freude', BWV 227, The Sixteen/ensemble directed by Harry Christophers
Hyperion CDA 66369
❡ Warlock, 'Sleep', Ian Partridge (tenor)/Jennifer Partridge (piano)
Etcetera KTC 1078
❡ Mendelssohn, Piano Trio in C minor (Finale: Allegro appassionato), Beaux Arts Trio
Philips 432 125 2

26 APRIL 1997
Adam Phillips, psychoanalyst and writer

❡ Webern, Five Pieces for Orchestra, Op. 10, London Symphony Orchestra/Pierre Boulez
Sony Classical CD 45845/A
❡ Billy Myles, 'Have You Ever Loved a Woman?', Derek and the Dominoes (Eric Clapton/Duane Allman/Bobby Whitlock/Carl Radle/Jim Gordon)
Polydor 847 090 2
❡ Schumann, *Fantasiestück*, Op. 12 ('Des Abends'), Alfred Brendel (piano)
Philips 411 049 2
❡ Bax, Nonet, Nash Ensemble/Ian Brown
Hyperion CDA 66807
❡ Lucinda Williams, 'Lines around your Eyes', Lucinda Williams
Chameleon 3705 61351 2

❡ Bob Dylan, 'Tangled up in Blue', Bob Dylan
CBS CD 69097
❡ Wagner, Prelude to *Das Rheingold*, Helen Donath, Edda Moser, Anna Reynolds (Rhinemaidens)/Berlin Philharmonic Orchestra/Herbert von Karajan
DG 415 142 2
❡ Boulez, . . . *explosante-fixe* . . ., Ensemble Intercontemporain/Pierre Boulez
DG 445 833 2
❡ Janáček, String Quartet No. 1, 'Kreutzer Sonata' (first movement, Con moto), Medici Quartet
Nimbus NI 5113

The psychoanalyst who first pointed out to me that people reveal more when talking about music or anything other than themselves. Having made that observation, he then became somewhat more guarded himself! A refreshing choice of music and an illuminating take on it.

3 MAY 1997
Siobhan Davies, choreographer

❡ Stravinsky, *Les noces* (conclusion), Libuse Domaninska (soprano), Marie Mrázová (contralto), Ivo Zidek (tenor), Dalibor Jedlička (bass)/Czech Philharmonic Chorus/Zdeněk Kozina, Jan Marcol, Peter Toperczer, Arnost Wilde (pianos)/Percussion section of the Czech Philharmonic Orchestra/Karel Ančerl
Supraphon 11 1946–2
❡ Scarlatti, Sonata in B minor, Pierre Hantaï (harpsichord)
Astrée E 8502
❡ Gavin Bryars, *Three Elegies for Nine Clarinets* (No. 2), Roger Heaton (clarinets)
Clarinets Classics CC 0009
❡ Handel, 'Se m'ami, oh caro' (from *Aci, Galatea e Polifemo*), Carolyn Watkinson (Galatea)/London Baroque/Charles Medlam
Harmonia Mundi HM 901253
❡ Gerald Barry, *Flamboys* (conclusion), National Orchestra of Ireland/Robert Houlihan
Marco Polo 8.225 006

¶ Kevin Volans, Third Dance (from *White Man Sleeps*), Kevin Volans, Robert Hill (harpsichords)/Margriet Tindemans (viola da gamba)/Robyn Schulkowsky (percussion)
United CD 88034
¶ Steve Reich, *Clapping Music*, Russ Hartenberger, Steve Reich
Nonesuch 979169–2
¶ Bach, Contrapunctus I (from *The Art of Fugue*), Tatiana Nikolayeva (piano)
Hyperion CDA 66631

10 MAY 1997
Sir Roy Strong, writer and historian

¶ Prokofiev, 'Love Scene' (from *Romeo and Juliet*, Act I), Kirov Orchestra/Valery Gergiev
Philips 432 166–2
¶ Purcell, 'Fairest Isle' (from *King Arthur*), Sylvia McNair (soprano)/Academy of Ancient Music/Christopher Hogwood
Philips 446 081–2
¶ Elgar, Symphony No. 1, London Philharmonic Orchestra/Andrian Boult
EMI CDM 764013 2
¶ Richard Strauss, 'Countess's Reverie' (from *Capriccio*), Elisabeth Schwarzkopf (Countess)/Philharmonia/Wolfgang Sawallisch
EMI CDH 763657 2
¶ Puccini, closing quartet from Act III of *La bohème*, Montserrat Caballé (Mimì), Placido Domingo (Rodolfo), Judith Blegen (Musetta), Sherrill Milnes (Marcello)/London Philharmonic Orchestra/Georg Solti
RCA RD 80371
¶ Johann Strauss II, 'Klänge der Heimat', Czardas (from *Die Fledermaus*), Anneliese Rothenberger (Rosalinde)/Vienna Symphony Orchestra/Willi Boskovsky
EMI CMS 769354 2
¶ Morley, 'It was a Lover and his Lass', Alfred Deller (countertenor)/Desmond Dupré (lute)
EMI CDH 565501 2
¶ Tchaikovsky, 'Journey Sequence' (from *Nutcracker*, Act II), London Symphony Orchestra/André Previn
CFP CD-CFP 4706

17 MAY 1997
Paul Daniel, conductor

❡ Rodgers/Hammerstein, 'June is Bustin' Out All Over', Bryn Terfel (baritone)/Chorus of Opera North/English Northern Philharmonia/Paul Daniel
DG 449 163–2

❡ Monteverdi, 'Possente spirto' (from *L'Orfeo*), Anthony Rolfe Johnson (Orfeo)/English Baroque Soloists/John Eliot Gardiner
Archiv 419 250–2

❡ Schubert, 'Heimliches Lieben', Joan Rodgers (soprano)/Malcolm Martineau (piano)
BBC tape

❡ Bach, 'Aus Liebe will mein Heiland sterben' (from *St Matthew Passion*), Ann Monoyios (soprano)/English Baroque Soloists/John Eliot Gardiner
Archiv 427 648–2

❡ Berg, Act II, scene 3 from *Wozzeck*, Franz Grundheber (Wozzeck), Hildegard Behrens (Marie)/Vienna Philharmonic Orchestra/Claudio Abbado
DG 423 587–2

❡ Beethoven, Sonata in A flat, Op. 110 (first movement), Artur Schnabel (piano)
EMI CHS 763765 2

❡ David Bowie, 'Fame' (from *Stage*), David Bowie
EMI CDS 798617 2

24 MAY 1997
Peter Shaffer, playwright

❡ Marc Wilkinson, 'Chant of Resurrection – Final Lament' (from *The Royal Hunt of the Sun*), Artists from the National Theatre production/Marc Wilkinson
Decca SKL 4920

❡ Handel, 'Eternal Source of Light Divine' (from *Ode for the Birthday of Queen Anne*), Alfred Deller (countertenor)/Richard Rudolf (trumpet)/Oriana Concert Orchestra
Vanguard 08 5045 71

❡ Shakespeare, 'Deposition Scene' (from *Richard II*), John Gielgud
Columbia OL 5390

70

❡ Rossini, 'Zitto, zitto: piano, piano' (from *La cenerentola*, Act I), Luigi Alva (Don Ramiro), Renato Capecchi (Dandini)/London Symphony Orchestra/Claudio Abbado
DG 423 861–2
❡ Mozart, Kyrie (from Mass in C minor, K427), Margaret Marshall, Felicity Palmer (sopranos)/Academy of St Martin-in-the-Fields and Chorus/Neville Marriner
Philips 420 891–2
❡ Mozart, Piano Concerto in G, K453 (third movement, Allegretto), Edwin Fischer (piano)/Edwin Fischer Chamber Orchestra
EMI CHS 763719 2
❡ Mendelssohn arr. Toscanini, Octet Op. 20 (conclusion of first movement), NBC Symphony Orchestra/Arturo Toscanini
RCA GD 60283
❡ Britten, 'Since She Whom I Loved' (from *Holy Sonnets of John Donne*), Peter Pears (tenor)/Benjamin Britten (piano)
Decca 417 428–2
❡ Verdi, 'Si, pel ciel' (from *Otello*), Ramón Vinay (Otello)/Giuseppe Valdengo (Iago)/NBC Symphony Orchestra/Arturo Toscanini
RCA GD 60302

31 MAY 1997
Richard Eyre, director, Royal National Theatre

❡ Verdi, Sanctus (from Requiem), Atlanta Symphony Orchestra and Chorus/Robert Shaw
Telarc CD 80152
❡ Miles Davis, 'So What' (from *Kind of Blue*), Miles Davis (trumpet)/Julian Adderley (alto saxophone)/John Coltrane (tenor saxophone)/Bill Evans (piano)/Paul Chambers (bass)/James Cobb (drums)
Columbia 460603 2
❡ Mozart, Fantasia in C minor, Ivan Moravec (piano)
Supraphon 110 1559
❡ Sibelius, Symphony No. 5 (third movement, conclusion), City of Birmingham Symphony Orchestra/Simon Rattle
EMI CDC 749717 2
❡ Chuck Berry, 'School Day', Chuck Berry
See for Miles SEECD 320

♪ Coslow/Johnston, 'My Old Flame', Billie Holiday
Commodore 8.24055
♪ Bach, Suite No. 1 in G, BWV 1007 (first and second movements,
Prelude and Allemande), Heinrich Schiff (cello)
EMI CDS 74741 8
♪ Schoenberg, *Verklärte Nacht* (conclusion), Berlin Philharmonic
Orchestra/Herbert von Karajan
DG 427 424–2

Having tackled opera and musicals as well as theatre, Richard, not
surprisingly, failed to subscribe to David Hare's views regarding the lack
of realism in opera.

7 JUNE 1997
Michael Grade, TV executive and programme editor

♪ Wagner, *Siegfried* (end of final scene), Birgit Nilsson (Brünnhilde)/
Wolfgang Windgassen (Siegfried)/Vienna Philharmonic Orchestra/
Georg Solti
Decca 414 114 2
♪ Sibelius, Symphony No. 2 (third movement, Vivacissimo), London
Symphony Orchestra/Colin Davis
RCA 09026 68218 2
♪ Beethoven, Benedictus (from *Missa solemnis*) Luba Orgonasova
(soprano), Jadwiga Rappé (alto), Uwe Heilmann (tenor), Jan-Hendrik
Rootering (bass)/Adreas Röhn (violin)/Bavarian Radio Symphony
Orchestra and Chorus/Colin Davis
RCA 09026 60967 2
♪ Billy Strayhorn, 'Chelsea Bridge', Duke Ellington and his Orchestra,
Billy Strayhorn (piano)/Ben Webster (tenor saxophone)/Juan Tizol
(valve trombone), rec. 1941
Bluebird 74321 13181/C
♪ Sondheim, 'The Worst Pies in London' (from *Sweeney Todd*), Angela
Lansbury (Mrs Lovett)/band directed by Paul Gemignani (orig.
Broadway recording)
RCA 3379 2 RC/A
♪ Bruch, *Kol Nidrei*, Pablo Casals (cello) and unknown orchestra
Pearl Gemm CD 9349

¶ Richard Strauss, 'Traum durch die Dämmerung', Jessye Norman (soprano)/Geoffrey Parsons (piano)
Philips 416 298 2

14 JUNE 1997
Baroness (Mary) Warnock, philosopher and writer on the morality of science

¶ Trad., 'Mary Hamilton', Joan Baez
Vanguard 662097
¶ Boudleaux/Felice Bryant, 'Bye Bye Love', The Everly Brothers
Music Club MCCD 209
¶ Beethoven, Sonata in D minor, Op. 31, No. 2 (last movement, Allegretto), Alfred Brendel (piano)
Philips 412 575–2
¶ Bach (attrib.), Sonata in C, BWV 1033 (first and second movements, Andante and Allegro), Lisa Beznosiuk (flute)/Nigel North (lute)
Amon Ra CD-SAR 33
¶ Purcell, 'Rejoice in the Lord Always', Christopher Robson (alto), William Kendall (tenor), Stephen Roberts (bass)/Winchester Cathedral Choir/Brandenburg Consort/David Hill
Oiseau Lyre 444 620–2
¶ Boyce, Symphony No. 8 in D minor (last movement, Tempo di Gavotta), English Concert/Trevor Pinnock
Archiv 419 631–2
¶ Zelenka, Second Lamentation for Maundy Thursday, Michael Chance (countertenor)/Chandos Baroque Players
Hyperion CDA 66426
¶ Schubert, String Quartet movement in C minor, D703, Amadeus Quartet
DG 413 453–2

21 JUNE 1997
George Walden, writer, former politician

¶ Sonny Bono, 'The Beat Goes On', Cathy Rich (vocal)/Jay Corre (tenor saxophone)/Buddy Rich Big Band
Pacific CDP 837989 2
¶ Stravinsky, L'histoire du soldat (excerpt from Part I), John Gielgud (narrator)/Ron Moody (The Devil)/Tom Courtenay (The Soldier)/

73

Boston Symphony Chamber Players

DG 2530 609

¶ Mussorgsky, Prelude to *Khovanshchina*, Act I, London Symphony Orchestra/Claudio Abbado

RCA 09026–61354–2

¶ Burns/Rogers, 'Keen and Peachy', Woody Herman and his Orchestra

Affinity CD Charly 100

¶ Schubert, Sonata in A, D959 (second movement, Andantino), Alfred Brendel (piano)

Philips 411 477–2

¶ Wagner, 'Träume' (from *Wesendonck-Lieder*), Cheryl Studer (soprano)/Staatskapelle Dresden/Giuseppe Sinopoli

DG 439 865–2

¶ Bartók, *The Miraculous Mandarin* (opening), New York Philharmonic Orchestra/Pierre Boulez

Sony SMK 45837

¶ Purcell, 'Man that is Born of Woman' (from *Music for the Funeral of Queen Mary*), Monteverdi Choir and Orchestra/John Eliot Gardiner

Erato 2292–45123–2

28 JUNE 1997

Sheila Colvin, former arts administrator (Edinburgh and Aldeburgh festivals)

¶ Weill, 'Seeräuber-Jenny' (from *Die Dreigroschenoper*), Lotte Lenya (Jenny)/Orchestra of Sender Freies Berlin/Wilhelm Brückner-Rüggeberg

CBS CD 42637

¶ Oliver Knussen, *Coursing*, London Sinfonietta/Oliver Knussen

Unicorn-Kanchana UKCD 2010

¶ Antonio Carlos Jobim, *A Felicidade*, Antonio Carlos Jobim

Verve 830 783–2

¶ Verdi, Act I, scene 2 from *Falstaff*, Herva Nelli (Mistress Alice Ford), Nan Merriman (Mistress Meg Page), Cloe Elmo (Mistress Quickly), Teresa Stich-Randall (Nannetta), Frank Guarrera (Ford), Antonio Madasi (Fenton), Gabor Carelli (Dr Caius), John Carmen Rossi (Bardolph), Norman Scott (Pistol)/NBC Symphony Orchestra/Arturo Toscanini

RCA GD 60251

❡ Schubert, 'Pause' (from *Die schöne Müllerin*, D795), Ian Bostridge (tenor)/Graham Johnson (piano)
Hyperion CDJ 33025
❡ Tchaikovsky, Symphony No. 5 in E minor, Op. 64 (third movement, Waltz), Hallé Orchestra/John Barbirolli
Royal Classics ROY 6472
❡ Britten, 'Fanfare' and 'Villes' (from *Les illuminations*), Anthony Rolfe Johnson (tenor)/London Mozart Players/Jane Glover
ASV CDDCA 682

5 JULY 1997
Denis Quilley, actor

❡ Rodgers/Hammerstein, 'What's the Use of Wonderin'?' (from *Carousel*), Shirley Jones/Chorus and Orchestra/Alfred Newman
Capitol CDP 746635 2
❡ Haydn, Symphony No. 88 (finale, Allegro con spirito), Cleveland Orchestra/George Szell
Fontana CFL 1014
❡ Van Heusen/Burke, 'Here's That Rainy Day', Stan Getz
Verve 3113–072
❡ Lehár, 'Dein ist mein ganzes Herz' (from *The Land of Smiles*), Placido Domingo (tenor)/London Symphony Orchestra/Karl Heinz Loges
DG 413 451–2
❡ Lehár, 'Freunde das Leben ist lebenswert!' (from *Giuditta*), Fritz Wunderlich (tenor)/Südwestfunk Radio Orchestra/Emmerich Smola
Acanta 33567
❡ Britten, 'Hymn' and 'Sonnet' (from *Serenade*, Peter Pears (tenor)/Barry Tuckwell (horn)/English Chamber Orchestra/Benjamin Britten
Decca 417 153–2
❡ Poulenc, Nocturne No. 1, Pascal Rogé (piano)
Decca 425 862–2
❡ Debussy, String Quartet (second movement, scherzo), Quartetto Italiano
Philips 420 894–2
❡ Butterworth, 'Loveliest of Trees' (from *A Shropshire Lad*), Bryn Terfel (baritone)/Malcolm Martineau (piano)
DG 445 946–2

Lord Harewood, opera administrator and President of the English Football Association

❡ Janáček, Prelude to *Katya Kabanova*, Vienna Philharmonic Orchestra/Charles Mackerras
Decca 421 852 2 CD1
❡ Prokofiev, 'Death of Prince Andrei' (scene 12 of *War and Peace*), Yevgeny Kibkalo (Prince Andrei Bolkonsky)/Chorus and Orchestra of the Bolshoi Theatre, Moscow/Alexander Melik-Pashayev
Melodiya 74321 29350/C
❡ Schubert, 'Ungeduld' (from *Die schöne Müllerin*) with orchestral accompaniment, Richard Tauber (tenor)/unknown orchestra
Pearl Gemm CD 9381
❡ Beethoven, Symphony No. 9 (third movement, Adagio molto e cantabile) Philharmonia/Otto Klemperer, rec. 1957
EMI CDM 763 359 2
❡ Britten, 'Sunday Morning' (from *Peter Grimes*, Act II), Claire Watson (Ellen Orford)/Orchestra of the Royal Opera House/Benjamin Britten
Decca 414 577 2
❡ Wagner, opening of Act II of *The Valkyrie*, Norman Bailey (Wotan), Rita Hunter (Brünnhilde)/English National Opera Orchestra/Reginald Goodall
EMI CMS 763 920 2
❡ Verdi, 'Ah! Dite alla giovine' (from *La Traviata*, Act III), Maria Callas (Violetta), Alfredo Kraus (Germont)/Orchestra of the San Carlos Opera House, Lisbon/Franco Ghione, live rec. 1958
EMI CDC 749 187 2
❡ Schoenberg, 'Nun sag ich dir zum ersten Mal' (from *Gurrelieder*), Jessye Norman (Tove)/Boston Symphony Orchestra/Seiji Ozawa
Philips 412 511 2

Huge influence on British opera in the post-war years. Graphic account of the first performance of Peter Grimes *and a wonderful recall of other pivotal moments like the Goodall* Ring *with Norman Bailey as Wotan.*

13 SEPTEMBER 1997
Douglas Adams, writer

❡ Ligeti, *Éjszaka* (Night), Schola Cantorum of Oxford/Jeremy Summerly
Proudsound PROU CD 130
❡ Berlioz, 'The Shepherds' Farewell' (from *L'Enfance du Christ*), Choir of Trinity College, Cambridge/Graham Jackson (organ)/Richard Marlow
Conifer CDCF 501
❡ Brooker/Reid, 'Holding On', Procul Harum
Zoo Entertainment PD 90589
❡ Randy Newman, 'Glory Train' (from *Faust*), Randy Newman/James Taylor
Reprise 9362–45672–2
❡ Mozart, 'Non so più' (from *The Marriage of Figaro*, Act I), Frederica von Stade (Cherubino)/London Philharmonic Orchestra/Georg Solti
Decca 410 150–2
❡ Robbie McIntosh, 'Gone Dancing', Robbie McIntosh (guitar)
Artist's private tape
❡ Bach, Chromatic Fantasia and Fugue in D minor, BWV 903, George Malcolm (harpsichord)
Decca 444 390–2
❡ Britten, *Rejoice in the Lamb* (conclusion), Donald Francke (bass)/Purcell Singers/George Malcolm (organ)/Benjamin Britten
London 425 714–2

Owing to his premature death and the iconic status of The Hitchhiker's Guide to the Galaxy, *this has become rather a sought-after recording. He was full of ebullience and life.*

20 SEPTEMBER 1997
Dame Felicity Lott, singer

❡ Mozart, Serenade in B flat, K361 (third movement, Adagio), Wind Soloists of the Vienna Philharmonic Orchestra/Wilhelm Furtwängler
EMI CDH 763818 2
❡ Schubert, 'An die Leier', D737, Flora Nielsen (mezzo-soprano)/Gerald Moore (piano)
HMV HLM 7248

77

❡ Brahms, 'Der Abend', Op. 64, No. 2, The Songmakers'Almanac
(Felicity Lott, Ann Murray, Anthony Rolfe Johnson, Richard Jackson,
Graham Johnson)
Hyperion CDA 66053
❡ Handel, 'Va tacito' (from *Giulio Cesare*, Act I), James Bowman (Giulio
Cesare)/La Grande Écurie et la Chambre de la Roy/Jean-Claude
Malgoire
Astrée E 8558
❡ Jacques Brel, 'La chanson des vieux amants', Jacques Brel
K West KNEWCD 703
❡ Bach, 'Have Mercy, Lord' (from *St Matthew Passion*), Alfreda
Hodgson (contralto)/John Bacon (violin)/Thames Chamber
Orchestra/David Willcocks
ASV CDQSS 324
❡ John Rutter, *The Lord Bless You and Keep You*, Cambridge
Singers/City of London Sinfonia/John Rutter
Collegium COLCD 100
❡ Richard Strauss, *Capriccio* (conclusion of scene 7), Elisabeth
Schwarzkopf (Countess)/Philharmonia/Wolfgang Sawallisch
EMI CDS 749014 8

27 SEPTEMBER 1997
Sir Georg Solti, conductor

❡ Beethoven, 'Mir ist so wunderbar' (from *Fidelio*, Act I), Sona
Ghazarian (Marzelline), Hildegard Behrens (Leonore), Hans Sotin
(Rocco), David Kuebler (Jaquino)/Chicago Symphony
Orchestra/Georg Solti
Decca 410 228 2
❡ Richard Strauss, Trio from Act III of *Der Rosenkavalier*, Régine
Crespin (Marschallin), Yvonne Minton (Octavian), Helen Donath
(Sophie)/Vienna Philharmonic Orchestra/Georg Solti
Decca 417 496 2
❡ Mozart, sextet from Act III of *The Marriage of Figaro*, Jane Berbié
(Marcellina), Samuel Ramey (Figaro), Kurt Moll (Doctor Bartolo),
Philip Langridge (Don Curzio), Thomas Allen (Count Almaviva),
Lucia Popp (Susanna)/London Philharmonic Orchestra/Georg Solti
Decca 410 152 2

¶ Bartók, *Concerto for Orchestra* (second movement, 'Giuoco delle coppie'), World Orchestra for Peace/Georg Solti
Decca 448 901 2
¶ Wagner, Pogner's monologue from Act I of *Die Meistersinger von Nürnberg*, René Pape (Veit Pogner)/Chicago Symphony Orchestra and Chorus/Georg Solti
Decca 452 607 2
¶ Verdi, *Falstaff* (final scene), cast including Giuseppe Valdengo (Sir John Falstaff), Frank Guarrera (Ford)/NBC Symphony Orchestra/Arturo Toscanini, rec. 1950
RCA AT 301/C

We were lucky to be able to visit Solti in his home not long before his unexpected demise. He was as dynamic an interviewee as he was a conductor, those rolling shoulders muscular in their emphasis of music and speech. An extraordinary feeling of certainty of purpose.

4 OCTOBER 1997
Ian Craft, Director of the London Gynaecology and Fertility Centre

¶ Bruckner, *Os justi meditabitur*, Corydon Singers/Matthew Best
Hyperion CDA 66062
¶ Robert Simpson, Symphony No. 6 (conclusion), Royal Liverpool Philharmonic Orchestra/Vernon Handley
Hyperion CDA 66280
¶ Beethoven, Overture to *Fidelio*, Philharmonia/Otto Klemperer
EMI CDM 763611 2
¶ Bach, Partita No. 1 in B minor, BWV 1002 (fourth movement, Tempo di Borea), Viktoria Mullova (violin)
Philips 434 075–2
¶ Blow, 'Venus! . . . Adonis!' (from *Venus and Adonis*, Act I), Catherine Bott (Venus), Michael George (Adonis)/New London Consort/Philip Pickett
Oiseau Lyre 440 220–2
¶ Shostakovich, Symphony No. 8 (third movement, Allegro non troppo), Concertgebouw Orchestra/Bernard Haitink
Decca 411 616–2

◀ Richard Strauss, Love duet ('Aber der Richtige') (from *Arabella* Act II), Maria Reining (Arabella), Hans Hotter (Mandryka)/Vienna Philharmonic Orchestra/Karl Böhm, rec. Salzburg 1947
DG 445 342–2

11 OCTOBER 1997
Andrew Motion, poet and biographer

◀ Steve Reich, *Three Movements* (second movement), London Symphony Orchestra/Michael Tilson Thomas
Nonesuch 7559–79295–2
◀ Bach, Suite No. 6 in D, BWV 1012 (first movement, Prelude), Maurice Gendron (cello)
Philips 422 494–2
◀ Haydn, 'Und Gott schuf grosse Walfische' (from *The Creation*, Part II), José van Dam (Raphael)/Vienna Philharmonic Orchestra/Herbert von Karajan
DG 410 718–2
◀ Gluck, 'Ballet des ombres heureuses' (from *Orphée et Euridice*), Lyon Opera Orchestra/John Eliot Gardiner
EMI CDS 749834 2
◀ Britten, 'Sonnet' (from *Serenade*), Peter Pears (tenor)/Dennis Brain (horn)/English Chamber Orchestra/Benjamin Britten
Decca 417 153–2
◀ Bob Dylan, 'Love Minus Zero', Bob Dylan
CBS CD 62515
◀ Laurie Anderson, 'Let X = X' (from *Big Science*), Laurie Anderson
Warner Bros 7599–23674–2
◀ Beethoven, Sonata in B flat, 'Hammerklavier', Op. 106 (third movement), Alfred Brendel (piano)
Philips 446 093–2

18 OCTOBER 1997
Timothy Garton Ash, academic and writer

◀ Schubert, 'Erlkönig', Dietrich Fischer-Dieskau (baritone)/Gerald Moore (piano)
EMI CMS 565 670–2

❡ Mozart, Sinfonia concertante in E flat, K364 (last movement), Itzhak Perlman (violin), Pinchas Zukerman (viola)/Israel Philharmonic Orchestra/Zubin Mehta
DG 415 486–2
❡ Britten, 'Dirge' (from *Serenade*), Peter Pears (tenor)/Dennis Brain (horn)/Boyd Neel String Orchestra/Benjamin Britten
Decca 425 996–2
❡ Peter Fischer, 'Apfelböck oder die Lilie auf dem Felde', Therese Giehse
Heliodor Bibliothek 3321 010
❡ Smetana, *Vltava* (from *Má vlast*), Czech Philharmonic Orchestra/Rafael Kubelík
Supraphon 11 1208–2
❡ Anon., 'Bogurodzica', Capella Bydgostiensis pro Musica Antiqua/Stanislav Galonski
Muza XL 0294
❡ Beethoven, Violin Concerto, Op. 61 (last movement), David Oistrakh (violin)/French National Radio Orchestra/André Cluytens
EMI CDM 769261 2

25 OCTOBER 1997
Deborah MacMillan, painter and executor of the Kenneth MacMillan estate

❡ Blossom Dearie, 'Et tu Bruce', Blossom Dearie
Master Mix CDCHES
❡ Schubert, 'La Pastorella', Cecilia Bartoli (mezzo-soprano)/András Schiff (piano)
Decca 440 297 2
❡ Poulenc, 'O magnum mysterium' (from *Quatre motets pour le temps de Noël*), Choir of Trinity College, Cambridge/Richard Marlow
Conifer CDCF 151
❡ Mozart, Lacrimosa (from Requiem, K626), Monteverdi Choir/English Baroque Soloists/John Eliot Gardiner
Philips 420 197 2
❡ Biber, Prelude, Aria and Variations, 'The Annunciation' (from *The Five Joyful Mysteries*), John Holloway (violin)/Tragicomedia
Virgin Classics VCD 790838-A

❡ Sammy Fain/Jerry Seelen, 'I Hear the Music Now', Peggy Lee/Gordon Jenkins and his Orchestra
MCA DMCL 1794
❡ Schoenberg, Prelude to *Gurrelieder*, New York Philharmonic Orchestra/Zubin Mehta
Sony Classical S2K 480771
❡ Poulenc, Concerto for two pianos and orchestra (first movement), François-René Duchable, Jean-Philippe Collard (pianos)/Rotterdam Philharmonic Orchestra/James Conlon
Erato ECD 88140

1 NOVEMBER 1997
Edmund White, writer

❡ Haydn, Symphony No. 45, 'Farewell' (fourth movement), Philharmonia Hungarica/Antál Dorati
London 448 531–2
❡ Monteverdi, 'Tornate, o cari baci' (from 7th Book of Madrigals), Elisabeth Schwarzkopf, Irmgard Seefried (sopranos)/Gerald Moore (piano)
HMV HLM 7267
❡ Britten, *Cello Symphony*, Op. 68 (second movement), Raphael Wallfisch (cello)/English Chamber Orchestra/Steuart Bedford
Chandos CHAN 8363
❡ Fauré, 'Berceuse' (from *Dolly Suite*, Op. 56), Katia and Marielle Labèque (piano duet)
Philips 420 159–2
❡ Brahms, Clarinet Sonata in F minor, Op. 120, No. 1 (second movement), Franklin Cohen (clarinet)/Vladimir Ashkenazy (piano)
Decca 430 149–2
❡ Puccini, 'Chi il bel sogno di Doretta' (from *La rondine*, Act I), Angela Gheorghiu (Magda), William Matteuzzi (Prunier)/London Symphony Orchestra/Antonio Pappano
EMI CDC 556338 2
❡ Grever/Adams, 'What a Difference a Day Makes', Dinah Washington/Belford Hendricks Orchestra
Mercury 830 700–2
❡ Janáček, Sonata *1. x. 1905* (first movement), Mikhail Rudy (piano)
EMI CDC 754094 2

8 NOVEMBER 1997
Robert Ponsonby, former festival director and Controller of Music, BBC

§ Beethoven, *Diabelli Variations*, Op. 120 (Variation No. 24, Andante), Artur Schnabel (piano)
Pearl Gemm CD 9378
§ Brahms, *Liebeslieder Waltzer* Op. 52, Nos 1–6, Edith Mathis (soprano), Brigitte Fassbaender (alto), Peter Schreier (tenor), Dietrich Fischer-Dieskau (baritone)/Karl Engel, Wolfgang Sawallisch (piano)
DG 423 133 2
§ Schubert, 'Abendbilder', Peter Pears (tenor)/Benjamin Britten (piano)
BBS REGL 410
§ Janáček, *Mládí* (fourth movement), Sebastian Bell (flute/piccolo), Janet Craxton (oboe), Antony Pay (clarinet), Michael Harris (bass clarinet), Martin Gatt (bassoon), Philip Eastop (horn)
Decca 448 257 2
§ Albéniz, 'Triana' (*Iberia*, No. 5), Alicia de Larrocha (piano)
Decca 433 927 2
§ Verdi, end of Act I, scene 1 of *Falstaff*, Geraint Evans (Sir John Falstaff)/RCA Italiana Opera Orchestra/Georg Solti
Decca 417 169 2
§ Stravinsky, 'Pas de deux' (from *Divertimento: Le baiser de la fée*), L'Orchestre de la Suisse Romande/Ernest Ansermet
Ace of Diamonds SDD 247
§ Mozart, 'Non ti fidar, o misera' (from *Don Giovanni*, Act I), Sena Jurinac (Donna Elvira), Hilde Zadek (Donna Anna), Léopold Simoneau (Don Ottavio), George London (Don Giovanni)/Vienna Symphony Orchestra/Rudolf Moralt
Philips 438 675 2

15 NOVEMBER 1997
A. N. Wilson, writer

§ Bartók ed. Tibor Serly, Viola Concerto (third movement), Yehudi Menuhin (viola)/New Philharmonia Orchestra/Antál Dorati
EMI CDM 763 985 2
§ Mozart, Sonata in C, K330 (third movement, Allegretto), Mitsuko Uchida (piano)
Philips 422 120 2

❡ Bruckner, *Locus iste*, Christ Church Cathedral Choir, Oxford/
Stephen Darlington
Nimbus NI 5440
❡ Stanford, *Irish Rhapsody* No. 4 in A minor, Op. 141, 'The Fisherman
of Loch Neagh and What He Saw', Ulster Orchestra/Vernon Handley
Chandos 7002
❡ Haydn, Quoniam tu solus sanctus (from the 'Nelson' Mass),
Margaret Marshall (soprano), Carolyn Watkinson (contralto), Keith
Lewis (tenor), Robert Holl (bass)/Leipzig Radio Choir/Dresden
Staatskapelle/Neville Marriner
EMI CDC 474 424 2
❡ Beethoven, String Quartet in F, Op. 135 (first movement, Allegretto),
Quartetto Italiano
Philips 426 110 2
❡ Shostakovich, Symphony No. 10 (second movement, Allegro), Saint
Louis Symphony Orchestra/Leonard Slatkin
RCA RD 86597
❡ Richard Strauss, 'September' (from *Four Last Songs*), Jessye Norman
(soprano)/Leipzig Gewandhaus Orchestra/Kurt Masur
Philips 411 052 2

22 NOVEMBER 1997
György Ligeti, composer

❡ Nancarrow, Study No. 3a, Conlon Nancarrow (player piano)
Wergo WER 6168−2
❡ Trad., 'Gënding: Dhenggung Turulare', Langen Praja
Seven Seas KICC 5184
❡ Trad., 'Piéré', Etienne Ngbozo (small sanza and voice)/Joseph
Sasmba (large sanza)/Daniel Ngadike, Robert Tarapai, Raymond Doko
(voice, rattle and percussion sticks)
Ocorra C 580008
❡ Trad., Whistle Ensemble, Banda-Linda Ensemble
Auvidis/UNESCOD 8020
❡ Claude Vivier, *Lonely Child*, Susan Narucki (soprano)/Schönberg
and Asko Ensembles/Reinbert de Leeuw
Philips 454 231−2

¶ Beethoven, Sonata in C minor, Op. 11 (second movement), Alfred Brendel (piano)
Philips 446 701–2

29 NOVEMBER 1997
Maureen Duffy, writer, poet and dramatist

¶ Byrd, *Elegy on the Death of Thomas Tallis*, Ian Partridge (tenor)/Jaye Consort of Viols
Turnabout TV 34017
¶ Purcell, 'Symphony' (from *Come Ye Sons of Art*), King's Consort/ Robert King
Hyperion CDA 66598
¶ Trad. arr. Burleigh, 'Deep River', Paul Robeson
Memoir CDMOIR 426
¶ Trad. arr. Dolly Collins, 'Six Dukes', Shirley Collins
Harvest SHVL 771
¶ Mozart, Clarinet Concerto, K.622 (second movement, Adagio), Jack Brymer (clarinet)/Royal Philharmonic Orchestra/Thomas Beecham
EMI CDM 763408 2
¶ Purcell, 'Sound the Trumpet' (from *Come Ye Sons of Art*), Alfred Deller, John Whitworth (countertenors)/Oiseau Lyre Orchestra/ Anthony Lewis
Oiseau Lyre 444 620–2
¶ Adamson/McHugh, 'You're a Sweetheart', Al Bowlly/Orchestra/ Ronnie Munro
Happy Days UCD 400
¶ Handel, 'Non to basto, consorte' and 'Io t'abbraccio' (from *Rodelinda*), Teresa Stich-Randall (Rodelinda), Maureen Forrester (Bertarido)/Vienna Radio Symphony Orchestra
HMV CSD 3555

6 DECEMBER 1997
Eduardo Paolozzi, sculptor

¶ Piazzola, 'Songe d'une nuit d'été', L'Ensemble Paris Tango
Milan A294
¶ Britten, Prelude to *The Prince of the Pagodas*, Orchestra of the Royal Opera House/Benjamin Britten
London 421 856 2

♪ Count Basie/S. Martin, 'Miss Thing', Part 1, Count Basie and his Orchestra
CBS 460061 2
♪ Traditional Japanese, Azuma Kabuki Musicians
Columbia AML 4925
♪ Honegger, *Pacific 231*, New York Philharmonic Orchestra/Leonard Bernstein
Sony Classical MHK 62352
♪ Porter, Henneve, Palex, 'Vous faites partie de moi' (I've got you under my skin), Josephine Baker
Flapper Past CD 7059
♪ Stravinsky, first part of Bedlam scene (from *The Rake's Progress*, Act III), Alexander Young (Rakewell)/Sadler's Wells Opera Chorus/Royal Philharmonic Orchestra/Igor Stravinsky
Sony Classical SM2K 46299
♪ Charles Ives, *Central Park in the Dark*, Saint Louis Symphony Orchestra/Leonard Slatkin
RCA 09026 61222 2

Amazing how the music somehow echoed the bear-like man and his massive machine sculptures. The gathering momentum of Honnegger's Pacific 231 *said it all.*

13 DECEMBER 1997
Judith Weir, composer

♪ Trad. arr. Copper, 'The Sweet Primeroses', Bob and Ron Copper
Topic TSCD 600
♪ Stravinsky, *Oedipus Rex* (excerpt from Act II), Tatiana Troyanos (Jocasta), Lajos Kozma (Oedipus)/Chorus and Symphony Orchestra of RAI, Rome/Claudio Abbado
Memories HR 4128
♪ Brahms, Sextet No. 1 in B flat, Op. 18 (second movement), L'Archibudelli
Sony SK 68252
♪ Kevin Volans, *White Man Sleeps* (first movement), Smith Quartet
Landor CTLCD 111
♪ Trad., Dzil Duet (from Accra, Ghana), performers unknown
Nonesuch 7559–72082–2

❡ Britten, 'Carol' (from *Sacred and Profane*), The Sixteen/Harry Christophers
Collins 13432
❡ Bach, Gloria (from Mass in F, BWV 233), Gächinger Kantorei Stuttgart/Franz Liszt Chamber Orchestra of Budapest/Helmuth Rilling
Hännsler CD 98924
❡ Loewe, 'Herr Oluf', Kurt Moll (bass)/Cord Garben (piano)
Harmonia Mundi HMA 1905171

Very much her own person as a composer and in her choice of music.

20 DECEMBER 1997
Frederic Raphael, writer

❡ Bach, *Goldberg Variations*, BWV 988 (Theme and Variations 1–3), Glenn Gould (piano)
Sony SMK 52594
❡ Haydn, Cello Concerto No. 2 in D (third movement), Paul Tortelier (cello)/Württemburg Chamber Orchestra/Jörg Faerber
EMI CDM 769299 2
❡ Mozart, Sonata in C minor, K457 (first movement), Mitsuko Uchida (piano)
Philips 412 617–2
❡ Antonio Carlos Jobim, 'Desafinado', Stan Getz (tenor saxophone)/Charlie Byrd (guitar)/Keter Betts and Gene Byrd (bass)/Buddy Deppenschmidt and Bill Reichenbach (drums)
Verve 831 368–2
❡ Schumann, Piano Concerto, Op. 54 (second movement), Rudolf Serkin (piano)/Philadelphia Orchestra/Eugene Ormandy
Sony CD 46543
❡ Beethoven, Violin Concerto (excerpt from first movement), Nathan Milstein (violin)/Philharmonia/Erich Leinsdorf
EMI ZDMF 764830 2
❡ Monnot/Moustaki, 'Milord', Edith Piaf/Orchestra/Robert Chauvigny
Columbia 790562 2

'Manfred Stürmer' (a.k.a. John Sessions)

❡ Brahms, Clarinet Sonata in E flat, Op. 120, No. 2 (third movement, Andante), Franklin Cohen (clarinet)/Vladimir Ashkenazy (piano)
Decca 430 144 2

❡ Brahms, 'Denn es gehet dem Menschen' (No. 1 of *Vier Ernste Gesänge*, Op. 121), Dietrich Fischer-Dieskau (baritone)/Daniel Barenboim (piano)
DG 447 507 2

❡ Schoenberg, 'Sterne jubeln' (from *Gurrelieder*, Part I), Jessye Norman (Tove)/Boston Symphony Orchestra/Seiji Ozawa
Philips 412 512 2

❡ Richard Strauss, closing moments of *Salome*, Catherine Malfitano (Salome)/Kenneth Riegel (Herod)/Vienna Philharmonic Orchestra/Christoph von Dohnányi
Decca 444 180 2

❡ Webern, *Five Pieces for Orchestra*, Op. 10 (No. 2), Ensemble Intercontemporain/Pierre Boulez
DG 437 786 2

❡ Washington/Harline, 'Give a Little Whistle', Jiminy Cricket and Orchestra
RCA 2137 2-R

❡ Stravinsky, 'Dance of the Earth' (from *The Rite of Spring*, Part I), Oslo Philharmonic Orchestra/Mariss Jansons
EMI CDC 754 899 2

❡ Beethoven, Sonata No. 21 in C, 'Waldstein', Op. 53 (third movement, Prestissimo), Artur Schnabel (piano), rec. 1933
Sirio SO 53008

❡ Mahler, Symphony No. 2, 'Resurrection' (excerpt from first movement, Allegro maestoso), City of Birmingham Symphony Orchestra/Simon Rattle
EMI CDC 747 962 2

Susannah Clapp, journalist and theatre critic

❡ Moxy Fruvous, 'The King of Spain', Moxy Fruvous
Moxy Fruvous MF 292

❡ Schumann, 'Romance', Op. 94, No. 2, Heinz Holliger (oboe)/Alfred Brendel (piano)
Philips 416 898–2
❡ Bartók, *Duke Bluebeard's Castle* (opening), Walter Berry (Bluebeard), Christa Ludwig (Judith)/London Symphony Orchestra/István Kertész
Decca 443 571–2
❡ Weill, 'Alabama Song' (from *Mahagonny*), Lotte Lenya/Orchestra/ Roger Bean
CBS CD 42658
❡ Verdi, 'Volta la terrea' (from *Un ballo in maschera*, Act I), Sumi Jo (Oscar), Placido Domingo (Gustav III)/Vienna Philharmonic Orchestra/Herbert von Karajan
DG 427 635–2
❡ Beethoven, Sonata in F, 'Spring', Op. 24 (first movement, Allegro), Henryk Szeryng (violin)/Ingrid Haebler (piano)
Philips 446 521–2

10 JANUARY 1998
John Fortune, actor and comedy writer

❡ Skryabin, Piano Concerto in F sharp minor, Op. 20 (second movement, Andante), Vladimir Ashkenazy (piano)/London Philharmonic Orchestra/Lorin Maazel
Decca 417 252–2
❡ Bunny O'Riley, 'Dream Land', Bunny Wailer
Mango CID 9415
❡ Scarlatti, Sonata in A major, Kk 208, Inger Södergren (piano)
Calliope CAL 9670
❡ Charles Ives, *The Unanswered Question*, New York Philharmonic Orchestra/Leonard Bernstein
DG 429 220–2
❡ Haydn, String Quartet in B flat, 'Sunrise', Op. 76, No. 4 (third movement, Minuet), Orlando Quartet
Philips 6514 204
❡ Mugsy Spanier, 'Relaxin' at the Touro', Mugsy Spanier and his Ragtime Band (Mugsy Spanier (Cornet)/George Brunis (trombone)/Rod Cless (clarinet)/Nick Caiazza (tenor saxophone)/Joe Bushkin (piano)/Bob Casey (bass)/Don Carter (drums)), rec. 1939
CDS RPCD 609

♪ Scarlatti, Sonata in E major, Kk 381, Virginia Black (harpsichord)
CRD 3442

17 JANUARY 1998
Louis de Bernières, novelist

♪ Mikis Theodorakis, *Apagoghi*, Maria Farantouri with the Bouzoukis of Mikis Theodorakis
Worldwide series Greece SCX 6498
♪ Trad., 'Cieliot Lindo' (from 2 *Flamenco Guitars in Latin America*), Paco de Lucia and Ramon de Algeciras (guitars)
Philips 838 823 4
♪ Armando Rodrigues/Affonso Correia Leite, 'Cançao de Alcipe' (from the film *Bocage*), Alcino Frazao (guitar)
Movieplay SO 3008
♪ Bach, Brandenburg Concerto No. 4, BWV 1049 (first movement, Allegro), Michel Schwalbé (violin)/Karlheinz Zoeller and Matthias Rütters (flutes)/Berlin Philharmonic Orchestra/Herbert von Karajan
DG 431 174 2
♪ Frescobaldi arr. Segovia, 'Aria con variazione detta la Frescobalda', Julian Bream (guitar)
RCA 09026 61592 2
♪ Gounod, Sanctus (*Messe solennelle*), Laurence Dale (tenor)/Radio France Choirs/New Philharmonic Orchestra of Radio France/Georges Prêtre
EMI CDC 747 094 2
♪ Bruch, Concerto for Two Pianos (finale, Andante–Allegro), Martin Berkofsky and David Hagan (pianos)/Berlin Symphony Orchestra/Lutz Herbig
Turnabout 0012
♪ Chopin, Prelude No. 4 in E minor, Rudolph Kerer (piano)
Classics for Pleasure CFP 40284
♪ V Valencia, 'Mis Dolencias' (from *Music from the Andes*), Pablo Cárcamo
ARC EUCD 1378

Robert Gottlieb, American editor and critic

❡ George and Ira Gershwin, 'A Foggy Day', Earl Hines (piano)/Larry
Richardson (bass)/Richie Goldberg (drums)
Musidisc 500562
❡ Tchaikovsky, 'Adagio' from *Sleeping Beauty*, No. 8, 'Pas d'action',
National Philharmonic Orchestra/Richard Bonynge
Decca 425 469 2
❡ Giordano, finale to Act IV of *Andrea Chénier*, Beniamino Gigli
(Chénier), Maria Caniglia (Maddalena), Gino Conti (Schmidt)/
Orchestra of La Scala, Milan/Oliviero de Fabritiis
EMI CDH 769998 2
❡ Handy, 'St Louis Blues', Sidney Bechet and band
Camden 74321 487302
❡ Meyerbeer, 'O Paradiso' (from *L'africaine*), Enrico Caruso (Vasco da
Gama) and unknown orchestra, rec. 1907
Pearl Gemm CD 9309
❡ Bizet, Symphony in C (fourth movement, Allegro vivace), Orchestre
symphonique de Montréal/Charles Dutoit
Decca 452 102 2
❡ Porter, 'Ridin' High' (from *Red, Hot and Blue*), Ethel Merman/
Fairchild-Carroll and their Orchestra, rec. 1936
Conifer CMSCD 015

*Following a distinguished career at Knopf and the New Yorker, the editor
of John le Carré, Bill Clinton and Doris Lessing was able to turn his full
attention to his other passions, namely ballet, jazz and the largest
collection in the world of plastic handbags (or pocketbooks as they are
known in the US) . . . Oh, yes indeedy!*

Sir Roger Norrington, conductor

❡ Berlioz, 'Dido's Farewell' (from *Les Troyens*, Act V), Josephine Veasey
(Dido)/Orchestra of the Royal Opera House/Colin Davis
Philips 416 436 2
❡ Byrd, 'Justorum animae', Cambridge Singers/John Rutter
Collegium Records COLCD 110

¶ Berg, Violin Concerto, Thomas Zehetmair (violin)/Philharmonia/
Heinz Holliger
Teldec 2292 46449 2
¶ Schütz, Final chorus from *St Matthew Passion*, Heinrich Schütz
Choir/Roger Norrington
Decca 436 221 2
¶ Beethoven, String Quartet in F minor (first movement, Allegro con
brio), Emerson String Quartet
DG 423 398 2
¶ Bach, 'Ich habe genug' (opening aria of Cantata BWV 82), Dietrich
Fischer-Dieskau (baritone)/Munich Bach Orchestra/Karl Richter
Archiv 427 128 2
¶ Purcell, Chaconne ('Dance for Chinese Man and Woman'), London
Classical Players/Roger Norrington
EMI CDC 555 236 2

7 FEBRUARY 1998

Jeremy Sams, theatre director, translator and composer

¶ Ravel, end of *L'enfant et les sortilèges*, Choir and Symphony
Orchestra of Montreal/Charles Dutoit
Decca 440 333 2
¶ Schubert, 'Im Frühling', Dietrich Fischer-Dieskau (baritone)/Gerald
Moore (piano)
DG 437 233 2
¶ Chabrier, *À la musique*, Barbara Hendricks (soprano)/Women of the
Toulouse-Midi-Pyrénées Chorus/Orchestre du Capitole de Toulouse/
Michel Plasson
EMI CDC 754 004 2
¶ Lennox Berkeley, Prelude No. 4 (from 6 Preludes), Christopher
Headington (piano)
Kingdom KCLCD 2012
¶ Wolf, 'Wir haben beide . . .' (from *Italienisches Liederbuch*), Felicity
Lott (soprano)/Graham Johnson (piano)
Hyperion CDA 66760
¶ Sondheim, 'Move On' (from *Sunday in the Park with George*),
original Broadway cast recording, Mandy Patinkin (George),
Bernadette Peters (Dot)
RCA RD 85042

❡ Handel arr. Cedric Dent, 'Oh Thou that Tellest' (*The Messiah*), Stevie Wonder and Take 6
Reprise 7599 26980 2
❡ Jonathan Dove, 'Barbarina Alone' (from *Figures in the Garden*), Members of the Orchestra of the Age of Enlightenment
EMI CDC 754424 2
❡ Charles Trenet, 'L'âme des poètes', Charles Trenet
Columbia 746567 2

14 FEBRUARY 1998
Claire Tomalin, writer

❡ Schumann, 'Zwielicht' (from *Liederkreis*, Op. 39), Ian Partridge (tenor)/Jennifer Partridge (piano)
CFP CD-CFP 4651
❡ Duparc, *L'invitation au voyage*, Sarah Walker (mezzo-soprano)/ Roger Vignoles (piano)
Hyperion CDA 66323
❡ Tchaikovsky, Waltz scene (from *Eugene Onegin*, Act II), Anton Japridze (Captain), Yuri Mazurok (Onegin), Vladimir Atlantov (Lensky), Chorus and Orchestra of the Bolshoi Opera/Mark Ermler
Olympia OCD 115
❡ Beethoven, String Quartet in E minor, 'Razumovsky', Op. 59, No. 2 (third movement, Allegretto), Hungarian Quartet
EMI CZS 767236 2
❡ Bach, *Goldberg Variations*, BWV 988 (Theme and Variations 1–2), Glenn Gould (piano)
Sony SMK 52594
❡ Schubert, Octet in F, D803 (second movement, Adagio), Nash Ensemble
Virgin VC 545017–2
❡ Beethoven, Sonata in C minor, Op. 111 (second movement, Arietta), Alfred Brendel (piano)
Philips 446 701–2

Lord (Robert) Winston, fertility expert

❡ Bach, 'Jauchzet, frohlocket' (from *Christmas Oratorio*), The Sixteen/ Orchestra of The Sixteen/Harry Christophers
Collins 70282
❡ Rossini, Sextet from *La cenerentola*, Act III, Jennifer Larmore (Cenerentola), Raúl Giménez (Don Ramiro), Gino Quilico (Dandini), Alessandro Corbelli (Don Magnifico), Adelina Scarabelli (Clorinda), Laura Polverelli (Tisbe)/Orchestra of the Royal Opera House/ Carlo Rizzi
Teldec 4509 94553 2
❡ Schubert, Piano Trio in B flat, D898 (third movement, Scherzo), Beaux Arts Trio
Philips 412 620–2
❡ Richard Strauss, 'Dance of the Seven Veils' (from *Salome*), Chicago Symphony Orchestra/Fritz Reiner
RCA GD 60874
❡ Carlo Grossi, *Cantata Ebraica in dialogo*, Boston Camerata/Joel Cohen
Harmonia Mundi HM 1901021
❡ Trad., arr. Alpert/Bern, 'Bukovina 212', Itzhak Perlman (violin)/Brave Old World
EMI CDC 556209 2
❡ Wagner, 'Hagen Summons the Vassals' (from *Götterdämmerung*), Josef Greindl (Hagen)/Bayreuth Festival Chorus and Orchestra/Karl Böhm
Philips 412 488–2

Edward Said, writer, academic

❡ Bach, *Goldberg Variations*, BWV 988 (Canon at the ninth), Glenn Gould (piano)
Sony SMK 52594
❡ Schumann, 'Widmung' (from *Myrten*, Op. 25), Dietrich Fischer-Dieskau (baritone)/Christoph Eschenbach (piano)
DG 415 190–2

❡ Berlioz, final scene from Act II of *Les Troyens*, Berit Lindholm (Cassandra)/Orchestra and Chorus of the Royal Opera House/ Colin Davis
Philips 416 432–2
❡ Messiaen, 'Amen des anges, des saints, du chant des oiseaux' (from *Visions de l'Amen*), Yvonne Loriod, Olivier Messiaen (pianos)
Adès 13.233–2
❡ Berg, Act I, scene 1 from *Wozzeck*, Franz Grundheber (Wozzeck), Graham Clark (Hauptmann)/Staatskapelle Berlin/Daniel Barenboim
Teldec 0630–14108–2
❡ Wagner, Prelude to *Das Rheingold*, Vienna Philharmonic Orchestra/Georg Solti
Decca 414 101–2
❡ Chopin, Impromptu in F sharp, Op. 36, Artur Rubinstein (piano)
RCA RD 89911

We were fortunate to record the programme before he succumbed to leukaemia made all the more sad by his idiosyncratic brilliance.

7 MARCH 1998
James Bernard, film composer

❡ Lennox Berkeley, Serenade for Strings, Op. 12 (first movement, Vivace), London Philharmonic Orchestra/Lennox Berkeley
Lyrita SRCD 226
❡ Verdi, Love duet from *Otello*, Act I, Jon Vickers (Otello), Leonie Rysanek (Desdemona)/Rome Opera Orchestra/Tullio Serafin
RCA GD 81969
❡ Britten, 'Variation of the King of the South' (from *The Prince of the Pagodas*), London Sinfonietta/Oliver Knussen
Virgin VCD 791103–2
❡ Liszt, 'Les jeux d'eaux à la Villa d'Este' (from *Années de pèlerinage*), Lazar Berman (piano)
DG 437 206–2
❡ Debussy, *Syrinx*, Philippa Davies (flute)
IMP PCD 835
❡ Suk, 'Love Song', Op. 7, No. 1 (conclusion), Radoslav Kvapil (piano)
Unicorn DKPCD 9159
❡ Rachmaninov, 'Dnes spasenie' (from Vespers, Op. 37), Corydon Singers/Matthew Best

Hyperion CDA 6460
♫ Nellie Lutcher, 'Hurry On Down', Nellie Lutcher
Music for Pleasure CDDL 1266
♫ Gershwin, 'Embraceable You', Nat King Cole Trio
Capitol CDP 769792 2

14 MARCH 1998
John Sessions, actor, writer

♫ Stravinsky, Overture to *Pulcinella*, London Symphony Orchestra/
Claudio Abbado
DG 423 889 2
♫ Schubert, 'Im Abendrot', Lotte Lehmann (soprano), Erno Balogh
(piano)
RCA GD 87809
♫ Brahms, Symphony No. 4 (second movement, Andante moderato),
Cleveland Orchestra/George Szell
Sony Classical SBK 46330
♫ Shostakovich, Piano Concerto No. 2 (second movement, Andante),
Dmitri Shostakovich (composer's grandson) (piano)/I Musici de
Montreal/Maxim Shostakovich
Chandos CHAN 8442
♫ Mose Allison, 'Warhorse', Mose Allison (piano and vocal)/Earl May
(bass)/Paul Motian (drums)
Atlantic 587031
♫ Wagner, Prelude to *Die Walküre*, Vienna Philharmonic
Orchestra/Georg Solti
Decca 414 106 2
♫ Puccini, Act II, scene 2 of *Turandot*, Joan Sutherland (Turandot),
Peter Pears (Emperor), Luciano Pavarotti (Calaf)/John Aldiss Choir/
London Philharmonic Orchestra/Zubin Mehta
Decca 414 276 2
♫ Beethoven, String Quartet in A minor, Op. 132, (third movement,
Molto adagio: 'A Convalescent's Hymn of Thanksgiving to God, in the
Lydian mode'), Fitzwilliam String Quartet
Decca 411 643 2

21 MARCH 1998
Anthony Minghella, film director

❡ Van Morrison, 'This Weight' (from *The Healing Game*), Van
Morrison
Exile 537 101 2
❡ Puccini, 'E lucevan le stelle' (from *Tosca*, Act III), Placido Domingo
(Cavaradossi)/Philharmonia/James Levine
EMI CDZ 762 520 22
❡ Bach, Suite No. 1 in G (Prelude), Pablo Casals (cello)
EMI CDH 761 028 2
❡ Prince, 'Nothing Compares 2 U' (from *I Do Not Want What I
Haven't Got*), Sinead O'Connor
Ensign CCD 1759
❡ Bach, Prelude and Fugue in C minor (from *The Well-tempered
Clavier*, Book I), Glenn Gould (piano)
CBS M3K 4226
❡ Higginbotham/Drake/Fisher, 'Good Morning Heartache', Billie
Holiday
Verve 516871 2
❡ Gismonti, 'Palhaco' (Editions Gismoni SUISA), Jan Garbarek and
Magico
ECM 823 474 2
❡ Vivaldi, Stabat mater, James Bowman (countertenor)/Academy of
Ancient Music/Christopher Hogwood
Oiseau Lyre 414 329 2

28 MARCH 1998
Ruth Padel, poet and writer

❡ Razaf/Belledna, 'Kitchen Man', Bessie Smith/Clarence Williams
(piano)/Eddie Lang (guitar), rec. 1929
BBC BBCCD 602
❡ Theodorakis, 'Arnisi', Maria Farandouri/Orchestra/Mikis
Theodorakis
Melodiya 33D 018847
❡ Cole Porter, 'Night and Day', Fred Astaire/Leo Reisman and his
Orchestra, rec. 1932
RCA 9590—2-R

¶ Beethoven, String Quartet in A minor, Op. 132 (first movement, Assai sostenuto–Allegro), Lindsay String Quartet
ASV CDDCA 604
[¶ Trad., 'The Bold Irish Boy', Ruth Padel
recorded live]
[¶ Ruth Padel, 'Indian Red', Ruth Padel
recorded live]
¶ Verdi, conclusion of Act I of *La Traviata*, Maria Callas (Violetta)/ Giuseppe di Stefano (Alfredo)/Orchestra of La Scala, Milan/Carlo Maria Giulini, rec. 1955
EMI CMS 763628 2
¶ Bach, Concerto for Two Violins in D minor, BWV 1043 (second movement, Largo ma non tanto), Henryk Szeryng, Maurice Hasson (violins)/Academy of St Martin-in-the-Fields/Neville Marriner
Philips 422 250–2

4 APRIL 1998
Allan Gurganus, American writer

¶ Trad. arr. Patterson, 'My Lord, What a Morning', Jessye Norman (soprano)/Ambrosian Singers/Willis Patterson
Philips 416 462–2
¶ Dibdin arr. Britten, 'Tom Bowling', Peter Pears (tenor)/Benjamin Britten (piano)
London 430 063–2
[¶ Gurganus, 'Plays Well With Others', Allan Gurganus
recorded as part of programme]
¶ Laura Nyro, 'I Never Meant to Hurt You', Laura Nyro
Elite 015 CD
¶ Duruflé, Sanctus (from Requiem, Op. 9), Choir of Westminster Cathedral/Iain Simcock (organ)/James O'Donnell
Hyperion CDA 66757
¶ Brahms, Intermezzo, Op. 118, No. 2, Ivo Pogorelich (piano)
DG 437 460–2
¶ Mahler, 'In diesem Wetter' (from *Kindertotenlieder*), Janet Baker (mezzo-soprano)/Hallé Orchestra/John Barbirolli
EMI CZS 7 62707 2
¶ Tauber/Pinkard/Tracey, 'Them There Eyes', Billie Holiday
CBS OODP 576

♪ Bach, *Goldberg Variations*, BWV 988 (Aria), Glenn Gould (piano)
Sony SMK 52594

Lady Antonia Fraser, writer, historian

♪ Verdi, 'Ascolta! Le porte dell'asil s'apron già . . . Dio, che nell'alma
infondere' (from *Don Carlos*, Act II), Placido Domingo (Don Carlos),
Sherrill Milnes (Rodrigo)/Ambrosian Opera Chorus/Orchestra of the
Royal Opera House/Carlo Maria Giulini
EMI CDS 747701 8
♪ Gluck, 'Adieu, conservez dans votre âme' (from *Iphigénie en Aulide*),
Janet Baker (mezzo-soprano)/English Chamber Orchestra/Raymond
Leppard
Philips 422 950–2
♪ Wagner, 'Winterstürme' (from *Die Walküre*, Act I), Wolfgang
Windgassen (Siegmund)/Rome RAI Symphony Orchestra/
Wilhelm Furtwängler
EMI CZS 767131 2
♪ Mozart, 'E Susanna non vien! . . . Dove sono' (from *The Marriage of
Figaro*, Act III), Kiri te Kanawa (Countess Almaviva)/London
Philharmonic Orchestra/Georg Solti
Decca 410 150–2
♪ Byrd, Kyrie (from Mass for Four Voices), Choir of King's College,
Cambridge/David Willcocks
Decca 452 170–2
♪ Janáček, 'The Vixen's Dream' (from *The Cunning Little Vixen*, Act I),
Lucia Popp (Vixen)/Vienna Philharmonic Orchestra/Charles Mackerras
Decca 417 129–2
♪ Donizetti, 'Ohimè! sorge il tremendo fantasma' (from *Lucia di
Lammermoor*, Act II), Joan Sutherland (Lucia)/Orchestra of the Royal
Opera House/Richard Bonynge
Decca 410 193–2

Sir Ian McKellen, actor

♪ Julie Styne/Stephen Sondheim, 'Rose's Turn' (from *Gypsy*), Ethel
Merman/band directed by Milton Rosenstock
Columbia CK 32607

¶ Holst, *A Moorside Suite* (first movement), Grimethorpe Colliery Band/Elgar Howarth
Belart 450 023 2
¶ Frank Loesser, 'My Time of Day' and 'I've Never Been In Love Before' (from *Guys and Dolls*), Ian Charleson/Julie Covington/original National Theatre production/Tony Britten
Music for Pleasure CDMFP 5978
¶ Chopin, Polonaise in C minor Op. 40, No. 2, Maurizio Pollini (piano)
DG 413 795 2
¶ Elgar/Anthony Payne, realisation of sketches for Symphony No. 3 (part of first movement, Allegro molto maestoso), BBC Symphony Orchestra/Andrew Davis
NMC NMC D 053
¶ Grieg, Prelude and Wedding Scene from *Peer Gynt*, Academy of St Martin-in-the-Fields/Neville Marriner
EMI CDC 474 003 2
¶ Sondheim, 'Being Alive' (from *Company*), Dean Jones (Robert) and Company/Harold Hastings
Columbia CK 3550

25 APRIL 1998
Guy Woolfenden, composer and RSC musical director

¶ Tippett, *Concerto for Double String Orchestra* (second movement, Adagio cantabile), BBC Symphony Orchestra/Andrew Davis
Teldec 4509 94542 2
¶ Britten, 'Elegy' (from *Serenade*, Op. 31), Peter Pears (tenor)/Dennis Brain (horn)/Boyd Neel String Orchestra/Benjamin Britten
Decca 425 996 2
¶ Walton, Viola Concerto (first movement, Andante comodo), Nigel Kennedy (viola)/Royal Philharmonic Orchestra/André Previn
CDC 749628 2
¶ Verdi, 'Tutto nel mondo è burla' (from *Falstaff*, Act III), Philharmonia and Chorus/Herbert von Karajan
EMI CDC 749 670 2
¶ Grainger, 'Harkstow Grange' (from *A Lincolnshire Posy*), Royal Northern College of Music Wind Orchestra/Timothy Reynish
Chandos CHAN 9549

❡ Sondheim, 'Another Hundred People' (from *Company*), Pamela Myers (Marta)/original cast recording/Harold Hastings
Columbia CK 3550
❡ Purcell, 'Hear my prayer', Choir of Trinity College, Cambridge/Richard Marlow
Conifer CDCF 152

2 MAY 1998
Barbara Trapido, writer

❡ Britten, 'Dirge' (from *Serenade*, Op. 31), John Mark Ainsley (tenor)/ David Pyatt (horn)/Britten Sinfonia/Nicholas Cleobury
EMI CD EMX 2247
❡ Gluck, 'Dance of the Blessed Spirits' (from *Orfeo ed Euridice*), Michala Petri (recorder)/Lars Hannibal (guitar)
BMG Classics 09026 68769 2
❡ Purcell, *Come Ye Sons of Art* (second movement of *Ode on the Birthday of Queen Mary*, 1694), Alfred Deller (countertenor and director)/Deller Consort/Oriana Concert Choir and Orchestra
Vanguard 08 5060 71
❡ Bach, *Goldberg Variations*, BWV 988 (Aria and Variations 1–5), Glenn Gould (piano)
CBS CD 37779
❡ Alessandro Scarlatti, 'Già il sole dal Gange' (from *L'Honesta Negli Amori*), José Carreras/members of English Chamber Orchestra
Philips 434 926 2
❡ Haydn, Benedictus (from *Missa cellensis*), Jennifer Smith (soprano), Helen Watts (contralto), Robert Tear (tenor), Benjamin Luxon (bass)/ Choir of St John's College, Cambridge/Academy of St Martin-in-the-Fields/George Guest
Argo 417 306 1
❡ Trad., 'Nkosi Sikelel' iAfrika', Soweto String Orchestra
BMG CD BSP (WF)2031
❡ Mozart, 'Marche' (first movement of Cassatio in G, 'The Toy Symphony'), Academy of St Martin-in-the-Fields/Neville Marriner
Philips 416 386 2

9 MAY 1998
Alan Borg, Director of the Victoria and Albert Museum

❧ Beethoven, Grosse Fuge, Op. 133 (conclusion), Lindsay String Quartet
ASV CDDCA 602
❧ Beethoven, Symphony No. 5, Op. 67 (first movement, Allegro con brio), Orchestre Révolutionnaire et Romantique/John Eliot Gardiner
Archiv 439 900–2
❧ Bach, Partita No. 1 in B flat, BWV 825 (first movement, Praeludium), Glenn Gould (piano)
Sony SM2K 52597
❧ Ligeti, 'A Long Sad Tale' (from *Nonsense Madrigals*), The King's Singers
Sony SK 62311
❧ Wagner, Quintet from *Die Meistersinger von Nürnberg*, Act III, Catarina Ligendza (Eva), Christa Ludwig (Magdalene), Placido Domingo (Walther), Horst Laubenthal (David), Dietrich Fischer-Dieskau (Hans Sachs)/Orchestra of the Deutsche Oper Berlin/Eugen Jochum
DG 415 278–2
❧ Handel, 'Scherza infida' (from *Ariodante*), Lorraine Hunt (Ariodante)/Freiburg Baroque Orchestra/Nicholas McGegan
Harmonia Mundi HMU 907147
❧ Linley, 'Arise! Ye Spirits of the Storm' (from music for *The Tempest*), The Parley of Instruments Baroque Orchestra and Choir/Paul Nicholson
Hyperion CDA 66767
❧ Purcell, 'March' (from *Music for the Funeral of Queen Mary*), Baroque Brass of London/David Hill
Argo 436 833–2

16 MAY 1998
Bernard MacLaverty, novelist

❧ Anon., 'Esposa e Mare de Deu' (from *La Festa o Misteri D'Elx*), Capella del Misteri d'Elx/Manuel Ramos (director)
TRVE Musica 65031
❧ Purcell, 'Tis Women Makes Us Love', Deller Consort/Alfred Deller
Harmonia Mundi HM 90242

❧ Mahler, 'Wenn dein Mütterlein tritt zur Tür herein' (from *Kindertotenlieder*), Kathleen Ferrier (contralto)/Vienna Philharmonic Orchestra/Bruno Walter

EMI CDH 761 003 2

❧ Mozart, 'Il mio tesoro' (from *Don Giovanni*, Act II), John McCormack (Don Ottavio)/unknown orchestra

Nimbus NI 7820

❧ Shostakovich, Symphony No. 10 (second movement, Allegro), Scottish National Orchestra/Neeme Järvi

Chandos CHAN 8630

❧ Britten, Agnus Dei (from Missa Brevis in D), Choir of Westminster Cathedral/James O'Donnell (organ)/David Hill

Hyperion CDA 66220

❧ Janáček, Allegretto (from Sinfonietta), Bavarian Radio Symphony Orchestra/Rafael Kubelík

DG 437 254 2

❧ Schubert, 'Andantino' (No. 2 from *Moments musicaux*), Clifford Curzon (piano)

Decca 417 642 2

❧ Messiaen, ending of *Turangalîla-Symphonie*, Orchestre de la Bastille/Yvonne Loriod (piano)/Jeanne Loriod (ondes martenot)/Myung-Whun Chung

DG 431 781 2

23 MAY 1998
Frances Partridge, diarist

❧ Monteverdi, 'Zefiro torna', Paul Derenne, Hugues Cuenod (tenors)/Ensemble/Nadia Boulanger

EMI CDH 761025 2

❧ Richard Strauss, *Metamorphosen* (conclusion), New Philharmonia/John Barbirolli

EMI CDM 565078 2

❧ Mozart, Piano Concerto in B flat, K238 (first movement), Géza Anda (piano and director)/Salzburg Mozarteum Camerata Academica

DG 419 001–2

❧ Schubert, Piano Trio in E flat, D929 (second movement), Alexander Schneider (violin)/Pablo Casals (cello)/Mieczyslaw Horszowski (piano)

Sony SMK 58988

❡ Handel, 'O Sleep, Why Dost Thou Leave Me?' (from *Semele*), Norma Burrowes (Semele)/English Baroque Soloists/John Eliot Gardiner
Erato 2292–45982–2
❡ Trenet/Breton, 'Boum!', Charles Trenet/Wal-Berg's Orchestra
ASV CD AJA 5166
❡ Bach, Concerto for Two Violins in D minor, BWV 1043 (second movement, Largo ma non tanto), David and Igor Oistrakh (violins)/Royal Philharmonic Orchestra/Eugene Goossens
DG 419 833–2
❡ Beethoven, String Quartet in C sharp minor, Busch Quartet
EMI CHS 565308 2

We don't have many guests in their nineties, but at that point she was still a wry observer of the society that had surrounded her.

30 MAY 1998
William Boyd, writer

❡ Sondheim, 'Pretty Women' (from *Sweeney Todd*), Peabo Bryson (vocal)/Joshua Redman (tenor saxophone)/Brad Mehldau (piano)/Christian McBride (bass)/Brian Blade (drums)
Sony SK 66566
❡ Joseph Schwantner, Percussion Concerto (first movement, Con forza), Evelyn Glennie (percussion)/National Symphony Orchestra/Leonard Slatkin
RCA 09026 68692 2
❡ Fauré, Piano Quartet No. 1 in C minor, Op. 15 (third movement, Adagio), Domus
Hyperion CDA 66166
❡ Prokofiev, Cello Sonata in C, Op. 119 (second movement), Yo-Yo Ma (cello)/Emanuel Ax (piano)
Sony SK 46486
❡ Brahms, Horn Trio in E flat, Op. 40 (first movement, Andante–poco più animato), György Sebok (piano)/Arthur Grumiaux (violin)/Francis Orval (horn)
Philips 438 365–2
❡ Delius, Violin Sonata No. 3 (first movement, Slow), Alexander Barantschik (violin)/Israela Margalit (piano)
EMI CDC 5 55399 2

¶ Brahms, Kanon 13 (from *13 Kanonen*, Op. 113), Leipzig Radio Choir/
Wolf-Dieter Hauschild
Orfeo C 026974 H

6 JUNE 1998
Binjamin Wilkomirski, alleged Holocaust child survivor

¶ Trad. arr. Feidman, 'Tatei Freilach', Giora Feidman
Pläne 88748
¶ Trad. arr. Lasry, 'A Jewish Child of Poland', Sarah Gorby/Les
Structures Sonores Lasry-Bachet/Orchestra/Jacques Lasry
Arion ARN 64081
¶ Brahms, Clarinet Quintet in B minor, Op. 115 (first movement,
Allegro), Karl Leister (clarinet)/Amadeus Quartet
DG 437 646–2
¶ Mozart, 'In diesen heil'gen Hallen' (from *The Magic Flute*, Act II),
Kurt Moll (Sarastro)/Staatskapelle Dresden/Colin Davis
Philips 411 459–2
¶ Beethoven, Violin Concerto in D, Op. 61 (second movement,
Larghetto), Josef Suk (violin)/New Philharmonia Orchestra/Adrian
Boult
EMI CDZ 7 62510 2
¶ Mahler, Symphony No. 1 (second movement, Kräftig), London
Symphony Orchestra/Jascha Horenstein
Unicorn UKCD 2012

*Perhaps the most bizarre story of them all, our recording followed the
hugely acclaimed publication of his book* Fragments, *a profoundly
moving autobiography of Wilkomirski's childhood experiences of
surviving the camps in the Holocaust. I thought that there was something
strange about this clarinet-playing writer, but put it down to his
appalling experiences – except that it then transpired that he could not
have been where he said he was and that his book was made up. Which
leaves us with the uneasy conundrum of whether or not that invalidates
the power of what he wrote, even if it is fiction and not fact.*

13 JUNE 1998
Deborah Bull, dancer

❡ Sparre Olsen, *Old Village Songs from Lom* (Nos 1, 4, 5, 6), Atle
Sponberg (violin)/Gjovik Sinfonietta/Rolf Baeckkelund
Bergen Digital Studio BD 7026 CD
❡ Mozart, Laudate Dominum (from Vesperae solennes de confessore),
Kiri te Kanawa (soprano)/London Symphony Orchestra and Chorus/
Colin Davis
Philips 412 873 2
❡ Willie Nelson, 'Crazy', Patsy Cline
Pickwick POKS 524
❡ Bach, Chaconne (from Partita No. 2 in D, BWV 1004), Nathan
Milstein (violin)
DG 423 296 2
❡ Monti arr. Ifor James, *Czardas*, Philip Jones Brass Ensemble
Argo ZRS 895
❡ Poulenc, Piano Concerto (second movement, Andante con moto),
François-René Duchâble (piano)/Rotterdam Philharmonic Orchestra/
James Conlon
Erato ECD 88140

20 JUNE 1998
Blake Morrison, writer

❡ Mahler, 'Oft denk' ich, sie sind nur ausgegangen' (from
Kindertotenlieder), Kathleen Ferrier (contralto)/Vienna Philharmonic
Orchestra/Bruno Walter
EMI CDH 761003 2
❡ Stevie Wonder, 'Living for the City', Stevie Wonder
Motown 530757 2
❡ Gavin Bryars, Cello Concerto, 'Farewell to Philosophy' (second
movement, Più mosso), Julian Lloyd Webber (cello)/English Chamber
Orchestra/James Judd
Point 454 126–2
❡ Lennon/McCartney, 'Fixing a Hole' (from *Sgt Pepper*), The Beatles
Parlophone CDP 746442 2
❡ Miles Davis, 'Spanish Key' (opening), Miles Davis
CBS CD 66236

℘ Mozart, Rex tremendae (from Requiem, K626), Wiener
Singverein/Berlin Philharmonic Orchestra/Herbert von Karajan
DG 423 213–2
[℘ Blake Morrison, *The Ballad of the Yorkshire Ripper*, Blake Morrison,
recorded live during programme session]
℘ Rodgers/Hammerstein, 'Cock-Eyed Optimist' (from *South Pacific*),
Mitzi Gaynor/Orchestra/Alfred Newman
RCA ND 83681
℘ Philip Glass, *North Star*, Philip Glass Ensemble
Virgin CDV 2085
℘ Schubert, Piano Quintet in A, D667, 'Trout' (third movement,
Scherzo), András Schiff (piano)/Members of the Hagen Quartet/Alois
Posch (double bass)
Decca 411 975–2

27 JUNE 1998
Sir Anthony Caro, artist

℘ Stravinsky, 'Here I Stand' (from *The Rake's Progress*, Act I),
Alexander Young (Tom Rakewell)/Royal Philharmonic Orchestra/Igor
Stravinsky
Sony SM2K 46299
℘ Mozart, 'Là ci darem la mano' (from *Don Giovanni*, Act I), Eberhard
Wächter (Don Giovanni), Graziella Sciutti (Zerlina)/Philharmonia/
Carlo Maria Giulini
EMI CDS 747260 2
℘ Haydn, Symphony No. 104 in D, 'London' (finale, Spiritoso),
Philharmonia/Leonard Slatkin
RCA 09026 62549–2
℘ Schubert, 'Die liebe Farbe' (from *Die schöne Müllerin*, D795),
Dietrich Fischer-Dieskau (baritone)/Gerald Moore (piano)
DG 415 186–2
℘ Schubert, String Quintet in C, D956 (conclusion of second
movement, Adagio), Isaac Stern, Alexander Schneider (violins)/Milton
Katims (viola)/Pablo Casals, Paul Tortelier (cellos)
CBS CD 44853
℘ Trad., 'Early One Morning', Alison Truefitt (mezzo-soprano)/Richard
Knott (baritone)
National Museum of Wales NMW 100

¶ Brahms, 'Denn wir haben hie' (from *A German Requiem*, Op. 45), Dietrich Fischer-Dieskau (baritone)/Philharmonia Chorus and Orchestra/Otto Klemperer
EMI CDC 747238 2
¶ Mozart, Piano Concerto in D minor, K466 (second movement, Romance), András Schiff (piano)/Salzburg Mozarteum Camerata Academia/Sándor Végh
Decca 430 510–2

4 JULY 1998
Chris Smith, politician, writer

¶ Dvořák, Cello Concerto in B minor, Op. 104 (first movement), Mstislav Rostropovich (cello)/Royal Philharmonic Orchestra/Adrian Boult
Laserlight 16223
¶ Machaut, Gloria (from Messe de Notre Dame), Taverner Consort/Andrew Parrott
EMI CDC 747949 2
¶ Sibelius, Symphony No. 2 (exc. from third movement), Vienna Philharmonic Orchestra/Lorin Maazel
Decca 430 778–2
¶ Puccini, 'Mimì's Farewell' (from *La bohème*, Act III), Maria Callas (Mimì), Giuseppe di Stefano (Rodolfo)/Orchestra of La Scala, Milan/Antonino Votto
EMI CDC 747475 8
¶ Mahler, 'Der Abschied' (conclusion) (from *Das Lied von der Erde*), Kathleen Ferrier (contralto)/Vienna Philharmonic Orchestra/Bruno Walter
Decca 414 194–2
¶ Schubert, String Quintet in C, D956 (first movement), Amadeus Quartet/William Pleeth (cello)
DG 423 543–2
¶ Gershwin, 'Summertime' (from *Porgy and Bess*), Harolyn Blackwell (Clara)/Glyndebourne Chorus/London Philharmonic Orchestra/Simon Rattle
EMI CDS 747568 2
¶ Weill, 'Ballad of Mack the Knife' (from *Die Dreigroschenoper*), Ute Lemper/RIAS Berlin Chamber Ensemble/John Mauceri
Decca 458 931–2

Amanda Holden, translator, librettist

❧ Irving Berlin, 'You Can't Get a Man With a Gun', Ethel Merman/
Orchestra/Jay Blackston
World Music WM 88010
❧ Tchaikovsky, 'Lensky's Aria' (from *Eugene Onegin*), Fritz Wunderlich
(Lensky)/Bavarian State Opera Orchestra/Otto Gerdes
DG 435 145–2
❧ Mozart, Quintet in E flat for piano and wind (second movement,
Larghetto), Walter Gieseking (piano)/Sidney Sutcliffe (oboe)/Bernard
Walton (clarinet)/Dennis Brain (horn)/Cecil James (bassoon)
Testament SBT 1091
❧ Handel, 'Tu, preparati a morire' (from *Ariodante*), Anne Sofie von
Otter (Ariodante)/Les Musiciens du Louvre/Mark Minkowski
Archiv 457 281–2
❧ John Adams, Violin Concerto (third movement, Toccare), Gidon
Kremer (violin)/London Symphony Orchestra/Kent Nagano
Nonesuch 7559 79360–2
❧ Heiner Goebbels, *Black on White* (second movement), Ensemble
Modern
RCA 09026 68870–2
❧ Schumann arr. Debussy, Study Op. 56, No. 4 (Espressivo), Daniel
Blumenthal and Robert Groslot (pianos)
Marco Polo 8 223378
❧ Debussy, Cello Sonata (first movement, Prologue), Mstislav
Rostropovich (cello)/Benjamin Britten (piano)
Decca 417 833–2

Professor Sir Michael Howard, historian

❧ Johann Strauss II, *Emperor Waltz*, Vienna Philharmonic Orchestra/
Claudio Abbado
DG 437 687–2
❧ Verdi, Sanctus (from Requiem), Robert Shaw Chorale/NBC
Symphony Orchestra/Arturo Toscanini
RCA GD 60299

♪ Brahms, Violin Concerto in D, Op. 77 (second movement, Adagio), Yehudi Menuhin (violin)/Lucerne Festival Orchestra/Wilhelm Furtwängler
EMI CDH 763496 2
♪ Puccini, 'Che gelida manina' (from *La bohème*, Act I), Giuseppe di Stefano (Rodolfo)/Orchestra of La Scala, Milan/Antonino Votto
EMI CDS 747475 8
♪ Trenet, 'La mer', Charles Trenet/Orchestra/Albert Lasry
EMI CDP 794464 2
♪ Rodgers/Hammerstein, 'Oklahoma' (from *Oklahoma*), Gordon MacRae, Charlotte Greenwood, James Whitmore, Shirley Jones, Jay C. Flippen/Chorus and Orchestra/Jay Blackston
Angel ZDM 764691 2
♪ Mozart, 'Riconosci in questo amplesso' (from *The Marriage of Figaro*, Act III), Elisabeth Höngen (Marcellina), Erich Kunz (Figaro), Marjan Rus (Doctor Bartolo), Erich Majkut (Don Curzio), George London (Count Almaviva), Irmgard Seefried (Susanna)/Vienna Philharmonic Orchestra/Herbert von Karajan
EMI CMS 769639 2
♪ Schubert, Quintet in A, 'Trout' (first movement, Allegro vivace), András Schiff (piano)/ Members of the Hagen Quartet/Alois Posch (double bass)
Decca 411 975–2

25 JULY 1998
Corin Redgrave, actor and political activist

♪ Tippett, String Quartet No. 1 (second movement, Lento cantabile), Britten Quartet
Collins Classics 70062/A
♪ Puccini, 'Che gelida manina' (from *La bohème*, Act I), Luciano Pavarotti (Rodolfo)/Berlin Philharmonic Orchestra/Herbert von Karajan
Decca 421 050 2
♪ Irving Berlin, 'I'm Beginning to Miss You', Kika Markham (vocal)/ Liz Marcus (piano)
Private recording

¶ Britten, 'Romance' (from *Variations on a Theme of Frank Bridge*), English Chamber Orchestra/Sir Alexander Gibson
EMI CD EMX 2111
¶ Schoenberg, *Drei Klavierstücke*, Op. 11 (No. 1), Katharina Wolpe (piano)
Symposium 1107
¶ Freddie Mercury, 'Bohemian Rhapsody', Queen
EMI CDP 746033 2
¶ Beethoven, Violin Sonata No. 5 in F, 'Spring' (first movement, Allegro), Itzhak Perlman (violin)/Vladimir Ashkenazy (piano)
Decca 421 456 2

1 AUGUST 1998
Lord Gowrie, politician, writer, literary critic and former Arts Council Chairman

¶ Verdi, 'Solenne in quest'ora' (from *La forza del destino*, Act III), Enrico Caruso/Antonio Scotti, rec. 1906
Nimbus NI 7834
¶ Adès, *The Origin of the Harp* (Dolcissimo ed espressivo), chamber ensemble conducted by Thomas Adès
EMI 572 271 2
¶ Berg, 'Seele, wir bist du schöner' (No. 1 of *Five Orchestral Songs*, Op. 4), Jessye Norman (soprano)/London Symphony Orchestra/Pierre Boulez
Sony Classical SK 66826
¶ Brahms, Nachtwache II: 'Ruhn sie?' (No. 2 of *Funf Gesänge: Lieder und Romanzen*, Op. 104), Arnold Schoenberg Choir/Erwin Ortner
Teldec 4509 92058 2
¶ Schoenberg, Piano Concerto (third movement, Adagio), Alfred Brendel/SWF Symphony Orchestra of Baden-Baden/Michael Gielen
Philips 446 683 2
¶ Mozart, Kyrie (from Mass in C minor, K427), Monteverdi Choir/ English Baroque Soloists/John Eliot Gardiner
Philips 420 210 2
¶ Stravinsky, *Symphony of Psalms* (Part I), London Symphony Orchestra and Chorus/Michael Tilson Thomas
Sony Classical SK 53275

♪ Birtwistle, 'The Second Hunt and Temptation' (from *Gawain*, Act II), Anne Howells (Lady de Hautdesert), François le Roux (Gawain)/Orchestra of the Royal Opera House/Elgar Howarth
Collins Classics 7041 2 B
♪ Grainger/Robbins, 'T'Aint Nobody's Bizness If I Do', from *The Trumpet Kings Meet Joe Turner*, featuring Dizzy Gillespie, Roy Eldridge, Harry 'Sweets' Edison, Clark Terry (trumpets)
Pablo OJCCD 497 2

8 AUGUST 1998
Richard Ingrams, journalist and writer

♪ Brahms, Violin Sonata in A, Op. 100 (first movement, Allegro amabile), Josef Suk (violin)/Julius Katchen (piano)
Decca 421 092–2
♪ Schumann, Study No. 5 (from *Symphonic Studies*, op. posth.), Sviatoslav Richter (piano)
Revelation RV 10012
♪ Gershwin, 'Embraceable You', Oleta Adams (vocal)/Larry Adler (harmonica)
Mercury 522 727–2
♪ Rachmaninov, Prelude in G, Op. 32, No. 5, Vladimir Horowitz (piano)
DG 419 499–2
♪ Delius, Intermezzo from *Fennimore and Gerda*, Royal Philharmonic Orchestra/Thomas Beecham
EMI CDS 747509 2
♪ Mozart, Quintet in D, K593 (second movement, Adagio), Griller String Quartet/William Primrose (viola)
Vanguard 08.8024.71
♪ Bach, 'Widerstehe doch der Sünde' (from Cantata, BWV 54), Alfred Deller (countertenor)/Leonhardt Baroque Ensemble
Vanguard 08.5069.71

15 AUGUST 1998
Jenny Uglow, writer and editor

♪ Schubert, String Quintet in C, D956 (second movement, Adagio), Emerson String Quartet/Mstislav Rostropovich (cello)
DG 431 792 2

❡ Poulenc, Laudamus te (from Gloria), Choeur de la Radio Suisse Romande/Choeur Pro Arte de Lausanne/L'Orchestre de la Suisse Romande/Jesus López-Cobos
Decca 448 270 2
❡ Purcell, 'The Earth Trembled', Nicholas Witcomb (treble)/King's Consort/Robert King
Hyperion CCD 66644
❡ Handel, Concerto Grosso in E minor, Op. 6, No. 3 (fourth movement, Polonaise), English Concert/Trevor Pinnock
Archiv 410 897 2
❡ Brecht/Weill, 'Alabama Moon' (from *Mahagonny*), Lotte Lenya/The Three Admirals and Theo Mackeben's Jazzorchester Berlin
Conifer CDHD 188
❡ Anon., 'Flying Bomb Kwela' (Fire), SDV Swing Band
Rave RMG (cassette copy)
❡ Haydn, 'In Rosy Mantle Appears' and 'By Thee With Bliss' (from *The Creation*, Part III), Anthony Rolfe Johnson (Uriel), Michael George (Adam), Emma Kirkby (Eve)/Academy of Ancient Music/Choir of New College, Oxford/Christopher Hogwood
Oiseau Lyre 430 397 2
❡ Beethoven, Sonata in A flat, Op. 110 (final fugue), Alfred Brendel (piano)
Philips 446 701 2

29 AUGUST 1998
Lord Birkett, former theatre producer, film director

❡ Mozart, Symphony No. 34 in C, K338 (finale, Allegro vivace), London Philharmonic Orchestra/Thomas Beecham
Dutton CDEA 5008
❡ Chopin, Sonata No. 3 in B minor, Op. 58 (first movement, Allegro maestoso), Dinu Lipatti (piano)
EMI CDH 763038 2
❡ Bernhard Flies, 'Wiegenlied', Irmgard Seefried (soprano)/Hermann von Nordberg (piano)
Testament SBT 1026

❧ Puccini, 'Dovunque al mondo' (from *Madama Butterfly*, Act I), Jussi Björling (Pinkerton), Mario Sereni (Sharpless)/Rome Opera Orchestra/Gabriele Santini
EMI CMS 763634 2
❧ Richard Strauss, end of the Prologue from *Ariadne auf Naxos*, Sena Jurinac (Composer), Leonie Rysanek (Prima Donna), Walter Berry (Music Master)/Vienna Philharmonic Orchestra/Erich Leinsdorf
Decca 443 675–2
❧ Medtner, Piano Concerto No. 3 in E minor, Op. 60 (finale), Nikolai Demidenko (piano)/BBC Scottish Symphony Orchestra/Jerzy Maksymiuk
Hyperion CDA 66580
❧ Leo Weiner, Serenade, Op. 3 (first movement, Allegretto), Budapest Festival Orchestra/Georg Solti
Decca 458 929–2

5 SEPTEMBER 1998
Michael Dibdin, novelist

❧ Britten, *Cello Symphony*, Op. 68 (second movement, Presto inquieto), Mstislav Rostropovich (cello)/English Chamber Orchestra/Benjamin Britten
London 425 100–2
❧ Scarlatti, Sonata in D, Kk 33, Scott Ross (harpsichord)
Erato ECD 75405
❧ Will McTell, 'Statesboro Blues', The Allman Brothers Band
Polydor 831 615–2
❧ Palestrina, Kyrie (from Missa Benedicta es), Tallis Scholars/Peter Phillips
Gimell CDGIM 001
❧ Vivaldi, Cum dederit (from Nisi Dominus), Christopher Robson (countertenor)/King's Consort/Robert King
Meridian CDE 84129
❧ Charles Dibdin, 'Vaudeville' (from *The Ephesian Matron*), Bronwen Mills (Matron), Jane Streeton (Maid), Mark Padmore (Centurion), Andrew Knight (Father)/Opera Restor'd/Peter Holman
Hyperion CDA 66608

¶ Dufay, 'Quel fronte signorille in paradiso', Gothic Voices/Christopher Page
Hyperion CDA 66286
¶ Mozart, String Quartet in G, K387 (fourth movement, Molto allegro), Quatuor Mosaïques
Astrée E 8746

12 SEPTEMBER 1998
Alan Rusbridger, editor of the *Guardian*

¶ Valdemar Henrique, arr. Patrick Russ, 'Boi-Bumbá', Kathleen Battle (soprano)/Christopher Parkening (guitar)
EMI CDC 747196 2
¶ George Benjamin, Invention II (from *Three Inventions*), London Sinfonietta/George Benjamin
Nimbus NI 5505
¶ Billy Mayerl, 'Punch', Billy Mayerl (piano)
ASV CDAJA 5162
¶ Wagner, 'Wotan's Farewell' (from *Die Walküre*, Act III), Thomas Stewart (Wotan)/Berlin Philharmonic Orchestra/Herbert von Karajan
DG 415 145–2
¶ Beethoven, Sonata in E, Op. 109 (third movement), Alfred Brendel (piano)
Philips 412 575–2
¶ Weber, Clarinet Quintet in B flat, Op. 34 (third movement, Menuetto: Capriccio Presto), Paul Meyer (clarinet)/Carmina Quartet
Denon Chamber Orchestra 78801
¶ J. H. Maunder, 'Droop, Sacred Head' (from *Olivet to Calvary*), Choir of Guildford Cathedral/Peter Moorse (organ)/Barry Rose
CFP CDCFP 4619
¶ Finley Quaye, 'Your Love Gets Sweeter', Finley Quaye
Epic 488758 2

Has brought much greater arts coverage to the Guardian *as its editor; one small aspect of this was even a direct result of the programme.*

Bill Paterson, actor

❡ Berlioz, Tibi omnes (from Te Deum, Op. 22), London Symphony Chorus/London Philharmonic Choir etc./Martin Haselböck (organ)/ European Community Youth Orchestra/Claudio Abbado
DG 410 696–2
❡ Catalani, 'Ne andrò lontana' (from *La Wally*), Renata Tebaldi (Wally)/Monte Carlo Opera Orchestra/Fausto Cleva
Decca 425 417–2
❡ Trad., 'Martyrs', Alisdair Graham and congregation
Greentrax CDTRAX 9006
❡ Trad., Annalese Bain/Phil Cunningham's Reel/Andy Brown's Reel, Aly Bain (fiddle)/Violet Tulloch (piano)/Danny Thompson (bass)/ Chris Newman (guitar)
Whirlie CD 2
❡ Schubert, String Quartet in D minor, D810, 'Death and the Maiden' (first movement, Allegro), Chilingirian Quartet
Nimbus NI 5048
❡ Franck arr. Delsart, Sonata in A (fourth movement, Allegretto poco mosso), Jacqueline du Pré (cello)/Daniel Barenboim (piano)
EMI CDM 763184 2
❡ Britten, 'Dawn' (from *Four Sea Interludes from Peter Grimes*), BBC Symphony Orchestra/Andrew Davis
Teldec 9031–73126–2
❡ Betjeman/Parker, 'Eunice', Sir John Betjeman/Ensemble/Jim Parker
Virgin CASCD 1096

Alan Titchmarsh, gardener, broadcaster and writer

❡ Bizet, 'Au fond du temple saint' (from *The Pearl Fishers*, Act I), Jussi Björling, Robert Merrill (tenors)/RCA Victor Orchestra/Renato Cellini
RCA RD 495224
❡ Allegri, Miserere, Choir of King's College, Cambridge/Roy Goodman (solo treble)/David Willcocks
Decca 421 147 2
❡ Hughes, 'Cwm Rhondda' (Mecolico), Morriston Orpheus Choir/Bob Potter
DAMON DMT 3001

❡ Rachmaninov, Symphony No. 2 (first movment, Largo–Allegro moderato), Bolshoi Symphony Orchestra/Alexander Lazarev
Erato 4509 96360 2
❡ Vivaldi, Gloria in excelsis Deo (from Gloria in D major, RV 589), Choir of St John's College, Cambridge/Wren Orchestra/George Guest
ARGO 410 018 2
❡ Elgar, Cello Concerto (first movement), Jacqueline du Pré (cello)/English Chamber Orchestra/John Barbirolli
CDM 769 708 2
❡ Dvořák, Symphony No. 8 (first movement, Allegro con brio), London Philharmonic Orchestra/Charles Mackerras
EMI EMX 2216
❡ Metheny, 'Always and Forever', Pat Metheny (guitar etc.)/Charlie Haden (bass)/Paul Wertico (drums)/ Toots Thielemans (harmonica)/London Orchestra/Jeremy Lubbock
Geffen GED 24468

3 OCTOBER 1998
HRH The Duke of Kent
❡ Janáček, 'Boris and Katya's Farewell' (from last scene of *Katya Kabanova*), Elisabeth Söderström (Katya), Peter Dvorský (Boris)/ Vienna State Opera Choir/Vienna Philharmonic Orchestra/Charles Mackerras
Decca 421 853 2
❡ Schubert, 'Nacht und Träume', D827, Ann Murray (mezzo-soprano)/ Graham Johnson (piano)
Hyperion CDJ 33003
❡ Bach, Qui tollis peccata mundi (from Mass in B minor, Gloria), Monteverdi Choir/English Baroque Soloists/John Eliot Gardiner
Archiv 415 515 2
❡ Mozart, String Quartet in B flat, 'The Hunt', K458 (second movement, Adagio), Alban Berg Quartet
Teldec 9031 76998A
❡ Chopin, Nocturne in C minor, Op. 48, No. 1, Artur Rubinstein (piano)
RCA RD 89563 B

¶ Wagner, end of 'Dawn Duet' and part of 'Siegfried's Rhine Journey' (from *Götterdämmerung*), Birgit Nilsson (Brünnhilde), Wolfgang Windgassen (Siegfried)/Vienna Philharmonic Orchestra/Georg Solti
Decca 414 116 2

The Royal Family has a somewhat unfair reputation regarding the arts since the Duke and Duchess, Princess Alexandra and the Prince of Wales are all passionate about music and have spoken of their enjoyment at the way people describe their love of music on the programme. I fear that the studio must have appeared somewhat bohemian to the Duke but he entered into the spirit of things and revealed a real reverence for the classics and especially the first Viennese school.

10 OCTOBER 1998
Gilbert Kaplan, businessman and Mahler expert

¶ Prokofiev, 'Alexander's Entry into Pskov' (from *Alexander Nevsky*, Op. 78), London Symphony Orchestra and Chorus/Claudio Abbado
DG 419 603 2
¶ Copland, *Billy the Kid*, Saint Louis Symphony Orchestra/Leonard Slatkin
EMI CDC 747 382 2
¶ Wagner, final scene from *Der Fliegende Holländer*, José van Dam (Dutchman), Kurt Moll (Daland), Dunja Vefzovic (Senta), Peter Hofmann (Erik), Kaja Borris (Mary)/Chorus and Orchestra of the Vienna State Opera/Herbert von Karajan
EMI CDC 747 056 2
¶ Mahler, Symphony No. 6 (Andante), London Philharmonic Orchestra/Klaus Tennstedt
EMI CDC 747 051 2
¶ Mahler, 'Ich bin der Welt abhanden gekommen' (from *Rückert-Lieder*), Dietrich Fischer-Dieskau (baritone)/Berlin Philharmonic Orchestra/Karl Böhm
DG 415 191 2
¶ Mahler, Symphony No. 7 (first movement), Chicago Symphony Orchestra/James Levine
RCA RD 84581 A
¶ Charles Ives, Symphony No. 4 (third movement, Fugue: Andante moderato), London Philharmonic Orchestra/José Serebrier
Chandos CHAN 8397

❡ Mahler, Symphony No. 2 (ending), Ardwyn Singers/BBC Welsh Chorus/Cardiff Polyphonic Choir/Dyfed Choir/London Symphony Chorus/London Symphony Orchestra/Gilbert Kaplan
Pickwick DPCD 910

17 OCTOBER 1998
Tom Rosenthal, publisher and writer

❡ Janáček, Gloria (from *Glagolitic Mass*), Evelyn Lear (soprano)/ Bavarian Radio Choir and Orchestra/Rafael Kubelík
DG 429 182 2
❡ Verdi, 'O si per ciel marmoreo giuro' (from *Otello*, Act II), Ramón Vinay (Otello), Giuseppe Valdengo (Iago)/NBC Symphony Orchestra/Arturo Toscanini
RCA GD 60302 A
❡ Tchaikovsky, duet from *The Queen of Spades*, Act I
Philips 438 142 2
❡ Beethoven, 'O namenlose Freude!' (from *Fidelio*, Act II), Christa Ludwig (Leonore), Jon Vickers (Florestan)/Philharmonia/Otto Klemperer
EMI CDM 769 326 2
❡ Berlioz, 'Chanson d'Hylas' (from *The Trojans*, Act V), Ryland Davies (Hylas)/Royal Opera House Orchestra/Colin Davis
Philips 416 436 2
❡ Bach, Suite No. 1 in G (Prelude), Paul Tortelier (cello)
EMI CDC 747 090 2
❡ Britten, 'Now the Great Bear and Pleiades' (from *Peter Grimes*, Act I), Jon Vickers (Peter)/Royal Opera House Chorus and Orchestra/Colin Davis
Philips 432 579 2
❡ Falla, 'En los jardines de la Sierra de Córdoba' (from *Nights in the Gardens of Spain*), Philippe Entremont (piano)/Philadelphia Orchestra/Eugene Ormandy
CBS CD 46499
❡ Richard Strauss, 'Frühling' (from *Four Last Songs*), Lisa della Casa (soprano)/Vienna Philharmonic Orchestra/ Karl Böhm
Decca 425 959 2

24 OCTOBER 1998
Erich Segal, writer and academic

¶ Lennon/McCartney, 'Let it Be', The Beatles
Parlophone CD3R 5833
¶ Shostakovich, 'Waltz' (from *Jazz Suite* No. 1), Philadelphia
Orchestra/Mariss Jansons
EMI CDC 556601 2
¶ Salomone de Rossi Ebreo, 'Adon olam', Boston Camerata/Joel Cohen
Harmonia Mundi HM 1901021
¶ Tallis, Agnus Dei (from Mass for Four Voices), Oxford Camerata/
Jeremy Summerly (conductor)
Naxos 8 550576
¶ Chopin, Waltz in C sharp minor, Op. 64, No. 2, Artur Rubinstein
(piano)
RCA RD 89564
¶ Gilbert/Sullivan, 'When I was a Lad' (from *HMS Pinafore*), George
Baker (Sir Joseph Porter)/Glyndebourne Festival Chorus/Pro Arte
Orchestra/Malcolm Sargent
EMI CDD 747 779 2
¶ Gluck, 'Che farò senza Euridice?' (from *Orfeo ed Euridice*, Act I),
Derek Lee Ragin (Orfeo)/English Baroque Soloists/John Eliot
Gardiner
Philips 434 095 2
¶ Weill/Brecht, 'Mack the Knife', Louis Armstrong and his All Stars
Bluebird 74321 19706 2
¶ Mozart, Laudate Dominum (from Vesperae solennes de confessore),
Kiri te Kanawa (soprano)/London Symphony Orchestra/London
Symphony Orchestra Chorus/Colin Davis
Philips 412 873 2
¶ Bach, Suite No. 1 in G (Prelude), Ralph Kirshbaum (cello)
Virgin Classics 545 086 2

31 OCTOBER 1998
Rabbi Julia Neuberger

¶ Bellini, 'Casta diva' (from *Norma*, Act I), Maria Callas (Norma)/
Orchestra and Chorus of La Scala, Milan/Tullio Serafin
EMI CDM 763 091 2

¶ Haydn, Sonata in G minor, Hob XVI:44 (Allegretto), Andrew Wilde (Piano)
Collins Classics 30172
¶ Johann Strauss II, 'How Engaging, How Exciting' (from *Die Fledermaus*), Joan Sutherland (Rosalinde), Robert Gard (Eisenstein)/ Elizabethan Symphony Orchestra/Richard Bonynge
Decca 277D 1
¶ Leclair, Sonata for flute, viola da gamba and continuo in D major, Op. 2, No. 8 (fourth movement, Allegro assai), Badinage
Meridian CDE 84381
¶ Salamone de Rossi Ebreo, 'Baruch haba b'shem Adonai' (*Les Cantiques de Salomon*), Boston Camarata/Joel Cohen (director)
Harmonia Mundi HM 1901021
¶ Haydn, 'The Heavens are Telling' (from *The Creation*, Part I), Edith Mathis (Gabriel), Aldo Baldin (Uriel), Dietrich Fischer-Dieskau (Raphael)/Chorus and Academy of St Martin-in-the Fields/Neville Marriner
Philips 416 450 2
¶ Halévy, 'Eleazar's Song' (from *La juive*), Miriam Kramer (violin)/ Simon Over (piano)
ASV CD OS 6186
¶ Tom Phillips, 'Mine is the Life Song', Mary Wiegold (Soprano)/Mark van de Wiel (clarinet)
Largo 5138
¶ Schumann, 'Ich grolle nicht' (from *Dichterliebe*), Dietrich Fischer-Dieskau (baritone)/Christoph Eschenbach (piano)
DG 415 190 2

7 NOVEMBER 1998
Christopher Bruce, choreographer

¶ Schoenberg, 'Moondrunk' and 'Columbine' (Nos 1 and 2 from *Pierrot lunaire*), Lucy Shelton (soprano)/Da Capo Chamber Players
Bridge CD 9032
¶ Trad. arr. Incantation, 'Sikuriadas' and 'Ojos Azules' (Ghost Dances), Incantation
Cooking Vinyl COOK CD 69

❡ Handel, scenes 6 and 7 from Act II of *Agrippina*, Lisa Saffer (Poppea), Drew Minter (Ottone)/Capella Savaria/Nicholas McGegan Harmonia Mundi HMV 907064

❡ Dave Heath, 'Celtic Air' (from *The Four Elements*), BT Scottish Ensemble/Clio Gould (violin/director)
LINN CKD 073

❡ Mahler, 'Wenn dein Mütterlein tritt zur Tür herein' (from *Kindertotenlieder*), Dietrich Fischer-Dieskau (baritone)/Berlin Philharmonic Orchestra/Rudolf Kempe
EMI CDC 747 657 2

❡ Barry Guy, *Refrain, Chorale and Antiphon* (first section, 'After the Rain'), City of London Sinfonia/Richard Hickox
NMC NMC DO13S

❡ Trad., 'Barbara Allen', Mike Taylor (vocal)
Cooking Vinyl COOK CD 69

14 NOVEMBER 1998
Russell Hoban, writer

❡ Garbage, 'I'm Only Happy When It Rains', Garbage
Mushroom D 31450

❡ Donald Fragen arr. Paich, 'The Goodbye Look', Mel Tormé (vocals),The Party Paich Dek-Tette/Marty Paich
Concord Jazz CCD 4360

❡ McGhee/Terry, 'Freight Train', Sonny Terry and Brownie McGhee
Reactive Masters REA CD 510

❡ Monk, 'Round about Midnight', Sun-Ra and his Astro Infinity Arkestra/Hatty Randolph
Evidence ECD 22014 2

❡ Villoldo, 'El Choclo', Tita Merello
El Bandoneon EB CD 59

❡ Chopin, Mazurka in A minor, Op. 67, No. 4, Halina Czerny-Stefanska
MUZA PNCD 006

❡ Haydn, 'In the Beginning . . .' (from *The Creation*, Part I), Walter Berry (Raphael), Fritz Wunderlich (Uriel)/Vienna Singverein/Berlin Philharmonic Orchestra/Herbert von Karajan
DG 435 078 2

¶ Schubert, 'Der Leiermann' (from *Winterreise*), Dietrich
Fischer-Dieskau (baritone)/Alfred Brendel (piano)
Philips 411 463 2
¶ Carl Loewe, 'Tom der Reimer', Op. 135, Hermann Prey (baritone)/
Karl Enge (piano)
Philips 422 244 2

The Garbage was a particular delight and, for me, a discovery.

21 NOVEMBER 1998
Marina Mahler, interior designer

¶ Bach, Prelude No. 4 in C sharp minor (from *The Well-temperered
Clavier*, Book I), Glenn Gould (piano)
Sony Classical SM2K 52600
¶ Bach, Prelude No. 8 in E flat minor (from *The Well-temperered
Clavier*, Book I), Glenn Gould (piano)
Sony Classical SM2K 52600
¶ Wagner, extract from *Parsifal*, Act I, Arnold van Mill (Titurel),
George London (Amfortas)/Bayreuth Festival Orchestra/Hans
Knappertsbusch, rec. 1951
Teldec 9031 76047 2 B
¶ Bach, Partita No. 4 (second movement), Glenn Gould (piano)
Sony Classical M2K 52597/A
¶ Nono, '3 voci' (*Prometeo* Suite 1992), Berlin Philharmonic
Orchestra/Claudio Abbado
Sony Classical SK 53978

28 NOVEMBER 1998
Clive Swift, actor

¶ Berlioz, 'Le repos de la sainte famille' (from *L'enfance du Christ*),
Anthony Rolfe Johnson (narrator)/Monteverdi Choir/Lyon Opera
Orchestra/John Eliot Gardiner
Erato ECD 75335
¶ Chopin, Sonata in B minor, Op. 58 (first movement, Allegro
maestoso) Garrick Ohlsson (piano)
Arabesque Z6628
¶ Coates, 'Calling All Workers', The Victory Band
Empress RAJCD 819

¶ Richard Strauss, 'The Dinner' (from suite, *Le bourgeois gentilhomme*, Op. 60), Dresden Staatskapelle/Rudolf Kempe
EMI CDM 764349 2
¶ Trad., *Kol Nidrei*, Adolphe Attia (cantor)/Hervé Désarbre (organ)
Chant du Monde LDX 2741033
¶ Eric Ball, *Journey into Freedom*, John Foster Black Dyke Mills Band/
Major Peter Parkes
Chandos CHAN 4504
¶ Fauré arr. Bream, 'Mi-a-o' (from *Dolly Suite*, Op. 56), Julian Bream/
John Williams (guitars)
RCA 09026 61450 2

5 DECEMBER 1998
Gillian Moore, music educationalist and Artistic Director of the London Sinfonietta

¶ Burt Bacharach, 'Say a Little Prayer', Aretha Franklin
Virgin VTCD 80B
¶ Trad., *Tamuke* (Offering) for shakuhachi, Yoshikazu Iwamoto
(shakuhachi)
Continuum CCD 1013
¶ Ellington, 'Thanks for the Beautiful Land on the Delta' (*New Orleans Suite*), Duke Ellington Orchestra. Track features Harold Ashby (tenor saxophone), acc. Johnny Hodges, Russell Procope, Norris Turney
Atlantic 781376 2
¶ Ligeti, 'Movimento preciso e meccanico' (third movement of *Chamber Concerto*), London Sinfonietta/David Atherton
Decca 425 623 2
¶ Turnage, 'Junior Addict' (from *Blood on the Floor*), Martin Robertson (saxophone)/John Scofield (guitar)/Ensemble Modern/
Peter Rundel
Decca 455 292 2
¶ Purcell, 'The Frost Scene' (from *King Arthur*, Act III), Elisabeth Priday (Cupid), Stephen Varcoe (Cold Genius)/Monteverdi Choir (Chorus of Cold People)/English Baroque Soloists/John Eliot Gardiner
Erato ECD 88057
¶ Birtwistle, *The Mask of Orpheus*, Marie Angel (soprano), John Garrison (tenor)/BBC Symphony Orchestra/Andrew Davis
NMC NMCD 051

Armando Iannucci, journalist and actor

¶ Leiber/Stoller, 'Is That All There Is?', Peggy Lee
Connoisseur Collection VSOPCD 220
¶ John Adams, *Harmonium* (third movement, 'Wild Nights'), San
Francisco Symphony Orchestra and Chorus/Edo de Waart
ECM 821 465 2
¶ Nielsen, Symphony No. 5 (first movement), Royal Danish
Orchestra/Paavo Berglund
RCA RD 87884
¶ Tippett, 'How Can I Cherish my Man' and 'Steal Away' (from *A
Child of our Time*), Jessye Norman (soprano), Janet Baker (contralto),
Richard Cassilly (tenor), John Shirley-Quirk (bass)/BBC Singers/BBC
Choral Society/BBC Symphony Orchestra/Colin Davis
Philips 446 351 2
¶ P. D. Q. Bach, Madrigal 'My Bonnie Lass She Smelleth' (*The
Triumphs of Thusnelda*), Amateur Musica Antiqua of Hoople
Vanguard VSD 6536
¶ Bach, Sonata No. 1 in G minor, BWV 1001 (first movement, Adagio),
Nathan Milstein (violin)
DG 423 295 2
¶ Berg, Violin Concerto (finale, Adagio), Anne-Sophie Mutter (violin)/
Chicago Symphony Orchestra/James Levine
DG 437 093 2

Robert Craft, musician

¶ Stravinsky, *Three Japanese Lyrics*, Susan Narucki (soprano)/
Ensemble/Robert Craft
Music Masters 01612–67195–2
¶ Mozart, Serenade in B flat, K361 (finale), Members of the Columbia
Symphony Orchestra/Robert Craft
Sony SBK 62651
¶ Couperin, 'Incipit Lamentatio' and 'Quomodo sedet' (from *Leçons
des ténèbres*), Hugues Cuenod (tenor)/Daniel Pinkham
(harpsichord)/Alfred Zighera (cello)
Allegro ALX 3003

¶ Stravinsky, *Les noces* (1st tableau), Kate Winter (soprano), Linda Seymour (contralto), Parry Jones (tenor), Roy Henderson (baritone)/ BBC Chorus/Berkeley Mason, Leslie Heward, Ernest Lush, Edwin Benbow (pianos)/Percussion Ensemble/Igor Stravinsky
EMI CDS 754607 2
¶ Lassus, Kyrie (from Missa *Osculetur me*), Tallis Scholars/Peter Philips
Gimell CDGIM 018
¶ Beethoven, Symphony No. 5, Op. 67 (first movement, Allegro con brio), Berlin Philharmonic Orchestra/Wilhelm Furtwängler
Biddulph WHL 006
¶ Stravinsky, *Sektanskaya*, Rosalind Rees (soprano)/Elizabeth Mann (flute)/James Barnes (cimbalom)
Music Masters 01612–67195–2
¶ Mozart, Qui tollis (from Mass in C minor, K427), London Symphony Chorus/London Symphony Orchestra/Colin Davis
Philips 6500 235

26 DECEMBER 1998
'Lady Pilar Woffington' (a.k.a. John Sessions)

¶ Villa-Lobos, Aria from *Bachianas Brasileiras* No. 5, Arleen Augér (soprano)/The Yale Cellos/Aldo Parisot
Delos D/CD 3041
¶ Hunter/Garcia, 'Attics of My Life', The Grateful Dead
Warner 7599–27190 2
¶ Falla, 'Ritual Fire Dance' from *El amor brujo*, London Symphony Orchestra/Rafael Frühbeck de Burgos
IMP PCD 924
¶ Puccini, Introduction to *La fanciulla del West*, Orchestra of La Scala, Milan/Lorin Maazel
Sony Classical S2K 47189/A
¶ Wagner, Overture to *Der fliegende Holländer*, Berlin Philharmonic Orchestra/Seiji Ozawa
Philips 426 271 2
¶ Puccini, end of Act II of *Tosca*, Mirella Freni (Tosca)/Samuel Ramey Scarpia)/Philharmonia/Giuseppe Sinopoli
DG 431 777 2

♪ J. J. Cale, 'Cocaine', Eric Clapton (and band)
RSO Polydor 821 939 2

2 JANUARY 1999
Brian Rix, former actor and theatre manager

♪ Gene Roland, 'Exit Stage Left', Stan Kenton and his Orchestra
Capitol T 1985
♪ Jerome Kern, 'Ol' Man River' (from *Showboat*), Paul Robeson/
Mississippi Chorus/Drury Lane Theatre Orchestra/Herman Finck
World Records SH 240
♪ Gilbert/Sullivan, 'Painted Emblems', 'Ghosts', 'High Noon' (from
Ruddigore), John Reed (Sir Ruthven Murgatroyd), Donald Adams
(Sir Roderic Murgatroyd)/D'Oyly Carte Chorus/Orchestra of the
Royal Opera House/Isidore Godfrey
London 417 355–2
♪ Tchaikovsky, *Andante cantabile*, Op. 11, English String
Orchestra/William Boughton
Nimbus NI 7009
♪ Zamfir, 'Doina de Jale', Gheorghe Zamfir (panpipes)/Marcel Cellier
(organ)
Laserlight 15117
♪ Mahler, Symphony No. 3 (opening), London Symphony
Orchestra/Jascha Horenstein
Unicorn UKCD 2006
♪ Walter Donaldson, 'Makin' Whoopee', Count Basie and his Orchestra
Saga EROS 8131
♪ Tommy Watt, 'Crumpets for the Count', Tommy Watt and his
Orchestra
Parlophone PMC 1107

Very touching, talking about problems related to mental health.

9 JANUARY 1999
Gita Mehta, writer

♪ Trad., 'Raga Yaman', Bismillan Khan (shehnai)
EMI CD PMLP 5568
♪ *Gita Govinda* (scene II), Ragunath Panigrahi (vocal)
Auvidis A 6152

¶ Trad., 'Raga Sindhu Bhairati', Ravi Shankar (sitar)/Ali Akbar Khan (sarod)/Alla Rakha (tabla)
Apple 853 817 2
¶ Haydn, String Quartet in B flat major, Op. 76, No. 4 (first movement, Allegro), Amadeus Quartet
DG 415 869 2
¶ Nina Simone, 'Sugar in my Bowl', Nina Simone
RCA BMG 07863 66307 2
¶ Trad., 'Teré Biné', Nusrat Fateh Ali Khan (vocal)
Real World 78 62212
¶ Trad., 'Raga Yaman', Vilayat Khan (sitar)
EMI CD PMLP 5568
¶ Trad., 'Raga Lathangi', Balamurali Krishnan (vocal)
Moment MRCD 1015

Rather as with John Bird and contemporary music, this gave an irresistible glimpse into Indian music, narrated with such ebullient enthusiasm that the nature of the Rag and the staggering gifts of the best performers suddenly seemed blindingly obvious.

16 JANUARY 1999
John Burningham, illustrator and writer

¶ La Rocca/Shields, 'At the Jazz Band Ball', Bix Beiderbecke and his Gang, rec. 1927
Flapper PASTCD 9765
¶ Mozart, 'Deh, vieni all' finestra' (from *Don Giovanni*, Act II), Ingvar Wixell (Don Giovanni)/Orchestra of the Royal Opera House/Colin Davis
Philips 422 816 2
¶ Schubert arr. Liszt, *Erlkönig* S557a, Leslie Howard (piano)
Hyperion CDA 66953
¶ Donaudy, 'O del mio amato ben', Beniamino Gigli (tenor)/Orchestra da Camera, Milan/Ruggero Ricci
EMI CDH 763 392 2
¶ Bach, Prelude to Suite No. 3 for cello in C, BWV 1009, Janos Starker (cello)
Philips 416 606 2

♪ Olivieri/Poterat, 'J'attendrai', Tino Rossi/Orchestra directed by
Marcel Cariven, rec. 1938
EMI CDP 799102 2
♪ Trad., 'The Coolin', Felix Doran (Irish pipes)
Topic 12T 288
♪ Rossini, 'Una voce poco fa' (from *The Barber of Seville*, Act I), Luisa
Tetrazzini (Rosina)/unknown orchestra (rec. 1911)
Pearl Gemm CD 9224
♪ Consuelo Velasquez, 'Besame mucho', Quentin Verdu and his
Orchestra
Pathé PA 2222 CBT 5931
♪ Richard Strauss, 'Night', 'Sunrise', 'The Ascent' (from *An Alpine
Symphony*), Berlin Philharmonic Orchestra/Herbert von Karajan
DG 439 017 2

23 JANUARY 1999
John Fuller, poet and academic

[♪ John Fuller, Concerto for Double Bass, John Fuller
Recorded live]
♪ Shostakovich, String Quartet No. 8 in C minor, Op. 110 (fourth
movement, Largo), Duke Quartet
Collins 14502
♪ Poulenc, Trio (first movement, Presto), Francis Poulenc (piano)/
Pierre Pierlot (oboe)/Maurice Allard (bassoon)
Adès 202522
♪ Prokofiev, Piano Concerto No. 4 in B flat, Op. 53 (first movement,
Vivace), Vladimir Ashkenazy (piano)/London Symphony
Orchestra/André Previn
Decca 425 570–2
[♪ John Fuller, Trio, John Fuller
Recorded live]
♪ Bill Russo, 'Gazelle', Shelly Manne and his Men
Original Jazz Classics OJCCD 152–2
♪ Szymanowski, Violin Concerto No. 2, Op. 61 (third movement,
Andantino), Thomas Zehetmair (violin)/City of Birmingham
Symphony Orchestra/Simon Rattle
EMI CDC 555607 2

♪ Stravinsky, Violin Concerto (third movement, Aria II), Isaac Stern (violin)/Columbia Symphony Orchestra/Igor Stravinsky
Sony SMK 46295
♪ Britten, 'Calypso' (from *Cabaret Songs*), Jill Gomez (soprano)/ Martin Jones (piano)
Unicorn-Kanchana DKPCD 9138
♪ Lutyens, 'As I Walked Out One Evening', Anthony Rolfe Johnson (tenor)/Graham Johnson (piano)
Hyperion CDA 66709

A poet I rather treasure and one whose verse is endlessly informed by music.

30 JANUARY 1999
Tom Phillips, painter, writer

♪ Wagner, extract from Act III, scene 2 of *Götterdämmerung*, Wolfgang Windgassen (Siegfried)/Vienna Philharmonic Orchestra/Georg Solti
Decca 455 555 2
♪ Birtwistle, part of 1st and 2nd Lullabyes (from *Gawain*), Marie Angel (Morgan le Fay)/François le Roux (Gawain)/Orchestra of the Royal Opera House/Elgar Howarth
Collins Classics 70412 A/B
♪ Riley, *In C*, Members of the Center of the Creative and Performing Arts in the State University of New York at Buffalo/Terry Riley (Leader and Saxophone)
Edsel EDCD 314
♪ John Cage, Sonata 1 (*Sonatas and Interludes*), John Tilbury (prepared piano)
Decca HEAD 9
♪ Brahms, 'Denn alles Fleisch es ist wie Gras' (from *A German Requiem*, Op. 45), Philharmonia and Chorus/Otto Klemperer
EMI CDC 747 238 2
♪ Dvořák, String Quartet in F, Op. 96, 'American', Hungarian Quartet
Nixa CLP 1157
♪ Verdi, end of Act III of *Otello*, Ramón Vinay (Otello), Giuseppe Valdengo (Iago), Herva Nelli (Desdemona)/NBC Symphony Orchestra/Toscanini
RCA VICS 6120

❡ Schultze/Leip, 'Lili Marlene', Marlene Dietrich
EMI CDP 796 450 278
❡ Bach, final chorus from *St Matthew Passion*, Monteverdi Choir/
London Oratory Junior Choir/English Baroque Soloists/John Eliot
Gardiner
Archiv 427 648 2

6 FEBRUARY 1999
Sir Humphrey Maud, former diplomat

❡ Schubert, Sonata in A, D664 (second movement, Andante), Claudio
Arrau (piano)
Philips 432 344 2
❡ Piazzolla, 'Milonga' in D, Tomas Tichauer (viola)/Monica Cosachov
(piano)
Intramuros IRCO 227
❡ Bach, Bourrées I and II (from Suite No. 3 in C, BWV 1009), Pablo
Casals (cello)
EMI CDH 761028 2
❡ Purcell, Fantasia No. 1, Serenata of London
Carlton 30367 00032
❡ Pärt, *Cantus in Memory of Benjamin Britten*, Stuttgart State
Orchestra/Dennis Russell Davis
ECM 1275
❡ Davis/Silver, 'Chasing Shadows', Django Reinhardt (guitar)/Stephane
Grappelli (violin)/Quintet of the Hot Club of France, rec. 1935
Charly CPCD 8312 2
❡ Smith/Balcom, 'You've Been a Good Ole Wagon', Bessie Smith
(vocals)/Louis Armstrong (cornet)/Fred Longshaw (piano), rec. 1925
CBS 463339 2
❡ Mozart, String Quintet in G minor, K516 (first movement, Allegro),
Arthur Grumiaux, Arpad Gérecz (violins)/Georges Janzer, Max
Lesueur (violas)/Eva Czako (cello)
Philips 422 511 2

13 FEBRUARY 1999
Jo Shapcott, poet

[❡ Jo Shapcott, 'My Life Asleep', Jo Shapcott
recorded live during session]

❡ James MacMillan, *Tryst* (opening), BBC Scottish Symphony Orchestra/Jerzy Maksymiuk
Koch 3–1050–2
❡ Trad., Bubaran Hudan Mas, Pura Paku Alaman, Jogyakarta/K. R. T. Wasitodinin
Nonesuch 7559 72044–2
[❡ Jo Shapcott, 'The Mad Cow Talks Back', Jo Shapcott recorded live during session]
❡ John Adams, 'Hoe-down' (Mad Cow) (from *Gnarly Buttons*), Michael Collins (clarinet)/London Sinfonietta/John Adams
Nonesuch 7559 79465–2
❡ Bach, Canon circularis per tonos (from *A Musical Offering*, BWV 1079), Academy of St-Martin-in-the-Fields/Neville Marriner
Philips 442 556–2
❡ Prokofiev, Sonata No. 2 in D minor, Op. 14 (last movement, Vivace), Sviatoslav Richter (piano)
Praga PR 250 015
❡ Keith Jarrett, *My Song*, Keith Jarrett (piano)/Jan Garbarek (saxophone)/Palle Danilsson (bass)/Jon Christensen (drums)
ECM 821 406–2
❡ Trad., 'Torre del Viento', Remedios Amaya
EMI 72434 96166 2
❡ Britten, *Hymn to St Cecilia* (first part), Choir of King's College, Cambridge/David Willcocks
EMI CDM 764653–2
❡ Finzi, 'Wonder' (from *Dies natalis*), Wilfred Brown (tenor)/English Chamber Orchestra/Christopher Finzi
EMI CDM 565588 2

20 FEBRUARY 1999
Bernard Williams, philosopher

❡ Elgar, 'Repent and Be Baptized' (from *The Kingdom*, Part III), John Shirley-Quirk (St Peter)/London Philharmonic Choir and Orchestra/Adrian Boult
EMI CDM 764 210 2
❡ Mozart, Duo No. 1, K423 (third movement, Rondeau: Allegro), Itzhak Perlman (violin)/Pinchas Zukerman (viola)
RCA RD 60735

❡ Bach, Sarabande and Bourrée (from English Suite No. 1 in A major, BQV 806), András Schiff (piano)
Decca 421 641 2
❡ Debussy, Act II, scene 1 from *Pelléas et Mélisande*, François le Roux (Pelléas)/Maria Ewing (Mélisande)/Vienna Philharmonic Orchestra/Claudio Abbado
DG 435 345 2
❡ Berg, *Altenberglieder*, Juliane Banse (soprano)/Vienna Philharmonic Orchestra/Claudio Abbado
DG 447 749 2
❡ Richard Strauss, 'Zueignung', Op. 10 (Nos. 1–8), Lucia Popp (soprano)/Wolfgang Sawallisch (piano)
EMI CDC 749 318 2

Had longed to talk to this remarkable thinker about music and was not disappointed. Sadly he died soon after the recording.

27 FEBRUARY 1999
Philip Hensher, writer

❡ Adès, 'Fancy Aria' (from *Powder Her Face*, Act I), Valdine Anderson (Waitress)/Almeida Ensemble/Thomas Adès
EMI CDS 556649 2
❡ Stravinsky, 'First Pas de Trois' (from *Agon*), Los Angeles Festival Symphony Orchestra/Igor Stravinsky
Sony SM3K 46292
❡ Schoenberg, 'Premonitions' (No. 1 from *Five Pieces for Orchestra*, Op. 16), City of Birmingham Symphony Orchestra/Simon Rattle
EMI CDC 749857 2
❡ Fatboy Slim, 'Praise You', Fatboy Slim
Brassic Brassic11CD
❡ Busoni, Sonatina No. 1, Paul Jacobs (piano)
Nonesuch H 71359
❡ Weill, 'Bilbao-Song' (from *Happy End*), Gisella May/Orchestra/Heinz Rögner
Berlin Classics BC 2069–2
❡ Nørgård, Symphony No. 2 (conclusion), Danish National Radio Symphony Orchestra/Leif Segerstam
Chandos CHAN 9450

¶ Wolf, 'Heb' auf dein blondes Haupt' (from *Italian Songbook*), Peter Schreier (tenor)/Graham Johnson (piano)
Hyperion CDA 66760

Hardly surprising that he should include part of Powder Her Face, *for which he wrote the mischievous libretto. Since the opera was performed in my first year running the Cheltenham Festival, I too have a soft spot for it. As always a highly intelligent 'take' on the music.*

6 MARCH 1999
Adrian Noble, theatre director

¶ Keith Jarrett, The Cologne Concert, 1975, Part I, Keith Jarrett (piano)
ECM 810 067 2
¶ Monteverdi, 'Lament' (from *Il ritorno d'Ulisse in patria*), Trudeliese Schmidt (Penelope)/Monteverdi-Ensemble Opernhaus Zürich/ Nikolaus Harnoncourt
Teldec 8.35807/B
¶ Beethoven, 'Mir ist so wunderbar' (from *Fidelio*, Act I), Helen Donath (Marzelline), Helga Dernesch (Leonore), Karl Riddersbusch (Rocco), Horst R. Laubenthal (Jaquino)/Berlin Philharmonic Orchestra/Herbert von Karajan
CDM 763 077 2
¶ Bernstein, Psalm 23 (from *Chichester Psalms*), John Bogart (alto)/ Camerata Singers/New York Philharmonic Orchestra/Leonard Bernstein
Sony Classical SM3K 47162/B
¶ Bach, 'Erbarme dich' (from *St Matthew Passion*), Michael Chance (alto)/Elizabeth Wilcock (violin)/English Baroque Soloists/John Eliot Gardiner
Archiv 427 650 2
¶ Shaun Davey, *The Winter's End* (adapted from score for RSC production of *A Winter's Tale*), Ensemble featuring Liam O'Flynn (Uilleann pipes) and Matthew Manning (oboe and cor anglais)
Tara TARACD 3031
¶ Mozart, 'Signor guardate un poco' and 'Prayer trio' (from *Don Giovanni*, Act I), Maria Ewing (Donna Elvira), Carol Vaness (Donna Anna), Keith Lewis (Don Ottavio)/London Philharmonic Orchestra/Bernard Haitink
EMI CDS 747 038 2

❡ Purcell, Chaconne (from *The Fairy Queen*, Act V), Les Arts
Florissants/William Christie
Harmonia Mundi HM 901 309

13 MARCH 1999
Sir Jimmy Disprin (a.k.a. John Sessions)

❡ Rodgers/Hammerstein, 'There is Nothing Like a Dame' (from *South Pacific*), Ken Darby Male Chorus/original soundtrack recording
RCD ND 83681
❡ Richard Strauss, trio from Act III of *Der Rosenkavalier*, Anna Tomawa-Sintow (Marschallin), Agnes Baltsa (Octavian), Janet Perry (Sophie)/Vienna Philharmonic Orchestra/Herbert von Karajan
DG 423 853 2
❡ Mozart, 'In uomini, sin soldati sperare fedelta?' (from *Così fan tutte*, Act I), Cecilia Bartoli (Despina)/Vienna Chamber Orchestra/György Fischer
Decca 443 452 2
❡ Walton, 'Agincourt Song' (from *Henry V*), Philharmonia and Chorus/Sir William Walton (1946)
EMI CDH 565007 2
❡ Britten, opening of *Billy Budd*, Peter Pears (Edward Fairfax Vere)/London Symphony Orchestra/Benjamin Britten
London 417 429 2
❡ Vaughan Williams, Overture, *The Wasps*, London Symphony Orchestra/André Previn
RCA GD 87830
❡ Flanders/Swann, 'The Hippopotamus Song', Michael Flanders/Donald Swann
Parlophone CDP 797 465 2

20 MARCH 1999
Ursula Owen, publisher

❡ Verdi, 'Ah! si maledetto, sospetto fatale' (from *Don Carlo*), Boris Christoff (Filippo II), Elena Nicolai (Principessa d'Eboli), Tito Gobbi (Rodrigo), Antonietta Stella (Elisabetta di Valois)/Orchestra of Rome Opera/Gabriele Santini
EMI CMS 764642 2

♪ Schubert, 'Nacht und Träume' D827, Teresa Stich-Randall (soprano)/
Jacqueline Bonneau (piano)
Accord 201 452
♪ Lambert, *The Rio Grande* (opening), Della Jones (mezzo-soprano)/
Kathryn Stott (piano)/BBC Singers/BBC Concert Orchestra/Barry
Wordsworth
Argo 436 118–2
♪ Wagner arr. Caine, Liebestod (from *Tristan und Isolde*), Uri Caine
Ensemble
Winter and Winter 910 013–2
♪ Kern, 'The Folks who Live on the Hill', Peggy Lee/Orchestra/Frank
Sinatra
MFP CD-MFP 5878
♪ Messiaen, Louange à l'Éternité de Jésus (from *Quartet for the End of
Time*), Étienne Pasquier (cello)/Olivier Messiaen (piano)
Musidisc RC 719
♪ Richard Strauss, 'Morgen', Op. 27, No. 4, Dame Janet Baker (mezzo-
soprano)/Gerald Moore (piano)
EMI CDM 565009 2
♪ Haydn, Piano Trio No. 18 in E, Hob.XV: 28 (second movement,
Allegretto), Beaux Arts Trio
Philips 420 790–2

27 MARCH 1999
David Lodge, novelist and academic

♪ Trad. arr. Aretha Franklin, 'Going Down Slow' (from *Aretha Arrives*),
Aretha Franklin/Orchestra directed by Tom Dowd and Arif Mardin
RHINO 8122 71274 2
♪ Geoffrey Burgon, 'Young Martin in Love' (from music for *Martin
Chuzzlewit*), Alan Merrick Orchestra/Geoffrey Burgon
Destiny Music DMUSCD 107
♪ John Lewis, 'Django', Modern Jazz Quartet
Prestige OJCD 057 2
♪ Rodrigo, arr. Gil Evans, 'Concerto de Aranjuez' (from *Sketches of
Spain*), Miles Davis/Orchestra conducted by Gil Evans
CBS 460604

❦ Previn, 'The Five of Us (A Different Kind of Blues)', Itzhak Perlman (violin)/André Previn (piano)/Shelly Manne (drums)/Jim Hall (guitar)/Red Mitchell (bass)
EMI ASD 3965
❦ Van Morrison, 'Slim Slow Slider' (from *Astral Weeks*), Van Morrison (vocals/guitar)/Richard Davis (bass)/John Payne (soprano saxophone)
Warner K 246024
❦ Ravel, *Pavane pour une infante défunte*, Ulster Orchestra/Yan Pascal Tortelier
Chandos CHAN 9202
❦ Victoria, Motet: *O quam gloriosum*, Westminster Cathedral Choir/ David Hill
Hyperion CDA 66114

3 APRIL 1999
David Suchet, actor

❦ Vivaldi, Concerto for four guitars in B minor, RV 580 (fourth movement, Allegro), Los Romeros (guitars)/San Antonio Symphony Orchestra/Victor Alessandro
Philips 426 076–2
❦ Orff, 'O Fortuna' (from *Carmina Burana*), New Philharmonia Chorus and Orchestra/Rafael Frühbeck de Burgos
HMV 5 72156 2
❦ Mozart, 'Soave sia il vento' (from *Così fan tutte*, Act I), Kiri te Kanawa (Fiordiligi), Frederica von Stade (Dorabella), Jules Bastin(Don Alfonso)/Strasbourg Philharmonic Orchestra/Alain Lombard
Erato 2292–45683–2
❦ Saint-Saëns, Symphony No. 3, Op. 78 (conclusion), Imrich Szabo (organ)/CSR Symphony Orchestra of Bratislava/Stephen Gunzenhauser
Naxos 8.550138
❦ Salieri, Piano Concerto in C (third movement, Andantino), Pietro Spada (piano)/Philharmonia
ASV CDDCA 955
❦ Rachmaninov, Piano Concerto No. 1 (second movement, Andante), Sergei Rachmaninov (piano)/Philadelphia Orchestra/Eugene Ormandy
RCA 09026 612652

¶ Mozart, Clarinet Concerto, K.622 (second movement, Adagio),
Alfred Prinz (clarinet)/Vienna Philharmonic Orchestra/Karl
Böhm
DG 413 552–2
¶ Weber, *Grand Duo Concertant*, Op. 48 (finale, Rondo: Allegro), Janet
Hilton (clarinet)/Keith Swallow (piano)
Chandos CHAN 8366

10 APRIL 1999
Vikram Seth, writer

¶ Brian Wilson/Mike Love, 'Fun, Fun, Fun', The Beach Boys
Capitol CDP 746324 2
¶ Recording of nightingale and muntjac
British Trust for Ornithology
¶ Alec Roth, Duet between Arion and the Dolphin (from *Arion and
the Dolphin*), Richard Chew (Arion), Claire Bradshaw (Dolphin)/
East of England Orchestra/Nicholas Kok
Artist's special recording
¶ Weber, Clarinet Quintet in B flat, Op. 134 (third movement,
Menuetto), Mobius
EMI CDZ 573162 2
¶ Vivaldi, Manchester Sonata No. 1 in C (third movement, Largo),
Romanesca
Harmonia Mundi HMU 907089
¶ Schubert, 'Erster Verlust', D226, Ian Bostridge (tenor)/Julius Drake
(piano)
EMI CDC 556347 2
¶ Schubert, 'Der Kreuzzug', D932, Dietrich Fischer-Dieskau
(baritone)/Gerald Moore (piano)
Orfeo C 140101 A
¶ Trad., 'Raga Marwa', Ram Narayan (sarangi)/Subhash Chandra
(tabla)
Music Today CDA 91009
¶ Bach, 'Am Abend, da es kühle war' (from *St Matthew Passion*),
Dietrich Fischer-Dieskau (baritone)/Munich Bach Orchestra/Karl
Richter
Archiv 439 338–2

¶ Bach, Contrapunctus I (from *The Art of Fugue*), Paolo Borciani, Elisa Pegreffi (violins)/Tomasso Poggi (viola)/Luca Simoncini (cello)
Nuova Era 6744

Have sung Schubert with Vikram at the piano. Definitely not for broadcast!

17 APRIL 1999
Jonathan Rée, philosopher

¶ Janáček, *Osud*, Philip Langridge (Zivny)/Orchestra and Chorus of Welsh National Opera/Charles Mackerras
EMI CDC 749993 2
¶ Schubert, String Quartet in B flat, D112 (finale, Presto), Takács Quartet
Hungaroton HCD 12390–2
¶ Rousseau, 'J'ai perdu tout mon bonheur' (from *Le devin du village*), Danièle Borst (Colette)/Collegium Academicum of Geneva/Philippe Corboz
CBS 76716
¶ Britten, Canticle 2, *Abraham and Isaac* (conclusion), Anthony Rolfe Johnson (tenor)/Michael Chance (countertenor)/Roger Vignoles (piano)
Hyperion CDA 66498
¶ Mozart, 'Ich bin die erste Sängerin' (from *Der Schauspieldirektor*), Arleen Augér (Mademoiselle Silberklang), Reri Grist (Madame Herz), Peter Schreier (Monsieur Vogelsang)/Staatskapelle Dresden/Karl Böhm
DG 419 566–2
¶ Reicha, Quintet in A minor, Op. 100, No. 5 (second movement, Andante con variazioni), Michael Thompson Wind Quintet
Naxos 8.550432
¶ Wolf, 'Bei einer Trauung' (from *Mörike-Lieder*), Olaf Bär (baritone)/Geoffrey Parsons (piano)
EMI CDC 749054 2
¶ Schubert, 'Erlkönig', Thomas Quasthoff (baritone)/Charles Spencer (piano)
RCA 09026 61864 2

♪ H. J. Bach/Axelson arr. H. Frommermann, 'Kannst du pfeifen, Johanna', Comedian Harmonists
Via Media 16 173/2

24 APRIL 1999
Amelia Freedman, director and founder of the Nash Ensemble

♪ Neal Hefti, 'The Kid from Red Bank', Count Basie and his Orchestra
Vogue 600008
♪ Schubert, Trio in B flat, D898 (second movement, Andante un poco mosso), Alfred Cortot (piano)/Jacques Thibaud (violin)/Pablo Casals (cello)
EMI CDH 761024 2
♪ Fauré, 'Une sainte en son auréole' and 'Puisque l'aube grandit' (from La bonne chanson), Sarah Walker (mezzo-soprano)/Nash Ensemble
CRD 3389
♪ Brahms, Clarinet Quintet in B minor, Op. 115 (third movement, Andantino), Gervase de Peyer (clarinet)/Melos Ensemble
EMI CDM 763116 2
♪ Simon Holt, 'Eyes, to the Shadow' (from Canciones), Fiona Kimm (mezzo-soprano)/Nash Ensemble/Lionel Friend
NMC NMCD 008
♪ Debussy, 'Jeux de vagues' (from La mer), Cleveland Orchestra/ Pierre Boulez
DG 439 896−2
♪ Weill, 'My Ship' (from Lady in the Dark), Anne Sofie von Otter (mezzo-soprano)/NDR Symphony Orchestra/John Eliot Gardiner
DG 439 894−2
♪ Stein/Sondheim, 'Everything's Coming Up Roses' (from Gypsy), Ethel Merman/Orchestra/Milton Rosenstock
Columbia CK 32607

1 MAY 1999
Peter Porter, poet

[♪ Porter, 'A Brahms Intermezzo', Peter Porter (piano)
recorded during session]

❡ Josquin Desprez, 'Miserere mei, Deus' (conclusion), La Chapelle Royale/Philippe Herreweghe
Harmonia Mundi HM 901243
[❡ Schiller trans. Porter, 'The Gods of Greece', Peter Porter (reader) recorded during session]
❡ Schubert, 'Die Götter Griechenlands', Dietrich Fischer-Dieskau (baritone)/Karl Engel (piano)
EMI CDS 565670 2
❡ Bach, 'Schmücke dich, o liebe Seele', BWV 654, Helmut Walcha (Silbermann organ of St-Pierre-le-Jeune, Strasbourg)
Archiv 419 904-2
❡ Britten, 'Since She Whom I Loved' (from *Holy Sonnets of John Donne*), Peter Pears (tenor)/Benjamin Britten (piano)
EMI CDC 754605 2
❡ Vaughan Williams, Symphony No. 5 (first movement, Preludio: Moderato), London Philharmonic Orchestra/Adrian Boult
EMI CDC 747214 2
❡ Richard Strauss, *Die Frau ohne Schatten* (conclusion of Act I), Paul Schoeffler (Barak), Alfred Poell, Eberhard Wächter, Ljubomir Pantscheff (Watchmen)/Vienna Philharmonic Orchestra/Karl Böhm
Decca 425 981-2
❡ Stravinsky, 'The Sun is Bright' (from *The Rake's Progress*, Act I), Mack Harrell (Nick Shadow)/Chorus and Orchestra of the Metropolitan Opera/Igor Stravinsky
Philips ABL 3056
❡ Mozart, 'Seid uns zum zweiten Mal willkommen' (from *The Magic Flute*, Act II), Frank Höher, Michael Diedrich, Friedemann Klos (boys)/Staatskapelle Dresden/Colin Davis
Philips 411 459-2

This man had music coming out of his ears. Would make a great music critic.

8 MAY 1999
Susan Hill, writer

❡ Parry, *I Was Glad*, Choir of King's College, Cambridge/Cambridge University Musical Society/New Philharmonia Orchestra/Band of the Royal Military School of Music, Kneller Hall/Philip Ledger
EMI CDZ 762 528 2

♪ Elgar, 'Where Corals Lie' (from *Sea Pictures*, Op. 37), Janet Baker (mezzo-soprano)/London Symphony Orchestra/John Barbirolli
EMI CDC 556 219 2
♪ Schubert, 'Danksagung an den Bach' (from *Die schöne Müllerin*), Peter Pears (tenor)/Benjamin Britten (piano)
Decca 436 201 2
♪ Britten, 'Storm' (from *Four Sea Interludes from Peter Grimes*), Orchestra of the Royal Opera House/Benjamin Britten
Decca 414 578 2
♪ Lennox Berkeley, 'How Love Came In', Peter Pears (tenor)/Benjamin Britten (piano)
Eclipse ECS 545
♪ Bellini, Concertino for Oboe in E flat major (last movement, Allegro polonese), Nicholas Daniel (oboe/director)/Peterborough String
Helios CDH 88014
♪ Handel, 'Lord, I Trust Thee', Christ Church Cathedral Choir, Oxford/ Stephen Farr (organ)/Stephen Darlington (director)
Nimbus NI 5440
♪ Vaughan Williams, 'Bright is the Ring of Words', Benjamin Luxon (baritone)/David Willison (piano)
Chandos CHAN 8475
♪ Mozart, 'Der Vogelfänger bin ich ja' (from *The Magic Flute*, Act I), Dietrich Fischer-Dieskau (Papageno)/Berlin RIAS Symphony Orchestra/Ferenc Fricsay
DG 435 742 2
♪ Walford Davies, 'God Be in My Head', Choir of King's College, Cambridge/Stephen Cleobury (director)
Decca 460 021 2
♪ Britten, 'When You're Feeling Like Expressing Your Affection', Ian Bostridge (tenor)/Graham Johnson (piano)
Hyperion CDA 66823

15 MAY 1999
Sam West, actor and theatre director

♪ Haydn Wood, 'Roses of Picardy', Derek Oldham (tenor)/Orchestra
HMV CDHMV 3
♪ Brian Eno/David Byrne, 'The Jezebel Spirit', Brian Eno, David Byrne
EG EGCD 48

¶ Mussorgsky orch. Shostakovich, 'Serenade' (from *Songs and Dances of Death*), Sergei Leiferkus (baritone)/Royal Philharmonic Orchestra/ Yuri Temirkanov
RCA RD 60195
¶ Stravinsky, 'Mysterious Circles of Young Girls' and 'Glorification of the Chosen Victim' (from *The Rite of Spring*), Columbia Symphony Orchestra/Igor Stravinsky
Sony SM3K 46291
¶ Thelonius Monk, 'Raise Four', Thelonius Monk (piano)/Larry Gales (bass)/Ben Riley (drums)
CBS 460066
¶ Bach, Suite No. 3 in C, BWV 1009 (fourth movement, Sarabande), Ralph Kirshbaum (cello)
Virgin VCD 545086 2
¶ Knussen, 'When I Heard the Learn'd Astronomer' (from *Whitman Settings*, Op. 25), Lucy Shelton (soprano)/Peter Serkin (piano)
Virgin VC 759308 2
¶ Mendelssohn, Octet in E flat, Op. 20 (first movement, Allegro moderato, ma con fuoco), Academy Chamber Ensemble
Philips 420 400–2
¶ Ravel, Piano Trio in A minor (third movement, Passacaille), Borodin Trio
Chandos CHAN 8458

22 MAY 1999
Brian Sewell, art critic, journalist

¶ Richard Strauss, 'Beim Schlafengehen' (from *Four Last Songs*), Gundula Janowitz (soprano)/Berlin Philharmonic Orchestra/ Herbert von Karajan
DG 423 888–2
¶ Mussorgsky, 'Coronation Scene' (from *Boris Godunov*), Paris Russian Chorus/French National Radio Orchestra/Issay Dobrowen
EMI CHS 565192 2
¶ Purcell, 'The Blessed Virgin's Expostulation', April Cantelo (soprano)/George Malcolm (harpsichord)
Top Rank XRK 508

¶ Messiaen, 'Transports de joie' (from *L'ascension*), Olivier Messiaen (Organ of La Trinité, Paris)
EMI CZS 767400 2
¶ Verdi, 'Ah, veglia, O Donna' (from *Rigoletto*), Amelita Galli-Curci (Gilda), Giuseppe de Luca (Rigoletto)/Metropolitan Opera Orchestra/ Giulio Setti
Conifer CDHD 201
¶ Wagner, *Lohengrin* (conclusion), Astrid Varnay (Ortrud), Jess Thomas (Lohengrin)/Bayreuth Festival Chorus and Orchestra/ Wolfgang Sawallisch
Philips 446 337–2
¶ Schubert, 'Ganymed,' D544, Ian Partridge (tenor)/Jennifer Partridge (piano)
Enigma VAR 1019
¶ Bellini, 'Adalgisa, Alma constanza' (from *Norma*), Maria Callas (Norma), Ebe Stignani (Adalgisa)/Orchestra of La Scala, Milan/ Tullio Serafin
EMI CDS 747304 8

29 MAY 1999
Kenny Werner, jazz musician

¶ Elliott Carter, *Fragment for String Quartet* (1994), Arditti String Quartet
Montaigne MO 782091
¶ Schoenberg, *Five Orchestral Pieces*, Op. 16 (Nos 4 and 5), City of Birmingham Symphony Orchestra/Simon Rattle
EMI CDC 749 857 2
¶ Keith Jarrett, 'Landscape for Future Earth' (from album *Facing You*), Keith Jarrett (piano)
ECM 827 132 2
¶ Kenny Werner, 'Kandinsky/Back to Light' (from *Paintings*), Kenny Werner (keyboards) and band
Pioneer PICJ 1101
¶ Ravel, *Boléro*, Orchestre du Capitole de Toulouse/Michel Plasson
EMI CDC 747 648 2
¶ Beethoven, String Quartet, Op. 131 (first movement, Adagio), Végh Quartet
Valois V 4408

¶ Django Bates, 'Early Bloomer' (from *Winter Truce and Homes Blaze*), Django Bates/Delightful Precipice
JMT 514 023 2
¶ John Kander/Fred Ebb arr. Django Bates, 'New York, New York', Christine Tobin (vocals)/Django Bates and Human Chain/featuring Iain Ballamy (tenor saxophone)
JMT 514 023 2

Incredible ability to communicate, which must be why he is such a revered teacher as well as keyboard player and composer.

5 JUNE 1999
Mavis Cheek, novelist

¶ Brahms, 'Selig sind, die da Leid tragen' (opening of *A German Requiem*, Op. 45), New England Conservatory Chorus/Boston Symphony Orchestra/Erich Leinsdorf
RCA GD 86800
¶ C. Conrad/H. Magidson, 'The Continental', Fred Astaire
Dejavu
¶ Sondheim, 'Send in the Clowns' (from *A Little Night Music*), Judi Dench/Royal National Theatre production/Orchestra/Jo Stewart
TRING TRING 001
¶ Puccini, 'Te Deum' (from *Tosca*, Act I), Tito Gobbi (Scarpia), Renato Ercolani (Spoletta)/Choirs of the Théâtre National de l'Opéra/Orchestre de la Société des Concerts du Conservatoire/Georges Prêtre
EMI CDM 769 975 2
¶ Puccini, 'Mimì's Death Scene' (from *La bohème*, Act IV), Katia Ricciarelli (Mimì), José Carreras (Rodolfo)/Orchestra of the Royal Opera House/Colin Davis
Philips 416 494 2
¶ Shostakovich, Symphony No. 5 (first movement), London Symphony Orchestra/André Previn
RCA GD 86801
¶ Easter Mattins, Bells of the Monastery and Procession, Monastic Choir of Holy Trinity/St Sergius Monastery (Zagorsk)/Archemandite Matthew
Ikon Records CIKO 11

❡ Mozart, Piano Concerto No. 21 in C, K467 (second movement, Andante), Annie Fischer (piano)/Philharmonia/Wolfgang Sawallisch
EMI CDZ 767 002 2

12 JUNE 1999
Tony Palmer, film director

❡ Britten, 'Hyde Park Aria' (from *Owen Wingrave*), Benjamin Luxon (Owen Wingrave), Sylvia Fisher (Miss Wingrave), John Shirley-Quirk (Mr Coyle)/English Chamber Orchestra/Benjamin Britten
London 433 200–2
❡ Shostakovich, Piano Concerto No. 2 in F, Op. 102 (second movement, Andante), Dmitri Shostakovich (composer's grandson) (piano)/I Musici de Montreal/Maxim Shostakovich
Chandos CHAN 8443
❡ Bob Dylan, 'All along the Watchtower', Jimi Hendrix
Polydor 837 362–2
❡ Puccini, 'Vissi d'arte' (from *Tosca*, Act II), Maria Callas (Tosca)/Paris Conservatoire Orchestra/Georges Prêtre
EMI CDM 763087 2
❡ Glass, 'Mrs Alexander's Outburst' (from *Satyagraha*, Act II), Rhonda Liss (Mrs Alexander)/New York City Opera Orchestra/Christopher Keene
CBS CD 39672
❡ Moncayo, *Huapango* (opening), Royal Philharmonic Orchestra/ Enrique Bátiz
ASV CDDCA 871
❡ Vaughan Williams, *A London Symphony* (second movement, Lento), London Philharmonic Orchestra/Adrian Boult
Belart 461 008–2
❡ Billie Cowie, 'Kam Falla Mi', Daphne Scott-Sawyer (vocal)/Billie Cowie (accordion and guitars)
Divas 4
❡ Rachmaninov, Prelude in B minor, Op. 32, No. 10, Valentina Igoshina (piano)
Artist's private recording

Natasha Spender, pianist and widow of Stephen Spender

❡ Barber, Sonata, Op. 26 (second movement, Allegro vivace e leggero),
Vladimir Horowitz (piano)
RCA GD 66377
❡ Lennox Berkeley, Sonata Op. 20 (second movement, Presto),
Christopher Headington (piano)
Kingdom KCLCD 2012
❡ Bach, Sonata No. 1 in G minor, BWV 1001 (second movement,
Fugue), Arthur Grumiaux (violin)
Philips 438 737 2
❡ Schubert, Sonata in B flat (first movement), Alfred Brendel (piano)
Philips 422 062 2
❡ Britten, 'Joe Has Gone Fishing' (from *Peter Grimes*, Act I), Peter
Pears (Grimes)/Chorus and Orchestra of the Royal Opera House/
Benjamin Britten
Decca SXL 2150/2
❡ Mozart, 'Ach, ich fühls' (from *The Magic Flute*, Act II), Tiana Lemnitz
(Pamina)/Berlin Philharmonic Orchestra/Thomas Beecham, rec. 1937/8
Pearl Gemm CDS 9371 B
❡ Beethoven, String Quartet in A minor, Op. 132 (finale, Allegro
appassionato), Amadeus Quartet
DG 423 480 2

Leonard Ingrams, Chairman of Garsington Opera

❡ Richard Strauss, 'Verwandlung' and 'Mondlicht' from *Daphne*, Hilde
Güden (Daphne)/Vienna Symphony Orchestra/Karl Böhm
DG 423 581 2
❡ Anon, 'O Waly Waly', Patrick Shuldham-Shaw (voice)/Gerald Moore
(piano), rec. 1959
HMV B 9965 (mono 78)
❡ Anon, 'I Will Give My Love an Apple', Richard Lewis (voice)/Tina
Bonifaccio (harp)
Dutton CDCLP 4003
❡ Victoria, 'O vos omnes' (Tenebrae Responsories), Tallis Scholars/
Peter Phillips
Gimell CDGIM 022

§ Purcell, Fantasia for 4 viols in C minor, Z738, Wenzinger Consort of Viols
Archiv APM 14027
§ Bach, 'Friede über Israel' (Closing chorus of Whitsun Cantata BWV 34), Munich Bach Choir/Munich Bach Orchestra/Karl Richter
Archiv 439 381 2
§ Haydn, 'Un certo ruscelletto' (from *Il mondo della luna*, Act III), Luigi Alva (Ecclitico), Edith Mathis (Clarice)/Chamber Orchestra of Lausanne/Antál Dorati
Philips 432 423 2
§ Schumann, *Märchenbilder* Op. 113 (No. 3, Rasch), Paul Coletti (viola)/Leslie Howard (piano)
Hyperion CDA 66946
§ Hindemith, *Trauermusik*, Yuri Bashmet (viola/director)/Moscow Soloists
RCA RD 60464
§ Vaughan Williams, 'Evening Hymn' (No. 4 of Four Hymns for tenor, viola and piano), Ian Partridge (tenor)/Christopher Wellington (viola)/David Parkhouse (piano)
EMI CDM 565 589 2

3 JULY 1999
Peter Eyre, actor

§ Verdi, 'Dio che nell'alma infondere' (from *Don Carlo*), Robert Merrill (baritone), Jussi Björling (tenor)/RCA Victor Symphony/Renato Cellini, rec. 1951
RCA GD 87799
§ Bellini, 'Qui la voce sua soave' (from *I Puritani*, Part II), Maria Callas (Elvira)/Turin Radio Orchestra/Arturo Basile, rec. 1949
Rodolphe Productions RPC 32486
§ Chopin, Ballade No. 4 in F minor, Krystian Zimerman (piano)
DG 431 262 2
§ Messiaen, 'Ta voix' (from *Poèmes pour Mi*), Françoise Pollet (soprano)/Cleveland Orchestra/Pierre Boulez
DG 453 478 2
§ Schubert, 'Das Wirtshaus' (from *Winterreise*), Matthias Goerne (baritone)/Graham Johnson (piano)
Hyperion CDJ 33030

❡ Elgar, Piano Quintet in A minor, Op. 84 (first movement), Peter Donohoe (piano)/Maggini String Quartet
Naxos 8.553737
❡ Wagner, 'Liebestod' (from *Tristan und Isolde*), Linda Esther Gray (Isolde)/Orchestra of Welsh National Opera/Sir Reginald Goodall
Decca 443 686 2

10 JULY 1999
Paul Levy, journalist and food writer

❡ Tchaikovsky, Gremin's aria (from *Eugene Onegin*, Act III), Paata Burchuladze (Prince Gremin)/Dresden Staatskapelle/James Levine
DG 423 961 2
❡ Bach, 'Was willst du dich, mein Geist, entsetzen' (from Cantata, BWV 8, 'Liebster Gott, wann werd ich sterben?'), Ernst Haefliger (tenor)/Horst Schneider (oboe d'amore)/Munich Bach Orchestra/ Karl Richter
Archiv 439 388 2
❡ Schumann, 'Die beiden Grenadiere', Dietrich Fischer-Dieskau (baritone)/Gerald Moore (piano), rec. 1951
HMV HLM 154703 1
❡ Maschwitz/Strachey, 'These Foolish Things' (from *These Foolish Things*), Bryan Ferry
EG 823 021 2
❡ Cahn/Chaplin/Secunda, 'Bei mir bist du schöen', Andrews Sisters, rec. 1937
ASV CDAJA 5116
❡ Beethoven, Cello Sonata No. 4 in C major, Op. 102, No. 1 (first movement, Andante–Vivace), Mstislav Rostropovich (cello)/Sviatoslav Richter (piano)
Philips 412 256 2
❡ Berg, Violin Concerto (first movement), Thomas Zehetmair (violin)/Philharmonia/Heinz Holliger
Teldec 2292 46449 2
❡ Mozart, 'In diesen heil'gen Hallen' (from *The Magic Flute*, Act II), Harry Peeters (Sarastro)/English Baroque Soloists/John Eliot Gardiner
Archiv 449 168 2

Nichola McAuliffe, actress

♪ Glass, 'Dance V' (from *In the Upper Room*), Philip Glass Ensemble/
Michael Riesman
CBS CD 39539

♪ Britten, 'Moonlight' (from *Four Sea Interludes from Peter Grimes*),
BBC Symphony Orchestra/Andrew Davis
Teldec 9031–73126–2

♪ Schoenberg, 'Heimfahrt' and 'O alter Duft' (Nos 20 and 21 from
Pierrot lunaire), Mary Thomas (Sprechstimme)/Fires of London/
Peter Maxwell Davies
Unicorn RHS 319

♪ Vaughan Williams, 'Silent Noon' (from *The House of Life*), Thomas
Allen (baritone)/Geoffrey Parsons (piano)
Virgin VC 791102 2

♪ Trad., Tuvan throat singing, anon. artist
Smithsonian Folkways SF 40002

♪ Mozart, 'Il mio tesoro' (from *Don Giovanni*, Act II), Jerry Hadley
(Don Ottavio)/Scottish Chamber Orchestra/Charles Mackerras
Telarc CD 80420

♪ Trad., 'El soldado ricante', Anon. artists
Manzana 2-SNICD-79

♪ Wagner, Overture to *Rienzi*, London Philharmonic Orchestra/
Adrian Boult
EMI CDM 763122 2

Dr Anthony Stevens, psychologist

♪ Schubert, 'Wohin?' (from *Die schöne Müllerin*), Dietrich Fischer-
Dieskau (baritone)/Gerald Moore (piano)
EMI CDC 747 173 2

♪ Poulenc, 'Hommage à Schubert' (*Improvisations*, No. 12), Pascal Rogé
(piano)
Decca 417 438 2

♪ Debussy, String Quartet in G minor (first movement, Animé et très
décidé), Kodaly Quartet
Naxos 8.550249

❡ Kamilieris, 'Last Evening in the Taverna' (Hasapiko–Butcher's Dance), Stratos Dionsiou (vocal)
Columbia SCDG 3798
❡ Purcell, 'Sound the Trumpet' (from *Come Ye Sons of Art*), Alfred Deller, John Whitworth (countertenors)/L'Ensemble Orchestral de L'Oiseau-Lyre/Anthony Lewis
Oiseau Lyre OLS 102
❡ Walton, 'En famille' (from *Façade*), Dame Edith Sitwell (reciter)/ English Opera Group Ensemble/Anthony Collins (director)
London 425 661 2
❡ Stanford, 'The Little Admiral' (No. 4 from *Songs of the Fleet*), Benjamin Luxon (baritone)/Bournemouth Symphony Orchestra and Chorus/Norman del Mar
EMI CDM 565 113 2
❡ Cole Porter, 'Experiment', Mabel Mercer (vocals)/Cy Walter and Stan Freeman (piano)
Atlantic 81264 1
❡ Handel, 'From Harmony, From Heavenly Harmony' (from *Ode for St Cecilia's Day*), Robert Tear (tenor)/English Chamber Orchestra/ Philip Ledger
ASV CDC 747 329 2
❡ Elgar, 'The Swimmer' (from *Sea Pictures*, Op. 37), Janet Baker (mezzo-soprano)/London Symphony Orchestra/John Barbirolli
EMI CDC 747 329 2

31 JULY 1999
Lord Neill, QC

❡ Montsalvatge, Divertimento No. 2 (Habañera), Alicia de Larrocha (piano)
Decca 433 929–2
❡ Britten, conclusion of Act I, scene 1 from *Peter Grimes*, Peter Pears (Peter Grimes), James Pease (Balstrode)/Orchestra of the Royal Opera House/Benjamin Britten
Decca 414 577–2
❡ Janáček, conclusion of Act II from *Katya Kabanova*, Zdeněk Švehla (Kudrjas), Libuše Márová (Varvara), Peter Dvorský (Boris), Elisabeth Söderström (Katya)/Vienna Philharmonic Orchestra/Charles Mackerras
Decca 421 852–2

¶ Schumann, 'Im wunderschönen Monat Mai' and 'Das ist ein Flöten und Geigen' (from *Dichterliebe*), Wolfgang Holzmair (baritone)/ Imogen Cooper (piano)
Philips 446 086–2
¶ Beethoven, Septet in E flat, Op. 20 (second movement, Adagio cantabile), Gaudier Ensemble
Hyperion CDA 66513
¶ Haydn, Symphony No. 102 in B flat (finale, Presto), Philharmonia Hungarica/Antál Dorati
London 425 531–2
¶ Mozart, 'O voto tremendo' (from *Idomeneo*, Act III), Eberhard Büchner (High Priest of Neptune)/Leipzig Radio Chorus/Staatskapelle Dresden/Karl Böhm
DG 429 864–2
¶ Bach, 'Menuets I and II' and 'Gigue' (from Partita in B flat, BWV 825), Dinu Lipatti (piano)
EMI CDH 769800 2
¶ Liszt, *Gnomenreigen*, Sviatoslav Richter (piano)
Revelation RV 10011

7 AUGUST 1999
Stephen Bayley, style guru

¶ Puccini, 'Bimba dagli occhi pieni di malìa' (from *Madama Butterfly*), Renata Scotto (Butterfly), Carlo Bergonzi (Pinkerton)/Rome Opera Orchestra/John Barbirolli
EMI CMS 769654 2
¶ Handel, 'Ombra mai fu' (from *Xerxes*, Act I), David Daniels (Xerxes)/Orchestra of the Age of Enlightenment/Roger Norrington
Virgin VC 545326 2
¶ Weill, 'September Song' (from *Knickerbocker Holiday*), Walter Huston/Orchestra/Maurice Abravanel
Pearl GEMMCDS9189
¶ Jagger/Richards, 'Gimmie Shelter', The Rolling Stones
London 844 473–2
¶ Brahms, 'Denn alles Fleisch, es ist wie Gras' (from *A German Requiem*, Op. 45) (first part), Vienna Singverein/Berlin Philharmonic Orchestra/Herbert von Karajan
DG 427 252–2

℣ Scarlatti, Sonata in E, Kk 380, Scott Ross (harpsichord)
Erato ECD 75431
℣ Washington/Young, 'A Hundred Years from Today', Jack Teagarden and his Orchestra
Classics 874
℣ Schubert, 'An die Musik', Elisabeth Schwarzkopf (soprano)/Edwin Fischer (piano)
EMI CDH 764025 2
℣ Beethoven, Triple Concerto in C, Op. 56 (first movement, Allegro), Géza Anda (piano)/Wolfgang Schneiderhan (violin)/Pierre Fournier (cello)/Berlin Radio Symphony Orchestra
DG 429 934–2

14 AUGUST 1999
Django Bates, jazz musician

℣ Kreisler, *Caprice Viennois*, Michael Rabin (violin)/Hollywood Bowl Symphony Orchestra/Felix Slatkin
Royal Classics ROY 6463
℣ Nancarrow, Study for Player Piano No. 40A, Conlon Nancarrow (player piano)
1750 Arch S-1777
℣ Miles Davis, 'Sivad' (from *Live-Evil*), Miles Davis (trumpet)
Columbia C2K 65135
℣ Charles Ives, *Three Quarter-tone Pieces for Two Pianos* (No. 1, Largo), Herbert Henck, Deborah Richards (pianos)
Wergo WER 6221–2
℣ Romanian folk music, Anon. artists
Artists' private recording
℣ Bob Dylan, 'Just like a Woman' (from *Songs of the Poets*), Nina Simone
Edsel EDCD 347
℣ Keith Jarrett, 'Blossom' (from *Belonging*), Keith Jarrett (piano)/ Jan Garbarek (saxophone)/Palle Danielsson (bass)/Jon Christiansen (drums)
ECM 829 115–2
℣ Lester Young, 'Lester Leaps In' (from *Bird is Free*), Charlie Parker (saxophone)
Esquire 32–157

❡ Farmers Market, 'Nell in the Sky with Farmers' (from *Musik fra Hybridene*), Farmers Market
FX CD 182

Interestingly this inventive musician chose the same composer that I selected for John Peel (see p. 36). Also the composer who made different sound worlds collide so effectively – Charles Ives.

21 AUGUST 1999
Sophie Ryder, sculptor

❡ Trad. Mexican, 'La Iguana', Sones Jarochos
❡ A. Marly/H. Zaret, 'The Partisan' (from *Songs from a Room*), Leonard Cohen
Columbia CD 32074
❡ Morton Feldman, *Why Patterns?*, Dorothy Stone (flute)/Gaylord Mowrey (piano)/Arthur Jarvinen (glockenspiel)
New Albion NA 039 CD
❡ Bach, 'Herr, unser Herrscher' (end of opening chorus of *St John Passion*), Koor van de Nederlandse Bachvereniging/Amsterdam Baroque Orchestra/Ton Koopman
Erato 4509 94675 2 A
❡ Bach, 'Sicilienne' (second movement of Sonata in E flat major, BWV 1031, for flute and harpsichord), Jean-Pierre Rampal (flute)/Robert Veyron-Lacroix (harpsichord)
Erato 2292 45830 2
❡ A. Newley/L. Bricusse, 'Feeling Good', Nina Simone
Verve 5 16871 2
❡ Liszt, *Valse oubliée* No. 1 in A minor, Raphael Albermann (piano)
Edition Peters EP 7516 CD
❡ Debussy, 'Golliwog's Cakewalk' (from *Children's Corner*), Pascal Rogé (piano)
Decca 417 792 2
❡ A.-C. Jobim/G. Lees, 'Corcovado' (from *Quiet Nights of Quiet Stars*), Stan Getz (tenor saxophone)/Astrud Gilberto (vocal)/Gary Burton (vibes)/Kenny Burrell (guitar)/Gene Cherico (bass)/Helico Milito (drums)
Verve 821 725 2

154

¶ Scarlatti, Sonata in B minor (L 449/Kk 27), Richard Lester (harpsichord)
Private recording

28 AUGUST 1999
Robert David MacDonald, theatre director

¶ Thomas, 'Connais-tu le pays' (from *Mignon*), Conchita Supervia (Mignon)/Orchestra/Gustave Cloëz
Nimbus NI 7836
¶ Bach, 'Bist du bei mir', Elisabeth Schumann (soprano)/Orchestra/ L. Rosenek
HMV HQM 1187
¶ Richard Strauss, 'Recognition Scene' (from *Elektra*), Erna Schlüter (Elektra)/Paul Schoeffler (Orest)/Royal Philharmonic Orchestra/ Thomas Beecham
Preiser 90341
¶ Bellini, 'Mira, O Norma' (from *Norma*), Joan Sutherland (Norma), Marilyn Horne (Adalgisa)/London Symphony Orchestra/Richard Bonynge
Decca 436 303–2
¶ Verdi, 'Chi i bei di m'adduce ancora', Margaret Price (soprano)/ Geoffrey Parsons (piano)
DG 419 621–2
¶ Schubert, 'Nacht und Träume' D827, Irmgard Seefried (soprano)/ Gerald Moore (piano)
Testament SBT 1026
¶ Liszt, *Le triomphe funèbre du Tasse* (conclusion), Berlin Radio Symphony Orchestra/Karl Anton Rickenbacker
Koch 317682
¶ Prokofiev, 'Lullaby' (from *On Guard for Peace*), Irina Arkhipova (contralto), Tamarez Mironov (treble)/USSR Radio Symphony Orchestra and Chorus/Gennadi Rozhdestvensky
Olympia OCD 206

4 SEPTEMBER 1999
Rainer Hersch, comedian

¶ Handel arr. Hersch, 'The Arrival of the Queen of Sheba', Anon. artists
Artists' special recording

❡ Sousa arr. Horowitz, 'The Stars and Stripes For Ever', Vladimir Horowitz (piano)
RCA GD 87755
❡ Schubert, 'Abschied' and 'Die Taubenpost' (from *Schwanengesang*), Peter Schreier (tenor)/András Schiff (piano)
Decca 425 612–2
❡ Schoenberg, 'Musette' (from Suite, Op. 25), Glenn Gould (piano)
Sony SMK 62021
❡ Linzer/Randell, 'A Lover's Concerto', The Toys
Polydor 529 508–2
❡ Handel arr. Mervyn Warren, 'Why do the Nations?' (from *The Messiah: A Soulful Celebration*), Al Jarreau
Proper Choice CD
❡ Richard Strauss, *Metamorphosen* (conclusion), Berlin Philharmonic Orchestra/Wilhelm Furtwängler
Music and Arts CD 719
❡ Alkan, 'Comme le vent', Op. 39, No. 1 (from *Twelve Studies in Minor Keys*), Michael Ponti (piano)
Vox STGBY 653
❡ Bach, Concerto in A, BWV 1055 (third movement, Allegro ma non tanto), Glenn Gould (piano)/Columbia Symphony Orchestra/Vladimir Golschmann
Sony SM2K 52591

11 SEPTEMBER 1999
Jonathan Coe, writer

❡ Robert Wyatt, 'Sea Song', Robert Wyatt
Virgin CDV 2017
❡ Howells, 'Merry Eye', New Philharmonia Orchestra/Adrian Boult
Lyrita SRCS 69
❡ Poulenc, 'Déploration' (third movement of Oboe Sonata), Maurice Bourgue (oboe)/Pascal Rogé (piano)
Decca 421 581 2
❡ Kenny Wheeler, *Consolation* (Part VI, The Sweet Time Suite), featuring Norma Winstone (vocal)/John Taylor/Ray Warleigh(alto saxophone)/Dave Holland (bass)/Kenny Wheeler Orchestra
ECM 843 400 2

¶ Debussy, Sonata for Flute, Viola and Harp (second movement, Interlude: Tempo di Minuetto), Philippa Davis (flute)/Roger Chase (viola)/Marisa Robles (harp)
Virgin Classics VC 791148 2
¶ Miklós Rózsa, Violin Concerto, Op. 24 (second movement, Lento cantabile), Igor Gruppman (violin)/New Zealand Symphony Orchestra/James Sedares
Koch 3 7379 2

18 SEPTEMBER 1999
John Humphrys, broadcaster

¶ Beethoven, String Quartet in C sharp minor, Op. 131 (first movement, Adagio non troppo), Alban Berg Quartet
EMI CDS 754587 2
¶ Elgar, Cello Concerto, Op. 85 (third movement, Adagio), Yo-Yo Ma (cello)/London Symphony Orchestra/André Previn
CBS CD 39541
¶ Joseph Parry, 'Myfanwy', Morriston Orpheus Choir
Music for Pleasure CD-MFP 6027
¶ Ellington/Hodges, 'Weary Blues', Duke Ellington (piano)/Johnny Hodges (alto saxophone)/Harry Edison (trumpet)/Les Spann (guitar)/ Al Hall (bass)/Jo Jones (drums)
Verve 849 361–2
¶ Rodgers/Hart, 'Manhattan', Ella Fitzgerald/Buddy Bregman and his Orchestra
Polydor 835 610–2
¶ Paul Simon, 'The Sound of Silence', Simon and Garfunkel
CBS CD 63370
¶ Bach, Sarabande (from Suite No. 1 in G, BWV 1007), Pierre Fournier (cello)
DG 419 359–2
¶ Fauré, Sanctus (from Requiem, Op. 48), Elisabeth Brasseur Chorale/Paris Conservatoire Orchestra/André Cluytens
EMI CDC 747836 2
¶ Billy Strayhorn, 'Take the A Train', Duke Ellington Band
Bluebird 74321 13181–2

Keith Swanwick, music educationalist

❡ Schubert, 'Frühlingstraum' (from *Winterreise*, D911), Peter Pears (tenor)/Benjamin Britten (piano)
Decca 452 402–2
❡ Sousa, 'The Stars and Stripes For Ever', John Foster Black Dyke Mills Band/Roy Newsome
Chandos CHAN 4528
❡ Eboly, untitled piano composition, Julia Eboly (piano)
Artist's special recording
❡ Timbalada, 'Cadè O Timbau?', Timbalada
Verve 522 813–2
❡ Miles Davis, 'Flamenco Sketches' (from *Kind of Blue*), Miles Davis (trumpet)/Julian Adderley (alto saxophone)/John Coltrane (tenor saxophone)/Bill Evans (piano)/Paul Chambers (bass)/James Cobb (drums)
Columbia COL 460603 2
❡ Ligeti, *Musica ricercata* (first movement), Pierre-Laurent Aimard (piano)
Sony SK 62308
❡ Lennon/McCartney, 'Ticket to Ride', The Beatles
Parlophone CDP 746439 2
❡ Elgar, Symphony No. 2 in E flat, Op. 63 (third movement, Rondo: Presto), London Philharmonic Orchestra/Georg Solti
Decca 421 386–2

William Lyne, director, Wigmore Hall

❡ Schubert, 'Die Taubenpost', Peter Schreier (tenor)/András Schiff (piano)
Decca 425 612 2
❡ Haydn, String Quartet in B flat, Op. 76, No. 4 (fourth movement), Takács Quartet
Decca 425 467 2
❡ Johann Strauss II, 'Spiel ich die Unschuld vom Lande' (from *Die Fledermaus*), Elisabeth Schumann (soprano)/Vienna State Opera Orchestra/Karl Alwyn
Romophone 81019 2

❡ F. Couperin, 'Les barricades mysterieuses' (Livre de clavecin Book 2, Ordre 6), Wanda Landowska (harpsichord)
HMV ALP 1246
❡ Hahn, 'Tyndaris', Ian Bostridge (tenor)/Graham Johnson (piano)
Hyperion CDA 67142
❡ Handel, Act III, scene 5 from *Saul*, James Bowman (David)/Leeds Festival Chorus/English Chamber Orchestra/Charles Mackerras
Archiv 447 699 2
❡ Verdi, 'Dinne . . . alcun là non vedisti?' (from *Simon Boccanegra*, Act I), Mirella Freni (Amelia)/Piero Cappuccilli (Boccanegra)/ Orchestra of La Scala/Claudio Abbado
DG 415 693 2
❡ Schubert, Piano Trio in E flat D929 (Andante con moto), Alexander Schneider (violin)/Pablo Casals (cello)/Mieczyslaw Horszowski (piano)
Sony Classical SMK 58988
❡ Hahn, 'L'heure exquise' (from *Chansons grises*), Ninon Vallin (soprano)/Reynaldo Hahn (piano), rec. *c*.1928
HMV E 290946 1

9 OCTOBER 1999
John Carey, writer, academic

❡ Mendelssohn, Violin Concerto in E minor, Op. 64 (finale, Allegro molto vivace), Yehudi Menuhin (violin)/Philharmonia/Efrem Kurtz
EMI CDM 769003 2
❡ Beethoven, Piano Trio in B flat, 'Archduke', Op. 97 (fourth movement, Allegro moderato–Presto), Isaac Stern (violin)/Leonard Rose (cello)/Eugene Istomin (piano)
CBS CD 44839
❡ Haydn, 'The Heavens are Telling' (from *The Creation*, Part I), Emma Kirkby (soprano)/Anthony Rolfe Johnson (tenor)/Michael George (bass)/Academy of Ancient Music Orchestra and Chorus/Christopher Hogwood
Oiseau Lyre 431 397–2
❡ Allegri, Miserere, Choir of New College, Oxford/Edward Higginbottom
Erato 0630–14634–2

¶ Gilbert/Sullivan, 'If you're anxious for to shine' (from *Patience*), George Baker (Bunthorne)/D'Oyly Carte Opera Orchestra/Malcolm Sargent
Arabesque z 8095–2
¶ Verdi, 'Ah, fors'é lui' (from *La traviata*, Act I), Joan Sutherland (Violetta)/Orchestra of the Maggio Musicale, Florence/John Pritchard
Decca 411 877–2
¶ Bach, 'Bourrées 1 and 2' (from Suite No. 4 in E flat, BWV 1010), Paul Tortelier (cello)
EMI CDC 749035 2
¶ Weber, Clarinet Concerto No. 2 in E flat, Op. 74, Gervase de Peyer (clarinet)/London Symphony Orchestra/Colin Davis
Decca 433 727–2

16 OCTOBER 1999
Sidonie Goossens, harpist

¶ Berg, 'Liebesode' (No. 6 from *Seven Early Songs*), Heather Harper/ BBC Symphony Orchestra/Pierre Boulez
Columbia M 32162
¶ Elgar, Symphony No. 1 (third movement), BBC Symphony Orchestra/Adrian Boult
BBC Radio Classics DMCD 98A
¶ Vaughan Williams, *Serenade to Music*, 16 soloists/BBC Symphony Orchestra/Henry Wood, rec. 1938
Dutton CDAX 8004
¶ Delius, *Brigg Fair*, Royal Philharmonic Orchestra/Thomas Beecham, rec. 1958
EMI CDS 747509
¶ Britten, *Young Person's Guide to the Orchestra* (double bass and harp variations), BBC Symphony Orchestra/Malcolm Sargent
HMV BLP 1101
¶ Prokofiev, 'Prelude', Op. 12, No. 7 (originally for piano), Sidonie Goossens (harp)
HMV 7EP 7183
¶ Ravel, *Introduction and Allegro*, Osian Ellis/Melos Ensemble
Decca 421 154–2

❡ Britten, *Nocturne* for tenor, seven solo instruments and strings (third movement, 'Encinctur'd with a twine of leaves', with harp obbligato), Peter Pears (tenor)/English Chamber Orchestra/Benjamin Britten
Decca 417 153–2

23 OCTOBER 1999
Al Alvarez, writer

❡ Beethoven, Sonata in C minor, Op. 111 (second movement, Arietta), Alfred Brendel (piano)
Philips 446 701–2
❡ Sibelius, Symphony No. 4 in A minor, Op. 63 (opening of finale, Allegro), City of Birmingham Symphony Orchestra/Simon Rattle
EMI CDC 764121 2
❡ Pérotin, 'Viderunt omnes' (opening), Hilliard Ensemble/Paul Hillier
ECM 837 751–2
❡ Harry Ruby, 'There's a Girl in the Heart of Wheeling, West Virginia', Zero Mostel/Orchestra/Sol Kaplan
Vanguard VSD 79229
❡ Mozart, 'Di, scrivermi ogni giorno' (from *Così fan tutte*, Act I), Carol Vaness (Fiordiligi)/Delores Ziegler (Dorabella)/Dale Duesing (Guglielmo)/ John Aler (Ferrando)/London Philharmonic Orchestra
EMI CDC 747727 2
❡ Schubert, Notturno in E flat major, D897 (opening), András Schiff (piano)/Yuuko Shiokawa (violin)/Miklós Perényi (cello)
Teldec 0630–13151–2
❡ Janáček, 'The Barn Owl Has Not Flown Away' (from *On an Overgrown Path*), Mikhail Rudy (piano)
EMI CDC 7 54094 2
[❡ Alvarez, 'Ann Dancing', Al Alvarez
Recorded live during session]
❡ S. Silverstein, 'Everybody's Makin' It Big But Me', Dr Hook
Capitol CDESTV 2

30 OCTOBER 1999
Jim Crace, novelist

❡ Mahler arr. Caine, Symphony No. 5 (Funeral March), Uri Caine Ensemble
Winter and Winter 910 004–2

❡ Louis Sclavis, 'Moi c'est S'Mariano' (from *Clarinettes*), Louis Sclavis
IDA 004CD
❡ Poulenc, Sonata for Two Clarinets (third movement, Vif), Lucien
Aubert, Jacques di Donato (clarinets)
Adda 590042
❡ Julian Argüelles, 'Qaanaaq' (from *Skull View*), Julian Argüelles Octet
Babel BDV7919
❡ John Adams, 'The Day Chorus' (from *The Death of Klinghoffer*,
Act II), London Opera Chorus/Lyon Opera Orchestra/Kent Nagano
Elektra Nonesuch 7559–79281–2
❡ Paganini, Sonata in A, Op. 3, No. 1, Desmond Bradley (violin)/
Hermann Leeb (guitar)
RCA GL 25095
[❡ Crace, 'Being Dead' (opening), Jim Crace
Recorded live during session]
❡ Benedict Mason, *Lighthouses of England and Wales* (opening), BBC
Symphony Orchestra/Lothar Zagrosek
Collins 20042
❡ N'Dour/Rykiel, 'Tourista' (from *The Guide*), The Super Étoile
Columbia 4765082
❡ Schubert, Impromptu in F minor, D935, No. 1, Alfred Brendel (piano)
Philips 422 237–2

We share a fascination for Ben Mason's highly idiosyncratic Lighthouses
of England and Wales. *An atmospheric and accessible contemporary
work.*

6 NOVEMBER 1999
Robin Simon, art historian and critic

❡ Dr Caradog Roberts, 'I bob un sy'n ffyddlon' (tune: Rachie), London
Welsh Festival of Male Choirs
Black Mountain CDBM 510
❡ Verdi, 'E scherzo, od è follia' (from *Un ballo in maschera*, Act I),
Carlo Bergonzi (Riccardo), Shirley Verrett (Ulrica)/RCA Italiana
Opera Orchestra and Chorus/Erich Leinsdorf
RCA GD 86645/A
❡ Mozart, 'Notte e giorno faticar' (from *Don Giovanni*, Act I),
Giuseppe Taddei (Leporello)/Philharmonia/Carlo Maria Giulini
EMI CDC 747 260 2

❡ Schubert, 'Der Erlkönig', Bryn Terfel (baritone)/Malcolm Martineau (piano)
DG 445 294 2
❡ Byrd, 'Ave verum corpus', Choir of New College, Oxford/Edward Higginbottom
Erato 3984 21659 2
❡ Puccini, 'E gelida manina' (from *La bohème*, Act I), Tito Schipa (Rodolfo)/Orchestra of La Scala, Milan/Carlo Sabajno
Cedar AB 78530
❡ Handel, 'All We Like Sheep' (from *The Messiah*), Choir of Christ Church Cathedral, Oxford/Academy of Ancient Music/Christopher Hogwood
Oiseau Lyre 411 860 2
❡ Purcell, 'Dear Pretty Youth' (from *The Tempest*, Act IV), Rosemary Hardy (Dorinda)/Monteverdi Orchestra/John Eliot Gardiner
Erato 2292 45555 2
❡ Chopin, Fantasie-Impromptu in C sharp minor, Op. 66, Irene Scharrer (piano), rec. 1925
Pearl Gemm CD 9978
❡ Rossini, 'Largo al factotum' (from *The Barber of Seville*, Act I), John Rawnsley (Figaro)/London Philharmonic Orchestra/Sylvain Cambreling
VIDEO Castle Opera CV1 2016

13 NOVEMBER 1999
Anthony Sampson, writer

❡ Masekela/Samson, 'Thank you Madiba', Hugh Masekela (trumpet)
Columbia CDCOL 8000
❡ Bizet, 'Minuetto' (from *L'Arlésienne* Suite No. 2), Ulster Orchestra/ Yan Pascal Tortelier
Chandos CHAN 6600
❡ Verdi, finale from *Falstaff*, Act III, Leo Nucci (Ford), Renato Bruson (Falstaff) et al./Los Angeles Philharmonic Orchestra/Carlo Maria Giulini
DG 410 503–2
❡ Berlioz, *Harold in Italy* (first movement, 'Harold in the Mountains'), William Primrose (viola)/Boston Symphony Orchestra/Serge Koussevitzky
Biddulph WHL 028

¶ Bach, Suite No. 2 in D minor, BWV 1008 (first movement, Prelude), Mstislav Rostropovich (cello)
EMI CDS 553363 2
¶ Puccini, Gratias agimus Tibi (from Messa di Gloria), José Carreras (tenor)/ Philharmonia/Claudio Scimone
Erato 2292–45197–2
¶ Beethoven, Variations on 'Ein Mädchen oder Weibchen', Op. 66, Maurice Gendron (cello)/Jean Françaix (piano)
Philips 438 960–2
¶ Trad. arr. Linda, Mbube, Miriam Makeba/Belafonte Folk Singers/ Perry Lopez (guitar)
London HA 2332
¶ Mozart, final scene from The Marriage of Figaro, Thomas Allen (Count Almaviva), Samuel Ramey (Figaro), Lucia Popp (Susanna), Frederica von Stade (Cherubino), Kiri te Kanawa (Countess)/ London Philharmonic Orchestra/Georg Solti
Decca 410 150–2

20 NOVEMBER 1999
Gaia Servadio, writer

¶ Mussorgsky, 'Chorus of Priestesses' (from Salammbô), London Symphony Orchestra and Chorus/Claudio Abbado
RCA 09026–61354–2
¶ Mozart, 'Sento, o Dio' (from Così fan tutte, Act I), Sena Jurinac (Fiordiligi), Blanche Thebom (Dorabella), Erich Kunz (Guglielmo), Richard Lewis (Ferrando), Mario Borriello (Don Alfonso)/ Glyndebourne Festival Orchestra/Fritz Busch
Testament SBT 1040
¶ Rossini, William Tell, Sherrill Milnes (Tell), Elizabeth Connell (Hedwige), Della Jones (Jemmy), Luciano Pavarotti (Arnold)/ Ambrosian Opera Chorus/National Philharmonic Orchestra/Riccardo Chailly
Decca 417 154–2
¶ Debussy, Act III Interlude (Descent into the Vaults) from Pelléas et Mélisande, Orchestra of the Royal Opera House/Pierre Boulez
Sony SM3K 47265

❡ Berlioz, 'Appearance of the Ghost of Hector' (from *Les Troyens*, Act II), Jon Vickers (Aeneas), Dennis Wicks (Ghost of Hector)/ Orchestra of the Royal Opera House/Colin Davis
Philips 416 432–2
❡ Mozart, Symphony No. 40, K.550 (second movement, Andante), Philharmonia/Otto Klemperer
EMI CMS 763272 2
❡ Verdi, 'É tardi' (from *La traviata*), Maria Callas (Violetta)/Orchestra of La Scala, Milan/Carlo Maria Giulini
EMI CMS 764628 2
❡ Brahms, Symphony No. 2, Op. 73 (second movement, Adagio non troppo), NBC Symphony Orchestra/Arturo Toscanini
RCA GD60258

27 NOVEMBER 1999
John Morgan, style guru

❡ Bellini, 'Mira, O Norma' (from *Norma*), Montserrat Caballé (Norma), Fiorenza Cossotto (Adalgisa)/London Philharmonic Orchestra/Carlo Felice Cilario
RCA 09026 61458–2
❡ Handel, 'To Thee, Thou Glorious Son' (from *Theodora*), Roberta Alexander (Theodora), Jochen Kowalski (Didymus)/Concentus Musicus Wien/Nikolaus Harnoncourt
Teldec 2292 46447–2
❡ Poulenc, 'Reine des mouettes' (from *Métamorphoses*), Gérard Souzay (baritone)/Dalton Baldwin (piano)
Philips 438 964–2
❡ Haydn, Benedictus (from Missa Brevis Sancti Joannis de Deo, 'Little Organ Mass'), Dominik Orieschnig (soprano)/Martin Haselböck (organ)/Vienna Boys' Choir/Chorus Viennensis/Vienna Symphony Orchestra/Uwe Christian Harrer
Philips 420 162–2
❡ Brahms, Piano Trio No. 3 in C minor, Op. 101 (first movement, Allegro energico), Julius Katchen (piano)/Josef Suk (violin)/Janos Starker (cello)
Decca 425 523–2

♪ Schubert, Sonata in A, D664 (second movement, Andante), András Schiff (piano)
Decca 440 311–2
♪ Schumann, 'Im wunderschönen Monat Mai' (from *Dichterliebe*, Op. 48), Ian Bostridge (tenor)/Julius Drake (piano)
EMI CDC 556575 2
♪ Wagner, 'Wotan's Farewell' (from *Die Walküre*, Act III), Hans Hotter (Wotan)/Vienna Philharmonic Orchestra/Georg Solti
Decca 414 105–2

4 DECEMBER 1999
Jeremy Dixon, architect

♪ Nancarrow, Study No. 21 (Canon, X), Conlon Nancarrow (player piano)
Wergo WER 6223–2
♪ Schumann, 'Die alten bösen Lieder' (from *Dichterliebe*, Op. 48), Wolfgang Holzmair (baritone)/Imogen Cooper (piano)
Philips 446 086–2
♪ Richard Strauss, 'Ja, ist Sie da?' (from *Der Rosenkavalier*), Christa Ludwig (Octavian)/Elisabeth Schwarzkopf (Marschallin)/ Philharmonia/Herbert von Karajan
EMI CDS 749354 2
♪ Haydn, String Quartet in D, Op. 33, No. 6 (second movement, Andante), Kodály Quartet
Naxos 8.550789
♪ Alan Price, 'Poor People' (from *O Lucky Man!*), Alan Price
Warner 9362 46137 2
♪ Britten, 'The Children' (from 'Who Are These Children', Op. 84), Peter Pears (tenor)/Benjamin Britten (piano)
Decca SXL 6608
♪ Bach, *Goldberg Variations*, BWV 988 (Variation 25), Gustav Leonhardt (harpsichord)
Vanguard VBD 175
♪ Brahms, Intermezzo in B flat minor, Op. 117, No. 2, Ivo Pogorelich (piano)
DG 437 460–2

11 DECEMBER 1999
Victoria Glendinning, writer

¶ Mozart, 'Deh vieni, non tardar' (from *The Marriage of Figaro*, Act IV), Alison Hagley (Susanna)/English Baroque Soloists/John Eliot Gardiner
Archiv 439 874 2
¶ Lennon/McCartney, 'The Long and Winding Road', The Beatles
Parlophone CDP 746447 2
¶ John Tavener, *The Protecting Veil* (opening), Steven Isserlis (cello)/ London Symphony Orchestra/Gennadi Rozhdestvensky
Virgin Classics VD 791474 2
¶ Cole Porter, 'True Love' (from *High Society*), Bing Crosby/Grace Kelly/MGM Studio Orchestra/Johnny Green
Capitol CDP 793787 2
¶ Chopin, Etude in E major, Op. 10, No. 3, Peter Donohoe (piano)
EMI CDC 754 416 2
¶ Britten, 'One Ever Hangs Where Shelled Roads Part' (from *War Requiem*, Op. 66, Part V, Agnus Dei), Peter Pears (tenor)/Bach Choir/ London Symphony Chorus and Orchestra/Benjamin Britten
Decca 414 385 2
¶ Handel, 'O Lovely Peace' (from *Judas Maccabeus*), Choristers of St Nicholas College, Chislehurst
Columbia SEG 7705
¶ Mahler, Symphony No. 1 (end of finale), City of Birmingham Symphony Orchestra/Simon Rattle
EMI CDC 754647 2

18 DECEMBER 1999
Simon Schama, historian

¶ Juan Luis Guerra, 'Ojalá que llueva café', Café Tacuba
WEA 16718–2
¶ Janáček, *The Cunning Little Vixen*, Richard Novák (The Forester), Marie Koucká (The Frog)/Czech Philharmonic Orchestra/Václav Neumann
Supraphon 10 3472–2
¶ Carter/Jacobs, 'Sittin' on Top of the World', Howlin' Wolf
Chess MCD 11073

❡ Puccini, 'Dunque è proprio finita' (from *La bohème*, Act III), Jussi Björling (Rodolfo), Victoria de Los Angeles (Mimì), Robert Merrill (Marcello), Lucine Amara (Musetta)/RCA Victor Orchestra/Thomas Beecham
EMI CDS 747235 8
❡ Rodgers/Hart, 'Manhattan', Dinah Washington
Mercury 818 815–2
❡ Vivaldi, Flute Concerto in G minor, 'La notte', RV 439 (third movement, Largo: 'Il sonno'), William Bennett (flute)/English Chamber Orchestra/George Malcolm
EMI CD-EMX 9504
❡ Schubert, Quintet in C, D956 (third movement, Scherzo), Isaac Stern, Alexander Schneider (violins)/Milton Katims (viola)/Pablo Casals, Paul Tortelier (cellos)
Sony SMK 58992
❡ Schubert, Impromptu in G flat, D899, No. 3, Alfred Brendel (piano)
Philips 422 237–2
❡ Verdi, 'L'onore! Ladri' (from *Falstaff*, Act I), Tito Gobbi (Falstaff)/Philharmonia/Herbert von Karajan
EMI CMS 567083 2

25 DECEMBER 1999
Don Maguire (a.k.a. John Sessions)

❡ Copland, *Appalachian Spring*, Orpheus Chamber Orchestra
DG 427 335 2
❡ John Cage, *Fifty-six Marches* (third movement, 'A dip in the lake', for cello and toy instruments), Frances-Marie Uitti (cello and toy instruments)
Etcetera KTC 2016B
❡ Laurie Anderson, 'O Superman', Laurie Anderson
Warner D 257002
❡ J. Livingston/R. Evans, theme from *Bonanza*, unknown orchestra
Silva Screen RILM CD 024
❡ Charles Ives, Symphony No. 4 (Prelude: Maestoso), Mary Sauer (piano)/Chicago Symphony Orchestra and Chorus /Michael Tilson Thomas
Sony Classical CD 44039

♪ Lou Reed, 'I'll Be Your Mirror', The Velvet Underground and Nico
Verve 823 290 2
♪ Glass, Dance No. 2 for Organ, Michael Riesman (organ)
CBS CD 44765

8 JANUARY 2000
John Caird, theatre director

♪ Schubert, 'Wohin' (from *Die schöne Müllerin*), Dietrich Fischer-
Dieskau (baritone)/Gerald Moore (piano)
EMI CDC 747173 2
♪ Mozart, Oboe Quartet in F, K370 (third movement, Rondo: Allegro),
George Caird (oboe)/Members of the Coull Quartet
LDR LDRCD 1011
♪ Chopin, Sonata No. 3 in B minor (Finale), Vlado Perlemuter (piano)
Nimbus NI 5038
♪ Górecki, Symphony No. 3 (third movement), Dawn Upshaw
(soprano)/London Sinfonietta/David Zinman
Nonesuch 7559–79282–2
♪ Mozart, Sanctus (from Requiem, K626), Wiener Singverein/Berlin
Philharmonic Orchestra/Herbert von Karajan
DG 439 412–2
♪ Bach, Sinfonia No. 14 in B flat, BWV 800, Glenn Gould (piano)
Sony SMK 52596
♪ Mozart, 'Ruhe sanft, mein holdes Leben' (from *Zaïde*), Lucia Popp
(soprano)/Vienna Haydn Orchestra/István Kertész
Decca 421 311–2
♪ Bernstein, Finale: 'Make our Garden Grow' (from *Candide*),
National Theatre cast (1999)/Mark Dorrell
Front Row
♪ Beethoven, String Quartet in B flat, Op. 130 (fifth movement,
Cavatina: Adagio molto espressivo), Medici String Quartet
Nimbus NI 5254

15 JANUARY 2000
Jonathan Raban, travel writer

♪ Elgar, *Ecce sacerdos magnos*, Choir of Worcester Cathedral/Adrian
Partington (organ)/Donald Hunt
Hyperion CDA 66313

169

❡ Bach, Toccata and Fugue in D minor, BWV 565, Lionel Rogg
(Silbermann organ at Arlesheim)
Harmonia Mundi HMX 290773
❡ Don McLean, 'American Pie', Don McLean
Dino Entertainment DINCD 99
❡ Trad., 'The Oak and the Ash', Alfred Deller (countertenor)/Desmond
Dupré (guitar)
Vanguard 08 5064 71
❡ Purcell, 'March' (from *Music for the Funeral of Queen Mary*), Equale
Brass Ensemble/John Eliot Gardiner
Erato 4509–96553–2
❡ Mozart, Agnus Dei (from Coronation Mass, K317), Helen Donath
(soprano), Gillian Knight (mezzo-soprano), Ryland Davies (tenor),
Stafford Dean (bass)/John Alldis Choir/London Symphony
Orchestra/Colin Davis
Philips 438 800–2
❡ Britten, Dies irae (from *War Requiem*, Op. 66), Bach Choir/London
Symphony Chorus and Orchestra/Benjamin Britten
Decca 414 383–2
❡ Schubert, Quintet in A, 'Trout' (third movement, Scherzo), András
Schiff (piano)/Members of the Hagen Quartet/Alois Posch (double
bass)
Decca 411 975–2

22 JANUARY 2000
John Richardson, art critic and biographer

❡ Britten, 'I Know a Bank' (from *A Midsummer Night's Dream*,
Act I), Alfred Deller, London Symphony Orchestra/Benjamin Britten
London 425 664–2 and 665–2
❡ Rachmaninov, 'Aleko's Cavatina' (from *Aleko*), Nicolai Ghiaurov,
London Symphony Orchestra/Edward Downes
Decca 448 248–2
❡ Soler, Fandango, Rafael Puyana (harpsichord)
Philips 432 830–2
❡ Singer/Vedora/White, 'At the Hop', Danny and the Juniors
Pickwick PWKS 511
[❡ John Richardson, 'The Sorcerer's Apprentice', Michael Berkeley
Reader, recorded in situ]

¶ Puccini, 'O principe' (from *Turandot*, Act II), Eva Turner/Orchestra/
Stanford Robinson
EMI CDH 769791 2
¶ Stravinsky, The Birth of Apollo (from *Apollo*, Scene 1), Columbia
Symphony Orchestra/Igor Stravinsky
Sony SM3K 46292
[¶ John Richardson, The Sorcerer's Apprentice, John Richardson
Reader, recorded in situ]
¶ Brühne/Balz, 'Der Wind hat mir ein Lied erzählt' (from the film
La habañera), Zarah Leander
Historia H 602
¶ Liszt, 'O quand je dors', Felicity Lott (soprano)/Graham Johnson
(piano)
Harmonia Mundi HMC 901138
¶ Knepler/Welleminsky/Mackeben-Millöcker,' Ich schenk mein Herz'
(*Die Dubarry*), Elisabeth Schwarzkopf, Philharmonia/Otto
Ackermann
EMI CDC 747284 2

Following his years of work on Picasso I was keen to invite him to talk
about that whole period and the obvious parallels with Stravinsky. These
were, after all, the two great twentieth-century artists who had the
strength of personality to reinvent the past with complete authority.

29 JANUARY 2000
John Suchet, broadcaster and writer

¶ Beethoven, String Quartet in F, Op. 135 (third movement, Lento assai
e cantante tranquillo), Busch Quartet
EMI CHS 565308 2
¶ Kid Ory, 'Ory's Creole Trombone', Louis Armstrong and his Hot Five
ASV CDAJA 5148
¶ Verdi, 'Di Provenza il mar' (from *La traviata*, Act II), Mario Sereni
(Germont)/Orchestra of the National Theatre of Lisbon/Franco Ghione
EMI CDS 556330 2
¶ Wagner, Prelude to Act I of *Parsifal*, Berlin Philharmonic
Orchestra/Herbert von Karajan
EMI CMS 763469 2
¶ Christine/Rourke/Willemetz, 'Valentine', Maurice Chevalier
Pathé Marconi CDP 790667 2

❡ Canteloube, 'Rossignolet qui chantes' (from *New Songs of the Auvergne*), Netania Davrath (soprano)/Orchestra/Gershon Kingsley
Vanguard 08.8002.72
❡ Beethoven, 'Mir ist so wunderbar' (from *Fidelio*, Act I), Ingeborg
Hallstein (Marcellina), Christa Ludwig (Leonore), Gottlob Frick
(Rocco), Gerhard Unger (Jaquino)/Philharmonia/Otto Klemperer
EMI CMS 769324 2

5 FEBRUARY 2000
Susannah Fiennes, painter

❡ Schubert, Arpeggione Sonata in A minor (second movement,
Adagio), Nobuko Imai (viola)/Roger Vignoles (piano)
Chandos CHAN 8664
❡ Wagner, conclusion of Act I from *Parsifal*, Chorus of the Berlin
Opera/Kurt Moll (Gurnemanz), Hanna Schwarz (Voice from above)/
Berlin Philharmonic Orchestra/Herbert von Karajan
DG 413 247–2
❡ Handel, Dominus a dextris tuis (from Dixit Dominus), Westminster
Abbey Choir and Orchestra/Simon Preston
Archiv 423 594–2
❡ Schumann, 'Ich will meine Seele tauchen' (from *Dichterliebe*,
Op. 48), Ian Bostridge (tenor)/Julius Drake (piano)
EMI CDC 556575 2
❡ Bernstein, *Chichester Psalms* (first movement), Corydon Singers/
Rachel Masters (harp)/Gary Kettel (percussion)/Thomas Trotter
(organ)/Matthew Best
Hyperion CDA 66219
❡ Shostakovich, String Quartet No. 10 in A flat, Op. 118 (first
movement, Andante), Shostakovich Quartet
Olympia OCD 534
❡ Brahms, *Geistliches Lied*, Op. 30, Choir of Trinity College,
Cambridge/James Morgan (organ)/Richard Marlow
Conifer CDCF 503
❡ Bach, Prelude and Fugue in C sharp major (from *The Well-tempered
Clavier*, Book II), András Schiff (piano)
Decca 417 236–2

Barrie Gavin, TV director

❡ Elgar, Symphony No. 2 in E flat, Op. 63 (third movement, Rondo: Presto), London Philharmonic Orchestra/Georg Solti
London 421 386–2

❡ Verdi, 'Dinne . . . alcun là non vedesti?' (from *Simon Boccanegra*), Piero Cappuccilli (Boccanegra), Mirella Freni (Amelia)/Orchestra of La Scala/Claudio Abbado
DG 449 752–2

❡ Trad., 'Al Bahr al Gharan Wasal', Mustapha Marad
RealWorld 768 144–2

❡ Trad., 'Shady Grove', Doc Watson
Vanguard VMCD 7308

❡ Szymanowski, Stabat mater (last movement), Elzbieta Szmytka (soprano), Florence Quivar (mezzo-soprano), John Connell (baritone)/CBSO Chorus/City of Birmingham Symphony Orchestra/ Simon Rattle
EMI CDC 555121 2

❡ Bartók, String Quartet No. 4 (fifth movement, Allegro molto), Emerson Quartet
DG 423 657–2

❡ Boulez, *Notations* (No. 3, Très modéré), Orchestre de Paris/Daniel Barenboim
Erato 2292–45493–2

❡ Trad., 'Stroudwater', Donald Macleod and congregation
Grentrax CDTRAX 9006

I have often worked with him, and though he always maintains he is not a musician, he has a terrific understanding and love of all kinds of music. The Scottish Congregational singing was nothing short of sensational in its haunting, wailing ferocity. Some listeners took offence when I said that in its primal beauty it could be African and tribal. I meant it as a compliment!

Jatinder Verma, theatre director

❡ Page/Plant, 'Stairway to Heaven', Led Zeppelin
Atlantic 7467–82144–2

❡ Nusrat Fateh Ali Khan, 'Huq Ali Ali Haq', Nusrat Fateh Ali Khan and Party
RealWorld RWMCD 2
❡ Bernstein, 'America' (from *West Side Story*) (Original Broadway cast), Chita Rivera, Marilyn Cooper, Reri Grist and Shark Girls/ Orchestra/Max Goberman
Columbia CK 32603
❡ Bach, Concerto for Two Violins in D minor, BWV 1043 (second movement, Largo ma non tanto), Anne-Sophie Mutter, Salvatore Accardo (violins)/English Chamber Orchestra/Salvatore Accardo
EMI CDC 747005 2
❡ Trad., Raga Marwa, R. Fahimuddin Dagar (voice)/Gopal Das (pakhawaj)/Jyoti Pande, Amelia Cuni (tampuras)
Wergo SM 1081–2
❡ Mukesh, 'Awara Hoon' (from the film *Awara*), Mukesh
EMI CDF 130076
❡ Beethoven, Piano Concerto No. 5 in E flat, 'Emperor', Op. 73 (third movement, Rondo), Maurizio Pollini (piano)/Vienna Philharmonic Orchestra/Karl Böhm
DG 413 447–2
❡ Kris Kristoffersen, 'Help Me Make It Through the Night', Gladys Knight and the Pips
Motown 530 187–2
❡ Beethoven, Sonata in F minor, 'Appassionata', Op. 57 (first movement, Allegro assai), Emil Gilels (piano)
DG 419 162–2

26 FEBRUARY 2000
Gerald Sinstadt, sports commentator

❡ Britten, Finale from *A Midsummer Night's Dream*, John Shirley-Quirk (Theseus), Stephen Terry (Puck), Alfred Deller (Oberon), Elizabeth Harwood (Tytania), Richard Dakin, John Pryer, Ian Wodehouse, Gordon Clark (Fairies)/Choirs of Downside and Emanuel Schools/London Symphony Orchestra/Benjamin Britten
London 425 663–2
❡ Beethoven, String Quartet in B flat, Op. 18, No. 6 (first movement, Allegro con brio), Tokyo String Quartet
RCA 09026–61284–2

❡ Haydn, Symphony No. 46 in B (finale), Austro-Hungarian Haydn Orchestra/Adam Fischer
Nimbus NI 5532
❡ Tchaikovsky, 'If I Had Known', Op. 47, No. 1, Ljuba Kazarnovskaya (soprano)/Ljuba Orfenova (piano)
Naxos 8.554357
❡ Verdi, 'Rivedrai le foreste imbalsamente' (from *Aida*, Act III), Robert Merrill (Amonasro), Leontyne Price (Aida)/Rome Opera Orchestra/Georg Solti
Decca 417 416–2
❡ Mahler, 'Ging heut' Morgen übers Feld' (from *Lieder eines fahrenden Gesellen*), Dietrich Fischer-Dieskau (baritone)/Philharmonia/Wilhelm Furtwängler
HMV XLP 30044
❡ Lalo, Aubade: 'Vainement, ma bien aimée' (from *Le roi d'Ys*), Tino Rossi (Mylio)/Chorus and Orchestra/Marcel Cariven
Columbia FSX 140
❡ Charlie Barnet, 'Skyliner', Charlie Barnet and his Orchestra, rec. 1944
ASV CDAJA 5169

4 MARCH 2000
Piers Plowright, radio producer

❡ Haydn, String Quartet in D minor, Op. 76, No. 2, Kodály Quartet
Naxos 8 550314
❡ Trad., Sardinian shepherd's song: 'T'amo', Tenores di Bitti/S'Amore 'e' Mame
RealWorld CDR W 60
❡ Japanese rice-wine seller calling his wares
KICG 1011
❡ Beethoven, Sonata in F minor, 'Appassionata', Op. 57, Solomon (piano)
HLM 7100
❡ Quincey Jones, 'Count 'Em' (from *Compact Jazz*), Count Basie and his Orchestra
Verve 831 364–2
❡ Berlioz, 'Un bal' (second movement from *Symphonie fantastique*), Detroit Symphony Orchestra/Paul Paray
Mercury 434 238–2

❡ Johnny Mercer, 'I Love You' (from *The Johnny Mercer Songbook*),
Billie Holiday (vocal)
Verve 555 402–2
❡ Bach, Partita No. 1 in B flat major (Menuet I and II), Dinu Lipatti
(piano)
EMI 7243 5 66988 2
❡ Victoria, Kyrie (from Requiem, 1605), Westminster Cathedral Choir/
David Hill
Hyperion CDA 66250

11 MARCH 2000
Penelope Farmer, writer

❡ Mozart, Divertimento for String Trio in E flat, K563 (second
movement, Adagio), Grumiaux Trio
Philips 422 513–2
❡ Boulez, 'Complainte du lézard amoureux' (from *Le soleil des eaux*),
Halina Lukomska (soprano)/French National Radio Orchestra/Pierre
Boulez
Stradivarius STR 10029
❡ Szymanowski, Stabat mater (fifth movement), John Connell (bass)/
City of Birmingham Symphony Orchestra and Chorus/Simon Rattle
EMI CDC 555121 2
❡ Birtwistle, *Earth Dances* (conclusion), BBC Symphony Orchestra/
Peter Eötvös
Collins 20012
❡ Mankwane/Bopape, 'Izingubo Ezimhlophe', Mahotella Queens
Earthworks CDEWV 20
❡ Gubaidulina, 'Weib, siehe, das ist dein Sohn' (from *Sieben Worte*),
Maria Kliegel (cello)/Elsbeth Moser (bayan)/Camerata Transsylvanica/
György Selmeczi
Naxos 8.553557
❡ Janáček, *The Makropoulos Case*, Elisabeth Söderström (Emilia
Marty), Peter Dvorský (Gregor), Vladimir Krejčik (Vitek), Dalibor
Jedlička (Kolenatý), Václav Zítek (Prus)/Vienna Philharmonic
Orchestra/Charles Mackerras
Decca 430 372–2
❡ Haydn, String Quartet in E flat, Op. 76, No. 6 (third movement,
Menuetto: Presto), Kodály Quartet
Naxos 8.550315

John Cale, singer/songwriter

❡ B. Wilson/G. Usher, 'In My Room', The Beach Boys
Capitol CDP 793692 2
❡ Villa Lobos, *Bachianas Brasileiras* No. 5 (first movement, Aria),
Barbara Hendricks (soprano)/8 cellos from the Royal Philharmonic
Orchestra/Enrique Bátiz
EMI CDC 747 433 2
❡ Beck/Karl Stephenson, 'Loser', Beck
Geffen GFSTD 67
❡ John Cage, *4'33''*, Frank Zappa
Koch 3 7238 2/B
❡ Jonathan Richman, 'Roadrunner', Jonathan Richman and the
Modern Lovers
Rhino R2 70091
❡ Roy Harris, Symphony No. 3 (opening), Detroit Symphony
Orchestra/Neeme Järvi
Chandos CHAN 9474
❡ John Cale, 'Ari Sleepy Too' (from *Dance Music: Nico the Ballet*), Ice
Nine
Detour 3984 22122
❡ Lou Reed, 'Heroin' (from album *The Velvet Underground and Nico*),
The Velvet Underground
Verve 823 290 2

*He of the oh, so slow delivery. Check out his counterpart as realised by
John Sessions (p. 126).*

John Calder, publisher

❡ Beethoven, 'My Faithful Johnny' (from *Scottish Folk Song
Arrangements*, Op. 108), Dietrich Fischer-Dieskau (baritone)/Andreas
Röhn (violin)/Georg Donderer (cello), Karl Engel (piano)
DG 2530 262
❡ Stravinsky, 'I Burn, I Freeze' (from *The Rake's Progress*, Act III), John
Reardon (Shadow), Royal Philharmonic Orchestra/Igor Stravinsky
Sony Classical SM2K 46 299

❡ Richard Strauss, 'Es gibt ein Reich' (from *Ariadne auf Naxos*), Leontyne Price (Ariadne), Barry McDaniel (Harlekin), Edita Gruberová (Zerbinetta)/London Philharmonic Orchestra/Georg Solti
Decca 440 402–2
❡ Birtwistle, 'The Turning of the Seasons', (from *Gawain*), John Marsden (Ywain), Marie Angel (Morgan le Fay)/Chorus and Orchestra of the Royal Opera House/Elgar Howarth
Collins Classics 70412/A and B
❡ Mozart, Dies irae (from Requiem, K626), Wiener Singverein/ Berlin Radio Symphony Orchestra/Ferenc Fricsay
DG 4399 412–2
❡ Gluck, 'Divinités du Styx' (from *Alceste*), Kirsten Flagstad/Danish Radio Symphony Orchestra/Johann Hye Knudsen
Simax PSC 1823/A-C
❡ Webern, Five Orchestral Pieces, Op. 10 (No. 3, Sehr langsam), London Symphony Orchestra/Pierre Boulez
Sony SM 3K 45845
❡ Handel, 'Verdi prati' (from *Alcina*, Act II), Jochen Kowalski (Ruggiero)/Chamber Orchestra 'Carl Philipp Emmanuel Bach'/ Hartmut Haenchen
Capriccio 10213
❡ Schubert, 'Death and the Maiden', D531, Dietrich Fischer-Dieskau (baritone)/Gerald Moore (piano)
DG 415 188–2

1 APRIL 2000
Christopher Frayling, director, Royal College of Art

❡ Shostakovich, Symphony No. 7, 'Leningrad' (first movement), St Petersburg Philharmonic Orchestra/Vladimir Ashkenazy
Decca 448 814–2
❡ Ennio Morricone, 'La Resi dei Conti' (from *For a Few Dollars More*), Ennio Morricone
Camden 74321 66040–2/A
❡ Mozart, 'Der hölle Rache' (from *The Magic Flute*, Act II), Sumi Jo (Queen of the Night), Vienna Philharmonic Orchestra/Georg Solti
Decca 433 212–2

❡ Weill, 'Die Moritat von Mackie Messer' (from *Kleine Dreigroschenmusik*), Berlin State Opera Orchestra/Otto Klemperer
Symposium SYMCD1042
❡ Gluck, 'Che farò senza Euridice?' (from *Orfeo ed Euridice*, Act III), Kathleen Ferrier (Orfeo)/London Symphony Orchestra/Malcolm Sargent
Decca 458 270–2
❡ Rousseau, *Le devin du village*, Colette Janine Micheau/Louis de Froment Chamber Orchestra/Louis de Froment
Columbia CX 1503
❡ Ian Dury, 'Reasons to be Cheerful' (Part 3), Ian Dury and the Blockheads
Repertoire REP 4547-WY
❡ Elgar, 'Nimrod' (from *Variations on an Original Theme, 'Enigma'*, Op. 36), BBC Symphony Orchestra/Leonard Bernstein
CD: 413 490–2

8 APRIL 2000
David Cairns, music critic, writer

❡ Beethoven, String Quartet in A minor, Op. 132, Busch Quartet
EMI CHS 565308 2
❡ Mozart, Symphony No. 39 in E flat, K543, London Philharmonic Orchestra/Thomas Beecham
EMI CHS 763698 2
❡ Wagner, Overture to *Die Meistersinger von Nürnberg*, Royal Philharmonic Orchestra/Thomas Beecham
Music and Arts CD 631
❡ Fisher/Roberts, 'You Always Hurt the One You Love', Spike Jones and his City Slickers
RCA 74321–13576–2
❡ Elgar, 'Sanctus fortis' (from *The Dream of Gerontius*), Heddle Nash (Gerontius)/Huddersfield Choral Society/Liverpool Philharmonic Orchestra/Malcolm Sargent
Testament SBT 2025
❡ Verdi, 'È sogno? o realtà?' (from *Falstaff*, Act II), Frank Guarrera (Ford), Giuseppe Valdengo (Falstaff)/NBC Symphony Orchestra/Arturo Toscanini
RCA GD 60251

¶ Tippett, opening of Act II from *The Midsummer Marriage*, Orchestra of the Royal Opera House/Colin Davis
Lyrita SRCD 2217
¶ Britten, 'Mad Scene' (from *Peter Grimes*, Act III), Jon Vickers (Peter Grimes)/Chorus and Orchestra of the Royal Opera House/Colin Davis
Philips 432 578–2
¶ Stravinsky, 'Pas de quatre' (from *Agon*), Los Angeles Festival Symphony Orchestra/Igor Stravinsky
Sony SM3K 46292
¶ Bach, Brandenburg Concerto No. 5 in D, BWV 1050, Rudolf Serkin (piano)/Marcel Moyse (flute)/Adolf Busch (violin)/Adolf Busch Chamber Players
EMI CHS 764047 2

David Cairns's biography of Berlioz and his editing of the letters provide some of the greatest literary sources in music. As with Colin Davis (p. 37), it is interesting that a passion for Berlioz is coupled with a love of Tippett.

15 APRIL 2000
Kevin Carey, writer, broadcaster and director of HumanITy

¶ Byrd, 'Ave verum corpus', Tallis Scholars
Gimell CDGIMB 450
¶ Berio, *Sinfonia* (third movement), Swingle Singers, New York Philharmonic Orchestra/Luciano Berio
Columbia MS 7268
¶ Gary Burton/Keith Jarrett, 'Moon Child' (from *In Your Quiet Place*), Gary Burton/Keith Jarrett
RHINO R2 71594
¶ Mahler, Symphony No. 9 (finale), Vienna Philharmonic Orchestra/Bruno Walter
DG 423 564–2
¶ Dallapiccola, Largo (No. 1 from *Five Fragments of Saffo*), Julie Moffatt (soprano)/Ensemble Intercontemporain/Hans Zender
Erato 4509 98509–2
¶ Schubert, Sonata in B flat, D960 (second movement, Andante sostenuto), Alfred Brendel (piano)
Philips 422 062–2

❡ Bach, Prelude in D minor, BWV 851 (from *The Well-tempered Clavier*, Book I), Angela Hewitt (piano)
Hyperion CDA 67301/2
❡ Britten, Te Deum, Choir of Norwich Cathedral, Neil Taylor (organ)/ Michael Nicholas
Priory PRCD 470
❡ Rameau, Last recitative, aria and chorus from *Hippolyte et Aricie*, Mark Padmore (Hippolyte), Eirian James (Diane)/Les Arts Florissants/ William Christie
Erato 0630 15517–2

22 APRIL 2000
Phyllida Lloyd, theatre director

❡ Morris/Waller, 'Please Take Me out of Jail', Thomas 'Fats' Waller (organ and piano)/Morris's Hot Babies
Halcyon DHDL 115
❡ Verdi, 'Una macchia è qui tuttora' (from *Macbeth*, Act IV), Shirley Verrett (Lady Macbeth), Sergio Fontana (Doctor), Anna Caterina Antonacci (Gentlewoman)/Orchestra of the Teatro Comunale of Bologna/Riccardo Chailly
Decca 417 525–2
❡ Gilbert/Sullivan, conclusion of Act I from *The Mikado*, Felicity Palmer (Katisha), Anthony Rolfe Johnson (Nanki-Poo), Marie McLaughlin (Yum-Yum)/Chorus and Orchestra of the Welsh National Opera/Charles Mackerras
Telarc CD 80284
❡ Lewis Carroll, 'The Croquet Game' (from *Alice in Wonderland*), Fiona Shaw (reader)
Naxos NA 213712
❡ Poulenc, final scene from *Dialogues des Carmélites*, Brigitte Fournier (Soeur Constance), Catherine Dubosc (Blanche)/Chorus and Orchestra of Lyon Opera/Kent Nagano
Virgin VCD 759227 2
❡ Verdi, Recordare (from Requiem), Luba Orgonasova (soprano), Anne Sofie von Otter (mezzo-soprano)/Orchestre Révolutionnaire et Romantique/John Eliot Gardiner
Philips 442 142–2

¶ Britten, second duet from *Gloriana*, Act III, Josephine Barstow
(Elizabeth), Philip Langridge (Essex)/Orchestra of the Welsh National
Opera/Charles Mackerras
Argo 440 213–2

29 APRIL 2000
Dave Holland, jazz musician

¶ Strayhorn, UMMG, Duke Ellington
RCA NC86287
¶ John Coltrane, 'A Love Supreme' (Part 1), John Coltrane, featuring
Elvin Jones (drums), Jimmy Garrison (bass)
Impulse MCAD 5660 JVC-467
¶ Holland/Lojac, 'Homecoming', Dave Holland Quintet
ECM 1292 825 322–2
¶ Moten/Peer, 'Moten Swing', Oscar Peterson Trio
Verve 821 724–2
¶ 'Gloria's Step', Bill Evans Trio
Riverside RLP-9376
¶ Miles Davis/Gil Evans, 'My Ship', Miles Davis/Gil Evans
¶ Bela Bartók, *Concerto for Orchestra* and *Dance Suite*, Chicago
Symphony Orchestra/Georg Solti
Decca 400 052 2
¶ Charles Mingus, '2BS', Charles Mingus, featured soloists Booker
Ervin (tenor saxophone), Jaki Byard (piano)
Impulse MCAD39119

*Just one of several highly articulate jazz musicians and just one of several
who had worked with Miles Davis. All spoke of his innate musicianship
and his ability to take jazz into completely new vistas. This was coupled
with the most idiosyncratic and liquid tone. Helped to explain why Miles
has been requested more than any other jazz composer or musician.*

6 MAY 2000
Donna Leon, crime writer

¶ Mozart, 'Se viver non degg'io' (from *Mitridate, Rè di Ponto*, Act II),
Cecilia Bartoli (Sifare), Natalie Dessay (Aspasia)/Les Talens Lyriques/
Christophe Rousset
Decca 460 772–2

❡ Handel, 'Ombre pallide' (from *Alcina*, Act II), Renée Fleming (Alcina)/Les Arts Florissants/William Christie
Erato 8573–80233–2
❡ Bellini arr. Celso Valli, 'Casta diva' (from *Norma*, Act I), Filippa Giordano
Erato 3984–29694–2
❡ Handel, 'Vivi, tiranno' (from *Rodelinda*), David Daniels (Bertarido)/ Orchestra of the Age of Enlightenment/Roger Norrington
Virgin VC 545326 2
❡ Vivaldi, 'Anch'il mar par che sommerga' (from *Il Tamerlano*), Cecilia Bartoli (Idaspe)/Il Giardino Armonico/Giovanni Antonini
Decca 466 569–2
❡ Verdi, 'Di quella pira' (from *Il Trovatore*, Part III), Jussi Björling (Manrico)/Robert Shaw Chorale/RCA Victor Orchestra/Renato Cellini
RCA GD 86643
❡ Handel, 'Gird on thy Sword' (from *Saul*), Vienna State Opera Chorus/Concentus Musicus of Vienna/Nikolaus Harnoncourt
Teldec 4509–97504–2
❡ Trad. arr. Carl Doy, 'Haere ra e Hine', Kiri te Kanawa (soprano)/ Maori Group/Abbey Road Ensemble
EMI CDC 556828 2

13 MAY 2000
Kathleen Burk, historian

❡ Schubert, 'Der Leiermann' (from *Winterreise*), Dietrich Fischer-Dieskau (baritone)/Gerald Moore (piano)
EMI CDM 763560/2 2
❡ Beethoven, String Quartet No. 15 in A minor, Op. 132 (third movement, 'Heiliges Dankgesang eines Genesenen an die Gottheit, in der lydischen Tonart'), The Lindsays
ASV CD DCA 604
❡ Beethoven, 'Mir ist so wunderbar' (from *Fidelio*, Act I), Ingeborg Hallstein (Marzelline), Christa Ludwig (Leonore), Gottlob Frick (Rocco), Gerhard Unger (Jaquino)/Philharmonia/Otto Klemperer
EMI CDM 769325/6
❡ Praetorius, A group of 4 Voltas (from *Dances from Terpsichore*, 1612), New London Consort/Philip Pickett (director)
Oiseau Lyre 414 633–2

¶ Byrd, 'My Sweet Little Darling', Alfred Deller (countertenor)/
Wenziger Consort of viols
Vanguard 08 5068 71
¶ Monteverdi, Duo seraphim (from Vespers, 1610), Nigel Rogers, Andrew
King, Joseph Cornwell (tenors)/Taverner Players/Andrew Parrott
EMI CDC 747078/79 2
¶ Mozart, 'Placido è il mar' (from *Idomeneo*, Act II), Hillevi
Martinpelto (Elektra)/Monteverdi Choir, English Baroque Soloists/
John Eliot Gardiner
Archiv 431 676–2
¶ Dunstaple, Gloria in canon, Orlando Consort
Metronome MET CD 1009
¶ Monteverdi, 'Pur ti miro, pur ti godo' (from *L'incoronazione di
Poppea*, Act III), Carolyn Watkinson (Nerone)/Carmen Balthrop
(Poppea)/Il complesso barocco/Alan Curtis
Fonit Cetra LMA 3008
¶ Machaut, 'Douce dame jolie' (virelai), Margaret Philpot (Gothic
Voices)
Hyperion CDA 66087

20 MAY 2000
Kevin Coates, jeweller

¶ Sarasate, *Navarra*, Op. 33, David and Igor Oistrakh (violins)/Leipzig
Gewandhaus Orchestra/Franz Konwitschny
DG 459 016–2
¶ Vivaldi, 'Agitata da due venti' (from *Griselda*), Cecilia Bartoli
(mezzo-soprano)/Sonatori de la Gioiosa Marca
Decca 455 981–2
¶ Trad., Raga Jogeshwari (beginning of *Alap*), Ravi Shankar (sitar)/
Alla Rakha (tabla)
DG 2531 280
¶ Mozart, Canzonetta sull'aria (from *The Marriage of Figaro*),
Elisabeth Schwarzkopf (Countess), Anna Moffo (Susanna)/
Philharmonia/Carlo Maria Giulini
EMI CMS 763266 2
¶ Telemann, Sonata in B flat (first movement, Dolce et vivace), Duo
Vinaccia: Kevin Coates (mandolin)/Nel Romano (harpsichord)
Arion ARN 38333

❡ Handel, 'As Steals the Morn upon the Night' (from *L'Allegro, il Penseroso ed il Moderato*), Patrizia Kwella (soprano)/Maldwyn Davies (tenor)/English Baroque Soloists/John Eliot Gardiner
Erato ECD 88077
❡ Donizetti, 'Chi mi frena in tal momento' (from *Lucia di Lammermoor*, Act II), Giuseppe di Stefano (Edgardo), Rolando Panerai (Enrico), Maria Callas (Lucia)/Nicola Zaccaria
EMI CMS 763631 2
❡ Prokofiev, Aubade (Mandolin Dance) from *Romeo and Juliet*, London Symphony Orchestra/André Previn
EMI CDS 749012 8
❡ Messiaen, 'Intermède' (from *Quartet for the End of Time*), Joshua Bell (violin)/Steven Isserlis (cello)/Michael Collins (clarinet)
Decca 452 899–2

27 MAY 2000
Richard Sennett, sociologist and writer

❡ Schubert, Impromptu in G flat, D899, No. 3, Alfred Brendel (piano)
Philips 422 237–2
❡ Bach, Arioso (from Cantata No. 156), Maurice Maréchal (cello)/ Jean Doyen (piano)
Strings QT 99–301
❡ Bach (arr. Siloti), Air (from Orchestral Suite No. 3), Pablo Casals (cello)/Blas Net (piano)
Pearl GEMMCD 9128
❡ Trad., 'Swing Low, Sweet Chariot', Archie Shepp (saxophone)/Horace Parlan (piano)
SteepleChase SCCD 31079
❡ De Laserna (arr. Cassadó), *Tonadilla*, Pablo Casals (cello)/Blas Net (piano)
Pearl GEMMCD 9128
❡ Irving Berlin, 'Count your Blessings Instead of Sheep', Sonny Rollins (saxophone)
Prestige PRCD 6894
❡ Brahms, Intermezzo in B minor, Op. 119, No. 1, Radu Lupu (piano)
Decca 417 599–2
❡ Scarlatti, Sonata in C sharp minor, Kk 247, Murray Perahia (piano)
Sony SK 62785

❡ Fauré, Cello Sonata No. 2, Op. 117 (first movement, Allegro), Steven Isserlis (cello)/Pascal Devoyon (piano)
RCA 09026–68049–2

3 JUNE 2000
Karen Armstrong, writer on religious affairs

❡ Bob Dylan, 'Visions of Johanna' (from *Blonde on Blonde*), Bob Dylan
Columbia CGK 841
❡ The Quran, 'Surat al-Qadr', Seemi Bushra Ghazi (singer)
Michael Sells Approaching the Quran, the early rev
White Cloud Press TK 29
❡ Mozart, Clarinet Quintet, K581 (second movement, Larghetto),
Gervase de Peyer (clarinet)/Amadeus Quartet
DG 437 646–2
❡ Purcell, 'Thy hand, Belinda' and 'When I am laid in earth' (from
Dido and Aeneas), Jessye Norman (Dido)/English Chamber Orchestra/
Raymond Leppard
Philips 416 299–2
❡ Beethoven, String Quartet No. 15 in A minor, Op. 132 (excerpt from
third movement, 'Heiliges Dankgesang eines Genesenen an die
Gottheit, in der lydischen Tonart'), The Lindsays
ASV CD DCA 604
❡ Bach, Gigue (from Suite No. 5 in C minor, BWV 1011), Pablo Casals
(cello)
EMI CDH 761029–2
❡ Gregorian chant, 'Christus factus est' (Gradual for Palm Sunday),
Choir and Monks of Farnborough Abbey/Anthony Noble (director)
Herald HAVPCD 122

*I always enjoy a tussle over the nature of belief; blind faith versus
rational thought. Music of course can be a religion that elevates
regardless of sight.*

10 JUNE 2000
Jonathan Keates, critic and writer

❡ Handel, 'As with Rosy Steps the Morn' (from *Theodora*), Jennifer
Lane (Irene)/Philharmonia Baroque Orchestra/Nicholas McGegan
Harmonia Mundi HMU 907060

❡ Elgar, Symphony No. 1 in A flat, Op. 55 (fourth movement, conclusion), London Philharmonic Orchestra/Georg Solti
London 421387–2
❡ Berlioz, 'L'île inconnue' (from *Les nuits d'été*), Régine Crespin (mezzo-soprano)/Orchestre de la Suisse Romande/Ernest Ansermet
Decca 460 973–2
❡ Dvořák, Symphony No. 3 in E flat, Op. 10 (second movement, Adagio molto), London Symphony Orchestra/István Kertész
Decca 430 046–2
❡ Donizetti, 'La sacrilega parola' (from *Poliuto*), Ettore Bastianini (Severo), Maria Callas (Paolina), Franco Corelli (Poliuto), Piero de Palma (Nearco), Rinaldo Pelizzoni (Felice), Nicola Zaccaria (Callistene)/Orchestra and Chorus of La Scala, Milan/Antonino Votto
EMI CMS 565448 2
❡ Haydn, Overture to *Armida*, Lausanne Chamber Orchestra/Antál Dorati
Philips 432 438–2
❡ Purcell, 'O All Ye People, Clap Your Hands', Eamonn O'Dwyer, Mark Kennedy (trebles)/Charles Daniels (tenor)/Michael George (bass)/ Choir of New College, Oxford/King's Consort/Robert King
Hyperion CDA 66644
❡ Salvador/Dimey, 'Syracuse', Jean Sablon
DRG CDXP 606

17 JUNE 2000
Julia Somerville, broadcaster

❡ Bach, 'Erbarme dich' (from *St Matthew Passion*), Michael Chance (countertenor)/English Baroque Soloists/John Eliot Gardiner
Archiv 427 648–2
❡ Verdi, 'Ah! Dite alla giovine' (from *La traviata*, Act II), Leo Nucci (Germont), Angela Gheorghiu (Violetta)/Orchestra of the Royal Opera House/Georg Solti
Decca 448 119–2
❡ White/Allan, 'Strange Fruit', Nina Simone
Verve 518 198–2
❡ Bach, Prelude (from Suite No. 1 in G, BWV 1007), Pablo Casals (cello)
Pearl GEMS 0045

❡ Beethoven, String Quartet in B flat, Op. 18, No. 6 (opening of fourth movement, Adagio, 'La Malinconia'), Lindsay String Quartet
ASV CDDCS 305
❡ Richard Strauss, trio from *Der Rosenkavalier*, Act III, Elisabeth Schwarzkopf (Marschallin), Christa Ludwig (Octavian), Teresa Stich-Randall (Sophie)/Philharmonia/Herbert von Karajan
EMI CDS 556242 2
❡ Schubert, Quintet in C, D956 (opening of second movement), Lindsay String Quartet/Douglas Cummings (cello)
ASV CDDCA 537
❡ Cole Porter, 'It's All Right With Me', Frank Sinatra/Nelson Riddle and his Orchestra
MFP CD-MFP 6052

24 JUNE 2000
Robert Temple, expert on occult and Oriental studies

❡ Franck, Prelude (from *Prelude, Fugue and Variation*, Op. 18), Jörg Demus (piano)
Harmonia Mundi HM 423
❡ Wolves howling
Tonsil 003
❡ Lecuona, 'Rapsodia Cubana', Thomas Tirino (piano)/Polish National Radio Symphony Orchestra/Michael Bartos
BIS CD 794
❡ Skryabin, Study in D sharp minor, Op. 8, No. 12, Vladimir Horowitz (piano)
Sony S2K 53457
❡ Marais, 'La rêveuse' (from *4th Book of Pieces for the Viola da Gamba*), Jordi Savall (viola da gamba)/Rolf Lislevand (theorbo)/Pierre Hantaï (harpsichord)
Valois V 4640
❡ Saint-Saëns, Symphony No. 3 in C minor (second movement, Poco adagio), Peter Hurford (organ)/Montreal Symphony Orchestra/Charles Dutoit
Decca 431 720–2
❡ Bach, Fugue in C (from *The Well-tempered Clavier*, Book I), Glenn Gould (piano)
Sony SM2K 52600

¶ Tartini, Cello Concerto in D (second movement, Grave), Severino Zannerini (cello)/I Solisti Veneti/Claudio Scimone
Erato STU 70626
¶ Bonga, Mona ki ngi Xiça, Bonga
Playasound PS 65013

1 JULY 2000
Laurence Marks, TV scriptwriter

¶ Bach, 'Zion hört die Wächter' (from Cantata No. 140), South-West German Madrigal Choir/Consortium Musicum/Wolfgang Gönnenwein
Virgin VTCD 234
¶ Jimmy Rowles, 'The Peacocks', Stan Getz (tenor saxophone)/Bill Evans Trio
Milestone MCD 92492
¶ Ireland, 'Elegy' (from *A Downland Suite*), City of London Sinfonia/ Richard Hickox
Chandos CHAN 9376
¶ Marcello, Oboe Concerto in D minor (second movement, Adagio), Malcolm Messiter (oboe)/Guildhall String Ensemble/Robert Salter
RCA RD 60224
¶ Paul Desmond, 'Take Five', Dave Brubeck Quartet
CBS 462403–2
¶ Beethoven, Symphony No. 6, 'Pastoral', Op. 68 (first movement, Allegro ma non troppo), Vienna Philharmonic Orchestra/Wilhelm Furtwängler
EMI CDH 763034 2

8 JULY 2000
Ronald Rae, sculptor

¶ Shostakovich, Fugue No. 24 in D minor (from *24 Preludes and Fugues*), Vladimir Ashkenazy (piano)
Decca 466 068–2
¶ Vaughan Williams, *Flos campi* (last part, Moderato tranquillo), Christopher Balmer (viola)/Liverpool Philharmonic Choir/Royal Liverpool Philharmonic Orchestra/Vernon Handley
EMI CD-EMX 9512

❧ Shostakovich, String Quartet No. 9 (last movement, Allegro),
Fitzwilliam String Quartet
Decca 425 797–2
❧ Sibelius, *Tapiola*, Op. 112, Helsinki Philharmonic Orchestra/Paavo
Berglund
EMI 568646–2
❧ Schubert, Sonata in B flat, D960 (second movement, Andante
sostenuto), Jenö Jandó (piano)
Naxos DWNX 8.550475
❧ Warlock, *Capriol Suite* (second movement, Pavane), Royal
Philharmonic Orchestra/Malcolm Sargent
EMI CD-EMX 2141
❧ Bach, Prelude and Fugue in E, BWV 878 (from *The Well-tempered
Clavier*, Book II), Glenn Gould (piano)
Sony SM2K 52603

15 JULY 2000
Kyra Vayne, opera singer

❧ Mahler, 'Wenn dein Mütterlein tritt zur Tür herein' (from
Kindertotenlieder), Janet Baker (mezzo-soprano)/Hallé Orchestra/
John Barbirolli
EMI CZS 762707 2
❧ Massenet, 'Élégie', Feodor Chaliapin (bass)/Cedric Sharpe (cello)/
Ivor Newton (piano), rec. 1931
Conifer CDHD 226
❧ Scarlatti, Sonata in G minor, Kk 30 ('Cat's Fugue'), Scott Ross
(harpsichord)
Erato ECD 75403
❧ Shostakovich, 'Foxtrot' (from *Jazz Suite* No. 1), Royal
Concertgebouw Orchestra/Riccardo Chailly
Decca 433 702–2
❧ Mascagni, 'Voi lo sapete' (from *Cavalliera rusticana*), Rosa Ponselle
(Santuzza)/Orchestra/Romano Romani, rec. 1919
Nimbus NI 7846
❧ Johann Strauss II, Overture to *Die Fledermaus*, Vienna Philharmonic
Orchestra/Erich Kleiber, rec. 1933
Biddulph WHL 002

¶ Verdi, 'Ernani involami' (from *Ernani*, Act I), Kyra Vayne (Elvira)
Preiser 89996
¶ Chopin, Polonaise in A, Op. 40, No. 1, Artur Rubinstein (piano)
RCA RD 89814

22 JULY 2000
Sir Frank Kermode, writer and literary critic

¶ Alexander Goehr, *Sing, Ariel* (conclusion), Lucy Shelton, Eileen
Hulse, Sarah Leonard (sopranos)/Ensemble/Oliver Knussen
Unicorn-Kanchana DKPCD 9129
¶ Handel, 'Io t'abbraccio' (from *Rodelinda*, Act II), Teresa Stich-
Randall (Rodelinda), Maureen Forrester (Bertarido)/Vienna Radio
Orchestra/Brian Priestman
Westminster XWN 3320
¶ Britten, Variation V and scene 6 ('The Lesson') from *The Turn of the
Screw*, Michael Ginn (Miles), Lillian Watson (Flora), Helen Donath
(The Governess)/Orchestra of the Royal Opera House/Colin Davis
Philips 446 325–2
¶ Beethoven, String Quartet in B flat, Op. 18, No. 6 (fourth
movement), Talich Quartet
Calliope CAL 9633/4
¶ Bach, 'Ach Herr, lehre uns' (from *Gottes Zeit ist die allerbeste Zeit*,
BWV 106), Teresa Stich-Randall (soprano), Anton Dermota (tenor),
Hans Braun (baritone)/Vienna Bach Guild Choir and Orchestra/Felix
Prohaska
Vanguard 08.2009.71
¶ Mozart, 'Per pietà, ben mio' (from *Così fan tutte*, Act II), Margaret
Price (Fiordiligi)/National Philharmonic Orchestra/Otto Klemperer
EMI CMS 763845 2

29 JULY 2000
Elaine Feinstein, writer and poet

¶ Telemann, Concerto in E minor (last movement, Presto), John
Turner (recorder)/Stephen Preston (flute)/Academy of Ancient
Music/Christopher Hogwood
Oiseau Lyre 411 949–2
¶ Chopin, Nocturne in E, Op. 62, No. 2, Arthur Rubinstein (piano)
RCA RD 89563/B

[¶ Elaine Feinstein reads from *Gold*, Elaine Feinstein recorded live]
¶ Brecht/Eisler, 'Ballad of the Waterwheel', Sonja Kehler (singer)/
Ensemble/Bernd Wefelmeyer
Wergo WER 60078
¶ Brassens, 'Marinette', Georges Brassens
Philips 9101 045
¶ Verdi, Fugue from end of Act III of *Falstaff*, soloists led by Tito
Gobbi (Falstaff)/Philharmonia/Herbert von Karajan
EMI CDM 567085–2
¶ C. P. E. Bach, Concerto in A (slow movement), Feinstein Ensemble/
Martin Feinstein (flute)
Black Box BBM 1019
¶ Bach, 'Singet dem Herrn' (excerpt from Motet No. 1), Monteverdi
Choir, English Baroque Soloists/John Eliot Gardiner
Erato 2292–45979–2B
¶ Mozart, 'Dove sono i bei momenti' (from *The Marriage of Figaro*,
Act III), Lisa della Casa (Countess)/Vienna Philharmonic
Orchestra/Erich Kleiber
Decca 466 369–2
¶ King Oliver, 'West End Blues', Louis Armstrong and his Hot Five, rec.
Chicago, 28 June 1928
Giants of Jazz CD 0242
¶ Shostakovich, 'Lullaby' (from *From Jewish Folk Poetry*, Op. 79),
Nathalie Stutzman (contralto), Gothenburg Symphony
Orchestra/Neeme Järvi
DG 439 860–2

5 AUGUST 2000
Leo Schofield, Sydney Festival Director

¶ Amanda McBroom, 'Ship in a Bottle', Barbara Cook, recorded live at
Sadler's Wells, London, 26 July 1994
DRG 91430
¶ Gilbert/Sullivan, 'If You'll Give Me Your Attention' (from *Princess
Ida*, Act I), John Reed (King Gama)/D'Oyly Carte Opera Chorus/
Royal Philharmonic Orchestra/Malcolm Sargent
London 436 810–2

❡ Wagner, 'Dich, teure Halle, grüss' ich wieder' (from *Tannhäuser*, Act II), Birgit Nilsson (Elisabeth)/Deutsche Oper, Berlin/Otto Gerdes
DG 423 867–2
❡ Debussy, 'Dialogue du vent et de la mer' (from *La mer*), Boston Symphony Orchestra/Pierre Monteux
RCA 09026 61893–2
❡ Bruckner, Symphony No. 7 (recapitulation from Adagio), Cologne Radio Symphony Orchestra/Günter Wand
RCA GD 60075
❡ Verdi, 'O don fatale' (from *Don Carlos*, Act IV), Shirley Verrett (Princess Eboli)/Orchestra of the Royal Opera House/Carlo Maria Giulini
EMI CDC 747701/03–2
❡ Mozart, 'Come scoglio' (from *Così fan tutte*, Act I), Elisabeth Schwarzkopf (Fiordiligi)/Philharmonia/Herbert von Karajan
EMI CHS7 69635–2

12 AUGUST 2000
Simon Shorvon, Professor of Neurology

❡ Galina Ustvolskaya, Sonata No. 2 (first movement), Ivan Sokolov (piano)
Triton 17 014
❡ Prokofiev, 'The King with Grey Eyes' (from *Five Poems by Anna Akhmatova*), Galina Vishnevskaya (soprano)/Mstislav Rostropovich (piano)
Melodiya 74321 53237–2
❡ Sofia Gubaidulina, Bassoon Concerto (second movement), Valeri Popov (bassoon)/Russian State Symphony Orchestra
Chandos CHAN 9717
❡ John Coltrane, *Ascension* Part 1 (Edition 2), John Coltrane
Impulse GRP 21132
❡ Bach, 'Schlummert ein' (from Cantata *Ich habe genug*, BWV 82), Hans Hotter (bass)/Philharmonia/Anthony Bernard
EMI References 763198–2
❡ Elliott Carter, String Quartet No. 5 (tenth section, Adagio serena), Arditti Quartet
Auvidis Montaigne MO 782091

♪ Berg, extract from Act III of *Lulu*, Julia Migenes (Lulu), Brigitte Fassbaender (Geschwitz), Theo Adam (Jack)/Vienna State Opera Orchestra/Lorin Maazel
RCA 74321 57734–2
♪ Shostakovich, String Quartet No. 15 (second movement, Serenata), Beethoven Quartet
Praga PR 254 043

Another scientist with, it would seem, a natural way into complex contemporary music thanks to the mindset required for his work.

19 AUGUST 2000
Ronald Blythe, writer

♪ Butterworth, 'Is My Team Ploughing?' (from *A Shropshire Lad*), Stephen Varcoe (baritone)/City of London Sinfonia/Richard Hickox
Chandos CHAN 8743
♪ Peter Paul Nash, 'Et je joue' (No. 11 of *Apollinaire Choruses*), BBC Singers/Simon Joly
NMC NMCD 055
♪ Cole Porter, 'Begin the Beguine', Andrews Sisters, Glenn Miller Orchestra
RCA 09026 63113–2
♪ Bach, *Goldberg Variations*, BWV 988 (Variation 12, Canone alla Quarta), Pierre Hantaï (harpsichord)
Opus 111 OPS 30–84
♪ Tallis, 'If Ye Love Me', Tallis Scholars/Peter Phillips
Gimell CDGIM 007
♪ Britten, 'God Moves in a Mysterious Way' (from *St Nicolas*), Suffolk school choirs/Aldeburgh Festival Choir and Orchestra/Benjamin Britten
London 425 714–2
♪ Schubert, Quintet for piano and strings in A major, 'Trout', D667, András Schiff (piano)/members of the Hagen Quartet
Decca 458 608
♪ Tippett, *Fantasia Concertante on a Theme of Corelli*, Bournemouth Symphony Orchestra/Richard Hickox
Chandos CHAN 9233
[♪ Ronald Blythe reads from *First Friends* (published by Viking) recorded live]

¶ Duparc, *L'invitation au voyage*, Felicity Lott (soprano)/Graham Johnson (piano)
Harmonia Mundi HMA 190 1219T1

26 AUGUST 2000
Posy Simmonds, cartoonist

¶ Trad. arr Ry Cooder, 'Cancion mixteca' (from the soundtrack of *Paris, Texas*), Harry Dean Stanton (vocal)
Warner 925270–2
¶ Handel, Concerto grosso in B flat, Op. 3, No. 1 (first movement), Vienna Concentus Musicus/Nikolaus Harnoncourt
Teldec 4509 95500–2
¶ Hilda Paredes, *Permutaciones*, Irving Arditti (violin)
MODE 60
¶ Mozart, 'Dove sono i bei momenti' (from *The Marriage of Figaro*, Act III), Gundula Janowitz (soprano)/Orchestra of the Deutsche Oper, Berlin/Karl Böhm
DG 423 115–2
¶ Haydn, Sonata in E minor, Hob XVI: 34, Alfred Brendel (piano)
Philips 412 228–2
¶ Brassens, 'Les sabots d'Hélène', Georges Brassens
Philips 9101 045
¶ Bach, Prelude and Fugue in G minor, BWV 558 (from *The Well-tempered Clavier*, Book I), Simon Preston (organ)
DG 449 212–2
¶ Brahms, Clarinet Quintet (first movement), Gervase de Peyer (clarinet)/Melos Ensemble
EMI CDM 763116–2
¶ Schubert, Sonata in G major, D894, second movement, Andante, Lydia Artymiw (piano)
Chandos ABRD 1075

2 SEPTEMBER 2000
Richard Cork, art critic

¶ Beethoven, Symphony No. 7 (finale), Royal Philharmonic Orchestra/Colin Davis
EMI CDZ 569365–2

❡ Cork, Interlude from 'Colonel Bird', Adam Cork

❡ Nyman, 'Coupling' (from *The Cook, the Thief, his Wife and her Lover*), Michael Nyman Band/Michael Nyman
Venture DVENB 55/D

❡ Mozart, Lacrimosa (from Requiem, K626), Academy and Chorus of St Martin-in-the-Fields/Neville Marriner
Philips 432 087–2

❡ Paul Simon, 'Bridge over Troubled Water', Simon and Garfunkel
CBS CD 63699

❡ Weill, 'Alabama Song' (from *Mahagonny Songspiel*), Susanne Tremper (Jessie), Ute Lemper (Bessie)/RIAS Berlin Sinfonietta/John Mauceri
Decca 430 168–2

❡ Britten, 'Move Him into the Sun' (from *War Requiem*, Op. 66), Peter Pears (tenor), Galina Vishnevskaya (soprano)/Bach Choir/London Symphony Chorus/London Symphony Orchestra/Benjamin Britten
Decca 414 384–2

❡ Verdi, Lacrymosa (from Requiem), Luba Orgonasova (soprano), Anne Sofie von Otter (mezzo-soprano), Luca Canonici (tenor), Alastair Miles (bass)/Monteverdi Choir/Orchestre Révolutionnaire et Romantique/John Eliot Gardiner
Philips 442 143–2

Just as good on music as he is on art and managed, tellingly, to combine the two.

9 SEPTEMBER 2000
Asa Briggs, historian

❡ Brahms, Symphony No. 2, Op. 73 (third movement, Allegretto grazioso), Chicago Symphony Orchestra/Georg Solti
Decca 421 074–2

❡ Scarlatti, Sonata in A, Kk 24, George Malcolm (harpsichord)
Decca LXT 2918

❡ Scarlatti, Sonata in C, Kk 309, Scott Ross (harpsichord)
Erato ECD 75426

❡ Chopin, Waltz in D flat, 'Minute Waltz', Op. 64, No. 1, Krystian Zimerman (piano)
DG 2530 965

¶ Bach, 'Italian' Concerto, BWV 971 (first movement), Wanda Landowska (harpsichord), rec. 1936
Pearl GEMMCD 9265
¶ Schubert, 'Erlkönig', D328, Dietrich Fischer-Dieskau (baritone)/ Gerald Moore (piano)
EMI CMS 763559 2
¶ Chopin, Waltz in D flat, 'Minute Waltz', Op. 64, No. 1, Aleksandr Michalowski (piano)
IPL Veritas VPM 115
¶ Britten, 'Now the Great Bear and Pleiades' (from *Peter Grimes*, Act I), Peter Pears (Peter Grimes)/Orchestra of the Royal Opera House/Benjamin Britten
Decca 414 577–2
¶ Richard Strauss, *Don Quixote*, Op. 35 (Theme and Variations 1 and 2), Lynn Harrell (cello)/Cleveland Orchestra/Vladimir Ashkenazy
Decca 417 184–2
¶ Mozart, conclusion of Act I from *Così fan tutte*, Carol Vaness (Fiordiligi), Delores Ziegler (Dorabella), Dale Duesing (Guglielmo), John Aler (Ferrando), Lillian Watson (Despina), Claudio Desderi (Don Alfonso)/London Philharmonic Orchestra/Bernard Haitink
EMI CDS 747727 2

He was fascinated by the different timbre of various genres of keyboard music, hence two versions of Chopin's 'Minute Waltz'.

16 SEPTEMBER 2000
Eva Figes, writer

¶ Haydn, 'Von deiner Güt', o Herr und Gott' (from *Die Schöpfung*, Part III), Gundula Janowitz (Eve), Dietrich Fischer-Dieskau (Adam)/ Wiener Singverein/Berlin Philharmonic Orchestra/Herbert von Karajan
DG 435 077–2
¶ Bach, Concerto for Two Violins in D minor, BWV 1043 (second movement, Largo ma non tanto), Anne-Sophie Mutter, Salvatore Accardo (violins)/English Chamber Orchestra/Salvatore Accardo
EMI CDC 747005 2
¶ Beethoven, String Quartet in B flat, Op. 130 (fifth movement, Cavatina), Amadeus Quartet
DG 423 473–2

¶ Weill, 'Pirate-Jenny' (from *The Threepenny Opera*), Lotte Lenya (Jenny)/Orchestra of Sender Freies Berlin/Wilhelm Brückner-Rüggeberg
CBS MK 42637
¶ Meacham/Gray, 'American Patrol', Glenn Miller and his Orchestra
Phontastic PHONTCD 7670
[¶ Eva Figes, 'The Knot', Michael Berkeley
recorded live during programme]
¶ Schubert, Impromptu in G flat, D899, No. 3, Alfred Brendel (piano)
Philips 422 237–2
¶ Schubert, 'Der Lindenbaum' (from *Winterreise*), Dietrich Fischer-Dieskau (baritone)/Gerald Moore (piano)
EMI CMS 763559 2

23 SEPTEMBER 2000
Christopher Potter, publisher

¶ Mozart, 'Che vedesse il mio dolore' and 'Che del ciel, che degli Dei' (from *La clemenza di Tito*, Act II), Janet Baker (Vitellia)/Chorus and Orchestra of the Royal Opera House/Colin Davis
Philips 422 824–2
¶ Schubert, 'Der Leiermann' (from *Winterreise*), Harry Plunket Greene (bass-baritone)/Anon. pianist
EMI CHS 566150 2
¶ Sibelius, 'Var det en Dröm', Kirsten Flagstad (soprano)/London Symphony Orchestra/Øivin Fjelstad
Eclipse ECS 794
¶ Wagner, 'Waltraute's Meeting with Brünnhilde' (from *Götterdämmerung*, Act I), Christa Ludwig (Waltraute), Birgit Nilsson (Brünnhilde)/Vienna Philharmonic Orchestra/Georg Solti
Decca 414 115–2
¶ Ligeti, 'Piet Recognises Nekrotzar as Death (from *Le grand macabre*), Willard White (Nekrotzar), Graham Clark (Piet the Pot), Laura Claycomb (Amanda), Charlotte Hellekant (Amando)/London Sinfonietta Voices/Philharmonia/Esa-Pekka Salonen
Sony S2K 62312
¶ Newton/Tate, 'Somewhere a Voice is Calling', John Bonner (treble and bass-baritone)/piano
Columbia DB 1818

¶ Offenbach, 'Ah! quel diner' (from *La périchole*), Claudia Novikova (mezzo-soprano)/Orchestra

EMI CHS 769741 2

¶ Foreman Brown, 'The Yashmak Song', Elsa Lanchester/Ray Henderson (piano)

Legacy International CD 363

¶ Richard Strauss, *Gesang der Apollopriesterin*, Op. 33, No. 2, Felicity Lott (soprano)/Scottish National Orchestra/Neeme Järvi

Chandos CHAN 9159

30 SEPTEMBER 2000
George Benjamin, composer and conductor

¶ Debussy, Act I, scene 3 from *Pelléas and Mélisande*, Frederica von Stade (Mélisande), Richard Stillwell (Pelléas), Nadine Denize (Geneviève)/Berlin Philharmonic Orchestra/Herbert von Karajan

EMI CDM 567058–2

¶ Ligeti, Piano Concerto (fourth movement), Pierre-Laurent Aimard (piano)/Ensemble Intercontemporain/Pierre Boulez

DG 439 808–2

¶ Purcell, Fantasia 7 in C minor, Fretwork

Virgin Veritas 7243 5 45062–2

¶ Grisey, *Modulations*, Frankfurter Museumorchester/Sylvain Cambreling

Accord 206532

¶ Beethoven, Symphony No. 7, Op. 92 (end of finale), Vienna Philharmonic Orchestra/Carlos Kleiber

DG 447 400–2

¶ Birmanie Musique d'Art, 'Hnin thon tha hé min' (Season of mists), Hsaing Waing Orchestra

Ocora C559019/020

¶ Messiaen, 'L'épouse' (No. 5 from *Poèmes pour Mi*), Françoise Pollet (soprano)/Cleveland Orchestra/Pierre Boulez

DG 453 478--2

¶ Berg, 'Seele, wie bist du schön' (No. 1 from *Altenberglieder*, Op. 4), Margaret Price (soprano)/London Symphony Orchestra/Claudio Abbado

DG 449 714–2

❡ Berlioz, 'Queen Mab' scherzo (from *Roméo et Juliette*, Op. 17), London Symphony Orchestra/Colin Davis
Philips 446 202–2
❡ Bach, 'Herr, unser Herrscher' (from *St John Passion*), Monteverdi Choir and English Baroque Soloists/John Eliot Gardiner
ARCHIV 419 325–2
❡ Knussen, Fantastico ('Winter's Foil') (No. 1 from *Songs Without Voices*, Op. 26), Chamber Music Society of the Lincoln Center/ Oliver Knussen
Virgin 0 777 7 59308–2

A fastidious musician who pulled a couple of rabbits from the hat and discussed them with vision. A very good animal impersonator – not many people know that. We neigh, moo and bleat when we see each other at a concert or party!

7 OCTOBER 2000
Dr David Cohen, GP and arts patron

❡ Stravinsky, *Pulcinella* (Vivo), Columbia Symphony Orchestra/Igor Stravinsky
Sony SMK 46293
❡ Beethoven, *Variations on God Save the King*, Alfred Brendel (piano)
Vox CD3X 3017/A–C
❡ Berio, *Sinfonia* (excerpt from third movement, In ruhig fliessender Bewegung), New Swingle Singers/Orchestre National de France/ Pierre Boulez
Erato 4509 98496–2
❡ Trad., 'Brigg Fair', Joseph Taylor (singer)
Leader LEA 4050
❡ Trad., 'The 7.40 Train', Budapest Klezmer Band
Quintana QUI 903070
❡ Bach, Magnificat (opening chorus), Taverner Consort and Players/ Andrew Parrott
Virgin 7243 5 61340–2
❡ Schubert, Fantasy in C major, D934, György Pauk (violin)/Peter Frankl (piano)
Vox STGBY 611

❡ Berlioz, 'Trojan March' (Finale from Act 1 of *Les Troyens*), Berit Lindholm (Cassandra)/Chorus and Orchestra of the Royal Opera House/Colin Davis
Philips 416 433–2
❡ Sibelius, String Quartet in D minor, 'Voces intimae', Op. 56 (first movement), Jean Sibelius Quartet
Ondine ODE 773–2

14 OCTOBER 2000
Robyn Davidson, travel writer

❡ Mompou, *Cançon i Danse* No. 6, Alicia de Larrocha (piano)
RCA 09026–62554–2
❡ Australian Trad., 'Inma Ngintaka', Inma Singers from the Pitjantjatjana region
Desert Tracks 02–7512297
❡ Chopin, Nocturne in E flat, Op. 55, No. 2, Gnaz Friedman (piano)
Philips 456 784–2
❡ Scarlatti, Sonata in C, Kk 159, Ivo Pogorelich (piano)
DG 435–855–2
❡ Indian Trad., Raga Kambohji, Dagar Brothers
Maestros' Choice A 90111
❡ Mahler, 'Ich bin der Welt abhanden gekommen' (from *Rückert-Lieder*), Janet Baker (mezzo-soprano)/New Philharmonia/John Barbirolli
EMI CZS 762707 2
❡ Bob Dylan, 'Love Sick', Bob Dylan
Columbia 486936 2
❡ Ligeti, Chamber Concerto (fourth movement, Presto), Ensemble Modern/Peter Eötvös
Sony SK 58945
❡ Bach, Dona nobis pacem (from Mass in B minor, BWV 232), BBC Chorus/New Philharmonia Orchestra/Otto Klemperer
EMI CMS 763374 2
❡ Berlioz, 'La belle voyageuse', Op. 2, No. 4, Anne Sofie von Otter (mezzo-soprano)/Cord Garben (piano)
DG 445 823–2

Dave Liebman, jazz player and teacher

❡ John Coltrane, 'Crescent', John Coltrane
Jasmine JAS41
❡ Dave Liebman, 'Storm Surge' (The Elements: Water), Dave Liebman
Arkadia 71043
❡ Joni Mitchell, 'Woodstock', Joni Mitchell
Reprise K244085
❡ Charles Ives, *The Unanswered Question*, Orpheus Chamber
Orchestra
DG 439 869–2
❡ Miles Davis/Gil Evans, 'The Pan Piper' From *Sketches of Spain*
Columbia CK67473
❡ Earth Wind and Fire, 'That's the Way of the World', Earth Wind
and Fire
CBS CDCBS 32536
❡ Trad. arr. Gasparian, 'A Cool Wind Is Blowing', Djivan Gasparian
Gyroscope ASCD06

*Another famous player who seems blessed with truly catholic taste in
music. There goes that Earth, Wind and Fire again.*

Bryan Magee, philosopher, writer and broadcaster

❡ Richard Strauss, 'September' (from *Four Last Songs*), Elisabeth
Schwarzkopf (soprano)/Philharmonia/Otto Ackermann
EMI CDH 761001 2
❡ Elgar, Serenade for Strings, Op. 20 (second movement, Larghetto),
Academy of St Martin-in-the-Fields/Neville Marriner
Decca 417 778–2
❡ Wood/Mellin, 'My One and Only Love', Ella Fitzgerald
GRP GRP 26192/B
❡ Mozart, Piano Concerto in C, K467 (second movement, Andante),
Alfred Brendel (piano)/Academy of St Martin-in-the-Fields/Neville
Marriner
Philips 400 018–2

❡ Mozart, 'Farewell Quintet' (from *Così fan tutte*, Act I), Elisabeth
Schwarzkopf (Fiordiligi), Christa Ludwig (Dorabella), Alfredo
Kraus (Ferrando), Giuseppe Taddei (Guglielmo), Walter Berry
(Don Alfonso)/Philharmonia/Karl Böhm
EMI CMS 769331 2
❡ Sibelius, Symphony No. 4 in A minor, Op. 63 (second movement,
Allegro molto vivace), Vienna Philharmonic Orchestra/Lorin Maazel
Belart 461 325–2
❡ Wagner, 'Höchstes Vertraun' (from *Lohengrin*), Franz Völker
(Lohengrin)/Bayreuth Festival Orchestra/Heinz Tietjen
Teldec 9031–76442–2
❡ Mahler/Cooke, Symphony No. 10 (excerpts from finale),
Bournemouth Symphony Orchestra/Simon Rattle
EMI CDC 754406 2

Philosophy and Wagner sure do make exciting bedfellows.

4 NOVEMBER 2000
Jacqueline Mina, jeweller

❡ Greek Trad., Melody of the 'Teke' in minor scale, Manolis Papos
(bouzouki)
FM Records FM 686
❡ Brown/Henderson, 'The Thrill is Gone', Chet Baker
Capitol 792932 2
❡ Vaughan Williams, 'Linden Lea', Ian Bostridge (tenor)/Julius Drake
(piano)
EMI CDC 556830 2
❡ Bartók, *Contrasts* (third movement, Sebes [fast dance]), Melos
Ensemble
EMI CZS 572646 2
❡ Purcell, 'I Attempt From Love's Sickness To Fly', Nancy Argenta
(soprano)/Paul Nicholson (harpsichord)
Virgin VC 759324 2
❡ Bach arr. North, Sarabande (from Suite in G minor, BWV 1011),
Nigel North (lute)
Linn CKD 055
❡ Britten, 'I Know a Bank' (from *A Midsummer Night's Dream*, Act I),
Alfred Deller (Oberon)/London Symphony Orchestra/Benjamin Britten
London 425 663–2

♪ Ravel, *Introduction and Allegro*, Melos Ensemble
EMI CZS 572646 2
♪ Bullock/Whiting, 'When did you Leave Heaven?', Big Bill Broonzy
Vogue EPV 1107

11 NOVEMBER 2000
Helen Simpson, writer

♪ Monnot/Délécluse/Senlis, 'Les amants d'un jour', Edith Piaf/
Orchestra/Robert Chauvigny
Columbia 790562 2
♪ Debussy, 'De l'aube à midi sur la mer' (from *La mer*), Berlin
Philharmonic Orchestra/Herbert von Karajan
DG 439 008–2
♪ Mozart, Fantasia in C minor, K475 (first section, Adagio), Mitsuko
Uchida (piano)
Philips 412 617–2
♪ Gluck, 'Viens, suis un époux qui t'adore' (from *Orphée et Euridice*),
Anne Sofie von Otter (Orphée), Barbara Hendricks (Euridice)/Lyon
Opera Orchestra/John Eliot Gardiner
EMI CDS 749834 2
♪ Purcell, 'Drum Processional and March' (from *Music for the Funeral
of Queen Mary*), King's Consort/Robert King
Hyperion CDA 66677
♪ Pelham Humfrey (arr. Andrew Watts), 'Oh! That I Had But a Fine
Man', Maddy Prior and the Carnival Band
Park Records PRKCD 31
♪ Brahms, Sextet No. 1 in B flat, Op. 18 (opening of second movement,
Andante ma moderato), Yehudi Menuhin, Robert Masters (violins)/
Cecil Aronowitz, Ernst Wallfisch (violas)/Maurice Gendron, Derek
Simpson (cellos)
EMI CDM 763531 2
♪ Campion, 'Come, Cheerful Day', Emma Kirkby (soprano)/Anthony
Rooley (lute)
Hyperion CDA 66186
♪ Mike Westbrook, 'Utopia Blues' (excerpt), John Winfield/Mike
Westbrook Orchestra
ASC Records CD 13

❡ Ravel, 'Deux robinets coulent' (from *L'enfant et les sortilèges*),
Maurice Prigent (Arithmetic), Nadine Sautereau (The Child)/French
National Radio Orchestra/Ernest Bour
Testament SBT 1044

18 NOVEMBER 2000
Norman Rosenthal, Exhibitions Secretary, Royal Academy

❡ Henze, 'Das Paradies' (from *Six Songs from the Arabian*), Ian
Bostridge (tenor)/Julius Drake (piano)
EMI CDC 557112 2
❡ John Cage, *Europera 3* (conclusion), Long Beach Opera
Mode MODE 38/39
❡ Benjamin, *A Mind of Winter* (conclusion), Penelope Walmsley-
Clarke (soprano)/London Sinfonietta/George Benjamin
Nimbus NI 5075
❡ Stravinsky, 'Ivresse matinale' (from *Perséphone*), Vera Zorina
(Perséphone)/Gregg Smith Singers/Columbia Symphony Orchestra/
Igor Stravinsky
Sony SM2K 46300
❡ Schoenberg, *Herzgewächse*, Op. 20, Eileen Hulse (soprano)/
Members of the London Symphony Orchestra/Robert Craft
Koch 37263–2
❡ Wolf-Ferrari, 'Aprile o bella' (from *The Jewels of the Madonna*),
Tito Gobbi (Rafaele)/Chorus and Orchestra of Rome Opera/
Oliviero di Fabritiis
EMI CDM 736109 2
❡ Boulez, 'Improvisation I sur Mallarmé' (from *Pli selon pli*), Phyllis
Bryn-Julson (soprano)/BBC Symphony Orchestra/Pierre Boulez
Erato 2292–45376–2
❡ Weill, 'Life, Love, and Laughter' (from *The Firebrand of Florence*),
Thomas Hampson (Benvenuto Cellini)/London Sinfonietta and
Chorus/John McGlinn
EMI CDC 555563 2
❡ Messiaen, 'Noël' (from *Vingt regards sur l'Enfant-Jésus*), Pierre-
Laurent Aimard (piano)
Teldec 3984–26868–2

*Passion is not the word when it comes to contemporary arts; steam
locomotion comes more to mind and we could certainly do with a bit
more of this kind of enthusiasm.*

Rick Stein, chef

♪ Copland, 'Saturday Night Waltz' (from *Rodeo*), Detroit Symphony Orchestra/Antál Dorati
Decca 430 705–2

♪ Arnold, *The Padstow Lifeboat*, Op. 94, Grimethorpe Colliery Band/ Malcolm Arnold
Conifer 75605 51263–2

♪ Pura Fe, 'Mahk Jchi', Robbie Robertson and the Red Road Ensemble
Capitol CDEST 2238

♪ Thomas Wyatt, 'They Flee from Me', Ted Hughes
published by Faber

♪ Handel, 'I Know that My Redeemer Liveth' (from *The Messiah*), Heather Harper (soprano)/London Symphony Orchestra/Colin Davis
Philips 438 356–2

♪ Hooker, 'This is Hip', John Lee Hooker (guitar, vocals)/Ry Cooder (guitar)/Johnnie Johnson (piano)/Nick Lowe (bass)/Jim Keltner (drums)/Bobby King, Terry Evans, Willie Greene (vocals)
Silvertone ORECD 519

♪ Mozart, Concerto in C for Flute and Harp, K299 (opening of second movement, Andantino), Wolfgang Schulz (flute)/Nicanor Zabaleta (harp)/Vienna Philharmonic Orchestra/Karl Böhm
DG 413 552–2

♪ Verdi, 'Parigi, o cara, noi lasceremo' (from *La traviata*, Act III), Joan Sutherland (Violetta)/Luciano Pavarotti (Alfredo)/National Philharmonic Orchestra/Richard Bonynge
Decca 430 491–2

♪ Mendelssohn, Symphony No. 4 in A, 'Italian', Op. 90 (fourth movement, Saltarello: Presto), Vienna Philharmonic Orchestra/John Eliot Gardiner
DG 459 156–2

Agreed that mackerel was a very underrated fish. Needs to be fresh, though, otherwise the oil becomes rancid.

Maxwell Hutchinson, architect

❡ John Coltrane, 'Giant Steps', John Coltrane
Atlantic LC 1311
❡ Brahms, *Alto Rhapsody*, Christa Ludwig (mezzo-soprano), Vienna
Singverein/Vienna Philharmonic Orchestra/Karl Böhm
DG 439 441–2
❡ Albert King, 'Laundromat Blues', Albert King
Atlantic LC 0121
❡ Elgar, 'O salutaris', All Saints Choir/Harry Bramma
Priory PRCD490
❡ Cesar Franck, *Prelude, Fugue and Variation*, Piet Kee (organ)
Chandos CHAN 8891
❡ Antoine Forqueray, 'La Forqueray', Jordi Savall and Christoph Coin
(bass viola da gamba) Ton Koopman (harpsichord)
Telefunken 6.42366
❡ Fauré, *Cantique de Jean Racine*, Oxford Schola Cantorum, Oxford
Camerata/Jeremy Summerly
Naxos 8 550765
❡ Martin Codax, 'Mandad'ei comingo' (Cantigas de Amigo), Mara
Kiek (singer)/Sinfonye/Stevie Wishart (director)
Hyperion HYP 12
❡ Vaughan Williams, 'Down Ampney' (Come down, O love divine),
Trinity College Choir, Cambridge/Richard Marlow
Conifer 75605 51249–2

Canon Tom Wright, theologian

❡ Walford Davies, *Psalm 23*, Choir of Lichfield Cathedral/Robert
Sharpe (organ)/Andrew Lumsden
Lammas LAMM 104D
❡ Beethoven, Symphony No. 9, 'Choral', Op. 125 (end of fourth
movement), Yvonne Kenny (soprano), Sarah Walker (mezzo-soprano),
Patrick Power (tenor), Petteri Salomaa (bass)/Schütz Choir of
London/London Classical Players/Roger Norrington
EMI CDC 749221 2

❡ Original Dixieland Jazz Band, 'Livery Stable Blues', Original
Dixieland Jazz Band
RCA ND 90026
❡ Vaughan Williams, Symphony No. 5 in D (opening of first
movement), Philharmonia/John Barbirolli
EMI CDM 565110 2
❡ Bob Dylan, 'When the Ship Comes In', Peter, Paul and Mary
Warner WEP 613
❡ Sibelius, Symphony No. 4 in A minor, Op. 63 (second movement,
Allegro molto vivace), Gothenburg Symphony Orchestra/Neeme Järvi
BIS CD 263
❡ Handel, 'Comfort Ye' (from *Messiah*), John Wakefield (tenor)/
London Symphony Orchestra/Colin Davis
Philips 438 356–2
❡ Schubert, 'Gute Nacht' (from *Winterreise*), Dietrich Fischer-Dieskau
(baritone)/Gerald Moore (piano)
EMI CMS 763559 2

16 DECEMBER 2000
Patrick Gale, novelist

❡ Tippett, 'Dance, Clarion Air', Christ Church Cathedral Choir/
Stephen Darlington
Nimbus NI 5266
❡ Britten, 'From the Gutter' (from *Peter Grimes*, Act II), Yvonne
Barclay, Pamela Helen Stephen (Nieces)/Ameral Gunson (Auntie)/
Janice Watson (Ellen)/City of London Sinfonia/Richard Hickox
Chandos CHAN 9448
❡ Bach, Suite No. 3 in C, BWV 1009 (Prelude), Pablo Casals (cello)
Pearl GEMS 0045
❡ Messiaen, *O sacrum convivium*, Choir of Westminster Cathedral/
James O'Donnell
Hyperion WCC 100
❡ Trad. arr. Britten, 'O Waly, Waly', Kathleen Ferrier (contralto)/Phyllis
Spurr (piano)
Decca 433 475–2
❡ Mendelssohn, *Song without Words* in E, Op. 19, No. 1, Daniel
Barenboim (piano)
DG 453 061–2

❡ Mendelssohn, Octet in E flat, Op. 20 (fourth movement, Presto), Academy Chamber Ensemble
Philips 420 411–2
❡ Handel, Dominus a dextris tuis (from Dixit Dominus), Margaret Marshall, Felicity Palmer (sopranos)/Richard Morton, Alastair Thompson (tenors)/David Wilson-Johnson (bass)/Monteverdi Choir and Orchestra/John Eliot Gardiner
Erato ECD 88072

23 DECEMBER 2000
National Theatre of Brent

❡ Handel, 'Hallelujah Chorus' (from Messiah), Royal Philharmonic Chorus and Orchestra/Thomas Beecham
RCA 09026–61266–2
❡ Kancheli, 'A la duduki' (opening), Vienna Radio Symphony Orchestra/Dennis Russell Davies
ECM 457 850–2
❡ Addinsell, *Warsaw Concerto* (opening), Louis Kentner (piano)/ London Symphony Orchestra/Muir Matheson (from the 1941 film *Dangerous Moonlight*)
Conifer CDHD 302
❡ Elmer Bernstein, Prelude (from *The Ten Commandments*), Orchestra/Elmer Bernstein (from the original 1956 soundtrack)
TRAX MODEMCD 1010
❡ Philip Glass, 'The Funeral of Amenhotep III' (from *Akhnaten*), Stuttgart State Opera Chorus and Orchestra/Dennis Russell Davies
CBS M2K 42457
❡ Bartók, *Music for Strings, Percussion and Celeste* (opening of second movement), Berlin Philharmonic Orchestra/Seiji Ozawa
DG 437 993–2
❡ Wagner, 'Ride of the Valkyries' (from *Die Walküre*, Act III), Vienna Philharmonic Orchestra/Wilhelm Furtwängler
EMI CE26–5588
❡ Martin/Coulter, 'Congratulations', Cliff Richard
EMI CZD 202

Lord (Robert) Skidelsky, professor of political economy and writer

❡ Mussorgsky, 'Boris's Monologue' (from *Boris Godunov*), Boris Christoff (Boris)/French National Radio Orchestra/Issay Dobrowen
EMI CHS 565192 2
❡ Liszt, Sonata in B minor, Vladimir Horowitz (piano)
EMI CHS 763538 2
❡ Donizetti, *Anna Bolena*, Maria Callas (Anna), Gabriella Carturan (Smeton), Gianni Raimondi (Percy), Plinio Clabassi (Rochefort)/ Chorus and Orchestra of La Scala Milan/Gianandrea Gavazzeni
EMI CMS 764941 2
❡ Mozart, Laudate Dominum (from Vesperae solennes de confessore, K339), Vienna Boys' Choir/Vienna Chamber Orchestra/Hans Gillesberger
RCA 26.41324
❡ Anon., 'Pray my Kinsman', George Seversky/Ivan Basiliesky
Tanagra H08P 0917
❡ Mozart, Sinfonia concertante in E flat, K.364, Arthur Grumiaux (violin)/Arrigo Pelliccia (viola)/London Symphony Orchestra/Colin Davis
Philips PHCP 4919
❡ Verdi, Ingemisco (from Requiem), Nicolai Gedda (tenor)/ Philharmonia/Carlo Maria Giulini
EMI CDS 556250 2

A. C. Grayling, philosopher and writer

❡ Reynaldo Hahn, 'L'heure exquise', Felicity Lott (soprano)/Graham Johnson (piano)
Hyperion CDA 67141
❡ Debussy, Sonata for Flute, Viola and Harp (second movement, Interlude), Melos Ensemble
Decca 421 154–2
❡ Puccini, 'Un bel di' (from *Madama Butterfly*, Act II), Maria Callas (Madama Butterfly)/Orchestra of La Scala, Milan/Herbert von Karajan
EMI CDS 747959 2

¶ Haydn, String Quartet in B minor, Op. 33, No. 1 (Finale: Presto), Quatuor Mosaïques
Astrée E 8570
¶ Brahms, 'Feldeinsamkeit', Op. 86, No. 2, Pierre Fournier (cello)/ Mme Pellas-Lemon (piano)
EMI CZS 569708 2
¶ Bach, 'Ich habe genug' (First aria from Cantata, BWV 82), David Thomas (bass)/Taverner Players/Andrew Parrott
Hyperion CDA 66036
¶ Beethoven, *Choral Fantasy*, Op. 80 (last movement, Allegro), Alfred Brendel (piano)/London Philharmonic Choir and Orchestra/Bernard Haitink
Philips 420 347–2
¶ Schubert, *Moment Musical* in C sharp minor, D780, No. 4, Nikolai Demidenko (piano)
Hyperion CDA 67091

A provocative and unusual man with a particular interest in the delicacy of tone that is a special gift of many fine artists.

13 JANUARY 2001
Sir Michael Levey, Director of the National Gallery

¶ Richard Strauss, conclusion of Act III from *Die Frau ohne Schatten*, Paul Schoeffler (Barak), Christel Goltz (Barak's wife), Hans Hopf (Emperor), Leonie Rysanek (Empress)/Vienna State Opera Chorus/ Vienna Philharmonic Orchestra/Karl Böhm
Decca 421 981–2
¶ Weber, conclusion of Act I from *Oberon*, Julia Hamari (Fatima), Birgit Nilsson (Rezia)/Bavarian Radio Chorus and Symphony Orchestra/Rafael Kubelík
DG 419 038–2
¶ Puccini, Gratias agimus tibi (from Messa di Gloria), Werner Hollweg (tenor)/West German Radio Choir/Frankfurt Radio Symphony Orchestra/Eliahu Inbal
Philips 434 170–2
¶ Handel, 'See in Spate the High Cataract Storming' (from *Julius Caesar*), Janet Baker (Julius Caesar)/English National Opera Orchestra/Charles Mackerras
Chandos CHAN 3019

¶ Mozart, chorus and entrance of Sarastro (from *The Magic Flute*, Act I), Gerhard Hüsch (Papageno), Tiana Lemnitz (Pamina), Wilhelm Strienz (Sarastro)/Berlin Philharmonic Orchestra/Thomas Beecham
EMI CHS 761034 2
¶ Lennon/McCartney, 'When I'm Sixty-Four', The Beatles
Parlophone CDP 746442 2
¶ Bellini, 'Angiol di pace' (from *Beatrice di Tenda*), Luciano Pavarotti (Orombello), Josephine Veasey (Agnese), Joan Sutherland (Beatrice)/ London Symphony Orchestra/Richard Bonynge
Decca 433 706–2
¶ Tchaikovsky, Symphony No. 1 in G minor, 'Winter Daydreams' (opening of first movement), Oslo Philharmonic Orchestra/Mariss Jansons
Chandos CHAN 8402

20 JANUARY 2001
Robert Harbison, professor of architecture

¶ Ram/Rand, 'Only You (and You Alone)', The Platters
Dino Entertainment DINCD 47
¶ Bellini, 'Casta diva' (from *Norma*, Act I), Joan Sutherland (Norma)/ London Symphony Orchestra and Chorus/Richard Bonynge
Decca 425 488–2
¶ Stradella, 'Su coronatemi' and 'Chi nel comun gioire' (from *San Giovanni Battista*), Catherine Bott (Salome), Philippe Huttenlocher (Herod)/Les Musiciens du Louvre/Marc Minkowski
Erato 2292–45739–2
¶ Handel, 'Col saggio tuo consiglio' (from *Agrippina*), Derek Lee Ragin (Nero)/English Baroque Soloists/John Eliot Gardiner
Philips 438 009–2
¶ Mozart, opening of Act I finale from *Così fan Tutte*, Elisabeth Schwarzkopf (Fiordiligi), Christa Ludwig (Dorabella), Alfredo Kraus (Ferrando), Giuseppe Taddei (Guglielmo), Walter Berry (Don Alfonso), Hanny Steffek (Despina)/Philharmonia/Karl Böhm
EMI CMS 769331 2
¶ Schubert, 'Sei mir gegrüsst', D741, Dietrich Fischer-Dieskau (baritone)/Gerald Moore (piano)
DG 431 085–2

❡ Chopin, Nocturne in E flat, Op. 55, No. 2, Vladimir Ashkenazy (piano)
London 443 742–2

3 FEBRUARY 2001
Bob Willis, former Test cricketer

❡ Wagner, *Twilight of the Gods*, Rita Hunter (Brünnhilde), Aage Haugland (Hagen)/English National Opera Orchestra/Reginald Goodall
EMI CMS 764244 2
❡ Morrison, 'Queen of the Slipstream', Van Morrison
Mercury 832 585–2
❡ Mahler, Symphony No. 4 in G (fourth movement, Sehr behaglich), Elly Ameling (soprano)/Royal Concertgebouw Orchestra/Bernard Haitink
Philips 442 054–2
❡ Shostakovich, Symphony No. 8 in C minor, Op. 65 (third movement, Allegro non troppo), Moscow Philharmonic Orchestra/Kiril Kondrashin
Melodiya 74321 19841–2
❡ Dylan, 'Forever Young', Bob Dylan
CBS 83692
❡ Wagner, *The Rhinegold* (opening), Helen Attfield, Shelagh Squires, Valerie Masterson (Rhinemaidens)/English National Opera Orchestra/Reginald Goodall
EMI CMS 764110 2

How appropriate that the England fast bowler with one of the longest run-ups should choose an opera with the same distinction. A Wagner fanatic who would race from cricket grounds all over the world to catch the first act of an opera.

10 FEBRUARY 2001
Colin Thubron, travel writer

❡ Richard Strauss, 'Morgen', Op. 27, No. 4, Elisabeth Schwarzkopf (soprano)/Edith Peinemann (violin)/London Symphony Orchestra/ George Szell
EMI CDC 747276 2

¶ Schubert, 'Die Nebensonnen' (from *Winterreise*), Dietrich Fischer-Dieskau (baritone)/Gerald Moore (piano)
HMV ASD 552
¶ Peruvian Trad., 'Espiritu Inka', Wayna Picchu
ARC EUCD 1569 LC 05111
¶ Mahler, 'Der Abschied' (conclusion) (from *Das Lied von der Erde*), Christa Ludwig (mezzo-soprano)/New Philharmonia Orchestra/Otto Klemperer
EMI CDC 747231 2
¶ Cavalli, 'Non è crudel' and 'Amara servitù' (from *La Calisto*), Janet Baker (Diana)/London Philharmonic Orchestra/Raymond Leppard
Decca 436 216–2
¶ Puccini, 'Or son sai mesi' (from *La fanciulla del West*, Act III), Giovanni Martinelli (Dick Johnson)/Anon. pianist
RCA CDN 5105
¶ Giordano, 'Un di, all'azzuro spazio' (from *Andrea Chénier*), Giovanni Martinelli (Chénier)/Orchestra/Josef Pasternak
Pearl GEMS 0030
¶ Trad., 'Ecstatic Dances of the Whirling Dervishes', Anon. performers
ARC EUCD 1580 LC 05111
¶ Mussorgsky, 'The Winds are Howling', Boris Christoff (bass)/French National Radio Orchestra/Georges Tzipine
EMI CHS 763025 2
¶ Janáček, Kostelnička's aria (from *Jenůfa*, Act II), Eva Randová (Kostelnička)/Vienna Philharmonic Orchestra/Charles Mackerras
Decca 424 483–2

His choice of music has the same exoticism as his travel-inspired writing.

17 FEBRUARY 2001
Keith Sutton, Bishop of Lichfield

¶ Beethoven, Trio in B flat, 'Archduke', Op. 97 (opening of third movement, Andante cantabile), Alfred Cortot (piano)/Jacques Thibaud (violin)/Pablo Casals (cello)
EMI CDM 566989 2
¶ Elgar, *Cockaigne* Overture, Op. 40 (conclusion), BBC Symphony Orchestra/Andrew Davis
Teldec 9031–73279–2

♪ Wilbye, 'Draw On, Sweet Night', Cambridge Singers/John Rutter
Collegium COLCD 105
♪ Beethoven, Symphony No. 6, 'Pastoral', Op. 68 (storm and opening
of Shepherds' Hymn), London Philharmonic Orchestra/Adrian Boult
Vanguard SVC 12
♪ Britten, 'The Choirmaster's Burial' (from *Winter Words*, Op. 52),
Peter Pears (tenor)/Benjamin Britten (piano)
Decca 425 996–2
♪ Trad., 'Nkosi sikeleli Afrika', Anon. choir from Tanganyika
Folkways FH 5588
♪ Bach arr. Busoni, 'Nun komm' der Heiden Heiland', BWV 659, Alfred
Brendel (piano)
Philips 420 832–2
♪ Tippett, Nunc Dimittis, Finzi Singers/Andrew Lumsden (organ)/
Paul Spicer
Chandos CHAN 9265

24 FEBRUARY 2001
Jennifer Johnston, writer

♪ Trad., 'The Beatitudes', Nóirín Ní Riain/Monks of Glenstal
Gael Linn CEFCD 144
♪ Elgar, Cello Concerto in E minor, Op. 85 (first movement,
Adagio–Moderato), Jacqueline du Pré (cello)/London Symphony
Orchestra/John Barbirolli
EMI CDC 555527 2
♪ Cole Porter, 'Miss Otis Regrets', Ethel Waters
Classics 735
♪ Irving Berlin, 'Let's Face the Music and Dance', Ella Fitzgerald
Verve 516 871–2
♪ Mozart, Introitus (from Requiem, K626), Lynne Dawson (soprano)/
Philharmonia Chorus and Orchestra/Carlo Maria Giulini
Sony SK 45577
♪ Edens/Comden/Green, 'Moses' (from *Singin' in the Rain*), Gene
Kelly, Donald O'Connor, Bobby Watson/MGM Studio Orchestra/
Lennie Hayton
CBS AK 45394
♪ Schulze/Leip/Conner/Phillips, 'Lili Marlene', Marlene Dietrich
Music Club MCCD 178

¶ Schubert, 'The Shepherd on the Rock', D965, Heather Harper (soprano)/Thea King (clarinet)/Benjamin Britten (piano)
BBC BBCB 8011–2

Hugh Brody, sociologist and writer

¶ Trad., Innuit throat singing, Mary Karoo, Jinnie Innugark
Ocora C 559071
¶ Lehrer, 'Lobachevsky', Tom Lehrer
Lehrer TLP 1
¶ Beethoven, Cello Sonata in F, Op. 5, No. 1 (opening of second movement, Allegro), Jacqueline du Pré (cello)/Daniel Barenboim (piano)
EMI CMS 763015 2
¶ Bizet, 'Habañera' (from *Carmen*, Act I), Maria Callas (Carmen)/Choeurs René Duclos/Paris Opera Orchestra/Georges Prêtre
EMI CDS 747313 8
¶ Trad., White Mountain Apache Crown Dance
Smithsonian/Folkways SF 40410
¶ Bach, Violin Concerto in A minor, BWV 1041 (third movement, Allegro assai), Andrew Manze (violin and director)/Academy of Ancient Music
Harmonia Mundi HMU 907155
¶ Beethoven, Sonata in E flat, 'Les Adieux', Op. 81a (second and third movements), Artur Schnabel (piano)
EMI CHS 763765 2
¶ Mozart, Offertorium (from Requiem, K626), Nancy Argenta (soprano), Catherine Robbin (mezzo-soprano), John Mark Ainsley (tenor), Alastair Miles (baritone)/London Schütz Choir/London Classical Players/Roger Norrington
Virgin VM 561520 2
¶ Cohen, 'Suzanne', Leonard Cohen
Columbia 468600 2

Jacques Loussier, jazz pianist

♩ Pink Floyd, 'Another Brick in the Wall', Part 2 of *The Wall*, Pink Floyd
Harvest CDP 746036/37 2
♩ Ravel, Piano Concerto in G major (second movement), Krystian Zimerman (piano)/Cleveland Orchestra/Pierre Boulez
DG 449213–2
♩ Bach, Air on a G String, Jacques Loussier Trio
Telarc CD83411TK6
♩ Debussy, *L'isle joyeuse*, Jacques Loussier Trio
Telarc CD83511
♩ Errol Garner, 'That's My Kick', Errol Garner
MGM C8047
♩ Modern Jazz Quartet, 'Django', Modern Jazz Quartet
Prestige OJCCD 057–2
♩ Bach, 'Ich habe genug' (opening aria from Cantata No. 82), Hermann Prey (bass)/Gewandhausorchester/Kurt Thomas
Electrola E80572

John Napper, painter

♩ Bach, 'Kommt, ihr Töchter, helft mir klagen' (opening chorus from *St Matthew Passion*), London Oratory Junior Chorus/Monteverdi Choir/English Baroque Soloists/John Eliot Gardiner
Archiv 427 649–2
♩ Hindi Holi, Juthika Ray (vocals)
HMV 16499 OMC 16208
♩ Traditional Spanish arr. Graciano Tarragó, 'Jaeneras que yo canto', Victoria de los Angeles (soprano)/Renata Tarragó
EMI CDM 566941–2
♩ Trad., 'The Lady of Carlisle', Basil May
AAFS L1
♩ Sibelius, Symphony No. 4 in A, Op. 63 (first movement), Finnish Radio Symphony Orchestra/Jukka-Pekka Saraste
Finlandia 4509–9963–2/B

❡ Canteloube, 'Down There in the Limousin' (from *Songs of the Auvergne*), Jill Gomez (soprano)/Royal Liverpool Philharmonic Orchestra/Vernon Handley
Eminence CD-EMX9500
❡ The Beatles, 'Come Together', The Beatles
Parlophone CD3R 5814
❡ Ewan MacColl, 'Shoals of Herring', Ewan MacColl
Argo ZDA 53
❡ Respighi, 'The Birth of Venus' (from *Trittico botticelliano*), City of London Sinfonia/Richard Hickox
Collins Classics 13492

24 MARCH 2001
Ruth Fainlight, poet

❡ Mozart, Clarinet Quintet in A, K581 (third movement, Menuetto), Antoine de Bavier (clarinet)/New Italian Quartet
Decca LXT 2698
❡ Messiaen, 'Bonjour toi, Colombe verte' and 'Katchikatchi les étoiles' (from *Harawi*), Jane Manning (soprano)/David Miller (piano)
Unicorn-Kanchana UKCD 2084
❡ Anon., 'Sibil-la catalane', Montserrat Figueras (soprano)/La Capella Reial de Catalunya/Jordi Savall Fontalis
ES 8705
❡ Trad., Qsbah solo, Zaan of the Jilala de Tanger
Psalmodia Sub Rosa SUBCD 014–37
❡ Mortazzo/Molleda/Oliva/Rey, 'Antonio Vargas Heredia', Imperio Argentina
Polydor EPH 20531
❡ Trad., 'Ya Da Fik Ghzal', Mouzino
Les Artistes Arabes Associés AAA 062
❡ Trad., 'The Cuckoo', Shirley Collins
Topic TSCD 815
❡ Birtwistle, 'Tenebrae' (from *Pulse Shadows*), Christine Whittlesey (soprano)/Ensemble Intercontemperain/Pierre Boulez
DG 439 910–2

¶ Puccini, 'Como tu m'odil' and 'Vissi d'arte' (from *Tosca*, Act II), Tito Gobbi (Scarpia), Maria Callas (Tosca)/Orchestra of La Scala, Milan/ Victor de Sabata
EMI CDS 556304 2

31 MARCH 2001
Michael Henderson, cricket journalist

¶ Mahler, Symphony No. 9 (conclusion of first movement), Vienna Philharmonic Orchestra/Simon Rattle
EMI CDS 556580 2
¶ Schubert, 'Des Baches Wiegenlied' (from *Die schöne Müllerin*), Fritz Wunderlich (tenor)/Hubert Giesen (piano)
DG 447 452–2
¶ Janáček, *Jenůfa* (conclusion), Elisabeth Söderström (Jenůfa), Wieslav Ochman (Laca)/Vienna Philharmonic Orchestra/Charles Mackerras
Decca 414 483–2
¶ Beethoven, String Quartet in C sharp minor, Op. 131 (first movement, Adagio ma non troppo), Alban Berg Quartet
EMI CDS 754587 2
¶ Wagner, Quintet from *Die Meistersinger von Nürnberg*, Act III, Helen Donath (Eva), Theo Adam (Hans Sachs), René Kollo (Walther), Peter Schreier (David), Ruth Hesse (Magdalene)/Staatskapelle Dresden/ Herbert von Karajan
EMI CMS 567086 2
¶ Sibelius, Violin Concerto in D minor, Op. 47 (second movement, Adagio di molto), Maxim Vengerov (violin)/Chicago Symphony Orchestra/Daniel Barenboim
Teldec 0630–13161–2
¶ Sondheim, 'The Miller's Son' (from *A Little Night Music*), D. Jamin-Bartlett (Petra)/Orchestra/Harold Hastings
Sony SK 65284

Michael tipped me off about Wagner-loving cricketers. Would, I suspect, be very happy writing regularly about music with cricket thrown in as opposed to the other way round.

Glyn Moody, journalist

❡ Mozart, *A Musical Dice Game*, K516f (excerpt), Erik Smith, Neville Marriner
Philips 422 545–2
❡ Beethoven, 'March' (from *Fidelio*, Act I), Philharmonia/Otto Klemperer
EMI CDS 555170 2
❡ Adès, *Asyla* (third movement, Ecstasio), City of Birmingham Symphony Orchestra/Simon Rattle
EMI CDC 556818 2
❡ Sibelius, *Väinön virsi*, Op. 110 (opening), Finnish National Opera Chorus and Orchestra/Eri Klas
Ondine ODE 754–2
❡ Miles Davis, 'Nuit sur les Champs-Élysées', Miles Davis (trumpet)/ Barney Wilen (tenor saxophone)/René Urtreger (piano)/Pierre Michelot (bass)/Kenny Clarke (drums)
Fontana 836 305–23
❡ Trad., 'Lashgvash', The Rustavi Choir
Nonesuch 7559–79224–2
❡ Bach, Prelude in C, BWV 846 (from *The Well-tempered Clavier*, Book I), Leon Berben (harpsichord)
Brilliant Classics 99632/1
❡ Schubert, 'Meeres Stille', D216, Janet Baker (mezzo-soprano)/ Graham Johnson (piano)
Hyperion CDJ 33001
❡ Satie, *Vexations*, Peter Dickinson (piano)
Unicorn RHS 338
❡ Alkan, Grande Sonate: *Les Quatre Ages*, Op. 33 (first movement, 'Vingt ans', Très vite), Marc-André Hamelin (piano)
Hyperion CDA20794

Elizabeth Fritsch, potter

❡ Tigran Tahmizhan, 'A Cool Wind is Blowing', Kronos Quartet/ Djivan Gasparian (duduk)
Elektra Nonesuch 7559–79346–2

❡ Machaut, Agnus Dei (from Messe de Notre Dame), Oxford
Camerata/Jeremy Summerly
Naxos 8.553833
❡ Schubert, Quartettsatz, D703, Alberni Quartet
CRD 3318
❡ Schnittke, Concerto Grosso No. 1 (opening of fifth movement,
Rondo agitato), Gidon Kremer, Tatjana Grindenko (violins)/Yuri
Smirnov (harpsichord)/Chamber Orchestra of Europe/Heinrich Schiff
DG 439 452–2
❡ Berg, 'Liebesode' (from *Seven Early Songs*), Jessye Norman
(soprano)/London Symphony Orchestra/Pierre Boulez
Sony SK 66826
❡ Bach, Preludes Nos 5 in D and 10 in E minor (from *The
Well-tempered Clavier*, Book I), Sviatoslav Richter (piano)
RCA GD 60949
❡ Bud Powell, 'Tempus fugit', Bud Powell (piano)/Ray Brown (bass)/
Max Roach (drums)
Verve 517 955–2
❡ Schumann, 'Mondnacht' (from *Liederkreis*, Op. 39), Ruby Hughes
(soprano)/Alan Williams (piano)
Artists' private recording
❡ Britten, 'This Yonge Child' and 'Balulalow' (from *A Ceremony of
Carols*, Op. 28), James Clark (treble)/Osian Ellis (harp)/Choir of
King's College Cambridge/David Willcocks
EMI CDM 565112 2
❡ Shostakovich, String Quartet No. 3 in F, Op. 73 (second movement,
Moderato con moto), Fitzwilliam String Quartet
Decca 421 475–2

21 APRIL 2001
Michael Holroyd, biographer

❡ Purcell, *Dido and Aeneas* (opening of Act II), Academy of Ancient
Music
Oiseau Lyre 436 992–2
❡ Berwald, *Sinfonia singulière* (Scherzo and final Adagio), Swedish
Radio Symphony Orchestra/Esa-Pekka Salonen
Musica Sveciae MSCD 531

❡ Prokofiev, 'The Battle on the Ice' (from *Alexander Nevsky*), Chorus
of St Petersburg Teleradio Company
RCA 09026 61926–2
❡ Schumann, 'Arlequin' (from *Carnaval*, Op. 9), Artur Rubinstein
RCA RD 85667
❡ Burt Bacharach, 'Trains and Boats and Planes', Dionne Warwick
Rhino R271100
❡ Schoenberg, *Verklärte Nacht*, Berlin Philharmonic Orchestra/
Herbert von Karajan
DG 427 426–2 CD2

28 APRIL 2001
Dr Ralph Kohn, pharmacologist and singer

❡ Bach, 'Vergnügte Ruh', beliebte Seelenlust' (from Cantata, BWV 170),
Janet Baker (contralto)/Academy of St Martin-in-the-Fields/Neville
Marriner
Decca 430 260–2
❡ Beethoven, 'Adelaïde', Op. 46, Peter Schreier (tenor)/András Schiff
(piano)
Decca 444 817–2
❡ Ravel, 'Chanson hébraïque' (from *Chants populaires*), Ralph Kohn
(baritone)/Graham Johnson (piano)
Opera Omnia OP 692
❡ Mahler, 'Der Abschied' (conclusion) (from *Das Lied von der Erde*),
Kathleen Ferrier (contralto)/Vienna Philharmonic Orchestra/Bruno
Walter
Decca 414 194–2
❡ Mozart, 'Ein Mädchen oder Weibchen' (from *The Magic Flute*,
Act II), Erich Kunz (Papageno)/Vienna Philharmonic Orchestra/
Wilhelm Furtwängler
EMI CHS 565356 2
❡ Bach, 'Hat man nicht mit seinen Kindern' (from *Coffee Cantata*,
BWV 211), Theo Adam (bass)/Berlin Chamber Orchestra/Peter Schreier
Archiv 427 116–2
❡ Elgar, Violin Concerto in B minor, Op. 61 (conclusion of second
movement, Andante), Yehudi Menuhin (violin)/London Symphony
Orchestra/Edward Elgar
EMI CDS 754564 2

❡ Stradella, 'Pietà Signore', Beniamino Gigli (tenor)/Orchestra

EMI CDM 769235 2

5 MAY 2001
Neil Tennant, musician

❡ Richard Strauss, *Metamorphosen*, Vienna Philharmonic/Simon
Rattle

EMI CDC 5565802

❡ Kraftwerk, 'Computer Love', Kraftwerk

Elektra 3549–2

❡ Harburg/Arlen, 'Over the Rainbow', Eva Cassidy

Hot Records G2–10045

❡ Poulenc, Oboe Sonata (first movement, Elégie), Olivier Doise
(oboe)/Alexandre Tharaud (piano)

Naxos 8553611

❡ Noël Coward/Gertrude Lawrence, 'You Were There', Noël Coward

EMI 499923–2

❡ Shostakovich, Symphony No. 5 (first movement), Vienna
Philharmonic/Mariss Jansons

EMI CDC 5564422

❡ Messiaen, *Oraison*, Ensemble D'Ondes de Montreal

OHM CD3670

Met him at the Proms. Is unequivocal about what he does and does not
like and fortunately can argue the toss with his friend Janet Street-Porter
(p. 342). I have noticed that pop composers that I really like invariably
have a real interest in contemporary classical music.

12 MAY 2001
Alan Sillitoe, writer

❡ Shostakovich, *The Execution of Stepan Razin* (opening), Vitaly
Gromadsky (bass)/RSFSR Russian Chorus/Moscow Philharmonic
Orchestra/Kiril Kondrashin

HMV ASD 3442

❡ Prokofiev, 'Death of Mercutio' (from *Romeo and Juliet*), Bolshoi
Theatre Orchestra/Gennadi Rozhdestvensky

CDM LDX-A 8297

¶ Chopin, Prelude in D flat, Op. 28, No. 15, Artur Rubinstein (piano)
RCA GD 60047
¶ Berlioz, Overture to *Benvenuto Cellini*, BBC Symphony
Orchestra/Colin Davis
Philips 416 955–2
¶ Handel, 'Sing Ye to the Lord' (final chorus from *Israel in Egypt*),
Elizabeth Priday (soprano)/Monteverdi Choir and Orchestra/John
Eliot Gardiner
Erato 2292–45399–2
¶ Vaughan Williams, 'Seventeen Come Sunday' (from *English Folk
Songs* Suite), London Philharmonic Orchestra/Adrian Boult
PRT PVCD 8396
¶ Bellini, 'Casta diva' (from *Norma*, Act I), Maria Callas (Norma)/
Chorus and Orchestra of La Scala, Milan/Tullio Serafin
EMI CDS 556271 2
¶ Kern, 'Ol' Man River' (from *Showboat*), Paul Robeson/Chorus and
Orchestra of the original 1928 London production
EMI CDC 7478039 2

19 MAY 2001
Nicholas Fisher, Chief Superintendent of Police

¶ Louis Grabu, 'Injurious Charmer of My Vanquished Heart' (from
Rochester's play *Valentinian*), Emma Kirkby (soprano), David Thomas
(bass)/Consort of Musicke/Steven Devine (organ)/directed by Antony
Rooley (lute)
Etcetera KTC 1211 T8
¶ John Blow, 'A Pastoral Elegy on the Earl of Rochester', Andrew King
(tenor)/Consort of Musicke/Steven Devine (organ)/directed by
Antony Rooley
Etcetera KTC 1211
¶ Hans Kox, 'Sempre notte' (from *L'Allegria*), Lucia Meeuwsen
(mezzo-soprano)/Fine Arts Chamber Orchestra/Melvin Margolis
Babel 9262–1
¶ Prokofiev, 'Dance with Mandolins' (from *Romeo and Juliet*, Act II),
Cleveland Orchestra/Lorin Maazel
EMI 452 971–2

❡ Aaron Jay Kernis, 'How God Answers the Soul', Birmingham Bach Choir/Paul Spicer
Ninth Wave Audio Promotional CD
❡ Vaughan Williams, 'Bright is the Ring of Words' (from *Songs of Travel*), Thomas Allen (baritone)/City of Birmingham Symphony Orchestra/Simon Rattle
EMI CDC 7 47220 2
❡ Handel, 'He Spake the Word and He Gave them Hailstones for Rain' (from *Israel in Egypt*), Taverner Choir and Taverner Players/Andrew Parrott
EMI CDS 7540182
❡ Max Reger, 'Unser lieben Frauen Traum', carol, Thomanerchor/ Christoph Biller
GEMA TC1093
❡ Smetana, 'Skocna' (Hopping Dance) (from *Czech Dances* 2), Radoslav Kvapil (piano)
Unicorn-Kanchana DKPC(CD)9139
❡ John Joubert, Theme from *Temps Perdu*: Variations for String Orchestra, English String Orchestra/William Boughton
BMS 419CD

We've not had many policeman on the programme, and certainly none who share my love of the Earl of Rochester, who should be known not just for his erotic verse but also for some of the most touching lines ever written about yearning and growing old.

26 MAY 2001
Jenni Murray, broadcaster

❡ Clara Schumann, 'The Violet', Barbara Bonney (soprano)/Vladimir Ashkenazy (piano)
Decca 452 898–2
❡ Ethel Smyth, Sarabande in D minor (from *Four 4-part Dances*), Liana Serbescu (piano)
CPO 999 327–2/AandB
❡ Milhaud, *Le boeuf sur le toit*, Op. 58, Orchestre du Théâtre des Champs-Élysées/Darius Milhaud
EMI CDC 754604–2

♩ Elgar, *Pomp and Circumstance* March No. 1 in D, BBC Symphony Orchestra/Andrew Davis
Teldec 9031 73278 2
♩ Hildegard of Bingen, 'Ave Generoso' (A Feather on the Breath of God), Margaret Philpot (contralto)/Gothic Voices/Christopher Page
Hyperion CDA 66039
♩ Joan Baez, 'Diamonds and Rust', Joan Baez
AandM CDA 3234
♩ Bach/Hess, Jesu Joy of Man's Desiring, Myra Hess (piano)
Philips 456 834–2
♩ Canteloube, 'Baïlèro' (from *Songs of the Auvergne*), Victoria de los Angeles (soprano)/Orchestre des Concerts Lamoureux/Jean-Pierre Jacquillat
EMI CDC 747970 2

2 JUNE 2001
Albert Irvin, artist

♩ Mahler, Symphony No. 1 (conclusion of last movement), New York Philharmonic Orchestra/Leonard Bernstein
CBS MK 42194
♩ Irving Berlin, 'Isn't This a Lovely Day to be Caught in the Rain?', Fred Astaire, Ginger Rogers/Orchestra/Max Steiner (from the soundtrack of *Top Hat*)
EMI EMTC 102
♩ Beethoven, Sonata in B flat, 'Hammerklavier', Op. 106 (conclusion of first movement, Allegro), Alfred Brendel (piano)
Philips 446 909–2
♩ Morton Feldman, *Rothko Chapel*, University of California Berkeley Chamber Choir/David Abel (viola)/Karen Rosenak (celeste)/William Winant (percussion)/Philip Brett
New Albion NA039CD
♩ Shostakovich, Cello Concerto No. 1 in E flat, Op. 107 (first movement, Allegretto), Mstislav Rostropovich (cello)/Philadelphia Orchestra/Eugene Ormandy
CBS MPK 44850
♩ Boulez, *Éclat* (opening), Ensemble Intercontemperain/Pierre Boulez
Sony SMK 45839

¶ Barry Guy, *After the Rain* (opening), City of London Sinfonia/
Richard Hickox
NMC NMCD 013
¶ Simons/Mark, 'All of Me', Louis Armstrong and his All Stars
Sony SRCS 9512

*Ever since the programme, he has sent the most wonderful hand-painted
Christmas cards with vibrant stripes of colour that light up the room.
Loved colourful new music too!*

9 JUNE 2001
Geoffrey Robertson, QC

¶ Gilbert/Sullivan, 'When I, Good Friends, was Called to the Bar'
(from *Trial By Jury*), John Reed (The Learned Judge)/D'Oyly Carte
Opera Company/Orchestra of the Royal Opera House/Isidore Godfrey
Decca 417 358–2
¶ Wagner, 'Fire Music' (from *Die Walküre*, Act III), Hans Hotter
(Wotan)/Vienna Philharmonic Orchestra/Georg Solti
Decca 455 563–2
¶ Puccini, 'E lucevan le stelle' (from *Tosca*, Act III), Donald Smith
(Cavaradossi)/Tasmanian Symphony Orchestra/Vanco Cavdarski
HMV OASD 7584
¶ Weill, 'Foolish Heart' (from *One Touch of Venus*), Teresa Stratas
(soprano)/'Y' Chamber Orchestra/Gerard Schwarz
Nonesuch 979131–2
¶ Offenbach, 'Elle a fui, la tourterelle' (from *Tales of Hoffmann*,
Act III), Joan Sutherland (Antonia), Orchestre de la Suisse Romande/
Richard Bonynge
Decca 417 364/5–2
¶ The Sex Pistols, 'Pretty Vacant', The Sex Pistols
Virgin V 2086
¶ Verdi, 'Dieu, tu semas dans nos âmes' (from *Don Carlos*, Act II),
Placido Domingo (Don Carlos), Leo Nucci (Rodrigue, Marquis de
Posa)/Orchestra of La Scala, Milan/Claudio Abbado
DG 415 317/2–3
¶ Dylan, 'The Hurricane', Bob Dylan
Columbia 669379–2
¶ Ochs, 'Love Me, I'm a Liberal', Phil Ochs
AandM SP-4599

Sir Roger Penrose, mathematician

¶ Schubert, 'Nacht und Träume', D827, Ian Bostridge (tenor)/Julius Drake (piano)
EMI 7243 5 56347–2
¶ Stravinsky, 'The Masqueraders' (from *Petrushka*), Columbia Symphony Orchestra/Igor Stravinsky
Sony SMK 46293–2
¶ Bach, Et misericordia (duet from Magnificat), Caroline Trevor (alto), Howard Crook (tenor)/Taverner Players/Andrew Parrott
Virgin 7243 5 61340–2
¶ Mozart, Piano Concerto No. 27 in B flat (finale: Allegro), Alfred Brendel (piano)/Academy of St Martin-in-the-Fields/Neville Marriner
Philips 420 487–2
¶ Bach, 'Herr, unser Herrscher' (end of first chorus from *St John Passion*), Taverner Consort and Players/Andrew Parrott
Virgin 7243 5 45096–2
¶ Janáček, final scene from *The Makropoulos Case*, Elisabeth Söderström (Emilia Marty)Vienna Philharmonic Orchestra/Charles Mackerras
Decca 430 373–2
¶ Bach, 'Zerfliesse, mein Herz' (from *St John Passion*), Tessa Bonner (soprano)/Janet See (flute)/Paul Goodwin (oboe da caccia)/Andrew Manze (violin)/Taverner Players/Andrew Parrott
Virgin 7243 5 45096–2
¶ Bach, Concerto for oboe and violin in C minor, BWV 1060 (second movement, Adagio), Anthony Robson (oboe)/Elizabeth Wallfisch (violin), Orchestra of the Age of Enlightenment
Virgin 7243 5 45095–2

Mathematics and Bach seemed inevitable bedfellows here, but finely explained. He also included one of my very favourite songs, 'Nacht und Träume'.

Douglas Kennedy, novelist

¶ Bach, Chromatic Fantasy and Fugue in D minor, BWV 903 (Fugue), Angela Hewitt (piano)
Hyperion CDA 66746

❧ Zappa, 'G-Spot Tornado' (from *The Yellow Shark*), Ensemble Modern
Zappa CDZAP 57
❧ Mozart, 'Madamina, il catalogo e questo' (from *Don Giovanni*, Act I),
Bryn Terfel (Leporello)/Metropolitan Opera Orchestra/James Levine
DG 445 866–2
❧ Brahms, 'Wie lieblich sind deine Wohnungen', (from *A German
Requiem*, Op. 45), Monteverdi Choir/Orchestre Révolutionnaire et
Romantique/John Eliot Gardiner
Philips 432 140–2
❧ Shostakovich, Symphony No. 15 (third movement: Allegretto),
London Philharmonic Orchestra/Bernard Haitink
Decca 444 430–2
❧ Webern, *Six Pieces for Large Orchestra*, Op. 6 (Nos 3 and 4, Zart
bewegt and Langsam), London Symphony Orchestra/Pierre Boulez
Sony SM3K 45845
❧ Stravinsky, *Ebony Concerto* (finale), Benny Goodman (clarinet)/
Columbia Jazz Ensemble
Sony SM2K 46297
❧ Tallis, Sanctus (from *The Christmas Mass*), Tallis Scholars/Peter
Philips
Gimell 454 934–2

30 JUNE 2001
Nicholas Hytner, theatre director

❧ Britten, 'The Moon has Risen' (from *Curlew River*), Harold
Blackburn (Abbot)/English Opera Group/Benjamin Britten
London 421 858–2
❧ Haydn, String Quartet in C major, 'Emperor' (second movement),
Amadeus Quartet
DG 415 867–2
❧ Handel, 'Piangerò la sorte mia' (from *Giulio Cesare*, Act III), Ann
Murray (Cleopatra)/Orchestra of the Age of Enlightenment/Charles
Mackerras
Forlane UCD 16738
❧ Sondheim, 'Finishing the Hat' (from *Sunday in the Park with
George*), George and Mandy Patinkin
RCA RD85042

❡ Stravinsky, *Agon* (Coda), Columbia Symphony Orchestra/Igor Stravinsky
Sony Classical 46292/A-C
❡ Janáček, *Sinfonietta* (fifth movement, Andante con moto), Philharmonia/Simon Rattle
EMI CDC 747048–2
❡ Fitzgerald, 'Bewitched, Bothered and Bewildered', Ella Fitzgerald
Verve 517 899–2,900–2,901–2

The kind of conversation that gave confidence that the third boss of the National Theatre to appear on the programme (see Richard Eyre and Peter Hall, pp. 71 and 281) would be just as adventurous and successful as his predecessors.

7 JULY 2001
Martin Fuller, painter

❡ Schoenberg, *Moses und Aron* (opening), Franz Mazura (Moses)/ Chicago Symphony Chorus and Orchestra/Georg Solti
Decca 414 264–2
❡ Verdi, Agnus Dei (from Requiem), Elisabeth Schwarzkopf (soprano)/Christa Ludwig (mezzo-soprano)/Philharmonia Chorus and Orchestra/Carlo Maria Giulini
EMI CDS 556250 2
❡ Dixon/Henderson, 'Bye Bye Blackbird', Della Reese/Orchestra/John Cotter
RCA RD 7508
❡ Ellington/Russell, 'Don't Get Around Much Any More', Al Hibbler (vocals)/Rahsaan Roland Kirk (saxophone)/Hank Jones (piano)/Ron Carter (bass)/Oliver Jackson (drums)
Atlantic K 40457
❡ Michael Berkeley, Clarinet Concerto, Emma Johnson (clarinet)/ Northern Sinfonia/Sian Edwards
ASV CDDCB 1101
❡ Mingus, 'Wham Bam Thank You Ma'am', Charles Mingus (piano)/ Rahsaan Roland Kirk, Booker Irvin (saxophones)/Jimmy Knepper (trombone)/Doug Watkins (bass)/Dannie Richmond (drums)
Atlantic 7567 90667–2
❡ Oscar Brown Jr, 'Haze's Hips', Oscar Brown Jr
Columbia CX 64994

¶ Beethoven, String Quartet in C sharp minor, Op. 131 (finale: Allegro), Talich Quartet
Calliope CAL 9638

Nice little bit of artistic camaraderie: I have two of his canvases and he included a similarly expressionistic piece of mine.

14 JULY 2001
Annie Proulx, writer

¶ Spiritual (from *Beyond the Missouri Sky*), Charley Haden and Pat Metheny
Verve 314 537 130–2
[¶ Proulx, *Accordion Crimes*, Annie Proulx
published by Fourth Estate, extract from pp. 292–3]
¶ Austin Pitre, 'Les Flames d'Enfer' (from *Lou'siana Dance Party*),
Gazelle GCCD 3004
¶ Francis Poulenc, 'Hommage à Edith Piaf' (from *15 Improvisations*),
Eric Parkin (piano)
Chandos CHAN 8847
¶ Gilmore, 'Deep Eddy Blues', Jimmy Dale Gilmore
Hightone Records HCD 8018
¶ Adams, 'Toot Nipple' (from *John's Book of Alleged Dances*), Kronos Quartet
Nonesuch 7550 79485–2
¶ 'Los Illegales', Valerio Longoria
Rounder CD 6024
¶ Walser/Kronos Quartet, 'Rose Marie' (from *Down at the Skyvue Drive-In*), Don Walser and Kronos Quartet
Watermelon Records 31017–2
¶ Welch, 'Morphine' (from *Hell Among the Yearlings*), Gillian Welch
Almo Sounds AMSD 80021
¶ 'Jelly Roll Rag' (from *Max Roach Presents The Uptown String Quartet*), The Uptown String Quartet
Philips 838 358–2

21 JULY 2001
Lucy Irvine, former castaway

¶ Michael Berkeley, *Farewell*, The Joyful Company of Singers/Peter Broadbent
EMI CDC 556961–2
¶ Shostakovich, Foxtrot (from *Jazz Suite* No. 1), Royal Concertgebouw Orchestra/Riccardo Chailly
Decca 433 702–2
¶ Byrd, Sixth Pavan and Galliard, Glenn Gould (piano)
Sony Classical SMK 52589
¶ Bruckner, Symphony No. 4 in E flat, 'Romantic' (first movement, recapitulation), Vienna Philharmonic Orchestra/Karl Böhm
Decca 411 581–2
¶ Boccherini, Quintet in E, Op. 11, No. 5 (Minuetto), Isaac Stern, Cho-Liang Lin (violins)/Jaime Laredo (viola)/Yo-Yo Ma and Sharon Robinson (cellos)
Sony Classical SK 53983
¶ Broonzy, 'All by Myself', Big Bill Broonzy
CBS 63573
¶ Bach, 'Herr, unser Herrscher' (ending of first chorus from *St John Passion*), Bach Collegium, Japan/Masaaki Suzuki
BIS CD 921/2
¶ Satie, 'Profiter de ce qu'il a des cors aux pieds pour lui prendre son cerceau' (Taking advantage of the corns on his toes to take his hop away from him) (from *Peccadilles importunes*), Pascal Rogé (piano)
Decca 458 105–2 T22
¶ Anon., arr. Guido Haazen, Sanctus (from Missa Luba), Muungano National Choir, Kenya/Boniface Mganga
Philips 426 836–2

4 AUGUST 2001
Frances Spalding, writer and art historian

¶ Mussorgsky, 'Trepak' (from *Songs and Dances of Death*), Vassily Savenko (bass-baritone)/Michael Dussek (piano)
Meridian CDE 84399
¶ Terriss/Robledo, 'Three O'clock in the Morning', Della Reese/Orchestra/Mercer Ellington
RCA RD 27234

❡ Holiday/Herzog, 'Don't Explain', Billie Holiday
Universal 547 494–2
❡ Bréval, Sonata in C (first movement), London Suzuki Cello Group
Artists' private recording
❡ Borodin, String Quartet No. 2 in D (third movement, Nocturne),
Borodin Quartet
Decca 425 541–2
❡ Vivaldi, Laudamus te (from Gloria), Judith Nelson, Emma Kirkby
(sopranos)/Academy of Ancient Music/Simon Preston
Oiseau Lyre 414 678–2
❡ Glinka, Mazurka in C minor, Victor Ryabchikov (piano)
BIS CD 981
❡ Bach, 'Widerstehe doch der Sünde' (opening aria from Cantata,
BWV 54), Paul Esswood (countertenor)/Leonhardt Consort/Gustav
Leonhardt
Teldec 8.35304
❡ Rutter, 'The Lord Bless You and Keep You', Hampstead Parish
Church Choir/David Davies (organ)/Lee Ward
HPC CD 01

11 AUGUST 2001
Salley Vickers, writer

❡ Byrd, Mass for five voices: Credo, Tallis Scholars/Peter Phillips
Gimell CDGIM 345
❡ Rachmaninov, 'Nyne otpushchaeshi' (Nunc dimittis), from Vespers
(All-Night Vigil), John Bowen (tenor)/Corydon Singers/Matthew Best
Hyperion CDA 66460
❡ Mozart, String Quintet in G minor, K516 (first movement, Allegro),
Grumiaux Ensemble
Philips 416 488–2
❡ Schubert, Impromptu Op. 90, No.3 in G flat, Artur Schnabel (piano)
EMI CDH 761021–2
❡ Galuppi, Sonata No. 5 in C (first movement, Andante), Arturo
Benedetti Michelangeli (piano)
Philips 456 903–2
❡ Mozart, Piano Concerto No. 24 in C minor, K491 (second move-
ment, Larghetto), Solomon (piano), Philharmonia/Herbert Menges
EMI CDH 763707–2

♪ Elvis Presley, 'Are You Lonesome Tonight?', Elvis Presley
RCA PD 90100/A and B

Her combination of novelist and ex-Jungian analyst gives her an unusual insight into human emotions, particularly when coupled to the divine and the nature of belief.

18 AUGUST 2001
Richard Hoggart, cultural commentator

♪ Cochran/Howard, 'I Fall to Pieces', Patsy Cline
Trax TRXCD 5012
♪ Mozart, 'Là ci darem la mano' (from *Don Giovanni*, Act I), Tom Krause (Don Giovanni), Lucia Popp (Zerlina)/Vienna Haydn Orchestra/István Kertész
Decca 440 203–2
♪ Parry, 'Dear Lord and Father of Mankind', Choir of King's College, Cambridge/Stephen Cleobury
Decca 460 848–2
♪ Verdi, 'Pietà, rispetto, amore' (from *Macbeth*, Act IV), Piero Cappuccilli (Macbeth)/Orchestra of La Scala, Milan/Claudio Abbado
DG 415 688–2
♪ Beethoven, 'Prisoners' Chorus' (from *Fidelio*, Act I), Andreas Schulist, Wilfried Vorwol (Prisoners)/Bavarian Radio Symphony Orchestra and Chorus/Colin Davis
RCA 09026 68344 2
♪ Thackray, 'The Castleford Ladies' Magic Circle', Jake Thackray
EMI CDP 796271 2
♪ Beethoven, Violin Sonata in F, 'Spring', Op. 24 (second movement, Adagio molto espressivo), Itzhak Perlman (violin)/Vladimir Ashkenazy (piano)
Decca 410 554–2
♪ Verdi, Prelude to Act III of *La traviata*, New York Philharmonic Orchestra/Arturo Toscanini
RCA GD 60318

The kind of inspiring conversation that for me was up there with George Steiner and Isaiah Berlin. There was an utterly wonderful joker in the pack, Jake Thackray's hilarious 'The Castleford Ladies' Magic Circle'. Lifted me for days.

Anissa Helou, food writer

❡ Bach, 'Buss' und Reu' (from *St Matthew Passion*), Christa Ludwig
(contralto)/Philharmonia/Otto Klemperer
EMI CMS 763058 2
❡ Muhammed Abdenwahab, 'Laylat Hob', Oum Kolthoum
Sidi 94 SDCD 01B72
❡ Sakr, 'Al-Haleh Te'baneh ya Layla', Joseph Sakr
Artist's private recording
❡ Cohen, 'Suzanne', Leonard Cohen
Stylus SMD 975
❡ Kantemiroglu, 'Muhayyer Pesrev', Bezmârâ Ensemble
Kalan CD 161
❡ Sacko, 'Ousmane Sacko, par Ousmane Sacko', Ousmane Sacko and
Yakare Diabate
Ocora HMCD 83
❡ Beethoven, 'Nur hurtig fort, nur frisch gegraben' (from *Leonore*,
Act III), Edda Moser (Leonore), Karl Ridderbusch (Rocco)/
Staatskapelle Dresden/Herbert Blomstedt
Arabesque 8043–3
❡ Puccini, 'Mi chiamano Mimì' (from *La bohème*, Act I), Renata
Tebaldi (Mimì), Carlo Bergonzi (Rodolfo)/Orchestra of the Academy
of Santa Cecilia/Tullio Serafin
Decca 411 868–2
❡ Toulali, Moroccan cooking song, Hajj el-Hussein Toulali
TCK TCK 936

Lee Langley, novelist

❡ Simon Richmond, 'How to Score in Vienna' (from *Küntstruk*),
Palmskin Productions
Pussy CDLP020
❡ Sousa-Freitas-Campos, 'Caminhos de Deus (A fado)', Amalia
Rodrigues (singer)
Columbia SX 1520
❡ Schubert, String Quintet in C major (first movement, exposition),
Hollywood String Quartet/Kurt Reher (cello)
Testament SBT 1031

♪ Debussy, String Quartet in G minor (Scherzo, Assez vif et bien rythmé), Quartetto Italiano
Philips 420 894–2
♪ Frank Loesser, 'Baby It's Cold Outside', Ella Fitzgerald/Louis Jordan and his Tympany Five
Classics 1134
♪ Mozart, 'Non v'è più tempo . . . Di scrivermi' (from *Così fan tutte*, Act I), Paul Schoeffler (Don Alfonso), Lisa della Casa (Fiordiligi), Christa Ludwig (Dorabella), Anton Dermota (Ferrando), Erich Kunz (Guglielmo)/Vienna Philharmonic Orchestra/Karl Böhm
Decca 417 186–2
♪ Villa Lobos, *Bachianas Brasileiras* No. 5, Salli Terri (contralto)/ Laurindo Almeida (guitar)
Capitol p 8406
♪ Janáček, String Quartet No. 1, 'Kreutzer Sonata' (first movement, Adagio con moto), Vlach Quartet
Naxos 8.553895
♪ Billie Holiday, 'Gloomy Sunday', Billie Holiday/Teddy Wilson and his Orchestra
Columbia 474401–2
♪ Frederick the Great, Symphony in D major (first movement, Allegro assai), C. P. E. Bach Chamber Orchestra/Hartmut Haenchen
Capriccio 10064

8 SEPTEMBER 2001
Eva Hoffman, author and essayist

♪ Bartók, String Quartet No. 5 (third movement, Scherzo: alla bulgarese), Juilliard Quartet
CBS 61120
♪ Debussy, 'Pour les notes répétées' (from *Douze Études*), Mitsuko Uchida (piano)
Philips 422 412–2
♪ Schubert, Sonata in B flat, D960 (opening of first movement, Molto moderato), Alfred Brendel (piano)
Philips 422 062–2
♪ Franklin/White, 'Think', Aretha Franklin
Atlantic 8227–2

❡ Brahms, Violin Sonata in D minor, Op. 108 (first movement, Allegro), Itzhak Perlman (violin)/Vladimir Ashkenazy (piano)
EMI CDC 747403 2
❡ Trad. Yiddish, 'Fidl Volach', The Klezmorin
Arhoolie CD309
❡ Trad., Two duets from the Shopsko region of Bulgaria, Trakia Choir Soloists
Fontana 846 626–2
❡ Chopin, Etude in A minor, Op. 25, No. 11, Maurizio Pollini (piano)
DG 413 794–2
❡ Chopin, Mazurka in C sharp minor, Op. 6, No. 2, Artur Rubinstein (piano)
EMI CHS 764697 2

15 SEPTEMBER 2001
Angela Flowers, art gallery owner

❡ Debussy, Violin Sonata in G minor (first movement, Allegro vivo), Ginette Neveu (violin)/Jean Neveu (piano)
EMI CDH 763493 2
❡ Coots/Gillespie, 'You Go to My Head', Billie Holiday
CBS OODP 574
❡ Bach, Suite No. 5 in C minor, BWV 1011 (first movement, Prelude), Paul Tortelier (cello)
EMI CDC 749035 2
❡ Miles Davis, 'Blue in Green', Miles Davis (trumpet)/John Coltrane (tenor saxophone)/Bill Evans (piano)/Paul Chambers (bass)/James Cobb (drums)
Columbia COL 460603 2
❡ Vaughan Williams, 'The Roadside Fire' (from *Songs of Travel*), Bryn Terfel (baritone)/Malcolm Martineau (piano)
DG 445 946–2
❡ Wagner, 'Prize Song' (from *Die Meistersinger von Nürnberg*, Act III), René Kollo (Walther), Theo Adam (Hans Sachs), Karl Ridderbusch (Veit Pogner), Helen Donath (Eva)/Dresden Opera and Leipzig Radio Choruses/Staatskapelle Dresden/Herbert von Karajan
EMI CDS 749683 2
❡ Schubert, Impromptu in E flat, D899, No. 2, Edwin Fischer (piano)
Pearl GEMMCD 9216

♪ Ravel, 'Daybreak' (from *Daphnis and Chloë*), Berlin Philharmonic Orchestra/Herbert von Karajan
DG 423 217–2

22 SEPTEMBER 2001
Melvyn Bragg, broadcaster and writer

♪ Wagner, 'Liebestod' (from *Tristan und Isolde*, Act III), Kirsten Flagstad (Isolde)/Philharmonia/Wilhelm Furtwängler
EMI CDS 747322 8
♪ Elgar, Cello Concerto in E minor, Op. 85 (third movement, Adagio), Jacqueline du Pré (cello)/London Symphony Orchestra/John Barbirolli
EMI CDC 556219 2
♪ Beethoven, Kyrie eleison (from Missa Solemnis, Op. 123), Edda Moser (soprano), Hanna Schwarz (mezzo-soprano), René Kollo (tenor)/NOS Radio Chorus, Hilversum/Royal Concertgebouw Orchestra/Leonard Bernstein
DG 469 546–2
♪ Howard Goodall, 'Love Divine', Choir of Christ Church Cathedral/ Stephen Darlington
Metronome CD 1044
♪ Gluck, 'Che farò senza Euridice' (from *Orfeo ed Euridice*), Kathleen Ferrier (Orfeo)/London Symphony Orchestra/Malcolm Sargent
Decca 458 270–12
♪ Monroe, 'Blue Moon of Kentucky', Elvis Presley
RCA ND 90415
♪ Schubert, 'An die Musik', D547, Ian Bostridge (tenor)/Julius Drake (piano)
EMI CDC 556347 2
♪ Messiaen, 'Joie du sang des étoiles' (from *Turangalîla-Symphonie*), Peter Donohoe (piano)/Tristan Murail (ondes Martenot)/City of Birmingham Symphony Orchestra/Simon Rattle
EMI CDS 747463 2

29 SEPTEMBER 2001
Will Self, writer

♪ Hanighen/Williams/Monk, 'Round Midnight', Miles Davis Quintet
Columbia 469440 2

❡ Massive Attack, 'Unfinished Sympathy', Massive Attack
Polydor 527 925–2
❡ Waller, 'Ain't Misbehavin'', Fats Waller
Empress RAJCD 824
❡ Richard Strauss, 'Beim Schlafengehen' (from *Four Last Songs*), Jessye
Norman (soprano)/Leipzig Gewandhaus Orchestra/Kurt Masur
Philips 411 052–2
❡ Beethoven, Piano Trio in D major, 'Ghost', Op. 70, No. 1 (first
movement, Allegro vivace e con brio), Isaac Stern (violin)/Leonard
Rose (cello)/Eugene Istomin (piano)
Sony SBK 53514
❡ Lassus, Introitus (from Requiem for Four Voices), Pro Cantione
Antiqua/Mark Brown
Hyperion CDD 22012
❡ Dylan, 'Blind Willie McTell', Bob Dylan
Sony 468 086–2

*Have enjoyed his writing but was taken by (pleasant) surprise at the
authority and instinctive feel shown in his discussion of music.*

6 OCTOBER 2001
Andro Linklater, writer

❡ Faithfull, 'Broken English', Marianne Faithfull
Island 524 579–2/AandB
❡ John Marbeck, Credo (from his 'Book of Common Prayer Noted'),
Choir of St George's Chapel, Windsor/Sidney Campbell
LP: Argo ZRG 789
❡ Adams, 'Oh What a Day I Thought I'd Die' and 'Whip Her to Death'
(from *Nixon in China*, Act II), James Maddalena (Richard Nixon),
Carolann Page (Pat Nixon), Thomas Hammons (Henry Kissinger)/
Orchestra of St Luke's/Edo de Waart
Nonesuch 979177–2/A-C
❡ Maxwell Davies, 'Mrs Linklater's Tune', rec. of first performance,
St Magnus Festival, Julia Robinson Dean (violin)
Private recording
❡ Trad. arr. Redpath/Hovey, 'Nine Inch Will Please a Lady' (tune 'The
Quaker's Wife', words by Robert Burns), sung by Jean Redpath
Greentrax CDTRAX 114

¶ Nevin, 'The Rosary', Clara Butt (contralto)
Flapper PASTCD 7012
¶ 'La petite tonkinoise', Josephine Baker
Pro Arte CDD 3401
¶ Verdi, finale of Act II from *Un ballo in maschera*, Renato Bruson
(Renato), Katia Ricciarelli (Amelia), Ruggero Raimondi (Samuel),
Giovanni Foiani (Tom)/Chorus and Orchestra of La Scala, Milan/
Claudio Abbado
DG 453 148–2
¶ Javanese Gamelan, Ujung Laut (The shore), Gamelan orchestra from
the Sunda Country/Enip Sukanda
Ocora C 560097

*The only time that both host and guest collapsed into such hysterical
laughter that we had to stop. It had something to do with the fifth piece,
coupled with a story about the First World War and its weaponry.*

13 OCTOBER 2001
Alan Brownjohn, poet and novelist

¶ Tiffen le Martelot, 'La chanson d'un Dadaiste', Anna Andreotti,
David Choquet (voices)/Laurent Couvreur (piano)
Tristan G2J 50513
¶ Raducanu, 'Danny Blues', Johnny Raducanu (piano)
Alpha Sound CDAL 016
¶ Hahn, Conclusion of Act I, scene 1 from *Ciboulette*, François le Roux
(Roger), José van Dam (Duparquet), Nicolai Gedda (Antonin), Colette
Alliot-Lugaz (Zénobie)/Chorus/Monte Carlo Philharmonic Orchestra/
Cyril Diedrich
EMI CDS 749873 2
¶ Debussy, 'Clair de lune' (from *Fêtes galantes*), Maggie Teyte
(soprano)/Alfred Cortot (piano)
EMI CHS 761038 2
¶ Monteverdi, 'Chiome d'oro', Hugues Cuenod, Paul Derenne
(tenors)/Ensemble/Nadia Boulanger
EMI CDH 761025 2
¶ Rawsthorne, Symphony No. 2, 'A Pastoral Symphony' (fourth
movement, Andante), Tracey Chadwell (soprano)/London
Philharmonic Orchestra/Nicholas Braithwaite
Lyrita SRCD 291

¶ Warlock, 'Jillian of Berry' and 'Pretty Ring Time', Ian Partridge (tenor)/Jennifer Partridge (piano)
Etcetera KTC 1078
¶ Schubert, Sonata in A, D959 (third movement, Scherzo: Allegro vivace), Radu Lupu (piano)
Decca 425 033–2
¶ Beethoven, String Quartet in C sharp minor, Op. 131 (fifth movement, Presto), Lindsay String Quartet
ASV CDDCA 603
¶ Tippett, *The Mask of Time* (conclusion), Faye Robinson (soprano), Sarah Walker (mezzo-soprano), Robert Tear (tenor), John Cheek (bass)/BBC Symphony Orchestra and Chorus/Andrew Davis
EMI CDS 747705

20 OCTOBER 2001
Anne Karpf, journalist

¶ The Eagles, 'Hotel California', The Eagles
Asylum 7559–60509–2
¶ Chopin, Nocturne in C sharp minor, Op. 27, No. 1, Natalia Karp (piano)
BBC archive recording
¶ Abdullah Ibrahim, 'Someday Soon Sweet Samba' (from *Cape Town Revisited*), Abdullah Ibrahim Trio
Tip Toe Tip 8888362
¶ Brave Old World, 'Rufn Di Kinder Aheym' (from *Beyond The Pale*), Brave Old World
Pinorrek Records CD 5013
¶ Charles Mingus, 'Wednesday Night Prayer Meeting' (from *Blues and Roots*), Charlie Mingus
RHINO R2 75205
¶ Mozart, Clarinet Quintet in A major, K581 (first movement), Thea King (clarinet)/Gabrieli String Quartet
Hyperion CDA 66199
¶ Mahler, Symphony No. 1 (third movement), Israel Philharmonic Orchestra/Zubin Mehta
Decca 443 032–2
¶ Schubert, Fantasie in F minor, D940, Murray Perahia and Radu Lupu (piano duet)
Sony SK 39511

Jeffrey Tobias, oncologist

❡ Messiaen, 'Regard de la Vierge' (from *Vingt regards sur l'enfant Jésus*), Malcolm Troup (piano)
Continuum CCD 1004/5
❡ Prokofiev, Sonata No. 7 in B flat, Op. 83 (third movement, Precipitato), Sviatoslav Richter (piano), rec. 1958
Melodiya 74321–29470–2
❡ Handy, 'Spanish Lady', John Handy Group
CBS BPG 62678
❡ Shostakovich, Piano Quintet in G minor, Op. 57 (third movement, Scherzo), Victor Aller (piano)/Hollywood String Quartet
Testament SBT 1077
❡ Wagner, Siegmund and Sieglinde's love duet from *The Valkyrie*, Act I, Alberto Remedios (Siegmund), Margaret Curphey (Sieglinde)/ English National Opera Orchestra/Reginald Goodall
EMI CMS 763918–2
❡ Gurney, 'I Will Go with My Father A-ploughing', Ian Bostridge (tenor)/Julius Drake (piano)
EMI CDC 556830 2
❡ Janáček, opening of Act II from *From the House of the Dead*, Zdenék Svehla (Voice from the Steppe), Dalibor Jedlička (Goryanchikov), Jaroslava Janská (Alyeya)/Vienna State Opera Chorus/Vienna Philharmonic Orchestra/Charles Mackerras
Decca 430 375–2
❡ Stravinsky, 'Marche du soldat' (from *L'histoire du soldat*), Prague Chamber Harmony/Libor Pešek
Supraphon 11–0672–2
❡ Bach, Partita No. 1 in B flat, BWV 825 (first movement, Prelude), Dinu Lipatti (piano)
EMI CDM 566988 2
❡ Britten, Billy's monologue from *Billy Budd*, Act II, scene 3, Peter Glossop (Billy Budd)/London Symphony Orchestra/Benjamin Britten
London 417 428–2

3 NOVEMBER 2001
Jon Stallworthy, poet

❡ Britten, 'I Am the Enemy You Killed, My Friend', from *War Requiem*, Op. 66 (Libera me), Peter Pears (tenor), Dietrich Fischer-Dieskau (baritone), Galina Vishnevskaya (soprano)/Highgate School Choir/ Bach Choir/London Symphony Chorus/London Symphony Orchestra/Benjamin Britten
Decca 414 385–2
❡ Yeats, 'Dialogue of Self and Soul', read by Chris Curran
LP Argo RG449
[❡ Stallworthy, 'The Bright Cloud', read by Jon Stallworthy]
❡ Owen, 'Strange Meeting', read by Michael Sheen
Naxos NA210912/A
❡ Dylan Thomas, 'Fern Hill', read by Richard Burton
Argo RG29
❡ Gilbert/Sullivan, 'If You're Anxious for to Shine' (from *Patience*, Act I), George Baker (Bunthorne, A Fleshly Poet)/Pro Arte Orchestra/Malcolm Sargent
EMI CDC 747783–2
❡ Beethoven, Symphony No. 6 in F, 'Pastoral', Op. 68 (first movement), Vienna Philharmonic Orchestra/Karl Böhm
DG 447 433–2
[❡ John Masefield, 'Cargoes', read by Michael Berkeley]
❡ Dumont/Vaucaire, 'Non, je ne regrette rien', Edith Piaf (singer)
Columbia 790562–2

10 NOVEMBER 2001
Fred Hersch, jazz pianist/composer

❡ Duke Ellington, 'The Mooche' (from *Ellington Uptown*), Duke Ellington
Philips BBL 7003
❡ Hersch, 'Aria' (from *Songs Without Words*)
Nonesuch 79612–2
❡ Horta, 'Aqui Oh' (from *Toninho Horta*), Toninho Horta
World Pacific CDP 793865 2
❡ Coleman, 'Tomorrow is the Question' (from *Tomorrow is the Question*), Ornette Coleman
OJCCD 342–2

꘡ Davis, 'If I Were a Bell', Miles Davis
Columbia 4651912
꘡ Mitchell, 'River' (from *Blue*), Joni Mitchell
Reprise 244128
꘡ Bach, Brandenburg Concerto No. 4 in G (Presto), Taverner
Players/Andrew Parrott
EMI 749807/08 2
꘡ Ravel, 'Le gibet' (from *Gaspard de la nuit*), Martha Argerich (piano)
EMI 7243 5 57101 23

17 NOVEMBER 2001
John Gage, scholar/art critic

꘡ Berlioz, 'Rêveries – Passions' (first movement of *Symphonie
fantastique*, Op. 14), Detroit Symphony Orchestra/Paul Paray
Mercury 434 328–2
꘡ Chisholm/Lawrence/Cruz/Lopes/Martin, 'Never Be the Same Again',
Melanie C/Lisa 'Left Eye' Lopes
Virgin VTDCD 322
꘡ Schoenberg, *Three Piano Pieces*, Op. 11 (No. 1, Mässig), Maurizio
Pollini (piano)
DG 423 249–2
꘡ Trad. Bolivian, 'Yaravi', Los Calchakis
Barclay 920 014
꘡ Gluck, 'Che farò senza Euridice' (from *Orfeo ed Euridice*), Dietrich
Fischer-Dieskau (Orfeo)/Munich Bach Orchestra/Karl Richter
DG 463 519–2
꘡ Barbara, 'Göttingen', Barbara
Philips 437.200 BE
꘡ Beethoven, Symphony No. 6 in F, 'Pastoral', Op. 68 (finale:
'Shepherds' Song'), Berlin Philharmonic Orchestra/Herbert von
Karajan
DG 439 004–2
꘡ Allegri, Miserere (opening), Roy Goodman (treble)/Choir of King's
College, Cambridge/David Willcocks
Decca 430 092–2
꘡ Migliacci/Modugno, 'Volare', Domenico Modugno
Oriole MG 10023

Andrew Marr, political journalist and broadcaster

❡ Burns, 'Ye Jacobites By Name', from *The Complete Songs of Robert Burns*, Vol. 2, sung by Ian Bruce
Linn Records, CKD 051
❡ Bacharach/David, '24 Hours from Tulsa', Dusty Springfield
Philips 842 699–2
❡ Dylan, 'Sad Eyed Lady of the Lowlands' (from *Blonde on Blonde*), Bob Dylan
CBS CD 66012
❡ Mozart, 'Se vuol ballare' (from *The Marriage of Figaro*, Act I), Erich Kunz (Figaro)/Vienna Philharmonic Orchestra/Herbert von Karajan
EMI CDM 567069–2
❡ Shostakovich, Piano Concerto No. 2 (second movement, Andante), Leonard Bernstein (piano and conductor)/New York Philharmonic Orchestra
Sony Classical SM3K 47166/A–C
❡ Bach, Prelude and Fugue in F minor, BWV 857 (from *The Well-tempered Clavier*, Book I), Glenn Gould (piano)
Sony Classical SM2K 53600
❡ Marco Uccellini, 'Aria Quinta sopra La Bermagasca', Arcadian Academy/McGegan
Harmonia Mundi HMU 907066

Robert Anderson, Director, British Museum

❡ Dowland, 'I Saw My Lady Weep', Andreas Scholl (countertenor)/ Andreas Martin (lute)
Harmonia Mundi HMC 901603
❡ Charles Ives, *The Unanswered Question*, New York Philharmonic Orchestra/Leonard Bernstein
DG 429 220–2
❡ Richard Strauss, 'Frühling' (from *Four Last Songs*), Lisa della Casa (soprano)/Vienna Philharmonic Orchestra/Karl Böhm
Decca 425 959–2
❡ Mozart, 'God is our Refuge', K20, Leipzig Radio Choir/Gert Frischmuth
Philips 422 520–2

❡ Beethoven, Grosse Fuge, Op. 133 (opening), Amadeus Quartet
DG 423 473–2
❡ Brahms, Trio in E flat, Op. 40 (first movement, Andante), Dennis
Brain (horn)/Max Salpeter (violin)/Cyril Preedy (piano)
BBC BBCL 4048–2
❡ Bach, Sonata No. 3 in C, BWV 1005 (first movement, Adagio), Hilary
Hahn (violin)
Sony SK 62793
❡ Beethoven, 'Nimm sie hin denn, diese Lieder' (from *An die ferne
Geliebte*, Op. 98), Dietrich Fischer-Dieskau (baritone)/Gerald Moore
(piano)
EMI CZS 568509 2

8 DECEMBER 2001
Colin Gough, physicist

❡ Brahms, Violin Concerto in D, Op. 77 (cadenza and conclusion of
first movement), David Oistrakh (violin)/Staatskapelle Dresden/
Franz Konwitschny
DG 423 399–2
❡ Richard Strauss, 'Morgen', Op. 27, Elisabeth Schwarzkopf (soprano)/
Edith Peinemann (violin)/London Symphony Orchestra/George Szell
EMI CDM 566908 2
❡ Handel, 'Dopo notte' (from *Ariodante*), Janet Baker
(Ariodante)/English Chamber Orchestra/Raymond Leppard
Philips 426 450–2
❡ Beethoven, String Quartet in B flat, Op. 130 (fifth movement,
Cavatina), Hungarian Quartet
EMI 573798 2
❡ Mozart, Overture to *The Marriage of Figaro*, Royal Philharmonic
Orchestra/Colin Davis
EMI CDZ 762858 2
❡ Bach, Suite No. 1 in G, BWV 1007 (first movement, Prelude), Paul
Tortelier (cello)
EMI CDC 749035 2
❡ Wagner, *Götterdämmerung* (conclusion), Karl Ridderbusch (Hagen)/
Berlin Philharmonic Orchestra/Herbert von Karajan
DG 457 780–2

❡ Britten, 'Storm Interlude' (from *Peter Grimes*), Orchestra of the
Royal Opera House/Benjamin Britten
Decca 414 577–2

15 DECEMBER 2001
Irma Kurtz, agony aunt

❡ Britten, 'Dance of Death' (from *Our Hunting Fathers*), Peter Pears
(tenor)/London Symphony Orchestra/Benjamin Britten
BBC BBCB 8014–2
❡ Ravel, 'Five O'clock Foxtrot' (from *L'enfant et les sortilèges*), Joseph
Peyron (Teapot)/Denise Scharley (China cup)/French National Radio
Orchestra/Ernest Bour
Testament SBT 1044
❡ Sondheim, 'The Little Things You Do Together' (from *Company*),
Elaine Stritch and members of the original 1970 Broadway Cast/
Orchestra/Harold Hastings
Sony SK 65283
❡ Tchaikovsky, 'Letter Scene' (from *Eugene Onegin*, Act I), Galina
Gorchakova (Tatiana)/Kirov Orchestra/Valery Gergiev
Philips 446 405–2
❡ Bach, 'Ei, wie schmeckt der Coffee süss' (from *Coffee Cantata*,
BWV 211), Julia Varady (soprano)/Academy of St Martin-in-the-
Fields/Neville Marriner
Philips 412 882–2
❡ Boyce, Symphony No. 5 in D (third movement, Tempo di Minuetto),
English Concert/Trevor Pinnock
Archiv 419 631–2
❡ Purcell, Prelude and trio ('May the God of Wit Inspire') from *The
Fairy Queen*, Wynford Evans, Martyn Hill (tenors)/Stephen Varcoe
(bass)/English Baroque Soloists/John Eliot Gardiner
Archiv 419 221–2
❡ Janáček, Prelude from *The Cunning Little Vixen*, Vienna
Philharmonic Orchestra/Charles Mackerras
Decca 417 129–2 Disc 1

22 DECEMBER 2001
Modest Mussorgsky (a.k.a. John Sessions)

¶ Mussorgsky, 'Catacombs' (from *Pictures at an Exhibition*), Sviatoslav Richter (piano)
Philips 420 774–2
¶ Mussorgsky, Prelude to *Khovanshchina*, Royal Philharmonic Orchestra/Artur Rodzinski
EMI CZS 568742 2
¶ Rimsky-Korsakov, Symphony No. 3 in C, Op. 32 (first movement, Moderato assai–Allegro), St Petersburg State Symphony Orchestra/ André Anichanov
Naxos 8.550812
¶ Balakirev, *Islamey*, Andrei Gavrilov (piano)
Philips 456 787–2
¶ Borodin, *In the Steppes of Central Asia*, USSR Radio Symphony Orchestra/Vladimir Fedoseyev
Olympia OCD 121
¶ Glinka, Overture to *Ruslan and Lyudmila*, Kirov Orchestra/Valery Gergiev
Philips 446 746–2
¶ Mussorgsky, 'Boris's Death Scene' (from *Boris Godunov*), Nicolai Ghiaurov (Boris)/Vienna Philharmonic Orchestra/Herbert von Karajan
Decca 411 862–2

29 DECEMBER 2001
Joseph Connolly, novelist

¶ Gilbert/Sullivan, 'I've got a Little List (from *The Mikado*), Richard Suart (Ko-Ko)/Welsh National Opera Chorus and Orchestra/Charles Mackerras
Telarc CD 80284
¶ McCartney, 'Somedays', Paul McCartney
Parlophone CDPCSD 171
¶ Bach, Prelude in C minor, BWV 999, and Courante (from Suite No. 2, BWV 1099), Andrés Segovia (guitar)
Saga STFID 2160
¶ Elmer Bernstein, 'Man with the Golden Arm', Billy May and his Orchestra
Capitol CDEMS 1594

❡ Max Harris, 'Gurney Slade', Max Harris with his Group
Fontana H 822
❡ Irving Berlin, 'Top Hat, White Tie and Tails', Fred Astaire/Orchestra/
Max Steiner
BBC BBCCD 665
❡ Gershwin, *Rhapsody in Blue*, André Previn (piano and conductor)/
London Symphony Orchestra
EMI CDM 566891 2
❡ Burgon, 'Rain in Venice' (from *Brideshead Revisited*), Orchestra/
Geoffrey Burgon
Music for Pleasure CDMFP 6172
❡ Corelli, Concerto Grosso in F, Op. 6, No. 2 (first and second
movements), Philharmonia Baroque Orchestra/Nicholas McGegan
Harmonia Mundi HCX 3957014
❡ Vivaldi, 'Winter' (from *The Four Seasons*) (first movement, Allegro
non molto), Yehudi Menuhin (violin)/Camerata Lysy Gstaad/
Alberto Lysy
EMI CDC 749574

5 JANUARY 2002
Roger Graef, writer, film-maker and criminologist

❡ Weill, 'Speak Low' (from *One Touch of Venus*), Kurt Weill (singer and
piano)
Heritage LP H-0051
❡ Parker, 'Relaxing with Lee 2', Charlie Parker with Dizzy Gillespie
(trumpet)/Thelonius Monk (piano)/Curley Russell (bass)/Buddy Rich
(drums)
Verve 711 049
❡ Hellawell, 'a white room', Schubert Ensemble of London
NMC D075
❡ Richard Strauss, 'Aber der Richtige' (from *Arabella*, Act I), Julia
Varady (Arabella), Helen Donath (Zdenka)/Bavarian State
Orchestra/Wolfgang Sawallisch
Orfeo C 169 882/A
❡ Virgil Thomson/Gertrude Stein, end of Act II from *The Mother of Us
All*, Mignon Dunn (Susan B Anthony)/The Santa Fé Opera/Raymond
Leppard
New World NW 288/9–2

¶ Bloch, Concerto Grosso for string orchestra and piano obbligato (finale: fugue), George Schlick (piano)/Chicago Symphony Orchestra/ Rafael Kubelík

LP Mercury MG 50001

¶ Kodaly, Sonatina for cello and piano, Maria Kliegel (cello)/Jenö Jandó (piano)

NAXOS 8.554039

¶ Traditional North Hungarian lament, 'Jaj, jaj, énneken bánatos anyának!' (Alas, alas for me, a grieving mother!)

LPX 1187-a MMX 1795

¶ Amy Beach, Piano Quintet in F sharp minor, Op. 67 (second movement, Adagio espressivo), Diana Ambache (piano)/Ambache Ensemble

Chandos CHAN 9752

12 JANUARY 2002
Peter Kemp, literary critic

¶ Bach, Suite No. 1 in G, BWV 1007 (first movement, Prelude), Mstislav Rostropovich (cello)

EMI CDS 55363 2

¶ Wagner, 'Siegmund! Sieh auf mich' (from *Die Walküre*, Act II), Astrid Varnay (Brünnhilde), Wolfgang Windgassen (Siegmund)/ Bavarian Radio Orchestra/Leopold Ludwig

Heliodor 478438

¶ Beethoven, Sonata in G, Op. 31, No. 1 (opening of second movement, Adagio grazioso), Alfred Brendel (piano)

Philips 446 909–2

¶ Hahn, 'Sopra l'acqua indormenzada' (from *Venezia: Chansons en dialecte vénitien*), Anthony Rolfe Johnson (tenor)/Graham Johnson (piano)

Hyperion CDA 66112

¶ Schubert, 'Der Leiermann' (from *Winterreise*), Dietrich Fischer-Dieskau (baritone)/Gerald Moore (piano)

DG 415 187–2

¶ Handel, 'As Steals the Morn upon the Night' (from *L'Allegro, il Penseroso ed il Moderato*), Patrizia Kwella (soprano), Maldwyn Davies (tenor)/English Baroque Soloists/John Eliot Gardiner

Erato ECD 88077

❡ Verdi, 'Ben'io t'invenni' (from *Nabucco*, Act II), Elena Suliotis
(Abigaille)/Vienna State Opera Orchestra/Lamberto Gardelli
Decca 417 407–2
❡ Puccini, 'Tre sbirri, una carrozza' (from *Tosca*, Act I), Tito Gobbi
(Scarpia), Angelo Mercuriali (Spoletta)/Chorus and Orchestra of La
Scala, Milan/Victor de Sabata
EMI CDS 556304 2

19 JANUARY 2002
Jude Kelly, theatre director

❡ Brown/Freed, 'Singin' in the Rain', Gene Kelly
Blue Moon BMCD 7008
❡ Donizetti, 'Mad Scene' (from *Lucia di Lammermoor*, Act III), Joan
Sutherland (Lucia)/Paris Opéra Chorus/Paris Conservatoire
Orchestra/Nello Santi
Decca 421 305–2
❡ Haydn, Symphony No. 104 in D, 'London', Philharmonia Hungarica/
Antál Dorati
London 425 939–2
❡ Buchanan/Bell, 'A Walk across the Rooftops', The Blue Nile
Virgin QCD1
❡ Mitchell, 'Blue', Joni Mitchell
Reprise K 244128
❡ Cage, 'In a Landscape', Stephen Drury (piano)
Catalyst 9026–61980–2
❡ Elgar, 'Where Corals Lie' (from *Sea Pictures*, Op. 37), Janet Baker
(mezzo-soprano)/London Symphony Orchestra/John Barbirolli
EMI CDC 556219 2
❡ Irish Trad., 'Carrickfergus', Seán Ó Riada
Gael-Linn CEF 027

26 JANUARY 2002
Philip Pullman, writer

❡ Horton/Darling/Gabler, 'Choo choo ch'boogie', Louis Jordan
MCA DMCL 1718
❡ Prokofiev, Piano Concerto No. 2 in G minor, Op. 16 (second
movement, Scherzo: vivace), Vladimir Ashkenazy (piano)/London
Symphony Orchestra/André Previn
Decca 425 570–2

❡ Davis, 'Miles' (from *Milestones*), Miles Davis Sextet
CBS 460827 2
❡ Beethoven, *Egmont* Overture, Op. 84, Leipzig Gewandhaus
Orchestra/Kurt Masur
Philips 438 706–2
❡ Vivaldi, 'Sventurata navicella' (from *Giustino*), Cecilia Bartoli
(mezzo-soprano)/Il Giardino Armonico/Giovanni Antonini
Decca 466 569–2
❡ Tippett, *Concerto for Double String Orchestra* (third movement,
Allegro molto), BBC Symphony Orchestra/Andrew Davis
Teldec 4509–94542–2
❡ Pomus/Shuman, 'Save the Last Dance for Me', The Drifters
Marble Arch MACCD 156
❡ Medtner, Sonata-Skazka in C minor, Op. 25, No. 1 (second
movement, Andantino con moto), Marc-André Hamelin (piano)
Hyperion CDA 67222

*Always thought that His Dark Materials was exhilaratingly operatic, and
he finds a corresponding drama in the pieces of music he chose.*

2 FEBRUARY 2002
David McVicar, stage director

❡ Nina Simone, 'For All We Know', Nina Simone (vocals/piano)/
Jimmy Bond (bass)/Albert Heath (drums)
Charly CDGR 295
❡ Handel, 'Praise the Lord' (from *Solomon*, Act III), Gabrieli Consort
and Players/Paul McCreesh
Archiv 459 691–2
❡ Vladimir Martynov, first movement of *Come In!*, Gidon Kremer/
Tatjana Grindenko/Kremerata Baltica
Nonesuch 7559–7958
❡ Britten, 'And Farewell to Ye' (from *Billy Budd*, Act IV), London
Symphony Orchestra/Benjamin Britten
London 417 428–2
❡ Connick, 'If I Only Had a Brain', Harry Connick Jr (vocals/piano)
CBS 462996–2
❡ Mozart, 'Cieli, che vedo?' (from *Idomeneo*, Act III), Luciano
Pavarotti/Agnes Baltsa/Lucia Popp/Edita Gruberova
Decca 411 808–2

❡ Ravel, 'La flûte enchantée' from *Shéhérazade*, Régine Crespin (mezzo-soprano)/L'Orchestre de la Suisse Romande/Ernest Ansermet Decca 417 813–2
❡ Handel, 'Caro speme' (from *Giulio Cesare*), David Daniels/ Orchestra of the Age of Enlightenment/Roger Norrington Virgin Classics VC 545326–2

I got to know and like David when we were both working at Opera North. Like Richard Jones, he has a very direct approach to life and work.

9 FEBRUARY 2002
Hanif Kureishi, writer

❡ Zakir Hussein, 'Making Music', Zakir Hussein (tabla)/Jan Garbarek (saxophone)/Hariprasad Chaurasia (flute)/John McLaughlin (guitar) ECM 831 544–2
❡ John Cage, Sonata No. 1 (from *Sonatas and Interludes*), Boris Berman (piano)
NAXOS 8 554345
❡ Frisell, 'Outlaws', Bill Frisell
Nonesuch 7559–79615–2
❡ Lennon/McCartney, 'Hello, Goodbye', The Beatles
Apple 0777 7 97039–2
❡ Davis, 'IFE' (from *Big Fun*), Miles Davis
Columbia 489776–2/AandB
❡ Arvo Pärt, *Spiegel im Spiegel*, Tasmin Little (violin)/Martin Roscoe (piano)
HMV HMV 572315–2
❡ Steve Reich, 'America – before the war' (from *Different Trains*), Kronos Quartet
Nonesuch 7559 79176–2

As in the final piece, has a wonderfully hybrid sense of culture.

16 FEBRUARY 2002
Prof. Sir Tom Blundell, biochemist

❡ Bellini, 'Qual cor tradisti' (from *Norma*, Act II), Jane Eaglen (Norma), Vincenzo La Scola (Pollione)/Orchestra and Chorus of the Maggio Musicale, Florence/Riccardo Muti
EMI CDS 555471 2

¶ Mingus, 'Wednesday Night Prayer Meeting', Charles Mingus
Atlantic 781336–2
¶ Lewis Allen, 'Strange Fruit', Billie Holiday
Verve 521 429–2
¶ Verdi, 'Gia nella notte densa' (from *Otello*, Act I), Placido Domingo
(Otello), Cheryl Studer (Desdemona)/Orchestra of the Bastille
Opera/Myung-Whun Chung
DG 439 805–2
¶ Trad., 'Man Akteia Beparwah De Naal', Nusraat Fateh Ali Khan
Music Collection International NSCD 013
¶ Trad., 'Soukoura', Ali Farka Toure/Ry Cooder
World Circuit WCD 040
¶ Mozart, Concerto for Flute and Harp in C, K299 (second movement,
Andantino), Susan Palma (flute)/Nancy Allen (harp)/Orpheus
Chamber Orchestra
DG 427 677–2

23 FEBRUARY 2002
Christopher Hunt, arts consultant

¶ Batak traditional, 'Patahuak ni manuk', Gondang Hasapi Ensemble
New Albion NA 046
¶ Mozart, *Masonic Funeral Music*, K477, Columbia Symphony
Orchestra/Bruno Walter
Sony SMK 64486
¶ Birtwistle, 'Morgan Goes Through into the Blizzard' (from *Gawain's
Journey*), Philharmonia/Elgar Howarth
Collins 13872
¶ Schubert, Sonata in G, D894 (third movement, Menuetto: Allegro
moderato), Alfred Brendel (piano)
Philips 456 573–2
¶ Mozart, Horn Concerto in D, K412 (second movement, Rondo:
Allegro), Jonathan Williams (horn)/Chamber Orchestra of Europe/
Alexander Schneider
ASV CDCOE 805
¶ Bach, 'Would you a Female Heart Inspire?' (from *Vauxhall Songs*),
Elsie Morison (soprano)/Boyd Neel Orchestra/Thurston Dart
Oiseau Lyre OL 50132

¶ Fauré, *Pièce*, Leon Goossens (oboe)/Clarence Raybould (piano)
Columbia DB 691
¶ Lennon/McCartney, 'Ticket to Ride', Cathy Berberian (soprano)/
Bruno Canino (piano)
Wergo WER 60054–50
¶ Song of a blackbird
BBC Sound Effects ECD 12
¶ Handel, 'Va tacito e nascosto' (from *Giulio Cesare*), James Bowman
(countertenor)/Andrew Clark (horn)/King's Consort/Robert King
Hyperion CDA 66483
¶ Bach, 'Angenehmes Wiederau' (from Cantata, BWV 30a), Gächinger
Kantorei/Stuttgart Bach Collegium/Helmuth Rilling
Hänssler 99139

2 MARCH 2002
Tony Lewis, former Test cricketer

¶ Haydn, Virgo virginum praeclara (from Stabat mater), Arleen Augér
(soprano), Alfreda Hodgson (contralto), Anthony Rolfe Johnson
(tenor), Gwynne Howell (bass)/London Chamber Choir/Argo
Chamber Orchestra/Laszlo Heltay
Decca 433 172–2
¶ Chopin, Nocturne No. 13 in C minor Op. 48, No. 1, Artur Rubinstein
(piano)
RCA 09026 63026–2
¶ Karg-Elert, Chorale improvisation 'Nun danket alle Gott', Robert
Joyce (organ of Llandaff Cathedral)
Qualiton (Wales) SQUAD 102
¶ Schubert, String Quintet in C major (first movement), The
Lindsays/Douglas Cummings (cello)
ASV CDDCS 243/B
¶ Handel, 'Vouchsafe O Lord' (from the *Dettingen Te Deum*), Bryn
Terfel (bass-baritone) Scottish Chamber Orchestra/Charles Mackerras
DG 453 480–2
¶ Joanna/Crugybar/Ebenezer, Medley of Welsh hymn tunes, Morriston
Orpheus Choir/Alwyn Humphries
EMI CC 214
¶ Beethoven, Violin Concerto in D, Op. 61 (first movement), Joseph
Szigeti (violin)/New York Philharmonic Orchestra/Bruno Walter
Sony Classical SMK64459

Sebastian Faulks, novelist

❡ Dionne Warwick, 'Heartbreaker', B. Gibb/R. Gibb/M. Gibb
Columbia STVCD 117/A and B

❡ Sibelius, Symphony No. 5 (third movement, Allegro molto), Berlin
Philharmonic/James Levine
DG 445 865–2

❡ Steely Dan, 'Doctor Wu' from *Katy Lied*, Phil Woods (alto saxophone
solo)
MCA DMCL 1800

❡ Riley, *In C*, Members of the Center of the Creative and Performing
Arts in the State University of New York at Buffalo/Terry Riley (leader
and saxophone)
Edsel EDCD 314

❡ Dionne Warwick, 'Do You Know the Way to San José', Burt
Bacharach
Dino Entertainment DIN CD16

❡ Ravel, Piano Concerto in G major (second movement, Adagio assai),
Krystian Zimerman/London Symphony Orchestra/Pierre Boulez
DG 449 213–2

❡ Gabriel Fauré, Sanctus (from Requiem, Op. 48), Choir and
Orchestra dell'Accademia Nazionale di Santa Cecilia/Daniele Rossi
(organ)/Myung-Whun Chung
DG 459 365–2

❡ Davis, 'It Never Entered My Mind', from *The Best of Miles Davis*,
Miles Davis
Sony SMN 496792–2

Simon Armitage, poet

❡ John Tavener, 'The Lamb', Choir of St John's College, Cambridge/
Christopher Robinson
Naxos 8.55256

❡ Ravel, 'Menuet' (from *Le tombeau de Couperin*), Werner Haas
(piano)
Philips 434 353–2

❡ O'Neill/Bradley, 'My Perfect Cousin', The Undertones
Dino DINCD 121

♪ Duruflé, Pie Jesu (from Requiem, Op. 9), Kiri te Kanawa (soprano)/Philharmonia/Andrew Davis
Sony SBK 67182
♪ Serious Drinking, 'Spirit of '66', Serious Drinking
Upright UPLP 3
♪ Engel, 'Montague Terrace in Blue', Scott Walker
Fontana WALKC 2
♪ Wolf, 'Auf ein altes Bild', Arleen Augér (soprano)/Irwin Gage (piano)
Hyperion CDA 66590
♪ Trad., 'He's got the Whole World in His Hands', Nina Simone
Charly CDGR 295
♪ Radiohead, 'Like Spinning Plates', Radiohead
Parlophone CDFHEIT 45101
♪ Pärt, *Cantus in Memory of Benjamin Britten*, Staatsorchester Stuttgart/Dennis Russell Davies
ECM 817 764–2

Will make fine librettist.

23 MARCH 2002
Anthony Burton, industrial historian

♪ Birtwistle, 'Clock 5' (from *Harrison's Clocks*), Joanna MacGregor (piano)
SNDC SC004
♪ Monk, 'Blue Monk', Thelonius Monk Trio
Prestige CDJZD 009
♪ Praetorius, 'La Bourrée' (from *Dances from Terpsichore*), Early Music Consort of London/David Munrow
EMI CDM 769024–2
♪ Weill, 'Bilbao Song', Ute Lemper (vocals)/RIAS Sinfonietta, Berlin/ John Mauceri
Decca 436 417–2
♪ Bartók, String Quartet No. 4 (second movement, Prestissimo, con sordino), Végh Quartet
Astrée E 7718
♪ Stravinsky, 'Dances of the Peasant and Bear' and 'Gypsy Girls' (from *Petrushka*), City of Birmingham Symphony Orchestra/Simon Rattle
EMI CDC 749053–2

❡ Gillespie/Parker, 'A Night in Tunisia', Dizzy Gillespie/Charlie Parker, rec. live in Toronto in 1953
Debut OJCCD 044–2
❡ Messiaen, <u>Chronochromie</u> (introduction), Cleveland Orchestra/ Pierre Boulez
DG 445 827–2
❡ Bach, 'Ei! wie schmeckt der Coffee süss' (from the *Coffee Cantata*), Emma Kirkby (soprano)/Lisa Besnosiuk (flute)/Academy of Ancient Music/Christopher Hogwood
Oiseau Lyre 417 621–2

30 MARCH 2002
Peter Parker, writer

❡ Stravinsky, 'No Word from Tom' (from *The Rake's Progress*, Act I), Deborah York (Anne Trulove)/London Symphony Orchestra/John Eliot Gardiner
DG 459 648–2
❡ Porter, 'Ev'ry Time We Say Goodbye', Annie Lennox
Chrysalis CCD 1799
❡ Křenek, final scene from *Jonny spielt auf*, Alessandra Marc (Anita), Marita Posselt (Yvonne), Dieter Scholz (Manager)/Cast/Leipzig Opera Chorus/Leipzig Gewandhaus Orchestra/Lothar Zagrosek
Decca 431 631–2
❡ Coward, 'Any Little Fish' (from *Cochran's 1931 Revue*), Noël Coward/ Ray Noble Orchestra
EMI Coward 11
❡ Weill, 'Das Lied von Schlaraffenland' (from *Der Silbersee*), Ernst Busch/Orchestra/Maurice Abravanel
Pearl GEMMCDS 9189
❡ Britten, 'Dance of Death' (from *Our Hunting Fathers*, Op. 8), Phyllis Bryn-Julson (soprano)/English Chamber Orchestra/Steuart Bedford
Collins 11922
❡ Somervell, 'The Lads in their Hundreds' (from *A Shropshire Lad*), Graham Trew (baritone)/Roger Vignoles (piano)
Meridian CDE 84185
❡ Trad. Brazilian, 'Soca Pilao' (Coffee Pounding), Victoria Kingsley with native drum
Artist's private recording

Clive James, writer and broadcaster

❡ Johnston/Burke, 'Pennies from Heaven', Billie Holiday/Teddie Wilson and his Orchestra
Flapper PASTCD 9756
❡ Kahn/Schwandt/Andre, 'Dream a Little Dream of Me', Mama Cass Elliot
Music for Pleasure CDMFP 50493
❡ Piaf/Dumont, 'La belle histoire de l'amour', Edith Piaf
EMI CDP 794465 2
❡ Donizetti, 'Chi mi frena in tal momento' (from *Lucia di Lammermoor*, Act II), Maria Callas (Lucia), Giuseppe di Stefano (Edgardo), Tito Gobbi (Enrico), Raffaele Arié (Raimondo), Valiano Natali (Arturo), Anna Maria Canali (Alisa)/Chorus and Orchestra of the Maggio Musicale, Florence/Tullio Serafin
EMI CMS 769980 2
❡ Johnston/Coslow, 'My Old Flame', Mae West/Duke Ellington and his Orchestra
Sandy Hook CDSH 2098
❡ Ida Cox, 'Nobody Knows You When You're Down and Out', Bessie Smith
BBC BBCCD 683
❡ Puccini, 'O soave fanciulla' (from *La bohème*, Act I), Jussi Björling (Rodolfo), Victoria de los Angeles (Mimì)/RCA Victor Orchestra/ Thomas Beecham
EMI CDS 747235 8
❡ Mayer/Mercer, 'Summer Wind', Frank Sinatra
Reprise 923927 2
❡ Travis, 'Sixteen Tons', Tennessee Ernie Ford
Capitol CDP 796834 2
❡ Bizet, 'Au fond du temple saint' (from *The Pearl Fishers*), Enrico Caruso (Nadir)/Mario Ancona (Zurga)/Orchestra/W. B. Rogers
Pearl GEMMCD 9361
❡ Lewis/Stock/Rose, 'Blueberry Hill', Fats Domino
Music For Pleasure CD-MFP 6047

I must admit to being surprised at how much I enjoyed this conversation. Sometimes well-known broadcasters are able to turn on the charm and yet leave you feeling that you have just been through the usual hoops, but

Clive's interest in music is so infectious and insightful that I found myself utterly engrossed, and pretty impressed by an intellect which is perhaps sometimes camouflaged by the easy wit.

13 APRIL 2002
Clare Francis, writer

❡ Richard Strauss, 'Hab' mir's gelobt' (from *Der Rosenkavalier*, Act III), Kiri te Kanawa (Marschallin), Anne Sofie von Otter (Octavian), Barbara Hendricks (Sophie)/Staatskapelle Dresden/Bernard Haitink
EMI CDS 754259 2

❡ Mozart, Lacrimosa (from Requiem, K626), Philharmonia Chorus and Orchestra/Carlo Maria Giulini
EMI CDZ 762518 2

❡ Tchaikovsky, 'Gremin's Aria' (from *Eugene Onegin*, Act III), Paata Burchuladze (Prince Gremin)/Staatskapelle Dresden/James Levine
DG 423 959–2

❡ Janáček, String Quartet No. 1, 'Kreutzer Sonata' (first movement, Adagio con moto), Vlach Quartet Prague
Naxos 8.553895

❡ Verdi, 'Esterrefatta fisso' (from *Otello*, Act III), Renata Tebaldi (Desdemona), Mario del Monaco (Otello)/Vienna Philharmonic Orchestra/Herbert von Karajan
Decca 411 618–2

❡ Tan Dun, 'Farewell' (from *Crouching Tiger, Hidden Dragon*), Yo-Yo Ma (cello)/Shanghai Symphony Orchestra/Tan Dun
Sony SK 89347

❡ Britten, 'And Farewell to Ye, Old *Rights o' Man*' (from *Billy Budd*, Act II), Peter Glossop (Billy)/London Symphony Orchestra/Benjamin Britten
London 417 428–2

❡ Liszt, 'Un sospiro', Leslie Howard (piano)
Hyperion CDA 67015

20 APRIL 2002
Wendy Cope, poet

[❡ Cope, 'Greek Island Triolets' and 'By the Round Pond' from *If I Don't Know*, and 'Strugnell's Haiku' from *Making Cocoa for Kingsley Amis*, Wendy Cope, pubished by Faber and Faber]

¶ Britten, 'There is No Rose' (from *A Ceremony of Carols*), Winchester College Quiristers/Sinead Williams (harp)/Christopher Tolley
Proud Sound PROU CD 147
¶ Bach, Suite in G major, (third movement, Courante), Pierre Fournier (cello)
DG 449 711–2
¶ Tallis, *Lamentations of Jeremiah*, Winchester Cathedral Choir/David Hill
Hyperion CDA66400
¶ Judith Weir, 'The Romance of Count Arnaldos', Mary Wiegold (soprano)/The Composers Ensemble/Dominic Muldowney
NMC D003
¶ Schubert, 'Im Frühling', Robert White (tenor)/Graham Johnson (piano)
Virgin Classics VC 790730–2
¶ Handel, Recorder Sonata in C (last movement, Allegro), Micaela Petri (recorder)/Keith Jarrett (harpsichord)
RCA RD 60441
¶ Mozart, Sonata in B flat, K570 (first movement, Allegro), Mitsuko Uchida (piano)
Philips 468 361–2
¶ Gluck, 'Che farò senza Euridice?' (from *Orfeo ed Euridice*), Kathleen Ferrier (Orfeo)/London Symphony Orchestra/Malcolm Sargent
Decca 458 270–2
¶ Beethoven, String Quartet in B flat, Op. 130 (fourth movement), The Lindsays
ASV CD DCA 602

27 APRIL 2002
Nigel Williams, novelist

¶ Muddy Waters, 'Trouble No More', Noël Coward
CHESS CHD 9291
¶ Elgar, *Salut d'amour*, Kyung-Wha Chung (violin)/Philip Moll (piano)
Decca 430 094–2
¶ Orlando Gibbons, 'This is the Record of John', Choir of King's College, Cambridge/Jacobean Consort of Viols/Simon Preston (organ)/David Willcocks
Decca 430 092–2

♪ Mozart, Piano Concerto in D minor, K466 (second movement, Romanze), Alfred Brendel (piano)/Academy of St Martin-in-the-Fields/Neville Marriner
Philips 446 229–2
♪ Bach, *Goldberg Variations*, BWV 988 (Aria), András Schiff (piano)
Decca 417 116–2
♪ Bach, Kyrie (from Mass in B minor), Leipzig Radio Choir, Dresden Staatskapelle/Peter Schreier
Philips 432 972–2
♪ Alaska, 'Hereafter', Private recording by permission of composers and performers

4 MAY 2002
Kathy Lette, novelist

♪ Fanny Mendelssohn, Piano Trio in D minor, Op. 11 (second movement, Andante espressivo), Clara Wieck Trio
Bayer BR 100094
♪ Brian Wilson, 'Surfer Girl', The Beach Boys
Capitol CDP 781295
♪ Smith, 'Kitchen Man', Bessie Smith
Golden Options GO 3811
♪ Richard Strauss, duet from the end of Act 1 of *Der Rosenkavalier*, Elisabeth Schwarzkopf (Marschallin), Christa Ludwig (Octavian)/Philharmonia/Herbert von Karajan
EMI 7243 5 67605 2
♪ Mozart, end of the finale of Act II from *Così fan tutte*, Lisa della Casa (Fiordiligi), Christa Ludwig (Dorabella), Anton Dermota (Ferrando), Erich Kunz (Guglielmo), Paul Schoeffler (Don Alfonso), Emmy Loose (Despina)/Vienna Philharmonic Orchestra/Karl Böhm
Decca 455 476–2
♪ Coward, 'I Went to a Marvellous Party', Noël Coward with Peter Matz (piano)
Sony CD 47253
♪ Blossom Dearie, 'I'm Hip', Blossom Dearie with Jeff Clyne (bass) and Johnny Butts (drums)
Redial 558 638–2

Mario Vargas Llosa, writer

❧ Orff, 'O Fortuna' (from *Carmina burana*), Chorus and Orchestra of the Deutsche Oper, Berlin/Eugen Jochum
DG 447 437–2
❧ Stravinsky, scene 2 from *The Firebird*, Columbia Symphony Orchestra/Igor Stravinsky
Sony SM3K 46291 CD1
❧ Sibelius, Violin Concerto in D minor, Op. 47 (second movement, Adagio di molto), Kyung-Wha Chung (violin), London Symphony Orchestra/André Previn
Decca 425 080–2
❧ Bruckner, Symphony No. 1 in C minor (Scherzo: Schnell), Chicago Symphony Orchestra/Daniel Barenboim
DG 435 068–2
❧ Mahler, end of first movement from Symphony No. 2, 'Resurrection', New York Philharmonic Orchestra/Leonard Bernstein
ONY SX12K 89499 CD23
❧ Mozart, appearance of the statue from *Don Giovanni*, Act II, Gottlob Frick (Statue), Eberhard Waechter (Don Giovanni), Giuseppe Taddei (Leporello)/Philharmonia and Chorus/Carlo Maria Giulini
EMI 7243 5 56232–2
❧ Dvořák, Symphony No. 9 in E minor, 'From the New World' (first movement), Berlin Philharmonic Orchestra/Klaus Tennstedt
HMV 7 67615–2

Niall Ferguson, historian

❧ Robert Burns, 'Hey ca' thro' and 'The deil's awa wi' the' exciseman', Janet Russell and Christine Kydd
Linn CKD 051
❧ Adderley, 'Mercy, Mercy, Mercy', Cannonball Adderly (alto saxophone)/Nat Adderley (cornet)/Joe Zawinul (piano)/Victor Gaskin (bass)/Roy McCurdy (drums)
Giants of Jazz CD 53132
❧ Schubert, 'Der Leiermann' (from *Winterreise*), Dietrich Fischer-Dieskau (baritone)/Gerald Moore (piano)
DG 415 187–2

❡ Wagner, 'Zu neuen Thater' (from the Prelude to Act I of *Götterdämmerung*), Brigit Nilsson (Brünnhilde), Wolfgang Windgassen (Siegfried)/Vienna Philharmonic Orchestra/Georg Solti
Decca 455 570–2 TK 4–7
❡ Bellini, 'Perfido! . . . Or basti!' and 'Vanne, si mi lascia, indegno' (from *Norma*, Act I), Maria Callas (Norma), Ebe Stignani (Adalgisa), Mario Filippeschi (Pollione)/Chorus and Orchestra of La Scala, Milan/Tullio Serafin
EMI 7243 5 56271 2
❡ Beethoven, Sonata in C, 'Waldstein', Op. 53 (first movement, Allegro), Artur Schnabel
EMI CHS 7 63765

25 MAY 2002
Arnold Wesker, playwright

❡ Shikeiki Saegusa, *Yamato Takeru* (excerpt from scene 3), Akemi Nishi (mezzo-soprano), Kazuo Kobayashi (tenor)/Shin Associates Chorus/Tokyo Symphony Orchestra/Naoto Ohtomo
Toshiba EMI TOCZ 9047
❡ Trad. Transylvanian Jewish, 'Khosid Wedding Dance', Muzsikás
Rykodisc HNCD 1373
❡ Schoenberg, *Gurrelieder* (conclusion), Hans Hotter (Speaker)/Choir of St Hedwig's Cathedral, Berlin/Städtischer Musikverein zu Düsseldorf/Berlin Radio Symphony Orchestra/Riccardo Chailly
Decca 430 321–2
❡ Nyman, String Quartet No. 3 (opening), Balanescu Quartet
Argo 433 093–2
❡ C. P. E. Bach, Magnificat anima mea (from Magnificat, Wq 215), Choir of King's College, Cambridge/Academy of St Martin-in-the-Fields/Philip Ledger
Decca 421 148–2
❡ Elgar, 'Sabbath Morning at Sea' (from *Sea Pictures*, Op. 37), Janet Baker (mezzo-soprano)/London Symphony Orchestra/John Barbirolli
EMI CDC 556219 2
❡ Trad. Jewish, 'Eili Eili', Cantor Solomon Rothstein
Columbia E 5226
❡ Loesser, 'Never Will I Marry', Barbra Streisand
CBS 32041

¶ McColl/Parker/Seeger, 'Singin' the Fishin'', Various artists
Topic TSCD 803

1 JUNE 2002
Howard Jacobson, novelist

¶ Mozart, 'Là ci darem la mano' (from *Don Giovanni*, Act I), Graziella Sciutti (Zerlina), Eberhard Waechter (Don Giovanni)/Philharmonia/ Carlo Maria Giulini
EMI 7243 5 56232 2
¶ Percy Grainger, 'Shallow Brown', John Shirley-Quirk (baritone)/ Ambrosian Singers/English Chamber Orchestra/Benjamin Britten
London 425 159–2
¶ Stewart/Gouldman, 'I'm Not In Love', 10cc
Polydor 515 006 2
¶ Lehár, 'Lippen schweigen' (from *The Merry Widow*, Act III), Richard Tauber (tenor)/Odeon-Künstler-Orchester/Erich Wolfgang Korngold
EMI CDM 564654–2
¶ Monteverdi, 'Ardo e scoprir', Boulanger Ensemble/Nadia Boulanger
Pearl GEMM CD 9994
¶ Vivian Ellis, 'This Is My Lovely Day' (from *Bless the Bride*), Lizbeth Webb and Georges Guétary/Michael Collins (musical director)
World Records SH 228
¶ Schubert, Piano Trio in B flat, D 898 (second movement, Andante un poco mosso), Jacques Thibaud (violin)/Pablo Casals (cello)/Alfred Cortot (piano)
EMI CDH 76058–2
¶ Bach, 'Schlummert ein, ihr matten Augen' (from Cantata No. 82, *Ich habe genug*), Janet Baker (mezzo-soprano)/Bath Festival Orchestra/ Yehudi Menuhin
EMI 7243 5 74284–2
¶ Puccini, 'Che gelida manina' (from *La bohème*, Act I), Jussi Björling (tenor)/RCA Victor Orchestra /Thomas Beecham
EMI 7243 5 67750 2

Sir Paul Nurse, Nobel prizewinner in Medicine (cell division research)

¶ Beethoven, Sonata in F minor, 'Appassionata', Op. 57 (second movement, Andante con moto), Emil Gilels (piano)
DG 419 162–2
¶ Purcell, 'Sound the Trumpet' (from Birthday Ode, *Come Ye Sons of Art*), Charles Brett and John Williams (countertenors)/Monteverdi Choir and Orchestra/John Eliot Gardiner
Erato 2292 45123–2
¶ Shostakovich, String Quartet No. 8, Op. 110 (second movement, Allegro molto), Borodin Quartet
EMI CDC 7 47507–2
¶ Brahms, 'Denn alles Fleisch, es ist wie Gras' (from *A German Requiem*, Op. 45), Prague Philharmonic/Giuseppe Sinopoli
DG 429 486–2
¶ Handel, Sonata in F (Larghetto and Allegro), Micaela Petri (recorder)/Keith Jarrett (harpsichord)
RCA RD 60441
¶ Philip Glass, Prelude to Act I of *Akhnaten*, Stuttgart State Opera/ Dennis Russell Davies
Sony M2K42457
¶ Schubert, String Quintet in C, D956 (second movement, Adagio), Emerson Quartet, Mstislav Rostropovich (cello)
DG 431 792–2
¶ Anon., Part of 'De grad'a Santa Maria' (from *The Pilgrimage to Santiago*), Catherine Bott (soprano)/New London Consort/Philip Pickett
Oiseau Lyre 433 148–2
¶ Britten, 'Now the Hungry Lion Roars' (from *A Midsummer Night's Dream*, Act III), Alfred Deller (Oberon), Elizabeth Harwood (Tytania), Stephen Terry (Puck), Richard Dakin, John Pryor, Ian Wodehouse and Gordon Clark (Fairies)/London Symphony Orchestra/Benjamin Britten
Decca 425 663–2

Guy Barker, jazz trumpeter

¶ Honegger, Largo for Strings, Orchestre Symphonique de
RTL/Leopold Hager
Timpani 1C 1016
¶ Douglas, 'Spring Ahead' (from *Stargazer*), Dave Douglas
Arabesque (AJO132)
¶ Perico Sambeat, 'Drume Negrita' from 'Perico', Perico Sambeat
Lola Records 724353320423
¶ Mingus, 'Solo Dancer' (from *The Black Saint and the Sinner Lady*),
Charles Mingus
Impulse IMP 11742
¶ Herrmann, 'Prelude' and 'Rooftop' from the soundtrack to *Vertigo*,
Muir Mathieson (conductor)
Varese Sarabande VSD 5759
¶ Martinů, Double Concerto for Two String Orchestras, Piano and
Timpani (first movement, Poco allegro), City of London Sinfonia/
Richard Hickox
Virgin Classics VC 791099–2
¶ Davis, 'Baby Won't You Please Come Home' (from *Seven Steps to
Heaven*), Miles Davis/Herbie Hancock/George Coleman/Tony
Williams/Ron Carter
Columbia 4669702
¶ Guy Barker, 'Underdogs' from *Soundtrack*, Guy Barker
Provocateur White Label
¶ Nancy Wilson, 'Lush Life', Nancy Wilson/Billy May Orchestra
Capitol PRDCD 3C

Sheena MacDonald, broadcaster

¶ Pärt, *Cantus in Memory of Benjamin Britten*, Royal Scottish National
Orchestra/Neeme Järvi
Chandos CHAN 7039
¶ Sveinsson, 'Somewhere Else Before', Esbjorn Sveinsson Trio
Act 9009–2
¶ Mozart, Qui tollis (from Mass in C minor, K427), London
Symphony Orchestra and Chorus/Colin Davis
Eloquence 468 141–2

¶ Shostakovich, Symphony No. 13, 'Babi Yar' (first movement, Adagio),
Sergei Aleksashkin (bass)/Men of the Chicago Symphony Chorus/
Chicago Symphony Orchestra/Georg Solti
Decca 444 791–2
¶ Berg, Act I, scene 1 from *Wozzeck*, Heinz Zednik (Captain)/Franz
Grundheber (Wozzeck)/Vienna Philharmonic Orchestra/Claudio
Abbado
DG 423 587–2
¶ Prokofiev, Piano Concerto No. 1 in D flat (opening, Allegro brioso),
Jorge Federico Osorio (piano)/Royal Philharmonic Orchestra/Enrique
Bátiz
ASV CDDCA 555
¶ John Adams, 'Meister Eckhardt and Quackie' (from *Harmonielehre*),
City of Birmingham Symphony Orchestra/Simon Rattle
EMI CDC 555051 2

29 JUNE 2002
George Steiner, Professor of Comparative Literature

¶ Schubert, 'Der Wanderer', D649, Matthias Goerne (baritone)/
Graham Johnson (piano)
Hyperion CDJ 33027
¶ Liszt, 'La lugubre gondola', Anner Bylsma (cello)/Reinbert De Leeuw
(piano)
LP Philips 411 117–1
¶ Oscar Hammerstein, 'Lover Come Back to Me', Dizzy Gillespie
RCA NL 89763/B
¶ Poulenc, 'C', Hugues Cuenod (tenor)/Geoffrey Parsons (piano)
Nimbus NIM 5027
¶ Dumont/Vaucaire, 'Non, je ne regrette rien', Edith Piaf
Replay RMCD 4069
¶ Handel (attrib.), arr. Siegfried Ochs, 'Dank sei Dir, Herr', Heinrich
Schlusnus (baritone)/State Opera Orchestra, Berlin/Hermann Weigert
Preiser 89205
¶ Gesualdo, 'Moro lasso al mio duolo', Singers of Ferrara/Robert Craft
Sunset Records LP 600
¶ Salamone de Rossi, 'Baruch haba b'shem Adonai', Boston
Camerata/Joel Cohen
Harmonia Mundi HM 1901021

He was an obvious choice for the programme, but would not countenance it for several years. When he finally relented, we had the kind of exhilerating exchange of ideas that brings out the best in me.

6 JULY 2002
Serena Sutcliffe, Master of Wine

❡ Haydn, Cello Concerto in C (first movement, Moderato), Steven Isserlis (cello)/Chamber Orchestra of Europe/Roger Norrington
RCA 09026 68578–2
❡ Schumann, 'Wenn ich in deine Augen seh' (from *Dichterliebe*, Op. 48), Peter Schreier (tenor)/Wolfgang Sawallisch (piano)
Philips 426 237–2
❡ Giovanni Gabrieli, Magnificat, Gabrieli Consort and Players/Paul McCreesh
Archiv 449 180–2
❡ Brahms, *Alto Rhapsody*, Op. 53 (conclusion), Christa Ludwig (contralto)/Philharmonia Men's Chorus and Orchestra/Otto Klemperer
EMI CDM 769650 2
❡ Theodorakis, 'The Train Leaves at Eight', Agnes Baltsa (mezzo-soprano)/Athens Experimental Orchestra/Stavros Xarhakos
DG 419 236–2
❡ Schubert, 'Liebesbotschaft' (from *Schwanengesang*, D957), Peter Schreier (tenor)/András Schiff (piano)
Decca 425 612–2
❡ Bach, *Ich habe genug*, BWV 82, Hans Hotter (baritone)/Sidney Sutcliffe (oboe)/Philharmonia/Anthony Bernard
EMI CDH 763198 2
❡ Tallis, Salvator Mundi, Theatre of Voices/Paul Hillier
Harmonia Mundi HMU 907154

13 JULY 2002
Rt Hon. Robert Carr, Prime Minister of New South Wales

❡ Janáček, closing scene from *Jenůfa*, Elisabeth Söderström (Jenůfa), Wieslaw Ochman (Laca)/Vienna Philharmonic Orchestra/Charles Mackerras
Decca 414 483–2

❡ Berlin, 'Moonshine Lullaby' (from *Annie Get Your Gun*), Bernadette Peters/1999 Broadway cast/Orchestra/Marvin Laird
Angel 7243 5 50812 2 5
❡ Kander/Ebb, 'Razzle Dazzle' (from *Chicago*), Terence Donovan and the company, 1981 Sydney Theatre Company cast recording
Polydor 539 192−2
❡ Verdi, 'Scene of the Flemish Deputies' (from *Don Carlo*, Act III), Ruggero Raimondi (Filippo II), Montserrat Caballé (Elisabetta), Placido Domingo (Carlo), Sherrill Milnes (Rodrigo), Delia Wallis (Tebaldo)/Ambrosian Opera Chorus/Orchestra of the Royal Opera House/Carlo Maria Giulini
EMI 7243 5 67401 2
❡ Ross Edwards, *Maninyas*, concerto for violin and orchestra (third movement), Dene Olding (violin)/Sydney Symphony Orchestra/Stuart Challender
ABC 438 610−2
❡ Wagner, Sachs's introduction and Quintet from *Die Meistersinger von Nürnberg*, Act III, Donald McIntyre (Sachs), Helena Doese (Eva), Paul Frey (Walther), Christopher Doig (David), Rosemary Gunn (Magdalena)/Elizabethan Philharmonic Orchestra/Charles Mackerras
Used by kind permission of Opera Australia
❡ Locke, 'Curtin Tune' (for Shadwell's *The Tempest, 1674*), Australian Brandenburg Orchestra/Paul Dyer
ABC Classics 456 692−2

20 JULY 2002
Anthony Gottlieb, economist

❡ Beethoven, Symphony No. 7 in A, Op. 92 (second movement, Allegretto), Philharmonia/Benjamin Zander
Telarc CD 80471
❡ Gershwin, 'I Got Rhythm' (two versions), Jack Gibbons (piano)
ASV CDWHL 2077
❡ Mahler, 'Das Trinklied vom Jammer der Erde' (first movement of *Das Lied von der Erde*), René Kollo (tenor)/Chicago Symphony Orchestra/Georg Solti
Decca 414 066−2

♪ Bach, Partita No. 5 in G, BWV 829 (first movement, Praeambulum), Glenn Gould (piano)
Sony SM2K 52597
♪ Rachmaninov, Piano Concerto No. 3 in D minor, Op. 30 (opening of first movement), Arcadi Volodos (piano)/Berlin Philharmonic Orchestra/James Levine
Sony SK 64384
♪ Bernstein, 'Conga!' (from *Wonderful Town*), Kim Criswell (Ruth)/ London Voices (Cadets)/Birmingham Contemporary Music Group/ Simon Rattle
EMI CDC 556753 2
♪ Brahms, opening of *A German Requiem*, Op. 45, Philharmonia Chorus and Orchestra/Otto Klemperer
EMI CDM 566903 2

27 JULY 2002
Stan Barstow, novelist

♪ Weill, 'This Is New' (from *Lady in the Dark*), Helen Forrest (vocals)/ Benny Goodman Orchestra
Columbia 471658 2
♪ Mozart, Serenade in D, 'Posthorn', K320 (first movement, Adagio maestoso–Allegro spirito), Cleveland Orchestra/George Szell
Sony SBK 48266
♪ Berlioz, 'Absence' (from *Les nuits d'été*, Op. 7), Janet Baker (mezzo-soprano)/New Philharmonia Orchestra/John Barbirolli
EMI CDM 769544 2
♪ Richard Strauss, Interlude in A flat (from *Intermezzo*), Royal Philharmonic Orchestra/Thomas Beecham
Biddulph WHL 056
♪ Puccini, 'Quando me'n vo'soletta' (from *La bohème*, Act II), Lucine Amara (Musetta), Robert Merrill (Marcello), Fernando Corena (Alcindoro), Victoria de los Angeles (Mimì), Jussi Björling (Rodolfo), John Reardon (Schaunard), Giorgio Tozzi (Colline)/RCA Victor Orchestra/Thomas Beecham
EMI CDS 747235 2
♪ Eric Ball, *Resurgam* (conclusion), Black Dyke Mills Band/James Watson
Polyphonic QPRL 061D

¶ Tchaikovsky, 'Pas de deux' (from *The Nutcracker*, Act II), Orchestra of the Royal Opera House/Mark Ermler
ROH ROH 305

3 AUGUST 2002
Mike Westbrook, jazz musician

¶ Mike Westbrook, 'Riding Down to Platterback' (from *Platterback*), Westbrook and Company
PAO Records 10530
¶ Mulligan arr. Gil Evans, 'MoonDreams' (from *Rebirth of the Cool*), Gerry Mulligan/featuring John Lewis, Wallace Roney (trumpet), Phil Woods (alto saxophone)
GRP 96792
¶ Parker, 'Donna Lee', Charlie Parker/Miles Davis/Bud Powell/Tommy Potter/Max Roach
Savoy ZD 70737
¶ Stravinsky, 'Petit concert' (from *L'histoire du soldat*), Aage Haugland (narrator)/Royal Scottish National Orchestra/Neeme Järvi
Chandos CHAN 9189
¶ Yancey, 'Death Letter Blues', Jimmy Yancey
Bluebird ND88334
¶ Ellington, '23rd Psalm' (from *Black, Brown and Beige*), Duke Ellington with Mahalia Jackson
COL 4684012
¶ Louis Armstrong, 'West End Blues', Louis Armstrong and His Hot Five
Columbia/Legacy C4K 63527
¶ Rossini, Overture to *The Barber of Seville*, New York Philharmonic Orchestra/Leonard Bernstein
Sony Classical SMK 47606
¶ Ornette Coleman, 'Lonely Woman' (from *The Shape of Jazz to Come*), Ornette Coleman, Don Cherry (cornets)/Charlie Haden (bass)/Billy Higgins (drums)
Atlantic 781339−2

10 AUGUST 2002
Timothy O'Brien, stage director

¶ Komeda, 'Sleep Safe and Warm', Stanko/Rydpal
ECM 1650 537 805−2

272

❡ Bach/Busoni, 'Wachet auf, ruft uns die Stimme' (from Cantata
No. 140), Solomon (piano)
EMI CZS5 69743–2
❡ Wagner, Quintet from *Die Meistersinger von Nürnberg*, Act III, Helen
Donath (Eva), Theo Adam (Hans Sachs), René Kollo (Walther), Peter
Schreier (Beckmesser), Ruth Hesse (Magdalene)/Dresden
Staatskapelle/Herbert von Karajan
EMI CDM 567090–2
❡ Franck, *Symphonic Variations*, Arthur Rubinstein (piano)/Symphony
of the Air/Alfred Wallenstein
RCA Red Seal 74321 846062
❡ Beethoven, 'Mir ist so wunderbar' (from *Fidelio*, Act I), Helga
Dernesch (Leonora), Karl Ridderbusch (Rocco), Helen Donath
(Marzelline), Horst Laubenthal (Jacquino)/Berlin Philharmonic
Orchestra/Herbert von Karajan
CDM 769291–2
❡ Janáček, conclusion of Act II from *The Cunning Little Vixen*, Lucia
Popp (Vixen Sharp-Ears), Eva Randová (Fox), Eva Zigmondová
(Owl), Gertrude Jahn (Jay), Ivana Mixová (Woodpecker)/Vienna State
Opera Chorus/Vienna Philharmonic Orchestra/Charles Mackerras
Decca 417 129–2
❡ Berg, Act I scene 2 from *Wozzeck*, Dietrich Fischer-Dieskau
(Wozzeck), Ernst Haefliger (Andras)/Deutsche Oper, Berlin/Karl
Böhm
DG 435 705–2
❡ Berlioz, 'Villanelle' (from *Les nuits d'été*), Régine Crespin (soprano)/
Orchestre de la Suisse Romande/Ernest Ansermet
Decca 417 813–2
❡ Stravinsky, Excerpt from Act III, scene 3 of *The Rake's Progress*,
Philip Langridge (Tom)/London Sinfonietta Voices/London
Sinfonietta/Riccardo Chailly
Decca 411 646–2

25 AUGUST 2002
Susan Wollenberg, academic

❡ William Byrd, 'Sing Joyfully', Magdalen College Choir, Oxford/John
Harper
CDCA 912

¶ Schubert, Piano Trio in E flat major, Op. 100 (Allegro), Haydn Trio, Wien
Teldec 843683
¶ Fanny Hensel-Mendelssohn, *Song without Words*, Françoise Tillard (piano)
Calliope CAL1213
¶ Salomone Rossi, 'Eftach na sefatai' (from *Les Cantiques de Salomon*), Boston Camerata/Joel Cohen
Harmonia Mundi HM 1901021
¶ Haydn, Horn Concerto No. 1 in D major (Allegro), Anthony Halstead (natural horn)/Hanover Band/Roy Goodman
Nimbus NI 5190
¶ C. P. E. Bach, Rondo in E minor, 'Abschied vom Silbermannschen Clavier', Gustav Leonhardt (clavichord)
RCA GD 71969
¶ Clara Schumann, 'Liebst du um Schönheit', Stella Doufexis (mezzo-soprano)/Graham Johnson (piano)
Hyperion CDJ 33104

31 AUGUST 2002
Anatole Kaletsky, economic journalist

¶ Tchaikovsky, *Manfred Symphony*, Op. 58 (first movement, Moderato con moto), Oslo Philharmonic Orchestra/Mariss Jansons
Chandos CHAN 8535
¶ Bach, 'Now from the Sixth Hour' and 'Be Near Me, Lord, When Dying' (from *St Matthew Passion*), Robert Tear (tenor), John Shirley-Quirk (baritone)/Bach Choir/Thames Chamber Orchestra/ David Willcocks
ASV CDQSS 324
¶ Szymanowski, 'The Fountain of Arethusa' (from *Myths*, Op. 30), David Oistrakh (violin)/Vladimir Yampolsky (piano)
Chant du Monde LDC 278 945
¶ Mozart, 'Sento, o Dio, che questo piede' (from *Così fan tutte*, Act I), Giuseppe Taddei (Guglielmo), Alfredo Kraus (Ferrando), Walter Berry (Don Alfonso), Elisabeth Schwarzkopf (Fiordiligi), Christa Ludwig (Dorabella)/Philharmonia/Karl Böhm
EMI CMS 769330 2

♫ Stravinsky, 'Russian Dance' (from *Three Movements from Petrushka*),
Maurizio Pollini (piano)
Philips 456 937–2
♫ Elgar, 'Go Forth Upon Thy Journey' (from *The Dream of Gerontius*,
Op. 38), John Shirley-Quirk (baritone)/Choir of King's College,
Cambridge/London Symphony Chorus and Orchestra/Benjamin
Britten
Decca 448 170–2
♫ Chopin, Nocturne in F, Op. 15, No. 1, Jacob Kaletsky (piano)
Artist's private recording
♫ Paganini, Violin Concerto No. 1 in D, Op. 6 (first movement, Allegro
maestoso), Leonid Kogan (violin)/Paris Conservatoire Orchestra/
Charles Bruck
Columbia CX 1562

7 SEPTEMBER 2002
Niamh Cusack, actress

♫ Bach, Suite in D major, S1012, Prelude, Yo-Yo Ma (cello)
CBS CD37867/B
♫ Brahms, Concerto for violin, cello and orchestra in A minor, Op. 102
(second movement, Andante),Yehudi Menuhin (violin), Mstislav
Rostropovich (cello)/London Symphony Orchestra/Colin Davis
BBC BBCL 4050 2
♫ Keith Jarrett, Part IIC from *The Köln Concert*, Keith Jarrett
ECM 810 067 2
♫ B. B. King, 'Every Day I Have the Blues', B. B. King
MCA MCLD 19252
♫ Trad. arr. Moore/O'Flynn/Krvine/Lunny, 'Raggle Taggle Gypsy',
Planxty
Shanachie SH79009
♫ Omara Portuondo, 'No me Ilores mas', Ibrahim Ferrer (vocals)
World Circuit WCD059
♫ Richard Strauss, Oboe Concerto in D major (first movement,
Allegro moderato), Martin Gabriel (oboe)/Vienna Philharmonic
Orchestra/André Previn
DG 452 483 2
♫ U2/Bono/The Edge, 'Stuck in a Moment You Can't Get Out Of', U2
Island CIDX770

Ronald Harwood, playwright

¶ Tchaikovsky arr. Ellington/Strayhorn, 'Sugar Rum Cherry' (from *The Nutcracker Suite*), Duke Ellington and his Orchestra
Columbia 472356 2
¶ Mozart, Symphony No. 40, K.550 (first movement, Molto allegro), New York Philharmonic Orchestra/Bruno Walter
Sony SMK 6477
¶ Britten, 'Be Slowly Lifted Up' and Lacrimosa (from *War Requiem*), Hans Wilbrink (baritone), Stefania Woytowicz (soprano)/Melos Ensemble/New Philharmonia Chorus and Orchestra/ Benjamin Britten and Carlo Maria Giulini (conductors)
BBC BBCL 4046–2
¶ Mahler, 'Wo die schönen Trompeten blasen' (from *Des Knaben Wunderhorn*), Christa Ludwig (mezzo-soprano)/Leonard Bernstein (piano)
Sony SM2K 47170
¶ Maschwitz/Sherwin, 'A Nightingale Sang in Berkeley Square', Hutch
Holland CB/H 1
¶ Schubert, Sonata in D, D850 (second movement, Con moto), András Schiff (piano)
Decca 440 306–2
¶ Beethoven, Quoniam (conclusion of Gloria from *Missa Solemnis*, Op. 123), Lucia Popp (soprano), Yvonne Minton (mezzo-soprano), Mallory Walker (tenor), Gwynne Howell (baritone)/Chicago Symphony Chorus and Orchestra/Georg Solti
Decca 425 844–2

Robert Fox, war correspondent

¶ Mozart, Sonata in D, K448 (third movement, Allegro molto), Murray Perahia, Radu Lupu (pianos)
CBS CD 39511
¶ Cohen, 'Alexandra Leaving', Leonard Cohen
Columbia 501202 2
¶ Butterworth, 'Loveliest of Trees' (from *A Shropshire Lad*), Thomas Allen (baritone)/Geoffrey Parsons (piano)
EMI CDM 567428 2

❡ Cimarosa, Oboe Concerto in C (first movement, Introduzione), Haakon Stotijn (oboe)/Netherlands Chamber Orchestra/Jaap Stotijn
CNR LTC 8013
❡ Mozart, 'Conoscete, signor Figaro' (from *The Marriage of Figaro*, Act II), Eberhard Waechter (Count), Giuseppe Taddei (Figaro), Anna Moffo (Susanna), Elisabeth Schwarzkopf (Countess), Piero Cappuccilli (Antonio)/Philharmonia/Carlo Maria Giulini
EMI CMS 763266 2
❡ Mozart, 'Ruhe sanft, mein holdes leben' (from *Zaïde*), Emma Kirkby (Zaïde)/Academy of Ancient Music/Christopher Hogwood
Oiseau Lyre 415 835–2
❡ Victoria, Kyrie (from Missa pro Defunctis), Westminster Cathedral Choir/David Hill
Hyperion CDA 66250
❡ Vivaldi, 'Veni, veni, me sequere' (from *Juditha Triumphans*), Birgit Finnilä (Judith)/Berlin Chamber Orchestra/Vittorio Negri
Philips 426 955–2

28 SEPTEMBER 2002
Jane Stevenson, writer

❡ Robert Johnson, 'Com Palefaced Deith', Carolyn Love (soprano)/ Coronach
CD CMF 008
❡ Antonio Durán de la Mota, 'Fuego, fuego, que el templo se abrasa', Ensemble Elyma and Cor Vivaldi/Gabriel Garrido
K617106
❡ Thomas Campion, 'My Sweetest Lesbia' (from *A Book of Airs*), Andreas Scholl (countertenor)/Andreas Martin (lute)
Harmonia Mundi HMC 901603
❡ Roberto di Simone, 'Villanella di Cenerentola' (from *La gatta Cenerentola*), Fausta Vetere (La gatta Cenerentola)/Orchestra/Antonio Sinagra
EMI 7243 4 96690–2
❡ Henry Purcell, 'What Power Art Thou?' (from *King Arthur*, Act III), Maurice Bevan (The Cold Genius)/The King's Musick/Roderick Skeaping
Harmonia Mundi HMA 190 200

❡ Fr Juan Pérez Bocanegra, 'Hanaq Pachaq', Coro de Camara Exaudi de la Habana/María Felicia Pérez
Editions Jade 74321 73083–2
❡ John Field, Nocturne No. 10 in E minor, Joanna Leach (piano)
Athene ATHCD1
❡ Schubert, 'Gute Nacht' (from *Winterreise*), Anton Dermota (tenor)/ Hilda Dermota (piano)
Telefunken NT 538
❡ Anon., 'In taberna quando sumus' (from *Carmina burana*), Clemencic Consort/René Clemencic
Harmonia Mundi HMA 190 336/8

5 OCTOBER 2002
Anna Enquist, Dutch psychoanalyst and novelist

❡ Mozart, 'Ah! soccorso' (from *Don Giovanni*, Act I), Eberhard Waechter (Don Giovanni), Giuseppe Taddei (Leporello), Gottlob Frick (Commendatore)/Philharmonia/Carlo Maria Giulini
EMI CDS 747260 2
❡ Bach, Sinfonia in F minor, BWV 795, Ivo Janssen (piano)
Void 9804
❡ Robert Heppener, 'A Girl' (from *Four Songs on Poems by Ezra Pound*), Susan Narucki (soprano)/Sepp Grotenhuis (piano)
Donemus CV 48
❡ Mozart, String Quartet in D minor, K421 (first movement, Allegro), Amadeus Quartet
DG 423 303–2
❡ Brahms, Cello Sonata in E minor, Op. 38 (second movement, Allegro quasi menuetto), Mstislav Rostropovich (cello)/Sviatoslav Richter (piano)
Intaglio INCD 705–1
❡ Britten, 'Pastoral' and 'Nocturne' (from Serenade, Op. 31), Martyn Hill (tenor)/Frank Lloyd (horn)/City of London Sinfonia/Richard Hickox
Virgin VC 790792–2
❡ Chopin, Studies in C major and A minor, Op. 10, Nos 1 and 2, Maurizio Pollini (piano)
DG 413 784–2

❡ Stravinsky, *Symphony of Psalms* (conclusion of third movement), Festival Singers of Toronto/CBC Symphony Orchestra/Igor Stravinsky
CBS CD 42434

12 OCTOBER 2002
Noël Annesley, Vice-chairman, Christie's

❡ Verdi, 'Ella giammai m'amò.' (from *Don Carlo*, Act IV), Boris Christoff (King Philip II)/Philharmonia/Jerzy Semkow
EMI CDM 769542 2
❡ Mozart, Violin Sonata in B flat, K378 (second movement, Andantino), Sviatoslav Richter (piano)/Oleg Kagan (violin)
EMI CZS 574293 2
❡ Gluck, 'O del mio dolce ardor' (from *Elena e Paride*, Act I), Teresa Berganza (soprano)/Orchestra of the Royal Opera House/Alexander Gibson
Decca 421 327–2
❡ Beethoven, Sonata in F minor, 'Appassionata', Op. 57 (third movement, Allegro ma non troppo), Sviatoslav Richter (piano)
Philips 456 949–2
❡ Schubert, 'Nähe des Geliebten', D162, Dietrich Fischer-Dieskau (baritone)/Gerald Moore (piano)
DG 457 747–2
❡ Mendelssohn, Octet in E flat, Op. 20 (first movement, Allegro moderato ma con fuoco), Vienna Octet
Decca 421 093–2
❡ Bach, 'Wir eilen mit Schwachen' (from *Jesu, der du meine Seele*, BWV 78), Teresa Stich-Randall (soprano), Dagmar Hermann (mezzo-soprano)/Vienna Bach Guild Orchestra/Felix Prohaska
Vanguard 08.2009.71

19 OCTOBER 2002
Mike Figgis, film director

❡ Holiday, 'Fine And Mellow', Billie Holiday
ESP LC 0546
❡ Ives, *The Unanswered Question*, New York Philharmonic Orchestra/Leonard Bernstein
DG 429 220–2

¶ E. Ory, 'Savoy Blues', Louis Armstrong and his Hot Five
ASV CDAJA 5117
¶ Bach, Suite No. 6 in D (Sarabande), Pierre Fournier (cello)
DG 419 360–2/361/2
¶ Bach, 'Wenn ich einmal soll scheiden' (from *St Matthew Passion*),
Das Neue Orchester/Christopher Spering
LXC5718 OPS 30 72/73
¶ Charlie Parker, 'Lester Leaps In', Count Basie/Lester Young, rec.
New York, 1952
Le Jazz CD3
¶ Beethoven, String Quartet No. 13 in B flat (fifth movement,
Cavatina), Quartetto Italiano
Philips 416 639–2 to 642–2
¶ Jarrett, 'Tribute', Keith Jarrett
ECM: 8471352

26 OCTOBER 2002
Kate Figes, writer

¶ Richard Strauss, 'Beim Schlafengehen' (from *Four Last Songs*), Jessye
Norman (soprano)/Leipzig Gewandhaus Orchestra/Kurt Masur
Philips 464 742–2
¶ Bach, Concerto for Two Violins in D minor, BWV 1043 (third
movement, Allegro), Itzhak Perlman and Pinchas Zukerman (violins)/
English Chamber Orchestra/Daniel Barenboim
EMI 5 74720–2
¶ Van Morrison, 'Someone Like You', Van Morrison
Mercury 832 58–2
¶ Dylan, 'Tangled Up in Blue', Bob Dylan
CBS CD 66509/B
¶ Bach, Contrapunctus XIIa and b from *The Art of Fugue* (Invertible
Fugue), Philomusica of London/George Malcolm
LP Argo ZRG 5422
¶ Schubert, Impromptu in A flat, D935, No. 2, op. posth., Wilhelm
Kempff (piano)
DG 459 412–2
¶ Chopin, Prelude in C, Op. 28, No. 1, Claudio Arrau (piano)
Philips 468 392–2

¶ Mozart, Kyrie (from Requiem, K626), Monteverdi Choir/English Baroque Soloists/John Eliot Gardiner
Philips 420 197–2

2 NOVEMBER 2002
Sir Peter Hall, theatre director

¶ Birtwistle, *Earth Dances* (excerpt), Cleveland Orchestra/Christoph von Dohnányi
Argo 452 104–2
¶ Schoenberg, *Moses und Aron* (conclusion), Franz Mazura (Moses), Philip Langridge (Aron)/Chicago Symphony Orchestra and Chorus/ Georg Solti
Decca 414 264–2
¶ Mozart, 'Gente, gente, all'armi, all'armi' (from *The Marriage of Figaro*, Act IV), Richard Stilwell (Count), Claudio Desderi (Figaro), Ugo Benelli (Don Basilio), Alexander Oliver (Don Curzio), Federico Davià (Antonio), Artur Korn (Bartolo), Gianna Rolandi (Susanna), Felicity Lott (Countess)/London Philharmonic Orchestra/Bernard Haitink
EMI CDS 749753 2
¶ Britten, 'Threnody' (from *Albert Herring*, Act III), John Noble (Vicar), Catherine Wilson (Nancy), Edgar Evans (Mayor), Sylvia Fisher (Lady Billows), Owen Brannigan (Superintendent Budd), Johanna Peters (Florence), April Cantelo (Miss Wordsworth), Sheila Rex (Mrs Herring)/English Chamber Orchestra/Benjamin Britten
London 421 849–2
¶ Beethoven, *Diabelli Variations*, Op. 120 (Variation 31, Largo, molto espressivo), Alfred Brendel (piano)
Philips 426 232–2
¶ Cavalli, 'Vivi, vivi a'nostri amori' (from *La Calisto*, Act II), Janet Baker (Diana), James Bowman (Endimione)/London Philharmonic Orchestra/Raymond Leppard
Decca 436 216–2
¶ Tippett, *Fantasia Concertante on a Theme of Corelli* (conclusion), Yehudi Menuhin, Robert Masters (violins)/Derek Simpson (cello)/ Bath Festival Orchestra/Michael Tippett
EMI CMS 763522 2

❡ Daugherty/Reynolds/Neiberg, 'I'm Confessin' That I Love You', Count Basie, Oscar Peterson (piano)/John Heard (bass)/Louis Bellson (drums)
Pablo CD 2310–896

Utterly outspoken and uncompromising and therefore invigorating in his choices and in discussion.

9 NOVEMBER 2002
Jane Gardam, novelist

❡ Mozart, Sinfonia Concertante in E flat, K247b (second movement, Adagio), John Anderson (oboe), Michael Collins (clarinet), Richard Watkins (horn), Meyrick Alexander (bassoon)/Philharmonia/ Giuseppe Sinopoli
DG 437 530–2
❡ Bishop Ken, 'Awake, My Soul, and With the Sun', Norwich Cathedral Choir/Katherine Dienes (organ)/David Dunnett
Priory PRCD 705
❡ Trad. Jamaican, 'Georgie Lyon', Charles Welsh and Chorus
Nonesuch H 72047
❡ Trad. arr. Quilter, 'Drink to Me Only', Kathleen Ferrier (contralto)/ Phyllis Spurr (piano)
Decca 467 782–2
❡ Archangelsky, The Creed, Feodor Chaliapin (bass)/Russian Metropolitan Church Choir, Paris/Nicolai Afonsky
Pearl GEMMCD 9314
❡ Mendelssohn, String Quartet in A, Op. 13 (first movement, Adagio–Allegro vivace), Hausmusik
Virgin VC 545104 2
❡ Schumann, 'Glückes genug' and 'Wichtige Begebenheit' and 'Träumerei' (from *Kinderszenen*, Op. 15), Alfred Brendel (piano)
Philips 446 948–2
❡ Garland/Razaf, 'In the Mood', Glenn Miller and his Orchestra
RCA PD 89260

Was interested in the difference a Russian choir makes as opposed to an English one and how sacred singing contrasts folk music.

16 NOVEMBER 2002
David Crystal, linguistics expert

¶ Borge, 'Caught in the Act', Victor Borge
CBS 32502
¶ Glass, *Powaqqatsi*, Hispanic Young People's Chorus/Orchestra/
Michael Riesman
Nonesuch 979 192–2
¶ Ramirez, Kyrie (from *Misa Criolla*), Los Fronterizos/Choir of the
Basilica of Socorro/Ariel Ramirez
Philips 814 055–2
¶ Monteverdi, Sonata sopra Sancta Maria (from Vespers, 1610), Tessa
Bonner (soprano)/Taverner Players/Andrew Parrott
EMI CDS 747078 8
¶ Anhalt, *Cento* (opening), Tudor Singers of Montreal/Istvan Anhalt
Radio Canada International 357
¶ Anderson, *O Superman* (opening), Laurie Anderson
Warner K 257002
¶ Nyman, 'Convening the Coven', Michael Nyman Orchestra/Michael
Nyman
Virgin CDVED 957
¶ Donegan, 'Rock Island Line', Lonnie Donegan
Pickwick PWK 076

23 NOVEMBER 2002
Colin Towns, record producer

¶ Davis, 'Blue in Green', Miles Davis
Columbia 4606032
¶ Weather Report, 'Teen Town', Weather Report
Columbia CD32358
¶ Thomas, 'A Child's Christmas In Wales', Dylan Thomas
¶ Debussy, 'Reverie', Paul Crossley (piano)
Sony SB4K87744
¶ Don Ellis Orchestra, 'Turkish Bath', Don Ellis Orchestra
Electric Bath/Columbia Records CK65522
¶ Elgar, *Salut d'Amour*, Bournemouth Sinfonietta/Norman del Mar
Chandos CHAN 8371

¶ Britten, 'Storm' (from *Four Sea Interludes from Peter Grimes*),
London Symphony Orchestra/André Previn
EMI 07777 6473628
¶ Stravinsky, *The Firebird*, London Symphony Orchestra/Kent Nagano
Virgin Classics VC540322
¶ Lennox, 'Thin Line between Love and Hate', Annie Lennox
RCA 74321 257172

30 NOVEMBER 2002
Richard Strange, actor

¶ Lauro, *Dos Valses Venezolanos* No. 1, Alirio Diaz (guitar)
Laserlight Classics 14 129
¶ Wagner, 'Liebestod' (from *Tristan und Isolde*), Philharmonia/Otto
Klemperer
EMI CDC 747254–2
¶ Weill, 'The Ballad of Mack The Knife' (from *The Threepenny Opera*,
Act I), Wolfgang Neuss/Orchestra of Sender Freies Berlin/Wilhelm
Brückner-Rüggeberg
CBS CD 42637
¶ Gavin Bryars, 'Jesus Blood Never Failed Me Yet', Tom Waits (vocals)/
Orchestra conducted by Michael Reisman
Point 438823–2
¶ Rodgers/Hart, 'Manhattan', Ella Fitzgerald
Polydor 835 610–2
¶ Liszt, *Les jeux d'eau à la Villa d'Este*, Alfred Brendel (piano)
Philips 446 943–2
¶ Fauré, Sanctus (from Requiem, Op. 48), Choir of Kings College,
Cambridge/New Philharmonia/David Willcocks
Classics for Pleasure CD-CFP 4570
¶ Ellington/Webster, 'I got It Bad and That Ain't Good', Ivy Anderson
(vocals)/Johnny Hodges (alto saxophone)/Duke Ellington and his
Famous Orchestra
Le Jazz
¶ Puccini, 'Vissi d'arte' (from *Tosca*, Act II), Maria Callas (Floria
Tosca)/Orchestra of La Scala, Milan/Victor de Sabata
EMI CDC 747176–2
[¶ Strange, 'You Will Die', Richard Strange (guitar and vocals)
Recorded live in the studio]

¶ Coulter, 'How Do I Love Thee?' (from *Intervention*), David Coulter
with Iain Morris
Fringecore FR004

7 DECEMBER 2002
Nicholas de Jongh, theatre critic

¶ Telemann, fourth movement from Concerto in A for flute, violin
and strings (from *Tafelmusik*, series 1), Collegium Aureum
Deutsche Harmonia Mundi 05472 77467–2
¶ Berlioz, 'The Death of the Two Lovers' (from *Roméo et Juliette*,
Part 4), London Symphony Orchestra/Colin Davis
Philips 416 964–2
¶ Schubert, String Quartet in D minor, 'Death and the Maiden', D810,
(Theme and Variation 1 from second movement), Quartetto Italiano
Philips 446 163–2
¶ Mozart, Piano Concerto No. 27 in B flat, K595, Clifford Curzon
(piano)/English Chamber Orchestra/Benjamin Britten
Decca 417 288–2
¶ Bach, Gigue from Suite in D Major, BWV 1012, Ralph Kirshbaum
(cello)
Virgin VBD5 61609–2
¶ Schubert, Sonata in A, D959 (first movement), Mitsuko Uchida
(piano)
Philips 456 579–2
¶ Mahler, Symphony No. 9 (end of finale), New Philharmonia
Orchestra/Otto Klemperer
EMI 7234 5 67036–2
¶ Richard Strauss, *Elektra* (ending), Hildegard Behrens (Elektra),
Nadine Secunde (Chrysothemis)/Tanglewood Festival Chorus/Boston
Symphony Orchestra/Seiji Ozawa
Philips 422 574–2

14 DECEMBER 2002
Simon McBurney, theatre director

¶ Trad. American, 'Mary Don't You Weep', Aretha Franklin
Atlantic R2 75627

♪ Beethoven, Violin Concerto in D, Op. 61 (first movement, cadenza and conclusion), Bronislaw Huberman (violin)/Vienna Philharmonic Orchestra/George Szell
EMI CDH 763194 2
♪ Trad. Russian, 'I Light the Fire', Veronika Oucholin
Playa Sound PS 65189
♪ Shostakovich, 'Gallop' (from *Hypothetically Murdered*, Op. 31a), City of Birmingham Symphony Orchestra/Mark Elder
Cala CACD 1020
♪ Trad. Georgian, 'Gogo shavtvala', Rustavi Folk Choir of Georgia/ Anzor Erkomaishvili
Beaux 2005
♪ Bellini, 'Casta diva' (from *Norma*, Act I), Maria Callas (Norma)/ Chorus and Orchestra of La Scala, Milan/Tullio Serafin
EMI CMS 763000 2
♪ Trad. Hebridean, 'Mo rùn Ailein', Miss Mary Morrison and Chorus
Greentrax CDTRAX 9003
♪ John Cage, Sonata No. 5 (from *Sonatas and Interludes*), Joanna MacGregor (prepared piano)
Sound Circus SC 002
♪ Chopin, Study in C, Op. 10, No. 1, Maurizio Pollini (piano)
DG 413 794–2
♪ Trad. Spanish, 'Alma Gitana', Ramon El Portugues
Nuevos Medios NM 15691
♪ Schnittke arr. Bashmet, Trio Sonata (first movement, Moderato), Moscow Soloists/Yuri Bashmet
RCA RD 60446

21 DECEMBER 2002
Peter Moores, philanthropist

♪ Wagner, 'Brünnhilde's Battle Cry' (from *The Valkyrie*, Act II), Rita Hunter (Brünnhilde)/English National Opera Orchestra/ Reginald Goodall
Chandos OPER 0018
♪ Verdi, 'It Can't Be! . . . Give Me Freedom To Be Happy' (from *La traviata*, Act I), Valerie Masterson (Violetta)/John Brecknock (Alfredo)/English National Opera Orchestra/Charles Mackerras
Chandos CHAN 3023

❡ Donizetti, 'Coppia iniqua' (from *Anna Bolena*, Act II), Maria Callas (Anna)/Orchestra of La Scala, Milan/Gianandrea Gavazzeni
EMI CMS 566471 2
❡ Lennon/McCartney, 'Do You Want To Know a Secret?', The Beatles
Parlophone CDP 746435 2
❡ Richard Strauss, Marschallin's monologue (from *Der Rosenkavalier*, Act I), Yvonne Kenny (Marschallin)/London Philharmonic Orchestra/David Parry
Chandos CHAN 3022
❡ Puccini, 'In questa reggia' (from *Turandot*, Act II), Eva Turner (Turandot)/Orchestra/Stanford Robinson
Nimbus NI 7801
❡ Berlin, 'The Hostess with the Mostest on the Ball' (from *Call Me Madam*), Ethel Merman/Gordon Jenkins and his Orchestra
MCA MCAD 10521
❡ Saint-Saëns, 'Mon coeur s'ouvre à ta voix' (from *Samson and Delilah*, Act II), Marian Anderson (Delilah)/Orchestra/Lawrence Collingwood, rec. 1930
Pearl GEMMCD 9318
❡ Beethoven, Sonata in C, 'Waldstein', Op. 53 (second movement, Adagio molto), Claudio Arrau (piano)
Philips 454 686–2

29 DECEMBER 2002
Philip Franks, actor

❡ Britten, 'Sunday Morning' (from *Peter Grimes*, Act II), Heather Harper (Ellen Orford)/Orchestra of the Royal Opera House/Benjamin Britten
London 425 659–2
❡ Schumann, Piano Quartet in E flat, Op. 47 (Andante cantabile), Beaux Arts Trio/Samuel Rhodes (viola)
Philips 420 791–2
❡ Purcell, 'Chaconne' (from *King Arthur*, Act V), Les Arts Florissants/William Christie
Erato 4509–98535–2
❡ Bach, 'Es ist vollbracht' (from *St John Passion*), Kathleen Ferrier (contralto)/Ambrose Gauntlett (viola da gamba)/London Philharmonic Orchestra/Adrian Boult
Decca 433 474–2

❡ Mozart, 'Bei Männern, welche Liebe fühlen' (from *The Magic Flute*, Act I), Gundula Janowitz (Pamina), Walter Berry (Papageno)/ Philharmonia/Otto Klemperer
EMI CDC 555174–2
❡ Lennon/McCartney, 'You Never Give Me Your Money' (from *Abbey Road*), The Beatles
Parlophone CDP 746446–2
❡ John Adams, *Christian Zeal and Activity*, San Francisco Symphony Orchestra/Edo de Waart
Nonesuch 979144–2
❡ Shostakovich, String Quartet No. 8 in C minor, Op. 110 (second movement, Allegro molto), Brodsky Quartet
Teldec 9031 71702–2

4 JANUARY 2003
Sue Townsend, writer

❡ Hines, 'There Will Never Be Another You', Earl Hines (piano)
Dejavu Retro R2CD 40–32
❡ Brahms, 'Ich habt nun Traurigkeit' (from *A German Requiem*, Op. 45), Elisabeth Schwarzkopf (soprano)/Philharmonia/Otto Klemperer
EMI CDC 747238–2
❡ Beethoven, Violin Sonata in F, 'Spring', Op. 24 (first movement, Allegro), Pinchas Zukerman (violin)/Daniel Barenboim (piano)
EMI 7243 5 74454–2
❡ Piaf, 'Lovers For a Day', Edith Piaf
EMI 838231–1
❡ Tchaikovsky, Violin Concerto in D (finale), Nigel Kennedy (violin)/ London Philharmonic Orchestra/Okko Kamu
EMI CDC 754127–2
❡ Teagarden, 'A Hundred Years From Today', Jack Teagarden and his Orchestra
CLASSICS CLASSICS 874
❡ Bach, Suite No. 1 in G (Prelude), Mstislav Rostropovich (cello)
EMI CDC 555364–2
❡ Shandileer, 'Happy' (from *Soca Gold* Vol. 3), Shandileer
HVCD 20

11 JANUARY 2003
Mike Gibbs, jazz musician

¶ Trad., 'When the Saints Go Marching In', Bunk Johnson and his
New Orleans Band
MM 7243 842940 2

¶ Debussy, Sonata for flute, viola and harp (first movement,
Pastorale), Philippa Davies (flute)/Roger Chase (viola)/Marisa Robles
(harp)
Virgin VBD 561427 2

¶ Herzog/Holiday, 'Don't Explain', Billie Holiday
MCA MCD 18767

¶ Charles Ives, *The Unanswered Question*, Chicago Symphony
Orchestra/Michael Tilson Thomas
CBS MK 42381

¶ Carisi, 'Springsville', Miles Davis/Orchestra/Gil Evans
CBS 460606 2

¶ Messiaen, 'Prière du Christ montant vers son Père' (from
L'ascension), Olivier Messiaen (organ of Saint-Trinité, Paris)
EMI CZS 767400 2

¶ Stravinsky, 'Danse sacrale' (from *The Rite of Spring*), Columbia
Symphony Orchestra/Igor Stravinsky
Sony SM3K 46291

18 JANUARY 2003
James Mirrlees, economist

¶ Schoenberg, Chamber Symphony No. 1, Op. 9 (conclusion),
Birmingham Contemporary Music Group/Simon Rattle
EMI CDC 555212 2

¶ Monteverdi, 'Pur ti miro' (from *L'incoronazione di Poppea*, Act III),
Sylvia McNair (Poppea), Dana Hanchard (Nerone)/English Baroque
Soloists/John Eliot Gardiner
Archiv 447 088-2

¶ Stravinsky, 'The Birth of Apollo' (from *Apollon musagète*), Academy
of St Martin-in-the-Fields/Neville Marriner
Decca 443 577-2

¶ Britten, 'Elegy' (from *Serenade*, Op. 31), Peter Pears (tenor)/Dennis
Brain (horn)/Boyd Neel String Orchestra/Benjamin Britten
Pearl GEMMCD 9177

❡ Stockhausen, *Gesang der Jünglinge* (opening), Electronic tape
DG LP 16133
❡ Goehr, 'Su l'orride paludi' and 'Sinfonia' (from *Arianna*, scene 6),
Chorus/Arianna Ensemble/William Lacey
NMC NMCD 054
❡ Beethoven, String Quartet in A minor, Op. 132 (finale, Allegro
appassionato), Busch Quartet
EMI CHS 565308 2
❡ Schubert, Fantasy in F minor, D940 (conclusion), Sviatoslav Richter,
Benjamin Britten (piano duet)
Decca 466 822–2

25 JANUARY 2003
Tim Winton, Australian novelist

❡ Arakel Siunetsi, 'Sirt im sasani', Anna Mailian (soprano)/Sharakan
Early Music Ensemble/Daniel Erazhist
Celestial Harmonies 13116–2
❡ Evans/Hewson/Clayton/Mullen, 'I Still Haven't Found What I'm
Looking For', Sensitive New Age Cowpersons
ABC 472 046–2
❡ McLaughlin, 'Luki', Shakti
Verve 014 164–2
❡ Phelps, 'Doxology', Kelly Joe Phelps
Rykodisc RCD 10393
❡ Vaughan Williams, Symphony No. 5 in D (third movement,
Romanza), London Philharmonic Orchestra/Adrian Boult
EMI CDC 747214 2
❡ Terry, 'Sonny's Thing', Sonny Terry (harmonica)/John Mayall
(harmonica and twelve-string electric guitar)/Brownie McGhee
(electric guitar)/Sugarcane Harris (violin)/Eddie Greene (drums)
AandM CD 0829
❡ Pärt, *Summa*, I Fiamminghi/Rudolf Werthen
Telarc CD 80387
❡ Peter Sculthorpe, *Djilile*, Alex Furman (piano)
Move MD 3031

Steven Pinker, scientist and writer

❧ Shearing/Forster, 'Lullaby in Birdland', Sarah Vaughan
Mercury 830 699–2
❧ Nelson, 'Stolen Moments', Oliver Nelson, Eric Dolphy, George
Barrow (saxophones)/Freddie Hubbard (trumpet)/Bill Evans (piano)/
Paul Chambers (bass)/Roy Haynes (drums)
MCA MCAD 5659
❧ Costello, 'God's Comic', Elvis Costello
Warner 925848–2
❧ A. and J. Neville, 'Yellow Moon', The Neville Brothers
A and M CDA 5240
❧ Jarre, 'Herman' (from the soundtrack of *Enemies: a Love Story*),
Orchestra/ Maurice Jarre
Varese Sarabande VSD 5253
❧ Lennon/McCartney, 'She Said She Said', The Beatles
Parlophone CDP 746441 2
❧ Bach, Brandenburg Concerto No. 2 in F, BWV 1047 (first movement,
Allegro), Emanuel Hurwitz (violin)/Richard Adeney (flute)/Peter
Graeme (oboe)/David Mason (trumpet)/English Chamber Orchestra/
Benjamin Britten
Decca 425 725–2
❧ Statman, 'Flatbush Waltz' (conclusion), Itzhak Perlman (violin)/The
Andy Statman Klezmer Orchestra
EMI CDC 555555 2

Elizabeth Jane Howard, novelist

❧ Bach, Double Concerto in C minor, BWV 1060 (first movement,
Allegro), András Schiff, Peter Serkin (pianos)/Camerata Bern
Decca 455 761–2
❧ C. P. E. Bach, Flute Concerto in A minor, Wq 166 (first movement,
Allegro assai), Stephen Preston (flute)/English Concert/Trevor
Pinnock
Archiv 427 132–2
❧ Mozart, Piano Concerto in B flat, K595 (third movement, Allegro),
Rudolf Serkin (piano)/London Symphony Orchestra/Claudio Abbado
DG 445 516–2

❡ Brahms, *Variations on the St Anthony Chorale* (Variations 5, 6 and 7), New York Philharmonic Orchestra/Arturo Toscanini
RCA GD 60317

❡ Richard Strauss, 'Noch glaub ich dem einen ganz mich gehörend' (from *Ariadne auf Naxos*), Edita Gruberova (Zerbinetta)/London Philharmonic Orchestra/Georg Solti
Decca 430 384–2

❡ Mozart, Horn Concerto No. 2 in E flat, K417 (third movement, Rondo), Dennis Brain (horn)/Philharmonia/Herbert von Karajan
EMI CDM 566898 2

❡ Scarlatti, Sonata in G, Kk 125, Nina Milkina (piano)
Unterschrift MICHALL

15 FEBRUARY 2003
Stephen Warbeck, film composer

❡ John Adams, *Short Ride in a Fast Machine*, City of Birmingham Symphony Orchestra/Simon Rattle
EMI CDC 555051–2

❡ The Pogues, 'And the Band Played "Waltzing Matilda" ' (from *Rum, Sodomy and the Lash*), The Pogues
Stiff SEEZ 5B

❡ Britten, 'Canto con moto' (from Suite for Cello No. 3, Op. 87), Steven Isserlis (cello)
Virgin 0777 75905229

❡ Eisler, 'Der Zerissene Rock' (from *Die Mutter*), Ernst Busch/Berliner Ensemble/Adolf Fritz Guhl
Berlin Classics 0092 302 BC

❡ Jarrett, 'All I Want' (from *The Mourning of a Star*), Keith Jarrett (piano)/Charlie Haden (bass)/Paul Motian (drums)
Atlantic K40309

❡ Messiaen, 'Louange a l'éternité de Jesus' (from *Quartet for the End of Time*), Erich Gruenberg (violin)/William Pleeth (cello)/Michel Béroff (piano)
EMI CDM 763947 2

❡ Parricelli/France, 'Shore Song' (from *Alba*), John Parricelli
Provocateur 1021

❡ Dylan, 'You Angel You' (from *Planet Waves*), Bob Dylan
CBS CD32154

22 FEBRUARY 2003
David Canter, psychological profiler

❡ Ligeti, *San Francisco Polyphony*, Swedish Radio Symphony
Orchestra/Elgar Howarth
Wergo WER 60163–50
❡ Palestrina, Gloria (from Missa *L'homme armé*), Soloists of the
Cappella Musicale di S. Petronio do Bologna/Sergio Vartolo
Naxos 8553315
❡ Luiz Bonfa, 'Manha de Carnaval', Ray Brown Trio
Evidence ECD 22076–2
❡ Lennon/McCartney, 'She's Leaving Home', The Beatles
Parlophone CDP 746442–2
❡ Bach arr. Webern, 'Ricercar' (from *The Musical Offering*), Berlin
Philharmonic Orchestra/Pierre Boulez
DG 447 099–2
❡ John Stafford Smith, 'The Star-Spangled Banner', Jimi Hendrix
ITM ITM 960004
❡ Françaix, Wind Quintet No. 1 (second movement, Presto), Prague
Wind Quintet
Praga PRD 250 126

1 MARCH 2003
Sir Peter Ustinov, actor, writer, director

❡ Prokofiev, Violin Concerto No. 2 in G minor, Op. 63 (second
movement, Andante assai), Jascha Heifetz (violin)/Boston Symphony
Orchestra/Charles Munch
RCA 09026 61779–2C
❡ Mozart, 'Il mio tesoro intanto' (from *Don Giovanni*, Act II), Luigi
Alva (Don Ottavio), Philharmonia/Carlo Maria Giulini
EMI 7243 5 56232–2
❡ Janáček, Organ solo (from *Glagolitic Mass*), Jan Hora (organ)
Supraphon 10 3575–2
❡ Moniuszko, 'The Wind Howls Among the Hills' (from *Halka*),
Leonid Sobinov (tenor)/unnamed orchestra and conductor
Symposium SYMCD 1239
❡ Britten, 'Sunday Morning' (from *Peter Grimes*, Act II), Heather Harper
(Ellen Orford), Orchestra of the Royal Opera House/Benjamin Britten
London 425 659–2

❡ Berlioz, 'Le spectre de la rose' (from *Les nuits d'été*), Janet Baker (mezzo-soprano)/New Philharmonia Orchestra/John Barbirolli
EMI CDM 769544–2
❡ Bononcini, 'Per la Gloria d'adoravi' (from *Griselda*), Luciano Pavarotti (tenor)/Bologna Teatro Communale Orchestra/Richard Bonynge
Decca 417 006–2

8 MARCH 2003
Daniel Libeskind, architect

❡ Bach, Suite in D minor, BWV 1008 (Prelude), Mstislav Rostropovich (cello)
EMI CDC 555365 2
❡ Coleman, 'Free Jazz' (opening), Ornette Coleman (saxophone)/ Eric Dolphy (bass clarinet)/Don Cherry (pocket trumpet)/Freddie Hubbard (trumpet)/Scott la Faro, Charlie Haden (bass)/Billy Higgins, Ed Blackwell (drums)
Atlantic 1364–2
❡ Messiaen, 'Sermon to the Birds' (conclusion) (from *Saint François d'Assise*), José van Dam (Saint François)/Hallé Orchestra/Kent Nagano
DG 445 176–2
❡ Beethoven, Sonata in C sharp minor, 'Moonlight', Op. 27, No. 2 (first movement, Adagio sostenuto), Vladimir Horowitz (piano)
CBS CD 34509
❡ Bach, Prelude and Fugue in F minor, BWV 881 (from *The Well-tempered Clavier*, Book II), Glenn Gould (piano)
Sony SM2K 52603
❡ Nono, *Fragmente – Stille*, 'An Diotima', LaSalle Quartet
DG 437 720–2
❡ Bartók, String Quartet No. 5 (fourth movement, Andante), Emerson String Quartet
DG 423 657–2
❡ Mozart, *A Musical Joke*, K522 (first movement, Allegro), Orpheus Chamber Orchestra
DG 429 783–2
❡ Tallis, *Spem in alium* (conclusion), Tallis Scholars/Peter Philips
Gimell CDGIM 006

15 MARCH 2003
Jon Lord, musician, ex-Deep Purple

❡ Lord, *Concerto for Group and Orchestra* (third movement, Vivace–Presto) London Symphony Orchestra/Paul Mann
Eagle Records EDGC124–3
❡ Stravinsky, 'Danse sacrale' (from *The Rite of Spring*), Oslo Philharmonic/Mariss Jansons
EMI 7548992
❡ Vaughan Williams, A London Symphony (second movement, Lento), London Philharmonic Orchestra/Adrian Boult
EMI CDCD7472132
❡ Davis/Evans, 'Gone' (from *Porgy and Bess*), Miles Davis/Gil Evans
CBS 450985 2
❡ Lennon/McCartney, 'Strawberry Fields Forever', The Beatles
Parlophone CD3R 5570
❡ Bach, arr. Elgar, Fantasia and Fugue in C minor (Fugue), London Philharmonic Orchestra/Leonard Slatkin
RCA 87862/AandB
❡ Bela Bartók, *Music for Strings, Percussion and Celesta* (fourth movement, Allegro molto), Oslo Philharmonic Orchestra/Mariss Jansons
EMI CDC 7540702

22 MARCH 2003
Virginia Nicholson, historical biographer

❡ Trad., 'The Water is Wide', Alfred Deller (countertenor)/Desmond Dupré (lute)
Vanguard 08 5064 71
❡ Gershwin, 'Bess, You Is My Woman Now' (from *Porgy and Bess*), Willard White (Porgy)/Cynthia Haymon (Bess)/London Philharmonic Orchestra/Simon Rattle
EMI CDS 749568 2
❡ Britten, Violin Concerto, Op. 15 (third movement, Passacaglia), Mark Lubotsky (violin)/English Chamber Orchestra/Benjamin Britten
London 417 308–2
❡ Delerue, 'Le tourbillon' (from the soundtrack of *Jules et Jim*), Jeanne Moreau
Philips 432 728

℥ Puccini, 'Quando m'en vo'soletta' (from *La bohème*, Act II), Ruth Ann Swenson (Musetta), Thomas Hampson (Marcello), Roberto Alagna (Rodolfo), Leontina Vaduva (Mimì)/Philharmonia/Antonio Pappano
EMI CDS 556120 2
℥ Stravinsky, *The Firebird* (conclusion), New York Philharmonic Orchestra/Pierre Boulez
CBS MK 42396
℥ Huey Smith, 'Sea Cruise', Frankie Ford
Ace CDCH 904
℥ Mozart, Et incarnatus est (from Mass in C minor, K.427), Sylvia McNair (soprano)/English Baroque Soloists/John Eliot Gardiner
Philips 420 210–2
℥ Anon., 'La cammesella', Roberto Murolo
Durium DRL 50016

29 MARCH 2003
André Brink, South African writer

℥ Dobar Veèer, 'Moja Draga', Klapa Singers
Unesco D 8276
℥ Mozart, 'Dove sono i bei momenti' (from *The Marriage of Figaro*, Act III), Kiri te Kanawa (Countess), London Philharmonic Orchestra/ Georg Solti
Decca 410 150–2
℥ Schubert, 'Nacht und Träume' D827, Gérard Souzay (baritone)/ Dalton Baldwin (piano)
Philips 438 514–2
[℥ André Brink, *The Other Side of Silence* (extract), read by André Brink]
℥ Haydn, 'Von deiner Güt', o Herr und Gott' (from *The Creation*, Part III), Edith Mathis (Eve), José van Dam (Adam)/Vienna Singverein/Vienna Philharmonic Orchestra/Herbert von Karajan
DG 410 720–2
℥ Hardy, 'Ce petit coeur', Françoise Hardy
Camden 74321 822322/B
℥ Chopin, Prelude in D flat major, 'Raindrop', Op. 28, No. 15, Vladimir Ashkenazy (piano)
Decca 443 739–2

¶ Mozart, Flute Sonata, K301 (second movement, Allegro), Jean-Pierre Rampal (flute)/John Steele Ritter (piano)
CBS CD 42142

¶ Beethoven, Symphony No. 3, 'Eroica' (finale, Allegro molto), Vienna Philharmonic Orchestra/Leonard Bernstein
DG 413 778–2

5 APRIL 2003
Toby Litt, novelist

¶ Parker, 'Koko', Charlie Parker's Reboppers
Savoy 70527

¶ Trad., 'Fifty Miles of Elbow Room', Rev. F. W. McGee
Truth TLP1001

¶ Dylan, 'I Dreamed I Saw St Augustine', Bob Dylan
Columbia 463359–2

¶ Schubert, 'Die Krähe', D911 (from *Winterreise*), Peter Schreier (tenor)/András Schiff piano
Decca 436122–2

¶ Adès, 'O Albion' (sixth movement from *Arcadiana*, Op. 12), Endellion Quartet
EMI CDZ 572271–2

¶ Nick Drake, 'Know', Karel Kryl
Island IMCD94 842923–2

¶ Mahler, 'Wenn dein Mütterlein tritt zur Tür herein' (from *Kindertotenlieder*), Janet Baker/Hallé Orchestra/John Barbirolli
EMI CDC 7477932

¶ Stravinsky, 'Here I Stand . . .' (from *The Rake's Progress*, Act I) Royal Philharmonic Orchestra/Igor Stravinsky
Sony Classical CD46299A

¶ Bach, Two and Three Part Inventions, No. 2 in C minor, Glenn Gould (piano)
CBS 42269B

¶ Saint-Saëns, 'Fossils' (from *Carnival of the Animals*), David Nettle and Richard Markham (pianos)/Aquarius/Nicholas Cleobury
Collins Classics 10962

¶ Kryl, 'Bratricku, zavirej vratka', Karel Kryl
Panton Records 8002011301

¶ Morrissey/Marr, 'Jeane', Sandie Shaw/The Smiths
WEA YZ0003

Peter Brookes, *Times* cartoonist

♫ Lehrer, 'The Vatican Rag', Tom Lehrer
Reprise 6179–2
♫ Stravinsky, 'Gently, Little Boat' (from *The Rake's Progress*, Act III),
Dawn Upshaw (Anne Trulove)/Chorus and Orchestra of Lyon Opera/
Kent Nagano
Erato 0630–12715–2
♫ Janáček, String Quartet No. 1, 'Kreutzer Sonata' (third movement,
Con moto), Belcea Quartet
Zig-Zag Territories zzт 010701
♫ Tchaikovsky, 'V vashem dome!' (from *Eugene Onegin*, Act II), Neil
Shicoff (Lensky), Thomas Allen (Onegin), Mirella Freni (Tatiana),
Anne Sofie von Otter (Olga), Rosemarie Lang (Madame Larina)/
Leipzig Radio Choir/Staatskapelle Dresden/James Levine
DG 423 959–2
♫ Maxwell Davies, 'Farewell to Stromness' (from *The Yellow Cake
Review*), Peter Maxwell Davies (piano)
Unicorn DKPCD 9070
♫ Shostakovich, String Quartet No. 8 in C minor, Op. 110 (first and
second movements), Borodin Quartet
Melodiya 74321 40715–2
♫ Handel, 'Cara sposa, amante cara' (from *Rinaldo*), David Daniels
(Rinaldo)/Orchestra of the Age of Enlightenment/Roger Norrington
Virgin vc 545326–2
♫ Mozart, 'Don Giovanni a cenar teco' (from *Don Giovanni*, Act II),
Gudjon Oskarsson (Commendatore), Peter Mattei (Don Giovanni),
Gilles Cachemaille (Leporello)/Soloists of the European Music
Academy of Aix-en-Provence/Mahler Chamber Orchestra/Daniel
Harding
Virgin vcd 545425 2

19 APRIL 2003
Matthew Parris, journalist and politician

♫ Davashe, 'Lakutshn Ilanga', Miriam Makeba
Music of the World cd 12514

❡ Taylor/Dallas, 'I Wish I Knew How It Would Feel To Be Free', Nina Simone

Camden 74321 69881–2

❡ Gounod, 'Judex' (from *Mors et Vita*), Orféon Donostiarra/Orchestra du Capitole de Toulouse/Michel Plasson

EMI CDS 754459 2

❡ Trad. Ukrainian, 'Moon in the Sky', Stepan Dmitrovich Shcherbak

Artist's private recording

❡ Gilbert/Sullivan, 'The Sun Whose Rays' (from *The Mikado*, Act II), Elsie Morison (Yum-Yum)/Pro Arte Orchestra/Malcolm Sargent

EMI CDS 747773 2

❡ Haydn, Violin Concerto in C, Hob. VIIa: 1 (second movement, Adagio), Arthur Grumiaux (violin)/English Chamber Orchestra/ Raymond Leppard

Philips 426 977–2

❡ Meyerbeer, 'Mi batte il cor . . . O Paradiso' (from *L'africaine*), Luciano Pavarotti (Vasco da Gama)/National Philharmonic Orchestra/ Oliviero de Fabritiis

Decca 430 470–2

❡ Smetana, 'Faithful Loving' (from *The Bartered Bride*, Act I), Peter Dvorský (Jeník)/Gabriela Beňačková (Mařenka)/Czech Philharmonic Orchestra/Zdeněk Košler

Supraphon 11 0641–2

❡ Rossini, 'Assisa a' piè d'un salice' (from *Otello*, Act III), Frederica von Stade (Desdemona)/Philharmonia/Jésus López-Cobos

Philips 432 456–2

❡ Arthur Smith, 'Duelling Banjos', Eric Weissberg and Steve Mandel (banjos)

Warner K 46214

26 APRIL 2003
Stanley Wells, Shakespeare scholar

❡ Vaughan Williams, 'Full Fathom Five' (from *Five Shakespeare Songs*), Choir of King's College, Cambridge/David Willcocks

Decca 430 093–2

❡ Adès, 'L'embarquement' and 'O Albion' (from *Arcadiana*), Endellion Quartet

EMI 5 72271–2

♪ Schubert, 'Auflösung', D807, Janet Baker (mezzo-soprano)/Geoffrey Parsons (piano)
BBC Legends BBCL 4070–2
♪ Martin Best, 'Who is Sylvia?' (from *The Two Gentlemen of Verona*), Martin Best (voice and guitar)/Edward Flower (guitar)
Grosvenor GRS 1013
♪ Shakespeare, 'O, What a Rogue and Peasant Slave Am I', from *Hamlet*, Act II, scene 2, John Gielgud
BBC Radio Collection ZBBZ 1691
♪ Berlioz, 'Fantasy on Shakespeare's *The Tempest*' (from *Lélio*, Op. 14b), London Symphony Chorus and Orchestra/Pierre Boulez
Sony Classical SM3K 64103/A
♪ Thomas Arne, 'Thou Soft-flowing Avon', April Cantelo/English Chamber Orchestra/Raymond Leppard
Oiseau Lyre SOL 60036
♪ Shakespeare, Sonnets Nos 29 and 36, read by Michael Williams
Penguin Audiobooks PEN 291
♪ Schubert, 'Hark, Hark, the Lark' ('Horch, horch, die Lerch', D889), Elisabeth Schumann (soprano)/Gerald Moore (piano)
EMI CDH 763041
♪ Britten, 'The Lovers' Awakening' (from *A Midsummer Night's Dream*, Act III), Peter Pears (Lysander), Thomas Hemsley (Demetrius), Josephine Veasey (Hermia), Heather Harper (Helena)/London Symphony Orchestra/Benjamin Britten
London 425 665–2

3 MAY 2003
Professor Malcolm Longair, astrophysicist

♪ Oscar Peterson, 'Chicago Blues' (from *The Trio*), Joe Pass (guitar)/ Niels-Henning Orsted Pedersen (bass)
Pablo OJCCD 992–2
♪ Messiaen, 'Regard de l'ésprit de joie' (from *Vingt regards sur l'enfant Jésus*), Pierre-Laurent Aimard (piano)
Teldec 3984 26868–2A
♪ Handel, 'Scherza infida' (from *Ariodante*, Act II), Lorraine Hunt/Freiburger Barockorchester/Nicholas McGegan
Harmonia Mundi HMU 907147

¶ Wagner, 'Muss ich dich so verstehn' (from *Tristan und Isolde*,
Act III), Wolfgang Windgassen (Tristan)/Bayreuther Festspiele/
Karl Böhm
DG 419 892–2
¶ John Adams, beginning of Act II, scene 2 from *Nixon in China*,
Orchestra of St Luke's/Edo de Waart (conductor)
Nonesuch 979177–2B

10 MAY 2003
Rick Moody, American writer

¶ Pärt, 'Für Alina', Werner Bärtschi (piano)
ECM 839 659–2
¶ Tchaikovsky, 'Valse sentimentale', Op. 51, No. 6, Clara Rockmore
(theremin)/Nadia Reisenberg (piano)
Delos D/CD 1014
¶ Monk, 'Gotham Lullaby', Meredith Monk
ECM 825 459–2
¶ Chopin, Nocturne in B flat minor, Op. 9, No. 1, Artur Rubinstein
(piano)
RCA RD 89563
¶ Jeffes/Richardson, 'Sheep Dip', Penguin Café Orchestra
EG EEGCD 38
¶ Webb, 'I'm Goin' Home', Ervin Webb/Prisoners from Parchman
Farm Dairy Camp, Mississippi
Rounder CD 1703
¶ Gilbert/Sullivan, 'The Sun Whose Rays' (from *The Mikado*, Act II),
Marie McLaughlin (Yum-Yum)/Orchestra of Welsh National Opera/
Charles Mackerras
Telarc CD 80284
¶ Fripp/Eno, 'Wind on Water', Robert Fripp (guitar)/Brian Eno (loops
and synthesiser)
EG EEGCD 3
¶ Zappa, 'Get Whitey', Ensemble Modern/Frank Zappa
Zappa CDZAP 57

Benedict Allen, explorer

❡ Son Montuno/José Ramón Sánchez, 'Soy Cubana', Omara
Portuondo (vocals)
Artex CD 025
❡ Alain Kounkou, 'Dansez', Soukouss Masters
CDJ 8806
❡ Richard Strauss, 'The Presentation of the Rose' (from *Der Rosenkavalier*, Act II), Teresa Stich-Randall (Sophie), Christa Ludwig (Octavian)/Philharmonia/Herbert von Karajan
EMI 7243 5 67605–2
❡ Trad. Mongolian, 'Song in Praise of the Altaï'
Ethnic B 6776
❡ Elgar, Cello Concerto in E minor, Op. 83 (third movement, Adagio), Jacqueline du Pré (cello)/London Symphony Orchestra/John Barbirolli
EMI CDM 763286–2
❡ Tchaikovsky, 'The Rose Adagio' (Pas d'action) (from *The Sleeping Beauty*, Op. 66), Philharmonia/Efrem Kurtz
Seraphim 7243 5 68537–2
❡ Bach, Recitative ('Da nahmen die Kriegsknechte'), chorus ('Gegrüsset seist du, Judenkönig') and chorale ('O Haupt voll Blut und Wunden') from *St Matthew Passion*, Part 2, Christoph Prégardien (Evangelist)/Arnold Schoenberg Choir/Vienna Concentus Musicus/ Nikolaus Harnoncourt
Teldec 8573–81036–2
❡ Trad. (from Papua New Guinea), Tofaril (singing) and Mariam (drumming)
Playsound PS 65107

Exotic travels are reflected by the choice of music heard in the land of origin.

James Wood, critic and novelist

❡ Parry, 'Never Weather-beaten Sail', Choir of St George's Chapel, Windsor/Christopher Robinson
Hyperion CDA 66273

❡ Bach, Sonatina (from Cantata, BWV 106, 'Actus Tragicus'), Bach Ensemble/Joshua Rifkin
Oiseau Lyre 417 323–2
❡ Brahms, Intermezzo in E flat, Op. 117, No. 1, Glenn Gould (piano)
Sony SM2K 52651
❡ Byrd, Agnus Dei (from Mass for Four Voices), Tallis Scholars/Peter Phillips
Gimell CDGIM 345
❡ William Harris, 'Faire is the Heaven', Cambridge Singers/John Rutter
Collegium COLCD 107
❡ Tallis, 'O nata lux', Cambridge Singers/John Rutter
Collegium COLCD 113
❡ Lennon/McCartney, 'The Fool on the Hill', The Beatles
Parlophone CDMMT 1
❡ Brahms, Piano Concerto No. 1 in D minor, Op. 15 (second movement, Adagio), Maurizio Pollini (piano)/Berlin Philharmonic Orchestra/Claudio Abbado
DG 447 041–2
❡ Beethoven, Sonata in E, Op. 109 (finale, Andante molto cantabile ed espressivo), Sviatoslav Richter (piano)
Philips 438 486–2

31 MAY 2003
John Banville, novelist

❡ Richard Strauss, Sextet from *Capriccio*, Vienna String Sextet
EMI CDC 555108–2
❡ Gerald Barry, *Triorchic Blues*, Noriko Kawai (piano)
NMCD 022
❡ Gabriel Fauré, Nocturne No. 12 in E minor, Op. 107, Paul Crossley (piano)
CRD 3407
❡ Trad., 'The Dear Irish Boy', Willie Clancy (uilleann pipes)
TOPIC 12T 175
❡ Britten, 'Before Life and After' (from *Winter Words*), Peter Pears (tenor)/Benjamin Britten (piano)
Decca 425 996–2

¶ Dmitri Shostakovich, Fugue No. 16 in B flat minor (from *24 Preludes and Fugues*, Op. 87), Tatiana Nikolayeva (piano)
Hyperion CDA 66442
¶ Purcell, 'Sound the Trumpet' (from *Come Ye Sons of Art Away*), Kathleen Ferrier (contralto), Isobel Baillie (soprano)/Gerald Moore (piano)
APR APR 5544

7 JUNE 2003
Tim Pigott-Smith, actor

¶ Ellington/Strayhorn, 'Brown Betty', Johnny Hodges (alto saxophone)/Duke Ellington Orchestra
LP: Rare Tune 5003 FC
¶ Shakespeare, 'Her Father Loved Me . . . Witchcraft I Have Used', from *Othello* Act I, scene 3, Laurence Olivier (Othello)
RCA RE 5520
¶ Puccini, 'The Death of Mimì' (from *La bohème*, Act IV), Barbara Hendricks (Mimì), José Carreras (Rodolfo), Angela Maria Blasi (Musetta), Gino Quilico (Marcello), Richard Cowan (Schaunard), Francesco Ellero d'Artegna (Colline)/French National Orchestra/ James Conlon
Erato ECD 75458
¶ Lennon/McCartney, 'Golden Slumbers', 'Carry That Weight', 'The End' (from *Abbey Road*), The Beatles
Parlophone CDP 7464462
¶ Bach, *Goldberg Variations*, BWV 988 (Aria), Glenn Gould (piano), rec. 1981
Sony Classical SM3K 87703
¶ Brassens, 'Chanson pour l'Auvergnat', Georges Brassens
LP: Philips 9101 045
¶ Piazzolla, 'Libertango, Guardia Vieja', Tom Pigott-Smith (violin)/ Michael Czerny (piano)/Morgan Szymanski (guitar)/Ian Hill (bandoneon)
Private recording
¶ Sibelius, Violin Concerto (first movement, excerpt), Yehudi Menuhin (violin)/London Philharmonic Orchestra/Adrian Boult
EMI CDM 763987 2

❡ Shakespeare, 'Fear No More the Heat of the Sun', from *Cymbeline*, Act IV, scene 2, Peggy Ashcroft
RCA RD 87843
❡ Mahler, 'Ich bin der Welt abhanden gekommen' (from *Rückert-Lieder*), Janet Baker (mezzo-soprano)/New Philharmonia Orchestra/John Barbirolli
EMI CDM 566981–2

14 JUNE 2003
Lynne Reid Banks, writer

❡ Bach, Concerto for Two Violins in D minor, BWV 1043 (first movement, Vivace), Yehudi Menuhin, Christian Ferras (violins)/Bath Festival Orchestra
EMI CZS 767310 2
❡ Bernstein, 'O, Happy We' (from *Candide*), Robert Rounseville (Candide), Barbara Cook (Cunegonde)/Orchestra/Thomas Krachmalnick
Sony SK 48017
❡ Gershwin, 'Bess, You is my Woman Now' (from *Porgy and Bess*), Willard White (Porgy), Cynthia Haymon (Bess)/London Philharmonic Orchestra/Simon Rattle
EMI CDS 749568 2
❡ Trad. arr. Finjan, 'I Wanna Fellow', Finjan
Red House RHR CD 57
❡ Menotti, 'Papers! Papers!' (from *The Consul*, Act II), Beverly O'Regan Thiele (Magda Sorel)/Camerata New York/Joel Revzen
Newport Classic NPD 85645–2
❡ Chopin, Prelude in D flat, 'Raindrop', Op. 28, No. 15, Artur Rubinstein (piano)
RCA GD 60047
❡ Schubert, 'Auf dem Wasser zu singen', D774, Elisabeth Schwarzkopf (soprano)/Edwin Fischer (piano)
EMI CDH 764026 2
❡ Mercer/De Paul, 'Jubilation T. Cornpone' (from the soundtrack *Li'l Abner*), Stubby Kaye (Marryin' Sam)/Chorus and Orchestra/Nelson Riddle
Philips BBL 7365

❡ Avissar/Levanon, 'Erev Ba', Aliza Kashi and Shimson Bar
Yisrafon EP 101
❡ Weill, 'Speak Low' (from *One Touch of Venus*), Lotte Lenya/
Orchestra/Maurice Levin
CBS MK 42658

21 JUNE 2003
Terry Farrell, architect

❡ Rogers/Hart, 'Here in My Arms' (from *Dearest Enemy*), Ella
Fitzgerald (vocal)/Orchestra arr. and cond. Buddy Bregman
Verve 821 580–2
❡ Benjamin, *Sudden Time* (opening), London Philharmonic
Orchestra/George Benjamin
Nimbus NI 1432
❡ Schubert, String Quintet in C, D956 (second movement, Adagio),
The Lindsays/Douglas Cummings (cello)
ASV CD DCA 537
❡ Lennon/McCartney, 'I'm Looking Through You' (from *Rubber Soul*),
The Beatles
Parlophone CDP 746440–2
❡ Beethoven, Allegro molto e vivace (Scherzo from Septet, Op. 20),
Gaudier Ensemble
Hyperion CDA 66513
❡ Kayranis, Inka Kenas
Indio Music DCD 946BLU
❡ Trad. from Connemara, 'The Piper's Broken Finger', Concertina solo
(Anonymous field recording)
Ocora C 580029
❡ Monteverdi, Antiphon: Trinitate Venerata, Psalm 147: Lauda
Jerusalem, The Sixteen Choir and Orchestra/Harry Christophers
Hyperion CDD 22028
❡ Mozart, 'Soave sia il vento' (from *Così fan tutte*, Act I), Elisabeth
Schwarzkopf (Fiordiligi), Christa Ludwig (Dorabella), Walter Berry
(Alfonso)/Philharmonia/Karl Böhm
EMI 7243 5 67382–2

Sir Martin Rees, astronomer

❧ Beethoven, String Quartet in E minor, Op. 59, No. 2 (second movement, Molto adagio), The Lindsays
ASV CDDCS 207
❧ Janáček, Organ solo and Intrada (from *Glagolitic Mass*), Thomas Trotter (organ)/Vienna Philharmonic Orchestra/Riccardo Chailly
Decca 460 213–2
❧ Rachmaninov, 'Rejoice, O Virgin Mother of God' (from *Vespers*, Op. 37), Choir of King's College, Cambridge/Stephen Cleobury
EMI CDC 556752 2
❧ Trad. Mongolian, Two xöömi songs, Anonymous singer
Chant du Monde CMX 374 1010.12
❧ Schumann, Piano Quintet in E flat, Op. 44 (third movement, Scherzo–Molto vivace), Martha Argerich (piano)/Dora Schwarzberg, Lucy Hall (violins)/Nobuko Imai (viola)/Mischa Maisky (cello)
EMI CDS 555484 2
❧ Handel, 'Descend, Kind Pity' (from *Theodora*), Paul Agnew (Septimius)/Gabrieli Players/Paul McCreesh
Archiv 469 061–2
❧ Haydn, 'In the Beginning' and 'Now Vanish Before the Holy Beams' (from *The Creation*, Part I), John Shirley-Quirk (baritone), Robert Tear (tenor)/Choir of King's College, Cambridge/Academy of St Martin-in-the-Fields/David Willcocks
EMI CMS 769894 2
❧ Bruckner, Te ergo, quaesumus (from Te Deum), Joan Rodgers (soprano), Catherine Wyn-Rogers (contralto), Keith Lewis (tenor), Alastair Miles (bass)/Joseph Fröhlich (violin)/Corydon Orchestra/Matthew Best
Hyperion CDA 66650
❧ Mahler, 'Urlicht' (from Symphony No. 2 in C minor, 'Resurrection'), Maureen Forrester (contralto)/London Symphony Orchestra/Gilbert Kaplan
Conifer 75605 51277 2

Absolutely stunning discussion on the comparable structures in music and science.

Tim Parks, novelist

❧ Mozart, 'Aprite un po' quegli occhi' (from *The Marriage of Figaro*, Act IV), Thomas Allen (Figaro)/Vienna Philharmonic Orchestra/Riccardo Muti
EMI CDC 747980
❧ John Dowland, 'Now O Now I Needs Must Part', Maddie Prior (vocal)/The Carnival Band
Ark PRKCD 31
❧ Mozart, 'Aprite, presto aprite' (from *The Marriage of Figaro*, Act II), Kathleen Battle (Susanna), Ann Murray (Cherubino)/Vienna Philharmonic Orchestra/Riccardo Muti
EMI CDC 747979
❧ Chopin, Waltz in G flat, Op. 70, No. 1, Artur Rubinstein (piano)
RCA RD 89564
❧ Bach, 'Jesus bleibet meine Freude' (from Cantata No. 147), Choir of Kings College, Cambridge/David Willcocks
Classics for Pleasure CD-CFP 4277
❧ Vivaldi, Concerto in G major for two mandolins (first movement, Allegro), Ugo Orlandi and Dorina Frati (mandolins)/I solisti Veneti/Claudio Scimone
Erato 4509 92132–2
❧ Old English folk song, 'Queen Eleanor's Confession', Tim Hart and Maddy Prior
Mooncrest CRESTCD 010
❧ Satie, *Gnossienne* No. 1, Aldo Ciccolini (piano)
EMI CDC 747474–2
❧ Paul Simon, 'The Boy in the Bubble' (from *Graceland*), Paul Simon
Warner 925447–2

Julian Bream, guitarist

❧ Fauré, 'Au bord de l'eau', Gérard Souzay (baritone)/Jacqueline Bonneau (piano)
Pearl GEMM 0159
❧ Janáček, Sonata *1.X.1905*, first movement, 'The Presentiment', from 'On the Street'), András Schiff (piano)
ECM 461 660–2

♪ Stravinsky, *Symphonies of Wind Instruments*, Netherlands Wind Ensemble/Edo de Waart
Philips 441 583–2
♪ Creamer/Layton, 'After You've Gone', Benny Goodman Sextet
Blu-Disc T 1002
♪ Reinhardt, 'Improvisation', Django Reinhardt (guitar)
ASV CDAJA 5267
♪ Chabrier, 'Idylle' (from *Suite Pastorale*), Orchestre du Capitole de Toulouse/Michel Plasson
EMI CDC 749652 2
♪ Falla, 'Nana' (from *Seven Spanish Folk Songs*), Victoria de los Angeles (soprano)/Gerald Moore (piano)
EMI CDH 764028 2
♪ Dowland, 'Stay, Time, Awhile thy Flying', Peter Pears (tenor)/Julian Bream (lute)
RCA 09026–61602–2

I've known him since childhood and he is still as scurrilous as ever. Loves to recall how Peter Pears, asked by William Walton why Bream appeared to be persona non grata at Aldeburgh for a couple of years, replied: 'His Dowland, my dear, it's slipping.' Now whenever I see him I ask how his Dowland is and if it is still slipping.

19 JULY 2003
Peter Gill, theatre director

♪ Stravinsky, 'The Tresses' (from *Les noces*), Anny Mory (soprano), Patricia Parker (mezzo-soprano), John Mitchinson (tenor), Paul Hudson (bass)/Martha Argerich, Krystian Zimerman, Cyprien Katsaris, Homero Francesch (pianos)/English Bach Festival Chorus and Percussion Ensemble/Leonard Bernstein
DG 423 251–2
♪ Schubert, 'Seligkeit', D433, Elly Ameling (soprano)/Dalton Baldwin (piano)
Philips 420 870–2
♪ Boulez, 'Conduite' (from *Le visage nuptial*), Phyllis Bryn-Julson (soprano), Elizabeth Laurence (mezzo-soprano)/BBC Symphony Orchestra/Pierre Boulez
Erato 2292–45494–2

❡ Rodgers/Hart, 'Manhattan', Ella Fitzgerald
Verve 821 579–2
❡ Mozart, 'Ruhe sanft mein holdes Leben' (from *Zaïde*), Irmgard
Seefried (soprano)/London Mozart Players/Harry Blech
Testament SBT 1026
❡ Bach arr. Webern, Ricercar (from *The Musical Offering*), London
Symphony Orchestra/Pierre Boulez
Sony SM3K 45845
❡ Josquin, Kyrie (from Missa *L'homme armé super voces musicales*),
A Sei Voci/Bernard Fabre-Garrus
Naïve E 8809
❡ Purcell, 'Sound the Trumpet' (from *Come ye Sons of Art*), Alfred and
Mark Deller (countertenors)/Kalmar Orchestra/Alfred Deller
Vanguard 08.5060.71
❡ Mahler, 'Nun seh' ich wohl' (from *Kindertotenlieder*), Janet Baker
(mezzo-soprano)/Hallé Orchestra/John Barbirolli
EMI CDM 566981 2

26 JULY 2003
Amanda Craig, writer

❡ Trad. arr. Barlow, 'I Had Four Brothers', Vivien Ellis/Tim Laycock/
Broadside Band
Saydisc CD-SDL 419
❡ Bach, arr. Myra Hess, 'Jesu, Joy of Man's Desiring', Dinu Lipatti
(piano)
Philips 456 892–2
❡ Mozart, 'Aprite un po' (from *The Marriage of Figaro*, Act IV), Samuel
Ramey (Figaro)/London Philharmonic Orchestra/Georg Solti
Decca 410 150–2
❡ Mendelssohn, *A Midsummer Night's Dream* (Overture, Op. 21),
Bavarian Radio Symphony Orchestra/Rafael Kubelík
DG 415 840–2
❡ Beethoven, 'Mir ist so wunderbar' (from *Fidelio*, Act I), Helga
Dernesch (Leonore), Karl Ridderbusch (Rocco), Helen Donath
(Marzelline), Horst R. Laubenthal (Jaquino)/Berlin Philharmonic
Orchestra/Herbert von Karajan
EMI CMS 769290 2

❡ Coward, 'Mad Dogs and Englishmen', Noël Coward/Ray Noble
Orchestra
BBC BBCCD 652
❡ Stravinsky, Appearance and Dance of the Firebird (from *The
Firebird*), Columbia Symphony Orchestra/Igor Stravinsky
Sony SM3K 46291
❡ Lennox/Stewart, 'Sisters are Doin' It for Themselves', Eurythmics/
Aretha Franklin
Castle CTVCD 112

2 AUGUST 2003
Adrian Lester, actor

❡ Elgar, Cello Concerto in E minor, Op. 85 (first movement,
Adagio–Moderato), Michaela Fukacová (cello)/Brno State
Philharmonic Orchestra/Libor Pešek
MCA MCD 10782
❡ Porter, 'I've Got You Under My Skin', Diana Krall
Verve IMPD 304
❡ Sondheim, 'These Are My Friends' (from *Sweeney Todd*), Len Cariou
(Sweeney Todd), Angela Lansbury (Mrs Lovett)/Orchestra/Paul
Gemignani(original Broadway cast)
RCA 3379–2-RC
❡ Vivaldi, 'Nulla in mundo pax sincera', Mária Zádori (soprano)/
Capella Savaria/Pál Németh
Quintana QUI 903063
❡ Paul Simon, 'Bridge over Troubled Water', Aretha Franklin
Atlantic 781668–2
❡ Harold Darke, 'In the Bleak Midwinter', Choir of Westminster
Cathedral/James O'Donnell (organ)/David Hill
IMP PCD 843
❡ Wonder, 'As', Stevie Wonder
Universal 066 502–2

9 AUGUST 2003
Richard Francis, biographer

❡ Adams, *Shaker Loops* (last movement, 'A Final Shaking'), Orchestra
of St Luke's/John Adams
Nonesuch 7559 79360–2

¶ Beethoven, Sonata in C, 'Waldstein', Op. 53 (second movement, Adagio molto), Alfred Brendel (piano)
Philips 438 472–2
¶ Biber, 'La battaglia', Concentus Musicus Wien/Nikolaus Harnoncourt
Archiv 437 081–2
¶ Mingus, 'Fables of Faubus', Jazz Workshop Inc.
CBS 45046–2
¶ Mozart, 'Voi che sapete' (from *The Marriage of Figaro*, Act II), Fiorenza Cossotto (Cherubino)/Philharmonia/Carlo Maria Giulini
EMI 763266–2
¶ Dylan, 'Just like a Woman', Nina Simone
Global RAD CD 84
¶ Bach, Prelude and Fugue in C sharp minor, BWV 872 (from *The Well-tempered Clavier*, Book 2), Glenn Gould (piano)
Sony SM2K 52603

16 AUGUST 2003

James Fenton, poet

¶ Gluck, 'Di questa cetra in seno' (from *Il Parnaso confuso*), Cecilia Bartoli (Erato)/Akademie für Alte Musik Berlin/Bernhard Forck
Decca 467 248–2
¶ Sapo Perapaskero, 'The Return of the Magic Horses', Taraf de Haïdouks
Cramworld CRAW 24
¶ Wagner, 'In fernem Land' (from *Lohengrin*, Act III), René Kollo (Lohengrin), Karl Ridderbusch (King Heinrich)/Chorus of the Deutsche Oper Berlin/Berlin Philharmonic Orchestra/Herbert von Karajan
EMI CMS 769314 2
¶ Zevon/Muldoon, 'MacGillycuddy's Reeks', Warren Zevon
Artemis 507838–2
¶ Mussorgsky, 'In the Corner' (from *The Nursery*), Boris Christoff (bass)/Alexandre Labinsky (piano)
EMI CHS 763023 2
¶ Harle, 'Hunting the Hare', John Harle (saxophone and percussion)/Andy Sheppard (saxophone)/Steve Lodder (keyboards)
Argo 452 605–2

❡ Cage, Sonata No. 5 (from *Sonatas and Interludes*), Joanna MacGregor (prepared piano)
Sound Circus SC 007
❡ Bach, *St Matthew Passion*, BWV 244 (conclusion), Deborah York, Julia Gooding (sopranos)/Magdalena Kozená, Susan Bickley (mezzos)/ Mark Padmore, James Gilchrist (tenors)/Peter Harvey, Stephan Loges (basses)/Gabrieli Players/Paul McCreesh
Archiv 474 200–2

23 AUGUST 2003
Orlando Figes, historian

❡ Trad. Russian, arr. Pokrovsky, 'Porushka', Dmitri Pokrovsky Ensemble
RealWorld CDRW 17
❡ Mussorgsky, 'The Great Gate of Kiev' (from *Pictures at an Exhibition*), Sviatoslav Richter (piano)
Philips 420 774–2
❡ Jimmy Witherspoon, 'Times are Gettin' Tougher than Tough', Jimmy Witherspoon (vocals)/Gerry Mulligan, Ben Webster (saxes)/ Jimmy Rowles (piano)/Leroy Vinnegar (bass)/Mel Lewis (drums)
Vogue LAE 12253
❡ Skryabin, Etude in D sharp minor, Op. 8, No. 12, Vladimir Horowitz (piano)
DG 419 499–2
❡ Bach, Violin Concerto in A minor, BWV 1041 (first movement, Allegro moderato), David Oistrakh (violin)/Royal Philharmonic Orchestra/Eugene Goossens
DG 419 855–2
❡ Rachmaninov, Nunc Dimittis (from Vespers, Op. 37), RSFSR Academic Russian Choir/Alexander Sveshnikov
HMV ASD 2973
❡ Schubert, *Moment Musical* in A flat, D780, No. 6, Alfred Brendel (piano)
Philips 422 076–2
❡ Shostakovich, String Quartet No. 12 in D flat, Op. 133 (first movement, Moderato), Beethoven Quartet
Melodiya C 01769

30 AUGUST 2003
Judith Flanders, writer

❧ Poulenc, Qui sedes ad dexteram patris (from Gloria), Kathleen Battle (soprano)/Tanglewood Festival Chorus/Boston Symphony Orchestra/Seiji Ozawa
DG 427 304–2
❧ Adams, *Shaker Loops* (last movement, A Final Shaking), Ensemble Modern/Sian Edwards
RCA 09026 68674–2
❧ Hindemith, The Four Temperaments (Variation 3, Phlegmatic), Hans Otte (piano)/Berlin Philharmonic Orchestra/Paul Hindemith
DG 427 407–2
❧ Stravinsky, 'Coda: Apollo and the Muses' (from *Apollon musagète*), Columbia Symphony Orchestra/Igor Stravinsky
Sony SM3K 46292
❧ Vivaldi, 'N'el suo carcere ristretto' (from Serenata a tre), Kurt Spanier (tenor)/Clemencic Consort/René Clemencic
Harmonia Mundi HMA 1901066
❧ Stradella, 'Volin'pure lontano dal sen" (from *San Giovanni Battista*), Catherine Bott (Salome)/Pascal Monteilhet, Yasunori Imamura (lute and theorbo)/Marc Minkowski
Erato 2292–45739–2
❧ Monteverdi, Nisi Dominus (from Vespers, 1610), Monteverdi Choir/ English Baroque Soloists/John Eliot Gardiner
Archiv 429 565–2
❧ Mozart, Piano Concerto in D, K175 (third movement, Allegro), Malcolm Bilson (fortepiano)/English Baroque Soloists/John Eliot Gardiner
Archiv 415 990–2

6 SEPTEMBER 2003
David Hughes, writer

❧ Nielsen, Clarinet Concerto, Op. 57 (first movement, Allegretto un poco), Niels Thomsen (clarinet)/Danish National Radio Symphony Orchestra/Michael Schønwandt
Chandos CHAN 8894

❡ Stravinsky, Octet (third movement, Finale), Nash Ensemble/Elgar Howarth

Classics for Pleasure CD-CFP 6044

❡ Bolcom, 'Graceful Ghost' (from *Three Ghost Rags*), William Bolcom (piano)

Nonesuch H 71257

❡ Bach, Fantasia and Fugue in G minor, BWV 542 (Fugue), John Scott (organ of St Peter Mancroft, Norwich)

Regent REGCD 105

❡ Thackray, 'Grandad', Jake Thackray

EMI CDP 796271 2

❡ Trad. Swedish, arr. Johansson, 'Folkvisor', Jan Johansson (piano)/ George Rydl (bass)

Heptagon HECD 000

❡ Stanford, Magnificat in C, Op. 115, Choir of King's College, Cambridge/James Vivian (organ)/Stephen Cleobury

EMI CDC 555535 2

❡ Ravel, 'Forlane' (from *Le tombeau de Couperin*), Jean-Yves Thibaudet (piano)

Decca 433 515–2

13 SEPTEMBER 2003
David Starkey, historian and broadcaster

❡ Mozart, Oboe Quartet in F, K370 (second movement, Adagio), Nicholas Daniel (oboe)/Members of The Lindsays

ASV CDDCA 968

❡ Haydn, Gloria (from 'Nelson' Mass), Margaret Marshall (soprano), Carolyn Watkinson (alto), Keith Lewis (tenor), Robert Holl (bass)/ Leipzig Radio Choir/Staatskapelle Dresden/Neville Marriner

EMI CDC 747424 2

❡ Verdi, 'Dio, che nell'alma infondere' (from *Don Carlo*, Act II), Eugenio Fernandi (Don Carlo), Ettore Bastianini (Rodrigo)/Vienna State Opera Chorus/Vienna Philharmonic Orchestra/Herbert von Karajan

DG 447 655–2

❡ Campion, 'It Fell on a Summer's Day', Ian Partridge (tenor)/Jakob Lindberg (lute)

Helios CDH 88011

❡ Purcell, March (from *Music for the Funeral of Queen Mary*), Equale Brass Ensemble/John Eliot Gardiner
Erato 4509–96553–2
❡ Henry VIII, 'Pastyme with Good Companye', I Fagiolini/Forbury Consort
Cantoris CRCD 2365
❡ Mozart, 'Dove sono i bei momenti' (from *The Marriage of Figaro*, Act III), Kiri te Kanawa (Countess)/London Philharmonic Orchestra/ Georg Solti
Decca 410 150–2
❡ Haydn, 'The Representation of Chaos' (from *The Creation*, Part I), Academy of St Martin-in-the-Fields/Neville Marriner
Philips 416 449–2
❡ Monteverdi, 'Pur ti miro, pur ti godo' (from *L'incoronazione di Poppea*, Act II), Magda László (Poppea), Richard Lewis (Nero)/Royal Philharmonic Orchestra/John Pritchard
EMI CZS 573842 2

21 SEPTEMBER 2003
John Simpson, journalist and broadcaster

❡ Grey/Wood/Gibbs, 'Runnin' Wild', Dick Robertson/Duke Ellington and his Famous Orchestra
Saville CDSVL 206
❡ Prokofiev, 'The Philosophers' (from *Cantata for the Twentieth Anniversary of the October Revolution*), Philharmonia Chorus and Orchestra/Neeme Järvi
Chandos CHAN 9095
❡ Gay, 'The Modes of the Court So Common are Grown' (from *The Beggar's Opera*), John Cameron (Macheath), Alexander Young (Filch)/ Pro Arte Chorus and Orchestra/Malcolm Sargent
CFP 575972 2
❡ Purcell, 'Behold, Upon My Bended Spear' (conclusion of *Dido and Aeneas*, Act II), David Thomas (Aeneas), Emma Kirkby (Dido), Judith Nelson (Belinda), Tessa Bonner (Spirit)/Taverner Choir and Players/ Andrew Parrott
Chandos CHAN 8306

❡ Britten, 'Captain Vere's Monologue' (from *Billy Budd*, Act II), Peter Pears (Captain Vere)/London Symphony Orchestra/Benjamin Britten
London 417 428–2
❡ Bartók, 'Stick Dance', 'Sash Dance' and 'In One Spot' (from *Six Romanian Folk Dances*), Zoltán Kocsis (piano)
Philips 434 104–2
❡ Anton Goosen, 'Om te breyten', Anton Goosen
Gallo GWVCD 15
❡ Berlioz, 'Nuit d'ivresse' (from *Les Troyens*, Act IV), Ben Heppner (Aeneas), Michelle DeYoung (Dido), Leigh Melrose (Mercury)/London Symphony Orchestra/Colin Davis
LSO Live LSO 0100

Was slightly expecting a hugely confident personality but (yet again) in talking about music, Simpson came over as human and compassionate. The music was not just an addendum but a genuine and interesting selection about which he clearly felt very strongly.

28 SEPTEMBER 2003
Zoe Wanamaker, actress

❡ Mahler, Symphony No. 9 (end of the first movement, Andante comodo), Berlin Philharmonic Orchestra/Herbert von Karajan
DG 439 025 and 6–2
❡ Styne/Merrill, 'Don't Rain on my Parade' (from *Funny Girl*), Barbra Streisand/Herbert Ross (musical director)
Columbia 462545–2
❡ Verdi, Lacrymosa (from Requiem), Maria Stader (soprano), Oralia Dominguez (mezzo-soprano), Gabor Carelli (tenor), Ivan Sardi (bass)/Berlin Radio Symphony Orchestra/Choir of St Hedwig's Cathedral/Ferenc Fricsay
DG 429 077/8–2
❡ Bach, Partita No. 1 in B flat major, BWV 825 (first movement), Glenn Gould (piano)
Sony Classical SM2K 52597
❡ Rodgers/Hart, 'My Funny Valentine', Miles Davis Quintet
COLUMBIA 471246–2

♪ Puccini, duet from the end of Act II of *Tosca*, Maria Callas (Tosca), Tito Gobbi (Scarpia), Angelo Mercuriali (Spoletta)/Orchestra of La Scala, Milan/Victor de Sabata
EMI CDC 747176–2
♪ Charlap/Leigh, 'I'm Flying from Peter Pan', Mary Martin (Peter Pan)/ Kathy Nolan, Robert Harrington and Joseph Stafford (the children)
RCA 3762–2-RG
♪ Bernstein, *West Side Story* (Prologue), Orchestra/Leonard Bernstein
DG 457 199–2

5 OCTOBER 2003
Michael Longley, poet

♪ Shostakovich, Cello Concerto No. 1, Op. 107 (third movement, Andantino), Mstislav Rostropovich (cello)/Philadelphia Orchestra/ Eugene Ormandy
CBS MPK44850
♪ Ives, 'The Housatonic at Stockbridge' (from *Three Places in New England*), Boston Symphony Orchestra/Michael Tilson Thomas
DG 2530 048
♪ Thomas Hanforth, Psalm 149, Choir of King's College, Cambridge/ David Willcocks
EMI 566784 2
♪ Janáček, conclusion of Act II of *The Cunning Little Vixen*, Lucia Popp (Vixen), Eva Randová (Fox), Eva Zigmundová (Owl), Gertrude Jahn (Jay), Ivana Mixová (Woodpecker)/Vienna State Opera Chorus/ Vienna Philharmonic Orchestra/Charles Mackerras
Decca 417 129–2
♪ Waller/Razaf, 'Lulu's Back in Town', Fats Waller and his Rhythm
BBC BBCCD 684
♪ Sibelius, Symphony No. 5 in E flat, Op. 82 (third movement, Allegro molto), City of Birmingham Symphony Orchestra/Simon Rattle
EMI CDM 764122 2
♪ Chopin, Nocturne in E flat, Op. 9, No. 2, Vladimir Ashkenazy (piano)
Decca 417 798–2
♪ Trad., 'The Lass from Killiecrankie', Len Graham/Fintan McManus
Clannagh CC 41
♪ Gershwin, 'I Loves You, Porgy', Billie Holiday
Columbia MOODCD 52

Jane Smiley, American novelist

♩ Trad., 'Down to the River to Pray', Alison Krauss
Mercury 170 069–2
♩ Trad., Ashokan Farewell, Jay Unger/Fiddle Fever
Rounder 116661–0505–2
♩ Beethoven, *Choral Fantasy*, Op. 80, Gabriela Lechner, Gretchen Eder
(sopranos), Elisabeth Mach (alto), Jorge Pita, Andreas Esders (tenors),
Gerhard Eder (bass)/Maurizio Pollini (piano)/Vienna State Opera
Chorus/Vienna Philharmonic Orchestra/Claudio Abbado
DG 419 779–2
♩ Mozart, Quintet in C major, K515 (first movement, Allegro), Alban
Berg Quartet/Markus Wolf (viola)
EMI CDC 749085 2
♩ Donizetti, 'Chi mi frena in tal momento' (from *Lucia di
Lammermoor*, Act II), Renato Cioni (Edgardo), Robert Merrill
(Enrico), Joan Sutherland (Lucia), Cesare Siepi (Raimondo), Kenneth
Macdonald (Arturo), Ana Raquel Satre (Alisa)/Orchestra of the
Academy of Santa Cecilia, Rome/John Pritchard
Decca 411 622–2
♩ Nitty Gritty Dirt Band, 'The Turn of the Century', Nitty Gritty Dirt
Band
MCA UVLD 12500
♩ Trad. arr. Terry, 'Shenandoah', Paul Robeson
Conifer CDHD 183
♩ Fuller, 'San Francisco Bay Blues', Peter, Paul and Mary
Warner WM 8172

Tom Courtenay, actor

♩ Bach, Suite No. 6 in D, BWV 1012 (Prelude), Yo-Yo Ma (cello)
Sony S2K 63203
♩ Dvořák arr. Kreisler, 'Songs My Mother Taught Me', Fritz Kreisler
(violin)/Carl Lamson (piano)
Pearl GEMMCD 9324
♩ Maschwitz/Stracey, 'These Foolish Things', Billie Holiday
Columbia CK 87067

¶ Beethoven, String Quartet in F, Op. 135 (third movement, Lento assai, cantate e tranquillo), Talich Quartet
Calliope CAL 9639
¶ Chopin, Waltz in F minor, Op. 70, No. 2, Dinu Lipatti (piano)
EMI CDM 566904 2
¶ Mozart, Divertimento in E flat, K563 (fourth movement, Andante), Grumiaux Trio
Philips PHCP 4972
¶ Schubert, 'Am See', Karl Erb (tenor)/Bruno Seidler-Winkler (piano)
Lebendige Vergangenheit 89208
¶ Cavanaugh/Rose/Stock, 'The Umbrella Man', Flanagan and Allen
Empress RAJCD 832
¶ Foster, 'Jeanie with the Light Brown Hair', Jussi Björling (tenor)/
Stockholm Royal Orchestra/Nils Grevillius
EMI CMS 566306 2

26 OCTOBER 2003
Allen Jones, painter

¶ Amsterdam/Sullivan/Baron, 'Rum and Coca Cola', Andrews Sisters
Castle Pie PIESD 234
¶ Puccini, 'Che il bel sogno di Doretta' (from *La rondine*, Act I), Ileana Cotrubas (Magda)/Philharmonia/John Pritchard
Sony SMK 60783
¶ Trad., 'Make Me a Pallet on the Floor', Ottilie Patterson/Chris Barber's Jazz Band
Polygon JTE 102
¶ Japanese traditional Geisha song, Anon. performers
OUP 113
¶ Trad. Irish, 'The March of the King of Laois', The Chieftains
Claddagh CC 10
¶ Wallace/Rule, 'Paying for that Back Street Affair', Kitty Wells
MCA MCF 2743
¶ Louiguy /Piaf, 'La vie en rose', Edith Piaf
MFP CD-MFP 6071
¶ Saint-Saëns, 'Mon coeur s'ouvre à ta voix' (from *Samson and Delilah*, Act II), Olga Borodina (Delilah), José Cura (Samson)/
London Symphony Orchestra/Colin Davis
Erato 3984–24756–2

¶ Bach, Brandenburg Concerto No. 3 in G, BWV 1048 (second and third movements), Basle Chamber Orchestra/Paul Sacher
Philips ABE 10058

Have for a long time enjoyed his saucy pieces – plastic ladies in the form of chairs, hat stands and ashtrays.

2 NOVEMBER 2003
Mary Ann Sieghart, journalist and assistant editor, *The Times*

¶ Brahms, 'How Lovely Are Thy Dwellings' (from *A German Requiem*, Op. 45), Monteverdi Choir/Orchestre Révolutionnaire et Romantique/ John Eliot Gardiner
Philips 432 140–2
¶ Mozart, Lacrimosa (from Requiem, K626), Westminster Cathedral Boys' Choir, Chorus and Orchestra of the Academy of Ancient Music/ Christopher Hogwood
Oiseau Lyre 411 712–2
¶ McHugh/Fields, 'I Can't Give You Anything But Love' (from *Fine and Mellow*), Ella Fitzgerald
Pablo PACD-2310–829–2
¶ Masekela/Gary/Michael, 'Bring Him Back Home', Hugh Masekela (trumpet) and his Band
Columbia 498266–2
¶ Redding, 'Try a Little Tenderness', Otis Redding
Atlantic 781298–2
¶ Wagner, Prelude to Act III of *Die Meistersinger von Nürnberg*, Berlin Philharmonic Orchestra/Herbert von Karajan
DG 439 022–2
¶ Cimarosa (arr. Benjamin), Oboe Concerto, Anthony Camden (oboe)/City of London Sinfonia/Nicholas Ward
Naxos 8.553433
¶ Richard Strauss, 'September' (from *Four Last Songs*), Kiri te Kanawa (soprano)/London Symphony Orchestra/Andrew Davis
CBS CD 76794

Asked her onto the programme because I enjoyed her column in The Times *and noticed that she was enthusiastic about the joy of amateur music making.*

Adam Thirlwell, novelist

❡ Webern, *Six Bagatelles*, Op. 9, Juilliard String Quartet
Sony Classical CD 45845A-C
❡ Brel, 'The Girls and the Dogs', Scott Walker (singer)
Fontana 838 212-2
❡ Lutoslawski, *Dance Preludes* (Nos 1–3), Duncan Prescott (clarinet)/
Ann Martin-Davis (piano)
ASV CDDCA 1046
❡ Stravinsky, 'Exaudi orationem meam, Domine' (from *Symphony of Psalms*), Russian State Academy Chorus/Russian State Symphony Orchestra/Igor Markevitch
Philips 442 583-2
❡ Adams, *Grand Pianola Music* (Part 3, 'On the Dominant Divide'), John Alley and Shelagh Sutherland (pianos), London Sinfonietta/John Adams
Elektra Nonesuch
❡ Belle and Sebastian, 'Seymour Stein', Belle and Sebastian
Jeepster JPRCD 003
❡ Mozart, 'Per pietà, ben mio, perdona' (from *Così fan tutte*, Act II), Elisabeth Schwarzkopf (Fiordiligi)/Philharmonia/Herbert von Karajan
EMI CDM 567064-2

Enjoyed his first novel, which has aspects of Così *running through it.*

Clare Morrall, writer and piano teacher

❡ Chopin, Prelude No. 17 in A flat, Evgeny Kissin (piano)
RCA 09026 635352
❡ Schubert, Impromptu D899, No. 1, Clifford Curzon (piano)
Philips 456 7582/7592
❡ Gilbert/Sullivan, 'I Have a Song to Sing, Oh!' (from *Yeoman of the Guard*), Thomas Allen, Sylvia McNair/Academy of St Martin-in-the-Fields/Neville Marriner
Philips 438 1392/140-2
❡ Bach, Concerto for Violin and Oboe in C minor, Elizabeth Wallfisch (violin)/Anthony Robson (oboe)/Orchestra of the Age of Enlightenment
Virgin Classics VC 5450952

♪ Handel, 'Io t'abbraccio' (from *Rodelinda*, Act II), Sophie Daneman (Rodelinda), Daniel Taylor (Bertarido), Raglan Baroque Players/ Nicholas Kraemer
Virgin Classics vct 545277 2/a-c
♪ Beethoven, Symphony No. 7 (fourth movement), London Classical Players/Roger Norrington
EMI CDC 7498162 London

23 NOVEMBER 2003
Robin Dunbar, evolutionary psychologist

♪ Reinhardt/Grappelli, 'Billets Doux', Django Reinhardt (guitar)/ Stephane Grappelli (violin)/Joseph Reinhardt, Eugene Vees (rhythm guitars)/Roger Grasset (bass)
JSP JSPCD 343
♪ Bach, Toccata and Fugue in D minor, BWV 565 (Fugue), Thomas Trotter (Klais Organ at Symphony Hall, Birmingham)
Symphony Hall SHCD 2
♪ Pérotin, 'Viderunt omnes', Hilliard Ensemble/Paul Hillier
ECM 837 751–2
♪ Lassus, Kyrie (from Missa *Entre vous filles*), Oxford Camerata/Jeremy Summerly
Naxos 8.550842
♪ Rodrigo, Concierto de Aranjuez (second movement, Adagio), Siegfried Behrend (guitar)/Berlin Philharmonic Orchestra/Reinhard Peters
DG 427 214–2
♪ Pärt, Magnificat, Theatre of Voices/Paul Hillier
Harmonia Mundi HMU 907182
♪ Trad. Scottish, arr. Capercaillie, 'Iain Ghlinn' Cuaich', Capercaillie Green Linnet SIF 1094
♪ Trad., 'Kali kali zulfon ke phande nah dalo', Nusrat Fateh Ali Khan and Party
RealWorld RWCD 3

Went back to some of the earliest music (Perotin) as befits an evolutionary psychologist specialising in the parallels in reproductive behaviour between animals and humans.

Quentin Blake, illustrator and children's author

❡ Janáček, String Quartet No. 2, 'Intimate Letters' (first movement, Andante–Allegro), The Lindsays
ASV CDDCA 749
❡ Britten, 'At the Railway Station, Upway' (from *Winter Words*, Op. 52), Peter Pears (tenor)/Benjamin Britten (piano)
Decca 425 996–2
❡ Verdi, 'Era la notte' and 'Si, pel ciel' (from *Otello*, Act II), Placido Domingo (Otello), Sherrill Milnes (Iago)/National Philharmonic Orchestra/James Levine
RCA 74321 39501 2
❡ Offenbach, 'Oui, c'est un rêve' (from *La belle Hélène*, Act II), Jane Rhodes (Hélène), Bernard Plantey (Paris)/Orchestra/Manuel Rosenthal
Philips 442 237–2
❡ Beethoven, String Quartet in F, Op. 135 (fourth movement, Grave ma non troppo tratto–Allegro), Hollywood Quartet
Testament SBT 3082
❡ Dowland, 'In Darkness Let Me Dwell', Alfred Deller (countertenor)/ Desmond Dupré (guitar)
EMI CDH 565501 2
❡ Brassens, 'Le parapluie', Georges Brassens
Philips 9101 043

Jill Balcon, actress

❡ Vaughan Williams, Symphony No. 5 (Romanza), Royal Philharmonic Orchestra/André Previn
Telarc CD-80158
❡ Fauré, 'Tarentelle', Op. 10, No. 2, Felicity Lott (soprano), Ann Murray (mezzo-soprano)/Graham Johnson (piano)
EMI CDC 749930–2
❡ Schubert, Sonata in B flat, D960 (fourth movement), Murray Perahia (piano)
Sony Classical S2K 87706
❡ Mozart, Piano Concerto No. 27 in B flat, K595 (third movement), Clifford Curzon (piano)/English Chamber Orchestra/Benjamin Britten
Decca 417 288–2

❡ Schubert, 'Sehnsucht der Liebe', D180, Philip Langridge (tenor)/
Graham Johnson (piano)
Hyperion CDJ 33004
❡ Porter, 'I've Got You Under My Skin', Ella Fitzgerald/Orchestra/
Buddy Bregman
Verve 821 990–2
❡ Trad. Irish, 'Believe Me If All Those Endearing Young Charms', John
McCormack (tenor), rec. 1911
Pearl GEMM CD 9338
❡ Janáček, String Quartet No. 2, 'Intimate Letters' (first movement),
Talich Quartet
Calliope CAL 9699
❡ Villa Lobos, Etude No. 7, Julian Bream (guitar)
RCA RD 89813
❡ Poulenc, Clarinet Sonata (third movement, Très animé), Janet
Hilton (clarinet)/Keith Swallow (piano)
Chandos 6589

28 DECEMBER 2003
Joanna Lumley, actress

❡ Chopin, Berceuse, Op. 57, Arthur Rubinstein (piano)
RCA 74321 34175–2
❡ Herrmann, 'Aria from Salammbô' (from the score for Citizen Kane),
Kiri te Kanawa, National Philharmonic Orchestra/Charles Gerhardt
RCA GD 80707
❡ Rossini, Overture to Semiramide, Concertgebouw Orchestra/
Eduard van Beinum
Decca 473 110–2
❡ Redding, 'I've Been Loving You Too Long' (from Otis Blue), Otis
Redding
Telstar TTVCD 3186/A and B
❡ Beethoven, 'Mir ist so wunderbar' (from Fidelio, Act I), Gwyneth
Jones (Leonore), Edith Mathis (Marzelline), Peter Schreier (Jacquino),
Franz Crass (Rocco)/Dresden Staatskapelle/Karl Böhm
DG 2720–009
❡ Josef Strauss, Sphärenklange, waltz, Op. 235, Vienna Boys Choir/
Friedrich Brenn
Philips NBR 6007

¶ Jim Parker, 'Business Women' (from *Banana Blush*), with John
Betjeman reading his own poem
Virgin VCCCD 19

Being married to a conductor, Stephen Barlow, has clearly given her
some insight into the musical profession. Still retains an endearing and
girlish enthusiasm for everything she tackles – very much the other side
of Patsy or even one of The Avengers.

4 JANUARY 2004
Sir John Meurig Thomas, Professor of Chemistry

¶ Richard Strauss, 'Beim Schlafengehen' (from *Four Last Songs*), Jessye
Norman (soprano)/Leipzig Gewandhaus Orchestra/Kurt Masur
Philips 464 742 2
¶ Franck, Violin Sonata in A major (last movement), Gidon Kremer
(violin)/Oleg Maisenberg (piano)
Praga PR 250 024
¶ Dvořák, Piano Trio in E minor (first movement), Suk Trio
Supraphon C375 7057
¶ Mozart, Divertimento, K136 (Presto), Consort of London/Robert
Haydon Clark
Collins Classics 13782
¶ 'Sussex Carol' and 'O Come All Ye Faithful', David Briggs (organ)/
Choir of King's College, Cambridge/Stephen Cleobury
Argo 4140422
¶ Said, 'Youm Wara Youm', Samira Said
EMI 07243 54098925
¶ 'Suo Gan', Bryn Terfel (baritone)/Orchestra of Welsh National
Opera/Gareth Jones
Deutsche Grammophon 463 5932
¶ Thomas L. Thomas, 'Cyfri'r Geifr', Enid Simon (harp)/Jacob
Hanneman (piano)
Qualiton DAF222
¶ Schubert, 'Ständchen', D920, Brigitte Fassbaender (mezzo)/Capella
Bavariae/Wolfgang Sawallisch (piano)
EMI CDM 5661402–1432

Rachel Kavanaugh, theatre director

❦ Tchaikovsky, opening of Act II of *Swan Lake*, USSR State Symphony Orchestra/Evgeny Svetlanov
Melodiya 74321 17082 2

❦ Loesser, 'Sit Down You're Rockin' the Boat' (from *Guys and Dolls*), Stubby Kaye/Chorus and Orchestra/Irving Actman
MCA MCAD 10301

❦ Ellington/Strayhorn, 'The Star-crossed Lovers' (from *Such Sweet Thunder*), Duke Ellington and his Orchestra
Columbia CK 65568

❦ Catalani, 'Ebben? ne andrò lontana' (from *La Wally*, Act I), Maria Callas (Wally)/Philharmonia/Tullio Serafin
EMI CDC 754702 2

❦ Ravel arr. Hancock, Piano Concerto in G (second movement, Adagio assai), Herbie Hancock (piano)/Orpheus Chamber Orchestra
Verve 557 797–2

❦ Handel, *Zadok the Priest*, King's Consort/Choir of the King's Consort/Robert King
Hyperion CDA67286

❦ Berlioz, 'Nuit paisible et sereine' (from *Beatrice and Benedict*, Act I), April Cantelo (Hero), Helen Watts (Ursula)/London Symphony Orchestra/Colin Davis
Decca 448 113–2

John Julius Norwich, writer

❦ Beethoven, 'Mir ist so wunderbar' (from *Fidelio*, Act I), Ingeborg Hallstein (Marzelline), Christa Ludwig (Leonore), Gottlob Frick (Rocco), Gerhard Unger (Jaquino)/Philharmonia/Otto Klemperer
EMI CDS 555170 2

❦ Mozart, Bassoon Concerto in B flat, K191 (second movement, Andante ma adagio), Klaus Thunemann (bassoon)/Academy of St Martin-in-the-Fields/Neville Marriner
Philips 422 390–2

❡ Verdi, 'Già nella notte densa' (from *Otello*, Act I), Kiri te Kanawa (Desdemona)/Luciano Pavarotti (Otello)/Chicago Symphony Orchestra/Georg Solti
Decca 440 203–2
❡ Schubert, 'Erlkönig', D328, Dietrich Fischer-Dieskau (baritone)/Gerald Moore (piano)
DG 431 085–2
❡ Rossini, Kyrie (from *Petite messe solennelle*), Choir of King's College, Cambridge/Katia and Marielle Labèque (pianos)/David Briggs (harmonium)/Stephen Cleobury
EMI CZS 568658 2
❡ Norworth/Bayes, 'Shine on Harvest Moon', Ruth Etting/Victor Young and his Orchestra
Sandy Hook CDSH 2033
❡ Monteverdi, Duo Seraphim (from Vespers, 1610), Robert Tear, Philip Langridge (tenors)/John Shirley-Quirk (baritone)/Monteverdi Choir and Orchestra/John Eliot Gardiner
Decca 414 572–2

I have known him and his family since childhood, and have always enjoyed his polymath and Renaissance passion for anything and everything cultural. Curiously his son-in-law, the historian Anthony Beevor (see p. 356) came over as something of a second-generation John Julius.

25 JANUARY 2004
Marcus du Sautoy, mathematician

❡ Britten, 'I Know a Bank' (from *A Midsummer Night's Dream*, Act I), James Bowman (Oberon)/City of London Sinfonia/Richard Hickox
Virgin VCD 759305 2
❡ Janáček, Sinfonietta, Op. 60 (first movement, Allegretto), Philharmonia/Simon Rattle
EMI CDC 747048 2
❡ Handel, 'Revenge, Revenge, Timotheus Cries' (from *Alexander's Feast*), Stephen Roberts (bass)/Concentus Musicus Wien/Nikolaus Harnoncourt
Teldec 8.35671

♪ Messiaen, 'Joie du sang des étoiles' (from *Turangalîla-Symphonie*), Peter Donohoe (piano)/Tristan Murail (ondes Martenot)/City of Birmingham Symphony Orchestra/Simon Rattle
EMI CDS 747463 2
♪ Dorothy Ker, Solo for cello, Chu-Chuan Liu (cello)
Artist's private recording
♪ Wagner, Prelude to *Parsifal*, Act I, Berlin Philharmonic Orchestra/ Herbert von Karajan
DG 413 347–2
♪ Britten, *Fanfare for St Edmundsbury*, Philip Jones Brass Ensemble
London 430 369–2
♪ Richard Strauss, 'Frühling' (from *Four Last Songs*), Lucia Popp (soprano)/London Philharmonic Orchestra/Klaus Tennstedt
EMI CDC 747013 2
♪ Shostakovich, String Quartet No. 8, Op. 110 (second movement, Allegro molto), Brodsky Quartet
Teldec 244 919–2

Needless to say we looked at music from a mathematical perspective. For instance, the Britten Fanfare has three trumpet solos that then ingeniously fit together as a chorus.

1 FEBRUARY 2004
Ross King, writer

♪ Dufay, 'Nuper rosarum flores', Hilliard Ensemble/Paul Hillier
EMI CDC 555207 2
♪ Palestrina, 'Assumpta est Maria', Tallis Scholars/Peter Phillips
Gimell CDGIM 020
♪ Bach, Concerto in D minor after Alessandro Marcello, BWV 974 (first movement), Glenn Gould (piano)
Sony SMK 52650
♪ Isaac, 'Quis dabit capiti meo aquam' (Lament on the Death of Lorenzo de Medici), London Pro Musica/Bernard Thomas
IMP PCD 825
♪ Korngold, 'Glück, das mir verblieb' (from *Die tote stadt*, Act I), Katarina Dalayman (Marietta), Thomas Sunnegårdh (Paul)/Royal Swedish Opera Orchestra/Leif Segerstam
Naxos 8.660060

❡ Tosti, *Ideale*, Alessandro Moreschi (castrato)
Opal CD 9823
❡ Handel, 'Cara sposa, amante cara' (from *Rinaldo*), David Daniels
(Rinaldo)/Orchestra of the Age of Enlightenment/Roger Norrington
Virgin VC 545326–2

8 FEBRUARY 2004
Andrew Sachs, actor

❡ Stravinsky, 'Vivo' (No. 4 from *Quatre Études*, Op. 7), Victor
Sangiorgio (piano)
Collins 1374–2
❡ Bach, Suite No. 4 in E flat, BWV 1010 (Allemande), Paul Tortelier
(cello)
EMI CDC 748035 2
❡ Sor, *Variations on a Theme of Mozart*, John Williams (guitar)
Decca 452 173–2
❡ Kozeluch, Clarinet Concerto in E flat (second movement, Poco
adagio), Emma Johnson (clarinet)/Royal Philharmonic Orchestra/
Günther Herbig
ASV CDDCA 763
❡ Rossini, 'Una voce poco fa' (from *The Barber of Seville*, Act I), Teresa
Berganza (Rosina)/Rossini Orchestra of Naples/Silvio Varviso
Decca 417 164–2
❡ Jelly Roll Morton, 'Wolverine Blues', Albert Nicholas (clarinet)
Vogue ZCVOD 2004
❡ Górecki, Symphony No. 3 (opening), London Sinfonietta/David
Zinman
Nonesuch 7559–79334–1
❡ Simon/Shabalala, 'Homeless' (from *Graceland*), Paul Simon/
Ladysmith Black Mambazo
Warner 9362 45408–2
❡ Gershwin, Piano Concerto in F (third movement, Allegro agitato),
Wayne Marshall (piano and conductor)/Aalborg Symphony Orchestra
Virgin VM 561243 2

Being a Fawlty Towers *addict, I could not but help but be tickled by the
presence of Manuel in my kitchen!*

15 FEBRUARY 2004
Lavinia Greenlaw, poet

❦ John Tavener, Song: 'The Western Wynde', Choir of St John's College, Cambridge/George Guest
Classics for Pleasure CDCFP 4654
❦ Janáček, 'Toť zrovna jde!' (from *Jenůfa*, Act II), Karita Mattila (Jenůfa), Anja Silja (Kostelnička), Jorma Silvasti (Laca)/Orchestra of the Royal Opera House/Bernard Haitink
Erato 0927 453302
❦ Dylan, 'Girl From the North Country' (from *Nashville Skyline*), Bob Dylan/Johnny Cash
CBS CD 63601
❦ Ian Wilson, *Hamelin*, Natalie Raybould (Girl), Eugene Ginty (Mayor), John Milne (Doctor)/David Brophy (music director)
RTE recording
❦ Kurtág, 'In memoriam Tamás Blum' (from *Signs, Games and Messages*), Ken Hakii (viola)
ECM New Series 1730 461 833–2
[❦ Greenlaw, 'Essex Rag' (from *Minsk*), read by Lavinia Greenlaw]
❦ Shostakovich, Piano Quintet Op. 57 (Prelude), Brodsky Quartet/ Christian Blackshaw (piano)
Challenge CC 72093
❦ Earth Wind and Fire, 'That's the Way of the World', Earth Wind and Fire
Columbia 467768–2
❦ Armstrong/Holiday, 'Do You Know What It Means to Miss New Orleans?', Louis Armstrong/Billie Holiday
A Touch of Magic DATOM 6
❦ Wreckless Eric, 'Whole Wide World', Wreckless Eric
Stiff STIFFCD 02

22 FEBRUARY 2004
Russell Taylor, cartoonist ('Alex')

❦ Bach, 'Mache dich mein Herze rein' (from *St Matthew Passion*), Cornelius Hauptmann (bass)/English Baroque Soloists/John Eliot Gardiner
Archiv 427 651–2

❡ Ellington/Strayhorn, 'Sonnet for Caesar', John Harle (saxophone)/
The John Harle Band
EMI CDC 75429–2
❡ Chopin, Mazurka in F minor, Op. 68, No. 4, Arthur Rubinstein
(piano)
RCA 09026 63050–2
❡ Gershwin, Piano Concerto in F (second movement), André Previn
(piano and conductor)/London Symphony Orchestra
EMI CDM 566891–2
❡ Lennon/McCartney, 'Julia' (from the 'White Album'), The Beatles
Parlophone CDP 746443–2
❡ Beethoven, Sonata in F minor, 'Appassionata', Op. 57 (second
movement), Daniel Barenboim (piano)
DG 419 602–2

29 FEBRUARY 2004
Michael Bywater, journalist

❡ Schoenberg, *Gurrelieder* (Introduction), Berlin Philharmonic
Orchestra/Simon Rattle
EMI CDS 5573303–2/A and B
❡ Newman, 'I Want Everyone to Like Me' (from *Bad Love*), Randy
Newman
Dreamworks Records 450 115–2
❡ Ligeti, *Volumina*, Gerd Zacher (organ)
DG 471 608–2
❡ Janáček, 'Pantomime' (from *The Cunning Little Vixen*), Vienna
Philharmonic Orchestra/Charles Mackerras
Decca 417 130–2
❡ Handel, 'Crystal Streams' (from *Susanna*), Jill Feldman (soprano)/
Philharmonia Baroque Orchestra/Nicholas McGegan
Harmonia Mundi HMU 907168–2
❡ Messiaen, 'Regard de l'ésprit de joie' (from *Vingt regards sur l'enfant
Jésus*), Pierre-Laurent Aimard (piano)
Teldec 3984–26868–2
❡ Hindemith, Organ Sonata No. 3 (third movement, 'So wünsch' ich
ihr'), Peter Hurford (organ)
Argo 417 159–2

¶ Monteverdi, 'Chioma d'oro' (from the Seventh Book of Madrigals),
Emma Kirkby and Evelyn Tubb (sopranos)/Consort of Musicke/
Anthony Rooley
Regis RRC 1060
¶ Bach, Organ Concerto in D minor, BWV 1059, Amsterdam Baroque
Orchestra/Ton Koopman (organ)
Erato 0630 16164–2
¶ Praetorius, In dulci jubilo, Gabrieli Consort and Players/Paul
McCreesh
Archiv 439 250–2

*Trained in medicine, qualified pilot and highly qualified organist. Would
probably have loved to have done any of these things to the highest level,
but it led to a particularly informed and rewarding conversation and I
was glad to be able to include the Ligeti – a work that has quickly
despatched many an unfit instrument and occasionally its operator!*

7 MARCH 2004
Shusha Guppy, singer/writer

¶ Debussy, 'Mes longs cheveux descendent' (from *Pelléas et Mélisande*,
Act III), Elisabeth Söderström (Mélisande)/Orchestra of the Royal
Opera House/Pierre Boulez
Sony SM3K 47265
¶ Trad., 'My Silver Gun', Shusha Guppy
Artist's private recording
¶ Schubert, Impromptu in G flat, D.899, No. 3, Wilhelm Kempff
(piano)
BBC BBCL 4045–2
¶ Puccini, 'Vissi d'arte' (from *Tosca*, Act II), Maria Callas (Tosca)/
Orchestra of La Scala, Milan/Victor de Sabata
EMI CDS 556304 2
¶ Brahms, Sextet in B flat, Op. 18 (second movement, Theme and
variations), Amadeus Quartet/Cecil Aronowitz (viola)/William Pleeth
(cello)
DG 439 490–2
¶ Dylan, 'Love Minus Zero', Bob Dylan
Columbia CD 32344
¶ Prévert/Cosma, 'Les feuilles mortes', Juliette Greco
Phonogram 830 955–2

♫ Chopin, Fantaisie-Impromptu in C sharp minor, Op. 66, Claudio
Arrau (piano)
Philips 426 634–2
♫ Payvar, 'The Warmth of Your Eyes', Shahidi/Orchestra
Ahang Rooz SARLP
♫ Mozart, Recordare (from Requiem, K626), Werner Pech (treble),
Hans Breitschopf (alto), Walther Ludwig (tenor), Harald Pröglhöf
(bass)/Vienna Hofmusikkapelle/Josef Krips
Eclipse ECS 715

14 MARCH 2004
Anthony Lane, film critic

♫ Bach, Christe eleison (from Mass in B Minor), Lynne Dawson
(soprano), Carol Hall (mezzo-soprano)/English Baroque Soloists/
John Eliot Gardiner
ARCHIV 415 515–2
♫ Finzi, *Dies natalis* (second movement, Rhapsody: 'Will you see the
infancy'), Wilfred Brown (tenor)/English Chamber Orchestra/
Christopher Finzi
EMI 763372–2
♫ Britten, *Hymn to the Virgin*, Choir of King's College, Cambridge/
Philip Ledger
HMV CSD 3774
♫ Brahms, Violin Sonata No. 1 in G, Op. 78 (first movement), Josef Suk
(violin)/Julius Katchen (piano)
Decca 421 092–2
♫ Stravinsky, 'Shrove-tide Fair' (from *Petrushka*, scene 1), Columbia
Symphony Orchestra/Igor Stravinsky
Sony SM3K 46291
♫ George and Ira Gershwin, 'They Can't Take That Away From Me',
Frank Sinatra/Nelson Riddle (arranger and conductor)
Capitol CDP 496986–2
♫ Debussy, 'Danseuses de Delphes' (from *Préludes*, Book 1), Paul
Roberts (piano)
Classical Recording Company CRC 501–2

Ray Dolan, neuroscientist

❡ Sibelius, Symphony No. 5 in E flat major, Op. 82 (third movement, Allegro molto), Finnish Radio Symphony Orchestra/Jukka-Pekka Saraste
Finlandia 4509 99960–2
❡ Hopkins, 'Trouble in Mind' (from *Autobiography in Blues*), Lightnin' Hopkins
Tradition TCD 1002
❡ Williams, 'Ramblin' Man', Hank Williams
Polydor 821 235–2
❡ Falla, 'Jota' (from *Suite populaire espagnole*), Itzhak Perlman (violin)/ Samuel Sanders (piano)
EMI CDM 763533–2
❡ Van Morrison, 'Country Fair' (from *Veedon Fleece*), Van Morrison
Polydor 537 456–2
❡ Liszt, 'Un sospiro' (from *Three Concert Studies*, S144), Jorge Bolet (piano)
Decca 417 523–2
❡ Rodrigo arr. Gil Evans, 'Concierto de Aranjuez' (from *Sketches of Spain*), Miles Davis (trumpet)/orchestra conducted by Gil Evans
CBS 460604–2

Reg Gadney, novelist

❡ 'Cuckoo clock' dialogue (from *The Third Man*), Orson Welles (Harry Lime)
Silva Screen FILMCD 367
❡ Parrish/Migliacci, 'Volare', Louis Armstrong and the All Stars
Gitanes Jazz 013 031–2
❡ Bellini, 'O rendetemi la speme' (from *I puritani*, Part III), Maria Callas (Elvira), Giuseppe di Stefano (Arturo), Rolando Panerai (Riccardo)/Orchestra of La Scala, Milan/Tullio Serafin
EMI CDS 747308 8
❡ Britten, Agnus Dei/'One ever hangs' (from *War Requiem*, Op. 66), Peter Pears (tenor)/London Symphony Chorus and Orchestra/ Benjamin Britten
Decca 414 383–2

♪ Edwin Bagley, 'National Emblem', Band of the Coldstream Guards/
Lt.-Col. Douglas A. Pope
Eclipse ECS 2172
♪ Gigout, Toccata in B minor, Jane Parker-Smith (organ of Coventry
Cathedral)
ASV CDDCA 539
♪ Bach, Concerto in F minor, BWV 1056, Glenn Gould (piano)/
Columbia Symphony Orchestra/Vladimir Golschmann
Sony SK 66531
♪ Karas, theme from *The Third Man*, Gertrud Huber (zither)
Silva Screen FILMCD 367

4 APRIL 2004
Richard Jones, theatre director

♪ Stravinsky arr. Crabb/Draugsvoll, 'Dance of the Puppets' (from
Petrushka), James Crabb, Geir Draugsvoll (accordions)
EMI CDZ 569705 2
♪ Tchaikovsky, 'Panorama' (from *The Sleeping Beauty*, Act II), Russian
National Orchestra/Mikhail Pletnev
DG 457 636–2
♪ Ravel, 'Fanfare' (from *L'Éventail de Jeanne*), City of Birmingham
Symphony Orchestra/Simon Rattle
EMI CDC 754204 2
♪ Janáček, 'Good Night!' (from *On an Overgrown Path*), András Schiff
(piano)
ECM 461 660–2
♪ Ligeti, 'Fanfares' (*Étude* No. 4), Pierre-Laurent Aimard (piano)
SK 62308
♪ Maxwell/Sigman, 'Ebb Tide', Frank Sinatra/Nelson Riddle and his
Orchestra
Capitol 496996–2
♪ Berlioz, 'Queen Mab' scherzo (from *Roméo et Juliette*, Op. 17),
NBC Symphony Orchestra/Arturo Toscanini
RCA GD 60274

¶ Wagner, 'Entrance of the Masters' (from *Die Meistersinger von Nürnberg*, Act I), Karl Ridderbusch (Pogner), Geraint Evans (Beckmesser), René Kollo (Walther), Theo Adam (Sachs), Zoltan Kelemen (Kothner)/Chorus of the Staatsoper Dresden/Dresden Staatskapelle/Herbert von Karajan
EMI CMS 567086 2
¶ Prokofiev, 'Refreshments for the Guests' (from *Cinderella*, Act II), Cleveland Orchestra/Vladimir Ashkenazy
Decca 410 162–2
¶ Grey, 'The Laughing Policeman', Charles Penrose
EMI 539265 2

A director whose work speaks particularly strongly to me. I love the slightly crazy way in which he informs us about ourselves by taking human behaviour and magnifying its comedy and its cruelty. Petrushka on these two accordions is a truly remarkable and appropriate act of virtuosity.

11 APRIL 2004
Loyd Grossman, broadcaster

¶ Albéniz arr. Yepes, 'Rumores de la caleta' (from *Recuerdos de viaje*), Narciso Yepes (guitar)
DG 474 666–2
¶ Burnett, 'Smokestack Lightnin'', Howlin' Wolf
Charly CDRB 2
¶ Mozart, Kyrie (from 'Coronation' Mass, K317), Edda Moser (soprano), Julia Hamari (mezzo-soprano), Nicolai Gedda (tenor), Dietrich Fischer-Dieskau (baritone)/Bavarian Radio Chorus and Symphony Orchestra/Eugen Jochum
EMI CDM 769023 2
¶ Keita, 'Yele n Na', Salif Keita
Mango CIDM 1073
¶ Gershwin, *Rhapsody in Blue* (conclusion), George Gershwin (piano, from a 1925 piano roll)
Nonesuch 7559–79287–2
¶ Shakira, 'Ojos así', Shakira
Sony 485719 6

¶ Beethoven, Symphony No. 9 in D minor, Op. 125 (second movement, Molto vivace), Berlin Philharmonic Orchestra/Herbert von Karajan
DG 415 832–2
¶ Trad., 'Tammurriata Nera', Nuova Compagnia di Canto Popolare
EMI 498404 2

18 APRIL 2004
Jane Lapotaire, actress

¶ Anon., 13th century, 'Domna, pos vos ay chausida' (Lady, since I have chosen you), Mara Kiek (voice)/Sinfonye/Stevie Wishart
Hyperion CDA 66283
¶ The Inkspots, 'If I Didn't Care', The Inkspots
President PLCD 535
¶ Schubert, Octet, Melos Ensemble of London
EMI CDM 769420–2
¶ Parry, 'There is an Old Belief' (*Songs of Farewell*, No. 4), Choir of Trinity College, Cambridge/Richard Marlow
Conifer CDCF 155
¶ Piaf, 'La foule', Edith Piaf
Columbia 746497–2
¶ Vaughan Williams, *The Lark Ascending*, Hugh Bean (violin)/ New Philharmonia Orchestra/Adrian Boult
EMI CDC 747218–2
¶ Allegri, Miserere, Roy Goodman (treble), Choir of King's College, Cambridge/David Willcocks
Decca 430 092–2
¶ Sibelius, Violin Concerto (first movement, Allegro moderato), Yehudi Menuhin (violin)/London Philharmonic Orchestra/Adrian Boult
EMI CDM 763987–2
¶ Trad., Wedding Song from Turkey (Istanbul) and Bosnia (Sarajevo), from *Songs of Spanish Sephardic Jews*, Fadia El-Hage and Belinda Sykes (voices)/Ensemble Sarband/Vladimir Ivanoff (director)
Deutsche Harmonia Mundi 05472 77372–2

Having read her savagely honest book about her radical brain surgery and how it affected her, I was wondering how she might cope. Clearly, though different in some ways from the pre-op person, she is making an amazing recovery and becoming a new and perhaps wiser self.

Geoffrey Hill, poet

❡ John Stafford Smith, 'The Star-Spangled Banner', Jimi Hendrix
Universal 170 322–2

❡ Bach, 'O Ewigkeit, du Donnerwort', BWV 513 (from the *Anna
Magdalena Notebook*), Benjamin Luxon (baritone)/Igor Kipnis
(harpsichord)/Catharina Meints (viola da gamba)
Nonesuch DB 79020

❡ Mussorgsky, 'Gnomus' (from *Pictures at an Exhibition*), Sviatoslav
Richter (piano)
Philips 456 946–2

[❡ Hill, 'The Orchards of Syon', Geoffrey Hill
read live during recording]

❡ Anon., 'Coventry Carol', Choir of Coventry Cathedral, rec. 1940
BBC Archive T 2823

❡ Elgar, 'R.P.A.' (Variation 5 from *Enigma Variations*), London
Symphony Orchestra/Adrian Boult
EMI CDC 747206 2

❡ Handel, 'I Know that my Redeemer Liveth' (from *The Messiah*),
Dora Labbette (soprano)/Symphony Orchestra/Thomas Beecham
Pearl GEMMCDS 9456

❡ Croft, Funeral Sentences (opening), Choir of Westminster Abbey/
Martin Neary
BBC 449 800–2

❡ Hugh Wood, 'Sabrina Fair' (from *Scenes from Comus*), Geraldine
McGreevy (soprano), Daniel Norman (tenor)/BBC Symphony
Orchestra/Andrew Davis
NMC NMCD 070

❡ Jones, *The Sleeping Lord*, David Jones
Argo PLP 1180

❡ Trad., 'The Ash Plant', 'The Black-Haired Lass', 'Jenny Picking
Cockles', Noel Hill/Tony MacMahon
Shanachie 34003

*Some have found his manner forbidding in its austerity. Once we were on
the same wavelength, however, I found a real magnificence in an
approach to music that is every bit as demanding as his way with words.*

2 MAY 2004
Richard Evans, historian

❡ Scarlatti, Sonata in B minor, Kk 27, Mikhail Pletnev (piano)
Virgin VCD 545123 2
❡ W. C. Handy, 'St Louis Blues', Charlie and his Orchestra, rec. 1940
Harlequin HQCD 03
❡ Bach, Prelude in C, BWV 547, Wolfgang Rübsam (Metzler organ at
Frauenfeld)
Philips 438 172–2
❡ Telemann, 'Der stürmende Æolus', 'Der angenehme Zephir' and
'Ebbe und Flut' (from Overture in C, 'Hamburger Ebb' und Flut'),
Musica Antiqua Köln/Reinhard Goebel
Archiv 413 788–2
❡ Weill, 'Introduction' and 'Ballad of Mack the Knife' (from *Die
Dreigroschenoper*), Kurt Gerron/Lewis Ruth Band/Theo Mackeben,
rec. 1930
Telefunken 0927 42663–2
❡ Richard Strauss, 'Im Abendrot' (from *Four Last Songs*), Gundula
Janowitz (soprano)/Berlin Philharmonic Orchestra/Herbert von
Karajan
DG 423 888–2
❡ Ullmann, Sonata No. 6, Op. 49 (second movement, Allegretto
grazioso), Gregor Weichert (piano)
CPO 999 087–2
❡ Hartmann, *Concerto funèbre* (fourth movement, Chorale–slow
march), Isabelle Faust (violin)/Munich Chamber Orchestra/Christoph
Poppen
ECM 465 779–2

9 MAY 2004
Miranda Seymour, writer

❡ Britten, 'Malo, Malo' (from *The Turn of the Screw*), David Hemmings
(Miles), Jennifer Vyvyan (Governess)/English Opera Group Orchestra/
Benjamin Britten
London 425 672–2
❡ Yvain/Willemetz/Charles, 'La Java', Mistinguett
Festival FLD 784

¶ Beethoven, Piano Concerto No. 1 in C, Op. 15 (third movement, Rondo: Allegro), Maurizio Pollini (piano)/Berlin Philharmonic Orchestra/Claudio Abbado
DG 439 770–2
¶ Legrand, 'Lola Song' (from the soundtrack *Les parapluies de Cherbourg*), Georges Blanès/Orchestra/Michel Legrand
Sony SM2K 62678
¶ Holbrooke, Piano Concerto No. 1, 'The Song of Gwyn ap Nudd', Hamish Milne (piano)/BBC Scottish Symphony Orchestra/Martyn Brabbins
Hyperion CDA 67127
¶ Trad. Cretan, 'Syrtos', Dora Stratou
Philips 6460410
¶ Prokofiev, 'Dance of the Oprichniks' (from *Ivan the Terrible*), Rotterdam Philharmonic Orchestra/Valery Gergiev
Philips 456 645–2
¶ Trad., 'Sometimes I Feel Like a Motherless Child', Odetta/Choir of the Church of the Master/Bill Lee (double bass)
Fontana FJL 409

16 MAY 2004
Martin Sixsmith, journalist

¶ Schoenberg, String Quartet No. 2, Op. 10 (fourth movement, Sehr langsam), Benita Valente (soprano)/Juilliard Quartet
Sony SMK 62 020
¶ Bartók, Piano Concerto No. 3 (second movement, Adagio religioso), Peter Donohoe (piano)/City of Birmingham Symphony Orchestra/Simon Rattle
EMI 0777 7 54871–2
¶ Schubert, 'Mut!' and 'Die Nebensonnen' (from *Winterreise*), Dietrich Fischer-Dieskau (baritone)/Alfred Brendel (piano)
Philips 464 739–2
¶ Messiaen, 'Louange à l'éternité de Jésus' (from *Quartet for the End of Time*), Trio Fontenay/Eduard Brunner (clarinet)
Teldec 0927 48749–2
¶ Richard Strauss, *Metamorphosen*, New Philharmonia Orchestra/John Barbirolli
EMI CDM 565078–2

¶ Penderecki, *Threnody for the Victims of Hiroshima*, Polish Radio
National Symphony Orchestra/Krysztof Penderecki
EMI CDZ 574303–2
¶ Shostakovich, Symphony No. 15 (first movement, Allegretto),
Moscow Radio Symphony Orchestra/Maxim Shostakovich
HMV ASD 2857

23 MAY 2004
Janet Street-Porter, broadcaster

¶ Philip Glass, 'Les soeurs' (from *La belle et la bête*), Janice Felty, Ana
Maria Martinez, Hallie Neill, John Kuether/Philip Glass Ensemble/
Michael Riesman
Nonesuch 7559–79660–2
¶ Sherrill/Wynette, 'Stand by your Man', Candi Staton
Honest Jons HJRCD 6
¶ Berlioz, 'Tuba mirum' (from *Grande messe des morts*, Op. 5), London
Symphony Chorus and Orchestra/Colin Davis
Philips 416 283–2
¶ Trad. Irish arr. Britten, 'The Salley Gardens', Ian Bostridge (tenor)/
Julius Drake (piano)
EMI CDC 556830 2
¶ Guaraldi, 'Cast your Fate to the Wind', Vince Guaraldi Trio
Fantasy OJCCD 4372
¶ Tennant/Lowe, 'It's a Sin', Pet Shop Boys
Parlophone 595093 2
¶ Donizetti, 'Mad Scene' (from *Lucia di Lammermoor*), Joan
Sutherland (Lucia), Pier Francesco Poli (Normanno), Nicolai
Ghiaurov (Raimondo)/Chorus and Orchestra of the Royal Opera
House/Richard Bonynge
Decca 410 193–2
¶ Bach, *Goldberg Variations*, BWV 988 (Variations 14–16), Glenn
Gould (piano)
CBS MYK 44868
¶ Rameau, 'Vaste empire de mers' (from *Les Indes galantes*, Première
entrée), Miriam Ruggeri (Émilie)/Les Arts Florissants/William Christie
Harmonia Mundi HMC 901367.69

She was as outspoken about aspects of Radio 3 she does not approve of as
she was appreciative of what she did like on the network. Hard on herself

too, I suspect. Famous friends mentioned freely but in the context of their love of music, for example, Neil Tennant, who also contributed an excellent programme (p. 220).

30 MAY 2004
Polly Devlin, writer

❧ Haydn, Sonata No. 1, 'Father Forgive Them' (from *Seven Last Words*), Moscow Academy of Ancient Music
CCN'C 02532
❧ Trad., 'On Raglan Road', Sinead O'Connor
EMI 7243 8 37691–2
❧ Beethoven, String Quartet in B flat, Op. 130 (Cavatina), Juilliard Quartet
Sony SB3K 89897
❧ Davis, 'So What' (from *Kind of Blue*), Miles Davis
Columbia Jazz Masterpieces CK 40579
❧ Heaney/Glackin, 'The Given Note' and 'The Fairy's Lament', Seamus Heaney and Paddy Glackin
RTE CD 191
❧ Mozart, Kyrie (from Mass in C minor), Monteverdi Choir/English Baroque Soloists/John Eliot Gardiner
Philips 420 210–2
❧ Trad., 'Standing In Yon Flowery Garden', Sarah Anne O'Neill/The Voice of the People
Topic TSCD 660
❧ Bach, Suite No. 1 in G, BWV 1007 (Prelude), Yo-Yo Ma (cello)
Sony Classical S2K 63203

6 JUNE 2004
Alain de Botton, philosopher and novelist

❧ Handel, 'Worthy is the Lamb' and 'Amen' (from *The Messiah*), Monteverdi Choir/English Baroque Soloists/John Eliot Gardiner
Philips 411 044–2
❧ Mozart, 'Exsultate, jubilate', K165, Teresa Stich-Randall (soprano)/ Orchestre de la Suisse Romande/Ernest Ansermet
Le Chant du Monde LDC 278 903 CM211

343

❡ Bach, Suite No. 3 in C, BWV 1009 (Prelude and Allemande), Maurice Gendron (cello)
Philips 442 295–2
❡ Bach, 'Das Lamm, das erwürget ist' (chorus from Cantata No. 21, *Ich hatte viel Bekümmernis*), boy soprano from the Vienna Boys' Choir, Paul Esswood (countertenor), Kurt Equiluz (tenor), Walker Wyatt (bass)/Vienna Boys' Choir/Chorus Viennensis, Concentus Musicus of Vienna/Nikolaus Harnoncourt
Teldec 4509–91756–2/A-F
❡ Bach, Agnus Dei (from the Mass in B minor, BWV 232), Michael Chance (countertenor), Monteverdi Choir and the English Baroque Soloists/John Eliot Gardiner
Archiv 469 778–2

13 JUNE 2004
Gerda Flockinger, jeweller

❡ Vivaldi, Concerto in C major, RV558 (first movement, Allegro molto), Il Giardino Armonico/Giovanni Antonini
Teldec 4509 91182 2
❡ Trad., 'Tabhari dom do Lámg' (Give me your hand), The Chieftains
Claddagh Records CC16CD
❡ Cage, *Suite for Toy Piano* (first and second movements), Joshua Pierce (toy piano)
Wergo WER 6158 2
❡ Shostakovich, Piano Quintet in G minor, Op. 57 (third movement, Scherzo), Hollywood String Quartet/Victor Aller (piano)
Testament SBT 1077
❡ Glass, String Quartet No. 3, 'Mishima' (second movement, 'November 25 – Ichigaya'), Kronos Quartet
Elektra Nonesuch 7559 79356 2
❡ Tchaikovsky, 'Dialogue' (No. 8 from *Piano Pieces*, Op. 72), Mikhail Pletnev (piano)
Chant du Monde LDC 278 953
❡ Trad. arr. Macgregor, 'Heil-ya-ho, Boys' (The Mingalay Boat Song), Robin Hall and Jimmie Macgregor/The Jim Johnston Band
Mercury SMCL 20169

❦ Richard Strauss, 'Beim Schlafengehen' (from *Four Last Songs*), Lisa della Casa/Vienna Philharmonic Orchestra/Karl Böhm, rec. 1953
Decca 425 959 2
❦ Taha/Khaled/Faudel, 'Menfi', Rachid Taha/Khaled/Faudel
Barclay (Polygram) 547 191 2
❦ Weill, 'Jealousy Duet' (from *The Threepenny Opera*), Inge Wolffberg (Lucy), Johanna von Kóczián (Polly)
BS CD 42637
❦ Strange/Davis, 'A Little Less Conversation' (extended remix), Elvis Presley/JXL Radio Edit Remix
RCA 82876 564012

20 JUNE 2004
Timothy West, actor

❦ Verdi, 'Willow Song' (from *Otello*, Act IV), Leonie Rysanek (Desdemona), Miriam Pirrazini (Emilia)/Rome Opera Orchestra/Tullio Serafin
RCA 09026 63180–2/B
❦ Poulenc, Piano Concerto (third movement, 'Rondeau à la Francaise'), Pascal Rogé (piano)/Philharmonia/Charles Dutoit
Decca 436 546–2
❦ Gretry, *Zémir et Azor* (Pantomime), Royal Philharmonic Orchestra/Thomas Beecham
EMI CDM 763401–2
❦ Dory Previn, 'Play it Again, Sam' (from *Reflections in a Mud Puddle*), Dory Previn
LP: United Artists UAG 29346
❦ Marin Marais, 'Le basque', Dennis Brain (horn)/Wilfred Parry (piano)
BBC BBCL 4048–2
❦ Schumann, 'Mondnacht' (from *Liederkreis*, Op. 39), Sophie Daneman (soprano)/Julius Drake (piano)
EMI CDZ 572828–2
❦ Rollins, 'St Thomas', Sonny Rollins (tenor saxophone)/Tommy Flanagan (piano)/Doug Watkins (bass)/Max Roach (drums)
Prestige OJCCD 291–2
❦ Mozart, 'Rondo' (from Serenade in B flat for 13 wind instruments, K361), London Mozart Players/Jane Glover
Novello NVLCD 103

❡ Rachmaninov, 'Only Begotten Son' (from the Liturgy of St John Chrysostom), Choir of the St Nicholas Church in Tolmachi at the State Tretyakov Gallery/Alexei Pouzakov
Artistotipia AN 127

27 JUNE 2004
Francis Wheen, journalist and biographer

❡ Mozart, 'Dalla sua pace' (*Don Giovanni*, Act I), Gösta Winbergh (Don Ottavio)/Berlin Philharmonic Orchestra/Herbert von Karajan
DG 419 180 2
❡ Thompson, 'Dundee Hornpipe'/'Poppy-Leaf Hornpipe' (trad.), Richard Thompson (all instruments)
Carthage CGLP 4409
❡ Purcell, 'When I am Laid in Earth' (from *Dido and Aeneas*), Catherine Bott (soprano)/Academy of Ancient Music/Christopher Hogwood
Decca 467 454 2
❡ Poppy, 'Do you Doubt?' (Ophelia), Margaret Cameron (mezzo-soprano)/ Andrew Poppy keyboards/percussion/samples
Impetus IMPCD 19426
❡ Rodrigo arr. Evans, 'Adagio' from 'Concerto de Aranjuez' (from *Sketches of Spain*), Miles Davis/Orchestra conducted by Gil Evans
CBS 460604 2
❡ Bach, *Goldberg Variations*, BWV 988 (Theme and Variation No. 1), András Schiff (piano)
ECM 472 185 2
❡ Gilbert/Sullivan, 'When All Night Long a Chap Remains' (from *Iolanthe*, Act II), John Rath (Private Willis)/D'Oyly Carte Orchestra/John Pryce-Jones
That's Entertainment CDTER2 1188B
❡ Frescobaldi, Toccata Chromatica, 'Per l'Elevatione', Laurence Cummings (organ)
Collins Classics 13602

A fine 'pricker of pomposity'. We had some amusing moments but his love of music is utterly serious even if the title of the penultimate piece might nowadays be open to interpretation.

Kevin Crossley-Holland, poet and children's author

❡ Janáček, String Quartet No. 1, 'Kreutzer Sonata' (first movement, Adagio–con moto), Panocha Quartet
Supraphon STU 0215–2131

❡ Anon., 'La quinte estampie real', David Munrow (oriental shawm)/ James Blades (nakers)
Decca 430 264 2

❡ Vaughan Williams, *Fantasia on a Theme by Thomas Tallis*, Sinfonia of London/John Barbirolli
EMI 0777 7 47537–2

❡ Crossley-Holland, 'The Nightingales', Lesley-Jane Rogers (soprano)
Celtic Magic – Campion Cameo 2026

❡ Nielsen, 'Springtime in Funen' and 'The Day, with Sun' (from *Springtime in Funen*), Inga Nielsen (soprano), Kim von Binzer (tenor)/ The University Choir 'Lille Muko'/Odense Symphony Orchestra/ Tamás Vetö
Unicorn-Kanchana DKP (CD) 9054

❡ Walther von der Vögelweide, 'Palästinalied' (from *Music of the Crusades*), James Bowman (countertenor)/James Tyler (lute)/ Christopher Hogwood (harp)/Early Music Consort/David Munrow
Decca 430 264 2

❡ Anon. 13th century, arr. R. L. Pearsall, 'In dulci jubilo', Choir of King's College, Cambridge/Stephen Cleobury
EMI 7243 5 73693–2

❡ Britten, 'Quartet of Swedes', 'Western Union Boy's Song' and 'Cooks' Duet' (from *Paul Bunyan*, Act I), Soloists, Chorus and Orchestra of the Plymouth Music Series/Philip Brunelle
EMI 7243 5 85139–2

❡ Mozart, quintet and chorus 'Di scrivermi ogni giorno' (from *Così fan tutte*, Act I), Lisa della Casa (Fiordiligi), Christa Ludwig (Dorabella), Anton Dermota (Ferrando), Erich Kunz (Guglielmo), Paul Schoeffler (Don Alfonso)/Vienna State Opera Chorus/Vienna Philharmonic Orchestra/ Karl Böhm
Decca 455 476–2

18 JULY 2004
David McKie, journalist

¶ Ravel, Violin Sonata (second movement, Blues: moderato), Chantal Juillet (violin)/Pascal Rogé (piano)
Decca 448 612–2
¶ Beethoven, Sonata in A flat, Op. 110 (first movement, Moderato cantabile molto espressivo), Alfred Brendel (piano)
Philips 438 374–2
¶ Britten, 'Midnight on the Great Western' (from *Winter Words*, Op. 52), Anthony Rolfe Johnson (tenor)/Graham Johnson (piano)
Hyperion CDH 55067
¶ Terry, 'Mumbles', Clark Terry/Oscar Peterson Trio
Laserlight 17432
¶ Bartók, *Music for Strings, Percussion and Celeste* (first movement, Andante tranquillo), Philharmonia Hungarica/Antál Dorati
Philips 426 661–2
¶ Chopin, Polonaise in A flat, Op. 53, Vladimir Ashkenazy (piano)
Decca 417 798–2
¶ Haydn, Piano Trio in G, Hob. XV: 15 (Finale, Allegro moderato),
Beaux Arts Trio
Philips 454 098–2

25 JULY 2004
Ed Smith, cricketer

¶ Wagner, Prelude to *Lohengrin*, Berlin Philharmonic Orchestra/ Herbert von Karajan
EMI 7243 5 66519–2
¶ Schubert, Quintet in A, 'Trout', D667 (first movement, Allegro vivace), András Schiff (piano)/members of the Hagen Quartet/Alois Posch (double bass)
Decca 411 975–2
¶ Beethoven, Piano Concerto No. 5 in E flat, 'Emperor', Op. 73 (second movement, Adagio un poco mosso), Wilhelm Kempff (piano)/Berlin Philharmonic Orchestra/Ferdinand Leitner
DG 427 240–2
¶ Dylan, 'Most of the Time' (from *Oh Mercy*), Bob Dylan
CBS 465800–2

♩ Wagner, 'Liebestod' (from *Tristan und Isolde*), Margaret Price
(Isolde)/Dresden Staatskapelle/Carlos Kleiber
DG 413 319–2
♩ Springsteen, 'Born to Run', Bruce Springsteen
CBS CD 80959
♩ Bach, Suite No. 1 in G major (Prelude), Mischa Maisky (cello)
DG 445 374–2

*Apart from being an international cricketer, Ed is highly articulate and
writes really well, both about cricket and its American cousin, baseball.
When his illustrious cricket career slows down he will, I suspect, become
a regular and brilliant commentator. Another cricketer who is mad about
musical Test matches, i.e. Wagner (see also Michael Henderson, p. 219
and Bob Willis, p. 213).*

1 AUGUST 2004
Kate Adie, foreign correspondent

♩ 'Shen khar, venakhi', Rustavi Choir/Ansor Erkomaishvili
Sony SMK 66823
♩ Puccini, opening of Act II of *La bohème*, Angela Gheorghiu (Mimì),
Roberto Alagna (Rodolfo), Simon Keenlyside (Marcello), Roberto de
Candia (Schaunard), Ildebrando D'Arcangelo (Colline)/Chorus and
Orchestra of La Scala, Milan/Riccardo Chailly
Decca 468 070–2
♩ Bruch, Violin Concerto No. 1 in G minor, Op. 26 (second movement,
Adagio), Kyung-Wha Chung (violin)/London Philharmonic
Orchestra/Klaus Tennstedt
EMI CDC 754 072 2
♩ Vaughan Williams, 'Folk Songs from Somerset' (from *English Folk
Song Suite*), London Symphony Orchestra/Adrian Boult
EMI CDC 747218 2
♩ Wagner, *Siegfried Idyll* (opening), Philharmonia/Otto Klemperer
EMI CMS 763277 2
♩ Carl Michael Bellman, 'Fjäriln vingad syns på Haga', Aksel Schiøtz
(tenor)/Banjo Lasse (lute)
Danacord DACOCD 455

♪ Gilbert/Sullivan, 'We're Called Gondolieri' (from *The Gondoliers*), Alexander Young (Marco)/John Cameron (Giuseppe)/Pro Arte Orchestra/Malcolm Sargent
EMI CMS 764394 2
♪ Shostakovich, 'Waltz' (from *Jazz Suite* No. 1), Royal Concertgebouw Orchestra/Riccardo Chailly
Decca 433 702–2

Several people commented on how this battle-worn correspondent came over as extraordinary jolly and youthful, almost as though there was a schoolgirl mentality which had given her the ability to deal with the dreadful things she had seen but which had also locked her into a kind of period manner. Not in the least intimidating.

8 AUGUST 2004
Edwin Thomas, writer

♪ Weber, 'Schütze, der im Dunkeln wacht' (from *Der Freischütz*, Act II), Peter Meven (Kaspar), Rolf Boysen (Samiel)/Bavarian Radio Chorus and Symphony Orchestra/Rafael Kubelík
Decca 417 119–2
♪ Dvořák, Symphony No. 9 in E minor, 'From the New World' (fourth movement, Allegro con fuoco), Cleveland Orchestra/Christoph von Dohnányi
Decca 421 082–2
♪ Merchant, 'This House is on Fire' (from *Motherland*), Natalie Merchant
Elektra 7559 62721 2
♪ Anne Dudley, *Jeeves and Wooster* (music from the TV series), The Dover Street Jazzomaniacs
EMI CDP 799010 2
♪ Howells, 'Here is the Little Door', Choir of St Paul's Cathedral/John Scott
Hyperion CDA 67269
♪ Maurice Jarre, 'Overture' to *Lawrence of Arabia* (from the original soundtrack), London Philharmonic Orchestra/Maurice Jarre
Varese Sarabande VSD 5263
♪ Mozart, Divertimento in D, K136 (first movement, Allegro), Moscow Virtuosi/Vladimir Spivakov
RCA RD 60066

Gillian Slovo, writer

¶ Arvo Pärt, *Tabula Rasa*, Gidon Kremer, Tatjana Grindenko (violins)/
Alfred Schnittke (prepared piano)/Lithuanian Chamber Orchestra/
Saulus Sondeckis
ECM 817 764–2
¶ Ibrahim, 'Mannenberg', Abdullah Ibrahim (piano)/Robbie Jansen and
Basil Coetzee (saxophones)/Paul Michaels (bass)/Monty Weber (drums)
Kaz Kaz CD 101
¶ Redding arr. Franklin, 'Respect', Aretha Franklin
Universal 9809935
¶ Shostakovich, Symphony No. 7, 'Leningrad' (third movement,
Adagio), New York Philharmonic Orchestra/Leonard Bernstein
Sony Classical SMK 47616
¶ Hammerstein/Kern, 'Ol' Man River' (from *Showboat*), Paul Robeson
Delta Music CD 6252
¶ Mafikizolo, 'Marabi', Mafikizolo
Columbia COL8212

*Was very moved to hear her talk about the murder of her mother (wife of
Joe Slovo) and, in that light, the resonances of truth and reconciliation in
South Africa.*

29 AUGUST 2004
Michael Rosen, children's novelist and poet

¶ Brassens, 'Le parapluie', Georges Brassens
Philips 9101 043
¶ Ferré, 'Paname', Léo Ferré
Barclay 80133
¶ Martin Luther, 'Ein feste Burg ist unser Gott', Westfälische Kantorei/
Wilhelm Ehmann
Cantate C 57616
¶ Franck, Violin Sonata in A (fourth movement, Allegretto poco
mosso), Christian Ferras (violin)/Pierre Barbizet (piano)
EMI 574872 2
¶ Beethoven, Symphony No. 6, 'Pastoral', Op. 68 (third movement,
'Peasants' Merrymaking'), Chicago Symphony Orchestra/Fritz Reiner
RCA GD 60002

¶ Billy Pigg, 'The Wild Hills of Wannies', J. R. Pigg, Dargai, Billy Pigg (Northumbrian pipes)
Leader LEA 4006
¶ Mozart, 'Non più andrai' (from *The Marriage of Figaro*, Act I), Samuel Ramey (Figaro)/London Philharmonic Orchestra/Georg Solti
Decca 410 150–2
¶ Davis, 'Freddie Freeloader' (from *Kind of Blue*), Miles Davis (trumpet)/Julian 'Cannonball' Adderley, John Coltrane (saxophones)/Wynton Kelly (piano)/Paul Chambers (bass)/Jimmy Cobb (drums)
Columbia CK 64935

5 SEPTEMBER 2004
Ian Jack, writer and editor of *Granta*

¶ Kern, 'I Still Suits Me' (from *Showboat*), Paul Robeson and Elizabeth Welch
Regis RRC 1056
¶ Verdi, 'Ehi! Taverniere!' (from *Falstaff*, Act III), José van Dam (Falstaff)/Berlin Philharmonic Orchestra/Georg Solti
Decca 440 650–2
¶ Schubert, 'An die Musik', Kathleen Ferrier (contralto)/Phyllis Spurr (piano)
Decca 430 096–2
¶ Lewis/Young/Conrad/Robinson, 'Singin' the Blues', Bix Beiderbecke with Frank Trumbauer and his Orchestra
Verve 549 080–2
¶ McColl, 'The Shoals of Herring', Ewan McColl and Peggy Seeger
Cooking Vinyl COOKCD 038
¶ Beethoven, Violin Sonata in A, 'Kreutzer', Op. 47 (first movement, Presto), Itzhak Perlman (violin)/Vladimir Ashkenazy (piano)
Decca 410 554–2
¶ Watt, 'The Kelty Clippie', John Watt
Living Tradition LTCD 3001
¶ Trad. Indian, 'Calamela', K. S. Gopalakrishnan (carnatic flute)
Wergo SM 1502–2

Hugo Morley-Fletcher, antiques expert

❡ Mascagni, 'Easter Hymn' (from *Cavalleria rusticana*), Renata Scotto (Santuzza), Jean Kraft (Mamma Lucia)/Ambrosian Opera Chorus/ National Philharmonic Orchestra/James Levine
RCA RD 83091

❡ Haydn, String Quartet in C, 'Emperor', Op. 76, No. 3 (first movement, Allegro), Amadeus Quartet
DG 471 762–2

❡ Beethoven, Piano Trio in B flat, 'Archduke', Op. 97 (second movement, Scherzo: Allegro), Pinchas Zukerman (violin), Jacqueline du Pré (cello), Daniel Barenboim (piano)
EMI 5 74447–2

❡ Mozart, Trio in E flat, 'Kegelstatt', K498, Gervase de Peyer (clarinet)/Cecil Aronowitz (viola)/Lamar Crowson (piano)
LP: HMV ASD 605

❡ Bruckner, Symphony No. 7 in E (finale), Royal Concertgebouw Orchestra/Bernard Haitink
Philips 446 580–2

❡ Monteverdi, 'Non morir, Seneca' (from *L'incoronazione di Poppea*, Act I), Glyndebourne Festival Chorus/Royal Philharmonic Orchestra/John Pritchard
EMI CDZ 573843–2

❡ Wagner, Overture to *Tannhäuser*, Vienna Philharmonic Orchestra/ Herbert von Karajan
DG 423 613–2

❡ Beethoven, String Quartet in C sharp minor, Op. 131 (first movement, Adagio ma non troppo e molto espressivo), Quartetto Italiano
Philips 454 062–2

❡ Vivaldi, Oboe Concerto in D minor, K454 (first movement, Allegro), Heinz Holliger (oboe)/Dresden Staatskapelle/Vittorio Negri
Philips 422 492–2

Jenny Agutter, actress

❡ Shostakovich, Prelude and Fugue No. 23, Keith Jarrett (piano)
ECM 437 189–2

♪ Brahms, Piano Concerto No. 2 in B flat, Op. 83 (fourth movement, Allegretto grazioso), Alfred Brendel (piano)/Concertgebouw Orchestra/Bernard Haitink
Philips 426 633–2
♪ Monteverdi, Lauda Jerusalem (from Vespers, 1610), Monteverdi Choir/English Baroque Soloists/His Majesty's Sagbutts and Cornetts/ John Eliot Gardiner
Archiv 429 565–2
♪ Schütz, 'O Jesu, nomen dulce', SWV 308, Andreas Scholl (countertenor)/Concerto de Viole/Basel Consort
Harmonia Mundi 901651
♪ Bernstein, 'Scherzo' (from *Symphonic Dances from West Side Story*), Royal Liverpool Philharmonic Orchestra/Carl Davis
Classics for Pleasure CD-CFP 4601
♪ Elgar, 'In Haven (Capri)' (from *Sea Pictures*), Janet Baker (mezzo-soprano)/London Symphony Orchestra/John Barbirolli
EMI SMS 763185–2
♪ Paul Reade, *The Victorian Kitchen Garden*, Emma Johnson (clarinet)/Skaila Kanga (harp)
BBC CD 705
♪ Schubert, Impromptu in F minor, D935, No. 1, András Schiff (piano)
Decca 425 638–2
♪ Amy Beach, Theme and Variations for flute and string quartet, Op. 80 (last variation), Helen Keen (flute)/The Ambache
Chandos CHAN 9752

26 SEPTEMBER 2004
Mark Tully, journalist and broadcaster

♪ Schubert, Symphony No. 8 in B minor (first movement, Allegro moderato), Bamberg Symphony Orchestra/Horst Stein
EURODISC 610 599
♪ John Tavener, *Song for Athene*, Westminster Abbey Choir/Martin Neary
Sony Classical SK 66613
♪ Hymn, 'O Come, O Come, Emmanuel', Choir of Old St Paul's Church/Leslie Shankland
OSP DCD 43701

❡ Percy Grainger, Irish Tune from County Derry ('Danny Boy'),
Grimethorpe Colliery Band/John Anderson
RCA 09026687515
❡ Khan, 'Allah Hoo', Ustad Nusrat Fateh Ali Khan
Star CD SR 056
❡ Trad., Raga: Bahar, Ustad Bismillah Khan (shehnai)/Prof. V. G. Joy
(violin)
HMV ASD 2312
❡ Bruckner, Te Deum (first section, Allegro), Maria Stader (soprano),
Sieglinde Wagner (contralto), Ernst Haefliger (tenor), Peter Lagger
(bass)/Berlin Philharmonic Orchestra/ Eugen Jochum
DG 457 743−2
❡ Alan Hovhaness, *Majnun Symphony* (Part I: 'Majnun'), Sidney Sax
(violin)/John Wilbraham (trumpet)/National Philharmonic Orchestra
of London/Alan Hovhaness
Crystal CD 803

Curiously potent mix of the Sacred, the Indian and the sentimental.

3 OCTOBER 2004
Dame Judi Dench, actress

❡ Shakespeare, 'When in Disgrace with Fortune and Men's Eyes'
(Sonnet No. 29), read by John Gielgud
LP Argo SPA 573
❡ Bach, Brandenburg Concerto No. 1 (third movement), English
Concert/Trevor Pinnock
Archiv 423 492−2
❡ Davis, 'Blue in Green' (from *Kind of Blue*), Miles Davis (trumpet)/
Cannonball Adderley (alto saxophone)/John Coltrane (tenor
saxophone)/Bill Evans (piano)/Paul Chambers (bass)/Jimmy Cobb
(drums)
Columbia Legacy CK 64935
❡ Rutter, 'What Sweeter Music', Choir of King's College, Cambridge/
Stephen Cleobury
EMI 5 56605−2
❡ Stravinsky, *The Rite of Spring* (opening), Columbia Symphony
Orchestra/Igor Stravinsky
Sony SM3K 46291

¶ Bernstein, Psalm 23 and Psalm 2 (vv. 1–4) (from *Chichester Psalms*), John Bogart (alto)/Camerata Singers/New York Philharmonic Orchestra/Leonard Bernstein
Sony SMK 60595
¶ Maxwell Davies, *An Orkney Wedding, with Sunrise*, George MacIlwham (bagpipes)/Royal Philharmonic Orchestra/Peter Maxwell Davies
Collins 14442
¶ Rachmaninov, Piano Concerto No. 3 in D minor, Op. 30 (first movement, Allegro ma non tanto), Vladimir Ashkenazy (piano)/ London Symphony Orchestra/André Previn
Decca 473 251–2

10 OCTOBER 2004
Antony Beevor, historian

¶ Knipper, 'Song of the Plains', Soviet Army Chorus and Band/Boris Alandrov
HMV 5 73045–2
¶ Corelli, Sonata for trumpet, two violins and continuo in D, Stephen Burns (trumpet)/unnamed ensemble
ASV CDQS 6081
¶ Knipper, Symphony No. 4 in D, Op. 41 (first movement), Oleg Biktomirov (tenor), Boris Shumilov (baritone)/Russian Academic Chamber Chorus/Moscow Symphony Orchestra/Veronika Dudarova
Olympia OCD 202
¶ Vivaldi, Suscitans a terra inopem (from Laudate pueri, RV601), Carolyn Sampson (soprano)/King's Consort/Robert King
Hyperion CDA 66819
¶ Haydn, String Quartet in C, 'Emperor', Op. 76, No. 3 (second movement, Poco adagio: Cantabile), Amadeus Quartet
DG 471 762–2
¶ Mozart, 'Bravo, signor padrone! . . . se vuol ballare' (*The Marriage of Figaro*, Act I), Cesare Siepi (Figaro)/Vienna Philharmonic Orchestra/Erich Kleiber
Decca 466 369–2
¶ Brahms, Cello Sonata No. 2 in F major, Op. 99 (second movement, Adagio affetuoso), Antonio Lysy (cello)/Ronan O'Hora (piano)
Tring International BES052

❡ Francesco Manfredini, Concerto for Two Trumpets in D major (first movement), Bernard Soustrot and Guy Touvron (trumpets)/Lucerne Festival Strings/Rudolf Baumgartner
Denon c 37 7544

17 OCTOBER 2004
Daniel Mason, novelist

❡ Bach, English Suite No. 2 in A minor, BWV 807 (first movement, Prelude), Glenn Gould (piano)
Sony SM2K 52606
❡ Dvořák, Bagatelle, Op. 9, No. 1, Members of the Prazak Quartet/ Jaroslav Tama (harmonium)
Praga PRD 250110
❡ Bach, 'Chaconne' (from Partita in D minor, BWV 1004), Christoph Poppen (violin)
ECM 461 895–2
❡ Mahler, Symphony No. 6 (opening of first movement), New York Philharmonic Orchestra/Leonard Bernstein
Sony SMK 60208
❡ Haydn, Sonata No. 50 in D, Hob.XVI, No. 37 (first movement, Allegro con brio), Julia Cload (piano)
Meridian ECD 84083
❡ Barber, *Adagio for Strings*, Philadelphia Orchestra/Eugene Ormandy
Sony SBK 63034
❡ Bach, Prelude in F sharp minor (from *The Well-tempered Clavier*, Book II), Glenn Gould (piano)
Sony SM2K 52603
[❡ Mason, extract from *The Piano Tuner*, Daniel Mason read live during recording session]

24 OCTOBER 2004
Christina Coker, chief executive of Youth Music

❡ Gibbons, 'The Silver Swan', Consort of Musicke/Anthony Rooley
Oiseau Lyre 585 714–2
❡ Mendelssohn, *Song without Words* in D, Op. 109, Jacqueline du Pré (cello)/Gerald Moore (piano)
EMI CDC 555529 2

♪ Stravinsky, 'Danse sacrale' (from *The Rite of Spring*), Philadelphia Orchestra/Riccardo Muti
EMI CDC 747408 2
♪ Farmer, 'Fair Phyllis', King's Singers
EMI EMX 2129
♪ Ladysmith Black Mambazo, 'Dlondlobalo Njalo', Ladysmith Black Mambazo
Wrasse WRASS 100
♪ Julian Joseph, 'Ode to the Time our Memories Forgot', Julian Joseph (piano)
Eastwest 9031–75122–2
♪ Benjamin, Invention I (from *Three Inventions for Chamber Orchestra*), John Wallace (flügelhorn)/London Sinfonietta/George Benjamin
Nimbus NI 5505
♪ Beethoven, String Quartet in C sharp minor, Op. 131 (fifth movement, Presto), Lindsay String Quartet
ASV CDDCS 403
♪ Irving Berlin, 'Let Yourself Go', Ginger Rogers/Jimmy Dorsey and his Orchestra
Past Perfect PPC 78113

I particularly wanted to discuss with her the music education of children of various ages, as this is an area for which we both have a passion.

31 OCTOBER 2004
Sir Harrison Birtwistle, composer

♪ Palestrina, 'Si ignoras te', Oxford Camerata/Jeremy Summerly
Naxos 8.550843
♪ Debussy, *Prélude à l'après-midi d'un faune*, Orchestre de la Suisse Romande/Ernest Ansermet
Decca 414 040–2
♪ Ravi Shankar, 'Yaman kalyan', Anoushka Shankar (sitar)
Angel 56969–2
♪ Boulez, Improvisation sur Mallarmé II, 'Une dentelle s'abolit' (from *Pli selon pli*), Christine Schäfer (soprano)/Ensemble Intercontemperain/Pierre Boulez
DG 471 344–2

❡ Stravinsky, *Symphonies of Wind Instruments*, Netherlands Wind
Ensemble/Edo de Waart
Philips 441 583–2
❡ Orbison, 'In Dreams', Roy Orbison
Orbison IM 00057–2

*Not as forbidding as he is sometimes made out to be, but hugely
interesting and a man of considerable dry wit. Traced a natural line
through the music – but who would have anticipated him being an
admirer of Roy Orbison's vocal dexterity?*

7 NOVEMBER 2004
Simon Goldhill, academic

❡ Adès, 'So That Is All' (from *Powder her Face*, Act II), Jill Gomez
(Duchess)/Valdine Anderson, Niall Morris (Rubberneckers)/Almeida
Ensemble/Thomas Adès
EMI CDS 55649 2
❡ Beethoven, String Quartet in C sharp minor, Op. 131 (first
movement, Adagio ma non troppo e molto espressivo), Busch Quartet
EMI CMS 565308 2
❡ Webern, *Five Movements*, Op. 5 (first movement, Heftig bewegt),
Schoenberg Quartet
Chandos CHAN 10083
❡ Handel, Dixit Dominus (opening chorus), Choir of King's College,
Cambridge/English Chamber Orchestra/Stephen Cleobury
Decca 421 294–2
[❡ Goldhill, excerpt from *Love, Sex and Tragedy*, Simon Goldhill
read live during programme recording session]
❡ Blow, 'Ah, Heav'n! What Is't I Hear?', James Bowman, Michael
Chance (countertenors)/King's Consort/Robert King
Hyperion CDA 66253
❡ Richard Strauss, 'Allein! Weh, ganz allein' (from *Elektra*), Birgit
Nilsson (Elektra)/Vienna Philharmonic Orchestra/Georg Solti
Decca 417 345–2

14 NOVEMBER 2004
George Duke, American jazz musician

♪ Duke, 'Brazilian Love Affair' (from *The Essential George Duke*), George Duke
Epic/Legacy 5161912
♪ Stravinsky, 'The Chosen One' (from *The Rite of Spring*), Columbia Symphony Orchestra/Stravinsky
CBS MK42433
♪ Debussy, 'Par les rues et par les chemins' (from *Ibéria*, No. 2 of *Images* for orchestra), Montreal Symphony Orchestra/Charles Dutoit
Decca 4255022
♪ Sly and the Family Stone, 'If You Want Me to Stay' (from *Fresh*), Sly and the Family Stone
Epic 4851702
♪ Hindemith, Trombone Sonata (first movement), Ensemble Villa Musica
MDG 304 06972
♪ Haydn, Sonata No. 50 (first movement), Rudolf Buchbinder (piano)
Teldec 835794
♪ Milton Nascimento/Lo Borges, 'Tudo que voce podia ser' (from Clube da Esquina), Lo and Marcio Borges/ASCAP
EMI 8304292
♪ Sarah Vaughan, 'So Many Stars' (from *Brazilian Romance*), Sergio Mendes/A. and M. Bergman
Columbia 4968562
♪ Davis, 'Blue in Green' (from *Kind of Blue*), Miles Davis
Columbia/Legacy CK64935

28 NOVEMBER 2004
Charles Mackworth-Young, consultant rheumatologist

♪ Schubert, 'An die Musik', D547, Dietrich Fischer-Dieskau (baritone)/ Gerald Moore (piano)
DG 463 503–2
♪ Varèse, *Hyperprism*, ASKO Ensemble/Riccardo Chailly
Decca 460 210–2

♪ Wagner, Prelude and opening of Act III of *Siegfried*, Thomas Stewart (Wotan), Oralia Dominguez (Erda)/Berlin Philharmonic Orchestra/Herbert von Karajan
DG 457 790–2

♪ Mozart, Symphony No. 39 in E flat, K543 (third movement, Minuet and Trio), London Mozart Players/Jane Glover
ASV CD DCA 615

♪ Bach, Prelude and Fugue in E flat major (from *The Well-tempered Clavier*, Book 2), Angela Hewitt (piano)
Hyperion CDA 67303/4

♪ Berg, String Quartet, Op. 3 (first movement, Langsam), Leipzig String Quartet
MD and G MDG 307 0996–2

♪ Byrd, Nunc Dimittis (from the Great Service), Tallis Scholars/ Peter Phillips
Gimell CDGIM 011

♪ Stravinsky, 'Mystic Circles of the Young Girls' and 'Glorification of the Chosen One' from *The Rite of Spring*, Philharmonia/Eliahu Inbal
Teldec 4509–91449–2

♪ Handel, 'Slow March' (from *Scipio*), Band of the Grenadier Guards/Major P. E. Hills
Bandleader BNA 5014

♪ Praetorius, 'Suite de Ballets' (from *Terpsichore*), Early Music Consort of London/David Munrow
EMI CDM 769024 2

5 DECEMBER 2004
James Hamilton-Paterson, writer

♪ Von Einem, Piano Concerto, Op. 20 (second movement, Adagio), Gerty Herzog (piano)/Berlin Radio Symphony Orchestra/Ferenc Fricsay
DG 445 404–2

♪ Rorem, 'The Boy with the Baseball Glove', Rufus Müller (tenor)/ Steven Blier (piano)
NewWorld 80575–2

♪ Elgar, *Mina*, Northern Sinfonia/Neville Marriner
EMI CDM 565593–2

❡ Richard Strauss, Suite in B flat for 13 Wind Instruments, Op. 4 (fourth movement, Introduction and Fugue), Netherlands Wind Ensemble/Edo de Waart
Philips 438 734–2
❡ E. T. A. Hoffmann, Sacrificium Deo (from Miserere in B flat minor), Camilla Nylund (soprano)/Concerto Bamberg/Rolf Beck
Koch 3–1148–2
❡ Haydn, String Quartet in F minor, Op. 20, No. 5 (fourth movement, Fuga a due soggetti), The Lindsays
ASV CDDCA 1057
❡ C. P. E. Bach, Concerto in G minor, W.32 (first movement, Allegretto), Miklós Spányi (fortepiano)/Concerto Armonico/Péter Szüts
BIS CD 786
❡ Bach, Trio Sonata in E flat, BWV 525 (third movement, Allegro), Christopher Herrick (Metzler organ of the Pfarrkirche St Nikolaus, Bremgarten)
Hyperion CDS 44121

12 DECEMBER 2004
Robert McCrum, editor, writer and journalist

❡ Britten, 'Elegy' ('O rose, thou art sick' (Blake)), from *Serenade for tenor, horn & strings*, Peter Pears (tenor), Dennis Brain (horn)/Boyd Neel String Orchestra/Benjamin Britten
Decca 425 996–2
❡ Gilbert/Sullivan, 'When all night long' ('The Nightmare Song') (*Iolanthe*, Act II), John Reed (Lord Chancellor)/New Symphony Orchestra of London/Isidore Duncan
Decca 414 145–2 CD2
❡ Jerome Kern, 'Bill' from *Showboat* (lyric by P. G. Wodehouse), Carol Bruce (Julie)/Orchestra conducted by Edwin McArthur
Sony Broadway SK 53330
❡ Milhaud, *Le boeuf sur le toit*, Op. 58, Lyon Opera Orchestra/Kent Nagano
Erato 2292 45820–2
❡ Cole Porter, 'Anything Goes' (from *Anything Goes*), Ella Fitzgerald Orchestra/Buddy Bregman
Verve 821 989–2

¶ Rossini, 'Kyrie' (from the *Petite messe solonnelle*), Katia and Marielle Labèque (pianos), David Briggs (harmonium), Choir of King's College, Cambridge/Stephen Cleobury
EMI CDC 747482–2 CD1
¶ Gershwin, 'Somebody Loves Me' (from *George White's Scandals of 1924*), Kiri te Kanawa, New Princess Theater Orchestra/John McGlinn
EMI CDC 747454–2
¶ Colin Matthews, *Fourth Sonata* (Part 1), London Sinfonietta/Oliver Knussen
Decca 474 316–2
¶ Frank Loesser, 'Adelaide's Lament' (from *Guys and Dolls*), Vivian Blaine (from original Broadway cast recording)
MCA MCAD 10301
¶ Gillian Welch, 'Honey Now' (from the album *Hell Among the Yearlings*)
ALMCD60

Really came alive when he described the goings-on in his brain, post-stroke, in terms of a piece by Colin Matthews which seemed to echo the fracture and dislocation of reality.

26 DECEMBER 2004
Stephen Fry, writer, actor and comedian

¶ Taylor/Lamb, 'I Wish I Knew How It Would Feel to be Free', Nina Simone
RCA ND 90376
¶ Alkan, 'La chanson de la folle au bord de la mer', Op. 31, No. 8, Ronald Smith (piano)
APR APR 7031
¶ Britten, 'So Abram Rose, and Clave the Wood' (from *War Requiem*, Op. 66), Peter Pears (tenor), Dietrich Fischer-Dieskau (baritone)/ Highgate School Choir/Bach Choir/London Symphony Chorus and Orchestra/Benjamin Britten
Decca 414 383–2
¶ Jankowski, 'A Walk in the Black Forest', Herb Alpert and the Tijuana Brass
A and M AML 965

❧ Mozart, 'Pa-pa-ge-na' (from *The Magic Flute*, Act II), Walter Berry (Papageno), Ruth-Margret Pütz (Papagena)/Philharmonia/Otto Klemperer
EMI CMS 567388 2
❧ Vivian Stanshall, 'The Intro and the Outro', The Bonzo Dog Doo Dah Band
Right RIGHT 010
❧ Beethoven, *Egmont* Overture, Op. 84, London Philharmonic Orchestra/Adrian Boult
Vanguard SVC 13
❧ Wagner, 'Isoldes Liebestod' (from *Tristan und Isolde*, Act III), Kirsten Flagstad (Isolde)/Philharmonia/Wilhelm Furtwängler
EMI CDS 747322 8

Like Clive James, an infectious, all-embracing intelligence. One of the few guests to choose something because it is so wonderfully ridiculous. The Herb Alpert had us rolling around.

9 JANUARY 2005
D. B. C. Pierre, novelist

❧ Juventino Rosas, 'Sobre las olas' (Over the waves), Berlin Philharmonic Orchestra/Robert Stolz
Eurodisc 258 665
❧ Shostakovich, Prelude No. 24 (from 24 *Preludes*, Op. 34), Tatiana Nikolayeva (piano)
Hyperion CDA 66620
❧ Harri Wessman, 'Water under Snow is Weary', Eva Tigerstedt (flute)/ Minna Pekonen (piano)/Tapiola Choir of Finland/Errki Pohjola
Finlandia FACD 921
❧ Britten, 'Tarantella' (finale) from *Diversions* for piano (left hand) and orchestra, Op. 21, Julius Katchen (piano)/London Symphony Orchestra/Benjamin Britten
Ace of Clubs Mono ACL 314
❧ Wagner, 'Schmerzen' (*Wesendonck-Lieder*, No. 4), Christa Ludwig (mezzo-soprano)/Philharmonia/Otto Klemperer
EMI CDM 764078–2
❧ Delius, 'I Stand as on Some Mighty Eagle's Beak' (*Songs of Farewell*, No. 2), Ambrosian Singers/Royal Philharmonic Orchestra/Eric Fenby
Unicorn UKCD 2077

¶ Schubert, 'Die junge Nonne', Kathleen Ferrier (contralto)/Phyllis
Spurr (piano)
Decca 430 096–2
¶ Jazz Jamaica, Theme from *Exodus* (from *Double Barrel*), Jazz Jamaica
Hannibal HNCD1421
¶ Beethoven, arr. William Finnegan, 'Moonlight' Sonata, Glenn Miller
Orchestra
Mercury 826 635–2
¶ Holst, 'Prelude' and 'Song of the Fishermen' (from *Japanese Suite*,
Op. 33), London Symphony Orchestra/Adrian Boult
Lyrita SRCD 222

16 JANUARY 2005
Jon Snow, broadcaster

¶ Bach, 'Herr, unser Herrscher, dessen Ruhm' (from *St John Passion*),
Monteverdi Choir/English Baroque Soloists/John Eliot Gardiner
Archiv 427 319–2
¶ Purcell, arr. Rees-Williams, 'When I am Laid in Earth', David
Rees-Williams Trio
Artist's private recording
¶ Poulenc, Organ Concerto (Allegro giocoso), Maurice Duruflé
(organ)/French National Radio Orchestra/Georges Prêtre
EMI CDC 747723 2
¶ Prokofiev, 'The Philosophers' (from *Cantata for the 20th Anniversary
of the October Revolution*), Philharmonia Chorus and Orchestra/
Neeme Järvi
Chandos CHAN 9095
¶ Schumann, *Études Symphoniques*, Op. 13 (Theme and Variation 1),
Rudolf Firkušný (piano)
EMI CDM 56608 2
¶ Mozart, Quoniam (from Mass in C minor, K427), Sylvia McNair,
Diana Montague (sopranos), Anthony Rolfe Johnson (tenor)/English
Baroque Soloists/John Eliot Gardiner
Philips 420 210–2

❡ Beethoven, Kyrie (from *Missa Solemnis*, Op. 123), Gundula Janowitz (soprano), Christa Ludwig (mezzo-soprano), Fritz Wunderlich (tenor), Walter Berry (bass)/Wiener Singverein/Berlin Philharmonic Orchestra/Herbert von Karajan
DG 423 913–2
❡ Howells, Magnificat (Collegium Regale), Choir of King's College, Cambridge/Peter Barley (organ)/Stephen Cleobury
Argo 430 205–2
❡ Rossini, Kyrie (from *Petite messe solennelle*), Raymond Allesandrini (piano)/Emmanuel Mandrin (harmonium)/Ensemble Vocal Michel Piquemal/Michel Piquemal
Accord 476 060–2

Nice to know that PP sometimes reaches the parts others don't, since Jon told me that he had a bigger response to this programme than to anything else he had done. He also said that his partner was amazed to hear him talk for the first time about the meaning of the soul.

23 JANUARY 2005
Shena Mackay, novelist

❡ Purcell, 'Thrice Happy Lovers' and 'The Plaint' (from *The Fairy Queen*, Act V), Alfred Deller (countertenor)
Harmonia Mundi HMC 90249
❡ Mozart, *Eine kleine Nachtmusik* (Rondo), Orpheus Chamber Orchestra
DG 419 192–2
❡ Holiday, 'It's Easy to Blame the Weather', Billie Holiday/Teddy Wilson Orchestra
Affinity CDAFS 1019/F
❡ Chopin, Mazurka in A minor, Op. 17, No. 4, Richard Goode (piano)
Nonesuch 7559–79452–2
❡ Birtwistle, 'Tenebrae' (from *Three Settings of Celan*), Christine Whittlesey (soprano)/Ensemble Intercontemporain/Pierre Boulez
DG 439 910–2
❡ Coleman, 'Lonely Woman' (from *Shape of Jazz to Come*), Ornette Coleman (alto saxophone)/Don Cherry (cornet)/Charlie Haden (bass)/Billy Higgins (drums)
Atlantic 781 339–2

¶ Germaine Tailleferre, Violin Sonata No. 1 (first movement), Renate
Eggebrecht (violin)/Angela Gassenhuber (piano)
Troubadisc TROCV01406
¶ Milhaud, *Le boeuf sur le toit*, Lyon Opera Orchestra/Kent Nagano
Erato 2292–45820–2
¶ Coward, 'If Love were All', Mabel Mercer
Atlantic SD 1301

30 JANUARY 2005
William Hague, politician and biographer

¶ Trad., arr. Cassidy, 'Wade in the Water', Eva Cassidy
Blix Street G210047
¶ Harris, 'Cry Me a River', Gene Harris with the Ray Brown Trio
Concord Jazz CCD4268
¶ Bach, Concerto for Two Violins in D minor, BWV 1043 (second
movement, Largo ma non tanto), Itzhak Perlman and Pinchas
Zukerman (violins)/English Chamber Orchestra/Daniel Barenboim
EMI 5 74720–2
¶ Stoltz, 'Wild Wind', Walkin', Jim Stoltz
Wild Wind Records WW003
¶ Chopin, Prelude in C minor, Op. 28, No. 20, Martha Argerich
(piano)
DG 463 663–3
¶ Rachmaninov, Piano Concerto No. 3 in D minor, Op. 30 (first
movement, Allegro ma non tanto), Vladimir Ashkenazy (piano)/
London Symphony Orchestra/André Previn
Decca 473 251–2
¶ Mozart, Sonata in C minor, K457 (third movement, Allegro assai),
Mitsuko Uchida (piano)
Philips 468 356–2

In talking about the pleasure he derived from music, he became
surprisingly endearing. We agreed that music should be compulsory for
politicians – would improve their capacity to think rationally as well as
their humanity.

6 FEBRUARY 2005
William Pye, sculptor

❡ Gluck, 'Dance of the Blessed Spirits' (middle section only), from *Orfeo ed Euridice*, Act II, William Bennett (flute)/ECO/Raymond Leppard
CBS CD44650

❡ Anouar Brahem Trio, 'Aube rouge a Grozny' (from the album *Astrakan Café*)
ECM 1718 159 494-2

❡ Schubert, 'Andante un poco moto' (second movement from the Piano Trio in B flat, D898), Jelly d'Aranyi (violin), Felix Salmond (cello), Myra Hess (piano)
APR CDAPR7012-2 CD2

❡ Berlioz, Trio for two flutes and harp (*L'enfance du Christ*, Part III), Richard Taylor and Francis Nolan (flutes), Renata Scheffel-Stein (harp) from the recording by Sir Colin Davis with the LSO
Philips 462 252-2 CD3

❡ Cesaria Evora, *Corregem irmon*
RCA 7 4321 4 53922

❡ Janáček, 'Andante' (first movement from *Mladi*), Members of the London Sinfonietta: Sebastian Bell (flute), Janet Craxton (oboe), Anthony Pay (clarinet), Michael Harris (bass clarinet), Philip Eastop (horn), Martin Gatt (bassoon)
Decca 4303752 CD2

❡ Berlioz, 'Royal Hunt and Storm' (from *The Trojans*, Act IV), Orchestra of the ROH, Covent Garden/Sir Colin Davis
Philips 456 143-2 CD3

13 FEBRUARY 2005
Josceline Dimbleby, cookery writer

❡ Albinoni, Oboe Concerto in D minor, Op. 9, No. 2 (second movement, Adagio), Heinz Holliger (oboe)/I Musici
Philips 420 255-2

❡ Kern, 'Bill' (from *Show Boat*), Helen Morgan/Orchestra/Victor Young
CBS A 55

¶ Richard Strauss, 'Cäcilie', Op. 27, No. 2, Jessye Norman (soprano)/
Leipzig Gewandhaus Orchestra/Kurt Masur
Philips 411 052–2
¶ Leiber/Stoller, 'I'm a Woman', Kate Dimbleby/Geoff Eales Trio
Black Box BBJ 2020
¶ Duparc, 'Chanson triste', Sarah Walker (mezzo-soprano)/Roger
Vignoles (piano)
Hyperion CDA 66323
¶ Schoebel/Erdman/Meyers, 'Nobody's Sweetheart', Al Bowlly/Roy Fox
and his Orchestra
Timeless CBC 1–005
¶ Monteverdi, 'Pur ti miro' (from *L'incoronazione di Poppea*, Act III),
Sylvia McNair (Poppea), Dana Hanchard (Nerone)/English Baroque
Soloists/John Eliot Gardiner
Archiv 447 088–2
¶ Pergolesi, Cujus animam (from Stabat mater), Emma Kirkby
(soprano)/Academy of Ancient Music/Christopher Hogwood
Oiseau Lyre 425 692–2
¶ Purcell, 'The Plaint' (from *The Fairy Queen*, Act V), Jennifer Smith
(soprano)/English Baroque Soloists/John Eliot Gardiner
Archiv 419 221–2

20 FEBRUARY 2005
Alfred Latham-Koenig, economic adviser

¶ Hahn, 'Paysage', Susan Graham (mezzo-soprano)/Roger Vignoles
(piano)
Sony SK 60168
¶ Debussy, Violin Sonata (second movement, Intermède), Ginette
Neveu (violin)/Jean Neveu (piano)
EMI CDH 763493–2
¶ Messiaen, 'Louange à l'immortalité de Jésus' (last movement of
Quartet for the End of Time), Gil Shaham (violin)/Myung-Whun
Chung (piano)
DG 469 052–2
¶ Shostakovich, Prelude and Fugue No. 1, Tatiana Nikolayeva (piano)
Hyperion CDA 66441
¶ Poulenc, 'Hotel', Felicity Lott (soprano)/Graham Johnson (piano)
Hyperion CDA 66147

♪ Poulenc, Flute Sonata (Cantilena), Jean-Pierre Rampal (flute)/
Robert Veyron-Lacroix
Erato 2292–45839–2
♪ Bach, Partita No. 1 in B flat, BWV 825 (Allemande), Dinu Lipatti
(piano)
Philips 456 892–2
♪ Duparc, 'La vie antérieure', Charles Panzéra (baritone)/Magdalena
Panzéra-Baillot (piano)
Pearl GEMM 9919
♪ Schubert, 'Pause' (from *Die schöne Müllerin*), Dietrich Fischer-
Dieskau (baritone)/Gerald Moore (piano)
EMI 7243 5 66146–2

27 FEBRUARY 2005
Noreena Hertz, economic globalisation expert and writer

♪ Archilei or Cavalieri, 'Dalle più alte sfere' (from *Intermedi per 'La
pellegrina'*), Emma Kirkby (soprano)/Taverner Players/Andrew Parrott
EMI CDC747998 2
♪ Abderrahmane Amrani, 'Ya Rayah', Rachid Taha
Barclay 539953–2
♪ Rachmaninov, Piano Concerto No. 2 in C minor, Op. 18 (first
movement, Allegro moderato), Barry Douglas (piano)/London
Symphony Orchestra/Michael Tilson Thomas
RCA 82876 55269 2
♪ Pete Townshend, 'Behind Blue Eyes', The Who
Polydor POCD 907
♪ Mozart, Requiem aeternam (from Requiem, K626), Karita Mattila
(soprano)/Swedish Radio Choir/Berlin Philharmonic Orchestra/
Claudio Abbado
DG 463 181–2
♪ Leonard Cohen, 'Suzanne', Leonard Cohen
Columbia 497995 2
♪ Pergolesi, Stabat mater (opening duet), Barbara Bonney (soprano)/
Andreas Scholl (countertenor)/Les Talens Lyriques/Christophe
Rousset
Decca 466 134–2
♪ Bach/Sankanda, 'Lasset uns den nicht zerteilen', Lambarena
Sony SXK 64542

Composers requested in order of frequency

222	Johann Sebastian Bach	16	Anonymous
216	Wolfgang Amadeus Mozart		Elmer Bernstein
157	Franz Schubert		Antonín Dvořák
154	Ludwig van Beethoven		Domenico Scarlatti
129	Traditional	15	John Adams
95	Benjamin Britten		William Byrd
73	Giuseppe Verdi		Lennon & McCartney
70	Igor Stravinsky		Modest Mussorgsky
68	George Frideric Handel		Cole Porter
64	Richard Wagner	14	Christoph Gluck
56	Frederic Chopin		Gilbert & Sullivan
55	Franz Joseph Haydn	13	Felix Mendelssohn
54	Johannes Brahms	12	Harrison Birtwistle
48	Henry Purcell		Charles Ives
46	Gustav Mahler		Franz Liszt
	Leoš Janáček		Stephen Sondheim
45	Dmitri Shostakovich		Michael Tippett
44	Giacomo Puccini	11	John Cage
41	Edward Elgar	10	Irving Berlin
38	Johann Strauss		Anton Bruckner
35	Richard Strauss		Gaetano Donizetti
33	Hector Berlioz		György Ligeti
31	Pyotr Ilyich Tchaikovsky	9	Philip Glass
28	Claudio Monteverdi		Jerome Kern
	Sergey Prokofiev		Arvo Pärt
27	Claude Debussy		Camille Saint-Saëns
26	Robert Schumann	8	Pierre Boulez
25	Maurice Ravel		César Franck
24	Francis Poulenc		Rodgers & Hart
	Arnold Schoenberg	7	Thomas Adès
23	Olivier Messiaen		Georges Brassens
	Ralph Vaughan Williams		Reynaldo Hahn
22	Jean Sibelius		Charles Mingus
21	Kurt Weill		Erik Satie
19	Miles Davis		Thomas Tallis
	Bob Dylan		William Walton
	Antonio Vivaldi		Anton von Webern
18	Alban Berg	6	Lennox Berkeley
	Gabriel Fauré		Georges Bizet
	George Gershwin		Henri Duparc
	Sergey Rachmaninov		Percy Grainger
17	Béla Bartók		Rodgers & Hammerstein
	Vincenzo Bellini		Frank Loesser
	Gioacchino Rossini		William Shakespeare

Carl Weber
5 Gregorio Allegri
C. P. E. Bach
Max Bruch
Joseph Canteloube
John Coltrane
Noël Coward
Frederick Delius
John Dowland
Charles Gounod
Guillaume de Machaut
Darius Milhaud
Van Morrison
Giovanni da Palestrina
Hubert Parry
John Rutter
John Taverner
Georg Philip Telemann
Tomás Victoria
Heitor Villa-Lobos
4 Samuel Barber
George Benjamin
Elliott Carter
Ornette Coleman
Aaron Copland
Manuel de Falla
Gerald Finzi
Orlando Gibbons
Paul Hindemith
Arthur Honegger
Franz Lehár
Lieber & Stoller
Peter Maxwell Davies
Joni Mitchell
Conlon Nancarrow
Michael Nyman
Jacques Offenbach
Charlie Parker
Michael Praetorius
Steve Reich
Salamone de Rossi Ebreo
Paul Simon
Alexander Skryabin
Karol Szymanowski
Hugo Wolf
3 Charles-Valentin Alkan
Joan Baez
Luciano Berio

Heinrich Biber
John Blow
Brecht/Weill
Gavin Bryars
George Butterworth
Thomas Campion
Pietro Cavalli
Emmanuel Chabrier
Leonard Cohen
François Couperin
Miles Davis/Gil Evans
Umberto Giordano
Henryk Górecki
Sofia Gubaidulina
Bernard Herrmann
Paul Hindemith
Billie Holiday
Gustav Holst
Herbert Howells
Antonio Carlos Jobim
Oliver Knussen
Orlandus Lassus
Jules Massenet
Giacomo Meyerbeer
Carl Nielsen
Giovanni Battista Pergolesi
Pérotin
Ottorino Respighi
Joaquin Rodrigo
Clara Schumann
Bedřich Smetana
Charles Stanford
Alessandro Stradella
Billy Strayhorn
Arthur Sullivan
Mikis Theodorakis
Peter Warlock
2 Isaac Albéniz
Laurie Anderson
Burt Bacharach
Eric Ball
Guy Barker
Gerald Barry
Amy Beach
The Beatles
Michael Berkeley
Giovanni Bononcini
Alexander Borodin

William Boyce
Jacques Brel
Nacio Brown & Arthur R. Freed
Buchanan & Bell
Geoffrey Burgon
Robert Burns
Ferrucio Busoni
Thomas Campion
Eva Cassidy
Arcangelo Corelli
Coslow & Johnston
Blossom Dearie
Josquin Desprès
Charles Dibdin
Dave Douglas
Guillaume Dufay
Dumont/Vacaire
Maurice Duruflé
Earth Wind & Fire
Duke Ellington
Duke Ellington/Billy Strayhorn
John Farmer
Morton Feldman
John Field
Stephen Foster
Girolamo Frescobaldi
John Fuller
John Gay
Mikhail Glinka
Edvard Grieg
Ivor Gurney
Barry Guy
W. C. Handy
Hildegard of Bingen
Billie Holiday & Arthur Herzog Jr
John Ireland
Maurice Jarre
Julian Joseph
John Kander/Fred Ebb
Ustad Nusrat Fateh Ali Khan
Lev Knipper
Ernest Křenek
Tom Lehrer
Carl Loewe
James MacMillan
Ladysmith Black Mambazo
Marin Marais
Bohuslav Martinů

Pietro Mascagni
Maschwitz/Stracey
Nikolai Medtner
Fanny Mendelssohn
Federico Mompou
Stanislaw Moniuszko
Thelonius Monk
Ennio Morricone
Gerry Mulligan
Randy Newman
Luigi Nono
Carl Orff
Niccolò Paganini
Krzysztof Penderecki
Edith Piaf
Astor Piazzolla
Jean-Philippe Rameau
Razaf/Belledna
Otis Redding
Lou Reed
Max Reger
John Richardson
Terry Riley
Jean Rousseau
Perico Sambeat
Alfred Schnittke
Heinrich Schutz
Jo Shapcott
Shel Silverstein
Nina Simone
Ethel Smyth
John Philip Sousa
Bruce Springsteen
John Stafford-Smith
Jake Thackray
Dylan Thomas
Charles Trenet
Galina Ustvolskaya
Edgard Varèse
Kevin Volans
Henry Walford Davies
Dionne Warwick
Gillian Welch
Mike Westbrook
Spencer Williams
Brian Wilson
Nancy Wilson
Stevie Wonder

Frank Zappa
1 Mohammed Abdenwahab
Adamson & McHugh
Cannonball Adderley
Richard Addinsell
Alaska
Tomaso Albinoni
Alexander Alexandrov
Lewis Allen
Mose Allison
Al Alvarez
Abderrahmane Amrani
Amsterdam, Sullivan & Baron
Laurie Anderson
Istvan Anhalt
Anouar Brahem Trio
John Antill
Alexander Archangelsky
Antonio Archilei or Emilio de
 Cavalieri
Julian Argüelles
Thomas Arne
Malcolm Arnold
Louis Armstrong
Louis Armstrong & Billie Holiday
Avissar & Levanon
H. S. Bach/Axelson
P. D. Q. Bach
Burt Bacharach/Hal David
Edwin Bagley
Mily Balakirev
Barbara
Charlie Barnet
Count Basie/S. Martin
Django Bates
Arnold Bax
Amy Beach
Sidney Bechet
Beck/Karl Stephenson
Belle and Sebastian
Belle Ciao
Carl Michael Bellman
Lennox Berkeley/Herrick
Chuck Berry
Franz Berwald
Martin Best
John Betjeman and Jim Parker
Acker Bilk

Birmanie Musique d'Art
Henry Rowley Bishop
Georges Bizet/Oscar Hammerstein II
Ernest Bloch
Fr Juan Pérez Bocanegra
Luigi Boccherini
William Bolcom
Luis Bonfa
Sonny Bono
Victor Borge
Dmitri Bortnyansky
Rutland Boughton
David Bowie
Malcolm Boyle
May Brahe
Brave New World
Bertolt Brecht/Hanns Eisler
Jean-Baptiste Bréval
André Brink
Benjamin Britten/W. H. Auden
Brooker and Reid
Big Bill Broonzy
Brown & Henderson
Foreman Brown
Oscar Brown Jr
John Browne
Brühne/Balz
Boudleaux and Felice Bryant
Bullock & Whiting
Chester Burnett
Ralph Burns and Shorty Rogers
Gary Burton & Keith Jarrett
Kate Bush
Cahn/Chaplin/Secunda
J. J. Cale
John Cale
Johnny Carisi
Hoagy Carmichael
Hoagy Carmichael & Johnny Mercer
Lewis Carroll
Carter & Jacobs
John Casken
Cavanaugh, Rose & Stock
Mark Charlap/Carolyn Leigh
Marc-Antoine Charpentier
Chisholm, Lawrence, Cruz, Lopes &
 Martin
Christine, Rourke & Willemetz

Domenico Cimarosa
Carroll Coates
Cochran & Howard
Martin Codax
Harry Connick Jr
Conrad/Magidson
Coots & Gillespie
Adam Cork
Elvis Costello
David Coulter
Noël Coward/Gertrude Lawrence
Billie Cowie
Ida Cox
Jim Crace
Creamer & Layton
William Croft
Kevin Crossley-Holland
Luigi Dalapiccola
Jean-Marie Damase
John Dankworth
Harold Darke
Daugherty, Reynolds & Neiberg
Mackay Davashe
Shaun Davey
Carl Davis
Miles Davis/Horace Silver
Georges Delerue
Paul Desmond
Dixon & Henderson
Don Ellis Orchestra
Walter Donaldson
Stefano Donaudy
Lonnie Donegan
Jonathon Dove
Nick Drake
Anne Dudley
George Duke
John Dunstaple
Antonio Durán de la Mota
Ian Dury
The Eagles
Easter Mattins
Julia Eboly
Edens, Comden & Green
Ross Edwards
Gottfried von Einem
Hanns Eisler
Duke Ellington/Bob Russell

Duke Ellington/Paul Webster
Duke Ellington/Johnny Hodges
Vivian Ellis
Lehman Engel
Brian Eno/David Byrne
Evans, Hewson, Clayton & Mullen
Cesaria Evora
Sammy Fain/Jerry Seelen
Marianne Faithfull
Farmers Market
Fat Boy Slim
Leo Ferré
Eva Figes
Mike Figgis
Peter Fischer
Fisher & Roberts
Ella Fitzgerald
Flanders & Swann
Bernhard Flies
Antoine Forqueray
Donald Fragen
Jean Françaix
Aretha Franklin
Aretha Franklin/Ted White
Frederick the Great
Robert Fripp & Brian Eno
Bill Frisell
Jesse Fuller
Giovanni Gabrieli
Baldassare Galuppi
Garbage
Garland & Razaf
Errol Garner
George and Ira Gershwin
Carlo Gesualdo
Eugène Gigout
Dizzy Gillespie and Charlie Parker
Jimmy Dale Gilmore
Gimbel & Fox
Egberto Gismonti
Leopold Godowsky
Heiner Goebbel
Simon Goldhill
Howard Goodall
Benny Goodman Orchestra
Anton Goosen
Louis Moreau Gottschalk
Louis Grabu

Grainger/Robbins
A. C. Green
Lavinia Greenlaw (reading)
Gregorian Chant
André Grétry
Grever & Adams
Grey
Grey, Wood & Gibbs
Gérard Grisey
Carlo Grossi
Vince Guaraldi
Juan Luis Guerra
Jacques Halévy
Oscar Hammerstein
Oscar Hammerstein and Jerome
  Kern
John Handy
Thomas Hanforth
Hanighen, Williams & Monk
Françoise Hardy
John Harle
Gene Harris with the Ray Brown
  Trio
Max Harris
Roy Harris
William Harris
Annie F. Harrison
D. Harrison/R. Elton
Karl Amadeus Hartmann
Seamus Heaney and Paddy Glackin
Dave Heath
Neal Hefti
Isaac Heinrich
Piers Hellawell
Valdemar Henrique
Henry VIII
Fanny Hensel-Mendelssohn
Hans Werner Henze
Robert Heppener
Johann Ritter von Herbeck
Robert Herrick/Henry Purcell
Fred Hersch
J. H. Hewitt
Heyman, Sour, Eyton & Green
Higginbotham/Drake/Fisher
Geoffrey Hill
Earl Hines
E. T. A. Hoffmann

Joseph Holbrooke
Dave Holland/Lojac
Simon Holt
John Lee Hooker
Lightnin' Hopkins
Toninho Horta
Horton, Darling & Gabler
Alan Hovhaness
Julia Ward Howe
John Hughes
Pelham Humfrey
Hunter/Garcia
Zakir Hussein
Ink Spots
Jagger & Richard
William Garret James
Horst Jankowski
Jazz Jamaica
Simon Jeffes & Geoff Richardson
Joanna, Crugybar, Ebenezer
Antonio Carlos Johim/Lees
Jonnie Johnson/Keith Richard
Robert Johnson
Johnston & Burke
David Jones
Quincy Jones
Janis Joplin
John Joubert
Kahn, Schwandt & André
Kamilieris
Giya Kancheli
Kantemiroglu
Anton Karas
Sigfrid Karg-Elert
Salif Keita
Bishop Thomas Ken
Stan Kenton
Dorothy Ker
Aaron J. Kernis
Aram Khachaturian
Albert King
B. B. King
Knepler, Welleminsky & Mackeben-
  Millöcker
Erland von Koch
Zoltán Kodály
Christopher Komeda
Erich Wolfgang Korngold

Alain Kounkou
Hans Kox
Leopold Kozeluch
Kraftwerk
Fritz Kreisler
Kris Kristofferson
Karol Kryl
György Kurtág
Robert La Bonga
Édouard-Victoir-Antoine Lalo
Constant Lambert
Blas de Laserna
Antonio Lauro
Jean-Marie Leclair
Ernesto Lecuona
Michel Legrand
Lennox & Stewart
Annie Lennox
John Lewis
Lewis, Stock & Rose
Lewis, Young, Conrad & Robinson
Dave Liebman
Matthew Linley
Linzer & Randall
J. Livingston & R. Evans
Matthew Locke
Jon Lord
Louiguy
Louiguy & Piaf
Nellie Lutcher
Martin Luther
Witold Lutoslawski
Elisabeth Lutyens
Mafikizolo
Kevin Malpass
Francesco Manfredini
John Marbeck
Benedetto Marcello
Bob Marley
A. Marly/H. Zaret
Wynton Marsalis
Martin & Coulter
Vladimir Martynov
Masekela & Samson
Hugh Masekela, Daly Gary,
    Thimothy Michael
Maschwitz & Sherwin
Maschwitz/Strachey

John Masefield
Benedict Mason
Daniel Mason
Massive Attack
Todd Matshikizia
Colin Matthews
J. H. Maunder
Maxwell & Sigman
Mayer & Mercer
Billy Mayerl
Amanda McBroom
Paul McCartney
Paul McCartney/Carl Davis
Ewan McColl
Ewan McColl, Charles Parker &
    Peggy Seeger
Jimmy McHugh and Dorothy
    Fields
Robbie McIntosh
John McLaughlin
Don McLean
Will McTell
Meacham & Gray
Peter Melville Smith
Gian Carlo Menotti
Saverio Mercadante
Mercer & De Paul
Johnny Mercer
Mabel Mercer
Natalie Merchant
Freddie Mercury
Pat Metheny
Migliacci & Modugno
Max Miller
Modern Jazz Quartet
José Pablo Moncayo
Meredith Monk
Monnot & Moustaki
Monnot, Délécluse & Senlis
Bill Monroe
Vittorio Monti
Xavier Montsalvatge
Thomas Morley
Morris & Waller
Blake Morrison
Morrissey/Marr
Mortazzo, Molleda, Oliva & Rey
Jelly Roll Morton

Bennie Moten/Peer
Moxy Fruvous
Mozart/Süssmayr
Mukesh
Stanley Myers
Billy Myles
Milton Nascimento/Lo Borges
Peter Paul Nash
N'Dour & Rykiel
Oliver Nelson
Willy Nelson
A. & J. Neville
Ethelbert Nevin
Mickey Newbury
Anthony Newley/Leslie Bricusse
Newton & Tate
Nitty Gritty Dirt Band
Per Nørgård
Norworth & Bayes
Laura Nyro
Phil Ochs
King Oliver
Stephen Oliver
Olivieri/Poterat
Sparre Olsen
O'Neill & Bradley
Roy Orbison
Original Dixieland Jazz Band
Bunny O'Riley
Edward 'Kid' Ory
Wilfred Owen
Ruth Padel
Jimmy Page & Robert Plant
Hilda Paredes
Jim Parker
John Parricelli/Martin France
Parrish/Migliacci
Joseph Parry
Dolly Parton
Ostad Faramarz Payvar
Sapo Perapaskero
Oscar Peterson
Kelly Joe Phelps
Tom Phillips
Piaf & Dumont
Billy Pigg
Pink Floyd
Austin Pitre

The Pogues
Pomus & Shuman
Andrew Poppy
Porter, Henneve, Palex
Omara Portuondo
Bud Powell
Elvis Presley
Prévert & Cosma
André Previn
Dory Previn
Alan Price
Prince
Pura Fe
Finley Quaye
Radiohead
Johnny Raducanu
Ram & Rand
Ramblers Dance Band
Ariel Ramirez
Alan Rawsthorne
Paul Reade
Max Reger
Reid/Shamblin
Reinhardt & Grappelli
Django Reinhardt
Jonathan Richman
Simon Richmond
Caradog Roberts
Robin/Rainger
La Rocca/Shields
Rodrigo/Davis/Evans
Armando Rodrigues
Gene Roland
Sonny Rollins
Ned Rorem
Juventino Rosas
Alec Roth
Jimmy Rowles
Miklós Rózsa
Harry Ruby
Bill Russo
Ousmane Sacko
Shikeiki Saegusa
Samira Said
Pascale Sakr
Antonio Salieri
Salvador & Dimey
Jacques Santer

Pablo de Sarasate
Alessandro Scarlatti
Friedrich Schiller
Schoebel, Erdman & Meyers
Schulze/Leip
Schulze, Leip, Connor, Phillips
Joseph Schwanter
Louis Sclavis
Peter Sculthorpe
Serious Drinking
Sex Pistols
William Shakespeare/Martin Best
Shakira
Shandileer
Ravi Shankar
Shearing & Forster
Percy Bysshe Shelley
Sherrill & Wynette
Simon & Shabalala
Roberto di Simone
Simons & Mark
Robert Simpson
Singer, Vedora, White
Arakel Siunetsi
Horace Silver
Julian Slade
Sly and the Family Stone
Arthur Smith
Bessie Smith
Huey Smith
Smith/Balcom
Antonio Soler
Somervell, Arthur
Son Montuno/José Ramón Sánchez
Fernando Sor
Sousa-Freitas-Campos
Mugsy Spanier
Jon Stallworthy
Vivian Stanshall
Andy Statman
Steely Dan
Stein/Sondheim
Stewart/Gouldman
Karlheinz Stockhausen
Richard Strange
Billy Strange/Mac Davis
Johann Strauss II
Johann Strauss Jr

Josef Strauss
Jule Styne/Bob Merrill
Jule Styne/Stephen Sondheim
Josef Suk
Esbjorn Svensson
Taha, Khaled, Faudel
Tigran Tahmizhan
Germaine Tailleferre
Tan Dun
Giuseppe Tartini
Tauber, Pinkard & Tracey
Taylor & Dallas
Taylor & Lamb
Jack Teagarden
Tennant & Lowe
Terriss & Robredo
Clark Terry
Sonny Terry
Sonny Terry & Brownie McGhee
Thomas L. Thomas
Richard Thompson
Virgil Thompson/Gertrude Stein
Tiffen le Martelot
Timbalada
Keith Tippett & Andy Sheppard
Thomas Tomkins
Francesco Paolo Tosti
El Hadj Houcine Toulali
Pete Townshend
Merle Travis
Trenet & Breton
Mark-Anthony Turnage
U2, Bono & The Edge
Marco Uccellini
Viktor Ullmann
V. Valencia
Van Heusen and Burke
Sarah Vaughan
Vaughan Williams/R. L. Stephenson
Don Van Vliet
Orazio Vecchi
Dobar Vecer
Consuelo Velasquez
Tomás Luis de Victoria
Angel Villoldo
Claude Vivier
Walther von der Vögelweide
Tom Waits

Index of interviewees